REINVENTING KHOMEINI

Reinventing Khomeini

21.00

Less 20%

16.80

Purchased by: _Robinson_

REINVENTING KHOMEINI

The Struggle for Reform in Iran

DANIEL BRUMBERG

The University of Chicago Press
Chicago and London

DANIEL BRUMBERG is assistant professor of government at Georgetown University. His articles and essays have appeared in a variety of publications, including *Inwal, Contemporary Sociology, American Arab Affairs, Harvard Middle East Papers,* and the *New York Times,* as well as in twenty edited collections. This is his first book.

The University of Chicago Press, Chicago 60637
The University of Chicago Press, Ltd., London
© 2001 by The University of Chicago
All rights reserved. Published 2001
Printed in the United States of America
10 09 08 07 06 05 04 03 02 01   1 2 3 4 5

ISBN: 0-226-07757-8 (cloth)
ISBN: 0-226-07758-6 (paper)

Library of Congress Cataloging-in-Publication Data

Brumberg, Daniel.
    Reinventing Khomeini: the struggle for reform in Iran / Daniel Brumberg.
        p.   cm.
    Includes bibliographical references and index.
    ISBN 0-226-07757-8 (cloth : alk. paper)—ISBN 0-226-07758-6
    (pbk. : alk. paper)
        1. Iran—Politics and government—1979–1997.   2. Iran—Politics and
government—1997–   3. Khomeini, Ruhollah.   4. Khâtamâ, Muòammad.
5. Islam and state—Iran.   I. Title.
DS381.8 .D36 2001
955.05'4—dc21

                                                                        00-057687

⊗ The paper used in this publication meets the minimum requirements of the American National Standard for Information Sciences—Permanence of Paper for Printed Library Materials, ANSI Z39.48-1992.

To the memory of my mother,
Zahava Brumberg

Contents

Acknowledgments

Reinventing Khomeini originated as a study of the political thought and leadership of Ayatollah Ruhollah Khomeini, Supreme Leader of the Islamic Republic of Iran from 1979 to 1989. I had initially assumed that the study, commissioned in 1992 by the Fundamentalism Project of the Academy of Arts and Sciences, would yield a straightforward account of how Khomeini actualized his revolutionary vision of Shi'ism during his regime. But as I pored over several hundred of his speeches during the winter of 1992 I discovered that this vision was anything but straightforward, coherent, or consistent. Khomeini's religiopolitical views swung from one perspective to another; what is more, during the last years of his life—and with nearly complete abandon after his death in June 1989—his followers exploited these competing notions of authority to advance various agendas of their own.

I tried to capture this complex dynamic in a long essay that was published in a volume edited by Scott Appleby, *Spokesmen for the Despised: Fundamentalist Leaders in the Middle East* (University of Chicago

Press, 1997). Alan Thomas of the Press suggested that I expand the essay into a book that would trace the link between Khomeini's legacy and the political change in post-Khomeini Iran. I readily agreed, in no small measure because I had come to appreciate how the ayatollah's story conveyed lessons that applied not merely to the evolution of "Islamic" politics in Iran, but also to the transformation of such politics in the wider Islamic world. President Mohammad Khatami's election in May 1997 confirmed my initial hunch that the politics of dissonant institutionalization—as I call it in this book—had become a broader, if not global, phenomenon, one that opened up possibilities for ideological change that conventional views of both Islamic politics and charismatic movements could not easily anticipate.

In pursuing this study I have benefited from the support of numerous individuals and institutions. Marvin Zonis of the University of Chicago Graduate School of Business was the first to spark my interest in Iran. During my graduate studies in Egypt, Marvin constantly encouraged me to keep an eye on the Arab world's Persian neighbor. I am grateful for his support, insights, and friendship, without which *Reinventing Khomeini* probably would not have been written.

Many other individuals contributed ideas and comments that strengthened this book. They include Scott Appleby, H. E. Chehabi, Michael Fischer, Nasser Hadian, Bernard Lynch, David Menashri, Baqer Moin, Sole Ozel, James Piscatori, Susanne and Lloyd Rudolph, Charles Tripp, John Voll, and Mark Warren. My wife, Laurie, offered valuable comments, particularly about the first chapter. She also performed heroic work on the index, for which I am very grateful. A number of my Georgetown University graduate students—particularly Tamara Wittes—provided insights that helped shape the theoretical contours of this study. Mara Leichtman helped proofread the first draft and undertook research for the conclusion. In addition, Lisa Tadayun and Vida Ghaffari assisted me with reading and selectively translating Persian materials. I am also grateful to Manuchehr Kouchak, who helped me with the daunting task of standardizing the transliterations of Persian and Arabic names and terms.

The editing of this book was—as it almost always is—an arduous task, one which Sandy Hazel of the University of Chicago Press handled with great skill and precision. Alan Thomas, our colleague at the Press, has been a steadfast and enthusiastic advocate whose patience and determination helped see this project through to completion.

Several institutions supported the research and/or writing of *Reinventing Khomeini*. I would like to thank Georgetown University, which granted me a Mellon Junior Faculty Award to pursue the initial research;

and the Earhart Foundation, which also provided generous funding. Anthony Sullivan, executive director of the Earhart Foundation, deserves particular mention for his friendship and encouragement. My thanks also to the International Forum on Democratic Studies, which hosted me as a Visiting Fellow during the early stages of my research and the final stage of writing. The hospitality of the entire staff, particularly that of director Marc Plattner and his colleague Art Kaufman, made my stay a productive and enjoyable experience. Melissa Mann, my research assistant while I was at the Forum, provided valuable help locating and retrieving the enormous amount of materials that I used in developing this project. I am also grateful to Peer Gatter, who provided invaluable assistance with Persian materials and many useful insights to boot.

My appreciation extends beyond the shores of the United States to the organizers of the International Congress on the Elucidation of the Islamic Revolution, which was held in early October 1999 in Tehran. They enabled me not only to share the results of my work with many Iranian scholars and students, but also to interview several individuals whose experiences and ideas figure in this book. I am particularly grateful to Professors Hadi Semati and Nasser Hadian of Tehran University, who hosted me before and after the conference despite busy schedules.

Finally, I think it is only fitting to mention the many scholars and authors whose studies of Iranian politics and history have influenced this book. Chapters 2, 3, and 4, in particular, owe much to the insights of Ervand Abrahamian, Said Amir Arjomand, Ahmad Ashraf, Shaul Bakhash, Bahman Baktiari, Mehrzad Boroujerdi, H. E. Chehabi, Hamid Debashi, Michael Fischer, Nikki Keddie, Alexander Knysh, Baqer Moin, Roy Mottahedeh, Asghar Schirazi, and Marvin Zonis. I can only hope that I have done some justice to the fascinating country of Iran, which many of these individuals still consider their second—if not first—home.

Introduction:
In Search of the "Real" Iran

> The government is . . . determined by the Majlis. . . . The executive branch must answer to the legislative branch. . . . It is here that we understand the words by His Eminence the Imam [leader of the *umma*, or Muslim community], . . . that "the Majlis heads all affairs." The Majlis is the manifestation of the nation's sovereignty. . . . The biggest mission of the Majlis is to defend national issues, and our national issues are linked to our religious issues. . . . The Majlis . . . is defending authorities, limits, rights. [It] is the forum where diversity inside a system is recognized. . . . Diversity should be accepted . . . [so] that problems are solved through discussions and the majority of votes. . . . This is the basis of independence.[1]
>
> —Presidential candidate Mohammad Khatami, February 1997

> Every day there is talk of . . . separating religion from politics . . . You should make the people understand that just as participating in an election is a duty, making a good choice is also a duty . . . The people accept the principle of receiving help from the clergy . . . No member of the clergy should think that he has no . . . duty in this respect. They should not say that the people should go and do whatever they like . . . You should issue . . . guidelines to the people.[2]
>
> —Supreme Leader Ayatollah 'Ali Khamene'i, speech to clerics, May 1997

> Which is the real Iran?
>
> —CNN reporter Christiane Amanpour, December 1997

Eighteen years after the Islamic Revolution, few students of Iranian politics would have predicted that a son of the revolution would so openly challenge the ruling clerics. But Mohammad Khatami—who for a decade had served as minister of Islamic Guidance—minced no words during the 1997 presidential elections. Not only did he assert that the *Majles* (Parliament) was the highest seat of national sovereignty, but he also implied that national issues could be determined by applying the principle of diversity in a free debate. Yet it was not merely his defense of pluralism, nationalism, and popular sovereignty that provoked his rivals. By maintaining that the "constitution is . . . the basis of the . . . political structure,"[3] Khatami implicitly questioned the principal conviction of the conservative clerical establishment, namely that Ayatollah 'Ali Khamene'i, as *faqih*, or "Supreme Leader," held absolute authority. This signaled more than mere political rivalry. The conservative clerics argued that because the founder of the Islamic revolution, the late Ayatollah Khomeini, had elaborated the doctrine of *velayat-e faqih*, or

"Rule of the Jurist" (which laid out the case for clerical rule under one Supreme Leader), any questioning of this doctrine constituted heresy. Yet here was Khatami insisting that notions such as limits, rights, and constitutional supremacy respected Khomeini's wishes! After all, hadn't Khomeini repeatedly asserted that the "The Majlis heads all affairs"?

Such claims provoked an ideological frenzy. Speaking for the conservative clerics, Ayatollah Mohammad Reza Mahdavi-Kani launched a bitter attack on Khatami supporters seeking to subordinate the *faqih*'s authority to the will of the people. "Beware!" he warned. "When they dare to . . . say that the legitimacy . . . of the guardianship [of the *faqih*] . . . is based on popular demand, then nothing will be left of your guardianship. . . . It is foolish not to prevent these deviations in the name of freedom."[4] Determined that nothing so trivial as "freedom" would obstruct them, Mahdavi-Kani's allies pulled out all the stops in their efforts to ensure that *Majles* Speaker 'Ali Akbar Nateq-Nuri, Khatami's chief opponent, would win the election. Khamene'i himself indirectly blessed this effort; he scoffed at the very notion that the people had a right to choose a presidential candidate without the clergy's guidance. Buoyed by the *faqih*'s support—and backed by the Ministries of Interior and Information, the police, and the regime's control over television, radio, and part of the semiofficial press—Khatami's opponents awaited victory. But to the dismay of the clerical establishment, Khatami won a record 70 percent of the nearly 30 million votes cast on 23 May 1997.

While his election represented a triumph of popular will over clerical absolutism, it hardly signaled a decisive victory for the reformers. As Supreme Leader, Ayatollah Khamene'i still led a formidable political alliance and possessed two powerful weapons: the many powers and institutional resources granted to his office by the Constitution; and the anti-Western ideology that Khomeini had championed—and that intellectuals such as Khatami himself had once promoted. In the ensuing year, Khamene'i turned these weapons against Khatami and his allies in the cabinet, the *Majles*, and the press, forcing them to defend themselves against the accusation that they were simply liberals in Islamic guise. Emboldened by these attacks, both the security forces and the judiciary made every effort to muzzle "liberal" intellectuals and clerics.

Yet the reformers had one crucial advantage that helped to deflect such attacks: eighteen years after the Islamic Revolution, the debate over the ideological legacy of that great event had not been settled in favor of any one vision of Islamic community. At the center of this debate was the legacy of Ayatollah Khomeini himself: but not the fire-breathing fundamentalist as many in the West perceived him, a blindly ambitious man who ruthlessly implemented a coherent doctrine in the name of Islam. The Khomeini who mattered most was a complex, ambiguous soul, a man who throughout his long life had absorbed diverse notions of political authority. For many Iranians, the fault lines in his ideology were obscured by the magical allure of his charisma. But behind his charisma, and woven into its very fabric, was a contradiction between Khomeini's belief that the people should play a role in choosing their government, and his strong commitment to revolutionary action and clerical rule under the leadership of a quasi-infallible, charismatic Supreme Leader.

Although many of his most zealous followers were unaware of this tension, it was of paramount importance to the ruling clerics and lay Islamic activists, who constituted the ruling elite. Throughout the eighties they invoked one or another aspect of Khomeini's multifaceted ideology to justify competing social and political agendas. The decisive battle to appropriate Khomeini's legacy erupted during the last two years of his life—after he issued, in January 1988, an edict declaring that the mundane interests of state take precedence over the timeless commands of religious faith. This remarkable development set the stage for a sweeping reform of the 1979 Constitution. Although undertaken with Khomeini's blessing, this reform weakened his greatest ideological innovation: *velayat-e faqih*. To the dismay of many clerics, the position of *faqih* was stripped of its charismatic-religious basis. This was achieved by separating the post of *faqih* from that of *marja'*, or "highest source of religious imitation." Henceforth, *political* skill, not divine inspiration or religious knowledge, was the chief qualification for holding the highest office in the land. In addition, while the first Constitution had stated that the *faqih* ruled by virtue of the people's recognition of his authority, the 1989 Constitution broke the charismatic bond between leader and followers by placing the selection of the *faqih* in the hands of a clerical body, the Council of Experts. Moreover, by maintaining the provision for the direct election of the president, the 1989 Constitution set up a potentially destabilizing conflict between the imperatives of rational authority, as embedded in the office of the president (and the *Majles*), and traditional authority, as reflected in the office of *faqih*.

In time, this and other contradictions would come to haunt Iran's leaders. For instead of resolving the central issue of political authority, the constitutional reforms of 1989 opened the door to a reformist movement that eagerly invoked the Imam's words to justify a more rational and democratic vision of political community. Thus the line from Khomeini's quest for revolutionary rebirth and clerical rule to Khatami's struggle for popular sovereignty and constitutional rights was neither fortuitous nor constructed out of a wholly new ideological cloth. Instead,

Khomeini's own complex legacy helped to enable Khatami and his reform movement. This said—and precisely because Khomeini's eclectic ideology was inspired by contending ideals such as clerical rule and popular sovereignty—it was virtually impossible for any one faction among his disciples to argue that its view of Islamic government was more authentic or revolutionary than the other. Thus, far from transcending the tensions that had animated Khomeini's legacy, in the wake of his death reformists and conservatives alike recast his vision in new and often beguiling ways.

Some readers may find this focus on the accommodation of contradiction and ideological ambiguity troubling. Many of the Imam's closest disciples, as well as some of his most ardent detractors, believe that his life was one long prophetic mission that culminated with his miraculous, if not inevitable, return to Tehran in February 1979. According to this account, the Imam forged a coherent ideology as a young man, and then, after much hardship, stoicism, and pain, revealed (or imposed) this doctrine when the moment was ripe.[5] Even those scholars and journalists who viewed the Islamic revolution through a more dispassionate lens have struggled with the phenomenon of contradiction. While the teleological assumptions of Marxism and modernization theory may have been supplanted by a postmodern sensibility, many scholars and journalists still cling to the idea that ideological and social tensions must eventually submit to the harmonizing exigencies of social and political reality. Consider the bewildered response of Cable News Network reporter Christiane Amanpour to the contrasting speeches given by President-elect Khatami and Supreme Leader Khamene'i during the December 1997 Summit of the Organization of Islamic Conference, or OIC (a meeting held that year in Tehran that brought the heads of state of almost all Islamic countries under one roof). Echoing Khomeini's xenophobia, Khamene'i warned that "[t]he West, with its comprehensive invasion, has . . . targeted our Islamic faith . . . [and has] exported the . . . disregard for religion and ethics [that will] . . . engulf the present Western civilization and wipe it out." In contrast, President Khatami spoke of a "Western civilization . . . whose accomplishments are not few" and of an "interdependent world . . . where the security of different regions is indivisible . . . [and requires] striving toward mutual trust."[6] Articulating her surprise, Amanpour asked Khatami this question:

> If a person from outer space had been watching the opening ceremonies of the OIC, he would have heard two completely different speeches; one . . . by Iran's spiritual leader talking about conflict, enemies and harping on the past; and then, yourself, talking about dialogue, understanding and

moving forward. Which is the real Iran; what are people meant to think about the thinking that is coming out of Iran today?[7]

That many academics were also surprised by Khatami's electoral victory and by the ensuing struggle over Khomeini's revolutionary legacy is understandable. After all, it was difficult to square these events with either of the two dominant theories of charismatic revolution. On one level, Khomeini may be the twentieth century's last example of a "pure" charismatic leader. His authority was born of a profound and genuinely felt crisis of identity. Khomeini sought to remedy this disenchantment through a revolutionary *cris de coeur* that was hostile to all forms of economic activity and political organization. When he reminded Iranians that the purpose of the revolution was *not* "to have less expensive melons,"[8] he affirmed the irrational if understandable aspiration for collective dignity that partly inspired the revolution. Yet if his charisma radiated a spiritual logic that could not be reduced to a vulgar struggle for power or wealth, his quest to forge a new identity for his people was also animated by a rational approach to politics and religion. Khomeini articulated a utilitarian instrumentalism that viewed religion as a useful tool for attaining collective political and social ends. Echoing the Third World ideologues of his day, he not only held that Islam was a "total ideology," but also insisted that this ideology could be represented by an elected *Majles* that articulated the "interests" of the Iranian people. Which, then, was the *real* Khomeini? And more important, which was the *real* Iran? Was the Islamic revolution an irrational quest for utopia? Or was it about creating institutions that could address the social and political interests of Iranians?

This book seeks to answer these difficult questions. Tracing the genesis and transformation of what I call a system of contending authorities, it will show how Khomeini's own efforts to accommodate competing visions of political community set the stage for an ideological struggle over his legacy in the nineties. Spurning all notions of linear development, particularly those that posit a neat path from revolutionary charisma to stable authority structures, I invite the reader to understand how a political system that strove to accommodate notions of rationality and constitutional rule to the imperatives of charismatic rule and clerical traditionalism encouraged change while limiting its ideological and political scope.

Beyond telling this particular story, this book offers a broader lesson that should interest social scientists seeking new insights into the dynamics of ideological change in authoritarian systems. Bridging the gap between the study of culture and political ideas on the one side, and historical institutionalist analysis on the other, it offers a sobering reminder that the images of authority that political actors bring to social and political conflicts are not mere rationalizations of material interests; nor are they reflections of some cultural essence. Viewed as integral elements of a state and its ideological legacies, these institutionalized images constitute decisive forces that can broaden or quickly limit the scope of political and ideological change.

Some may argue that such analysis entails a return to the much maligned field of cultural analysis. Why should we treat Iran as a case of Islamic or Middle Eastern exceptionalism? Would it not be more appropriate to view the struggle over Khomeini's legacy as we would any other contest for power—that is, as a wholly rational struggle between soft-liners and hard-liners, both of whom bringing to the political arena an array of material resources, political allies, and negotiating strategies?[9] The answer is that these universal power struggles are only part of the story. If we have learned anything from the study of transitions from authoritarianism, it is that certain types of authority, certain historically rooted notions of political community, and even distinct political routines can endure in complex and contradictory ways. The challenge is neither to dismiss these legacies by reaching for a master social theory, nor to exaggerate their effect by resorting to an equally unrevealing cultural essentialism. Rather, we must devise *appropriate* middle-range theories that allow us to trace the evolution of such legacies, and to assess their impact on the efforts of political elites to reform or defend existing authoritarian ideologies and institutions.

Toward this end, I begin by mapping an alternative strategy for explaining the genesis and evolution of charismatic movements and ideologies. As we shall see in chapter 1, both symbolic and instrumentalist theories view charisma as a vital—but ultimately ephemeral—form of authority. In the long run, it is argued, charisma is transformed or routinized into a stable form of legitimacy, be it based on custom and tradition or on modern, rational-legal authority. I argue that this linear view, largely inspired by Max Weber's analysis of authority, does *not* offer a compelling explanation for the contradictory dynamics by which competing visions of community shape, propel, or obstruct political change, particularly in an age of cultural, socioeconomic, and political globalization. In its place I sketch four concepts that together constitute the phenomenon of contending authorities: multiple biographies, multiple shared imaginations, dissonant institutionalization, and complex routinization. Using these four analytical guides, chapters 2 through 5 trace the genesis of Khomeini's charismatic authority and legacy. We shall see how Khomeini grafted onto this charismatic sensibility at least two other visions of authority. The first was radical, instrumentalist, and indirectly influenced by Western political thought. Its advocates, mainly lay intellectuals and some radical clerics affiliated with the Islamic Left, conceived of Shi'ism as a utilitarian resource that modern leaders could galvanize to elaborate and defend the social and political interests of the people. The second was traditional and homespun. Its advocates viewed Shi'ism as a body of divine truths that could be grasped and explained only by qualified clerics. For proponents of the first vision, the pragmatic exigencies of power, human will, and mundane interest determined what Islam was all about, whereas for advocates of the second, a transcendent Islam as enforced by a clerical elite determined the limits of power and the boundaries of "interest."

Chapter 6 analyzes the struggle over Khomeini's legacy during the eighties. It highlights how the clash between the rational logic of economic interests, and the transrational logic of charismatic experience, hindered the efforts of Khomeini's disciples to routinize his authority. We shall see that while Khomeini appreciated the need to institutionalize the revolution, his own commitment to a mystical ethos hindered his attempts to stabilize economic and political structures. Yet when he was finally convinced that the devastating human, economic, and social effects of the eight-year Iran–Iraq War threatened the very viability of the Islamic Republic, and when faced as well by the daunting problem of succession, Khomeini initiated the constitutional reforms that ultimately deprived the *faqih* of supreme religious authority. Although these reforms redistributed authority among the *faqih*, *Majles*, and president in ways that both strengthened *and* weakened the Supreme Leader, they also precipitated a struggle over the very nature of political authority, one that eventually reinforced the democratic legitimacy of the president.

Chapter 7 traces the ideological lines of this contest as it evolved in the early nineties. We shall see that while President 'Ali Akbar Hashemi Rafsanjani initially held out hope for limited democratic reforms, he soon embraced the traditional authority of the *faqih* and his conservative allies. Rafsanjani and Khamene'i skillfully deployed this "traditionalization strategy" by reinterpreting Khomeini's legacy in an effort to legitimate market reforms and authoritarian-patrimonialist rule. Joining forces, they tried to advance economic reconstruction by purging Islamic Leftists from the *Majles*. Accused of facilitating the West's "cultural onslaught," these self-proclaimed Children of the Revolution were persecuted by the very state they had helped to create. Chapter 8 considers the paradoxical consequences of this development. As we shall see, some of revolution's own ideologues, including Mohammad Khatami and Abdolkarim Soroush, responded by arguing for a pluralistic vision, which they argued was consistent with Khomeini's legacy and would address the disenchantment of a new generation. Indeed, the youth of Iran desperately sought a leader whose personal charisma and intellectual perspective would replace Khomeini's ascetic scowl with a joyous grin. Thus when Khatami surfaced in 1997—sporting Armani glasses and an infectious smile—and began to talk of an "Islamic civil society" and the need for a "civilizational dialogue," the foundation for change had been laid. Whether this vision is politically and intellectually tenable, or whether, in an age of globalization and diverse rationalities, Khomeini's multidimensional legacy has made it *easier* to accommodate contending notions of authority, is a question to which we will turn in the conclusion. In addition, the conclusion assesses the many obstacles encountered by President Khatami and his allies during his first three years in office.

A note on sources: This project originated as a study of Khomeini's speeches during the 1979–89 period, and subsequently blossomed into a more ambitious project. I have relied on Foreign Broadcast Information Service (FBIS) as well as some British Broadcasting Corporation (BBC) translations of these and other speeches by Iranian leaders, and on the extensive and detailed translations of *Majles* debates during the 1989–97 period. In addition, I have worked with several Persian readers to consult relevant original sources where necessary. Yet the choice of material was not dictated merely by its availability, but also by a systematic review of the secondary literature on the Islamic Revolution, which helped to identify the central questions to be investigated. Finally, a review of this manuscript by several Iranian colleagues based in Tehran provided extremely useful, and encouraging, assessments of my own analysis of the relevant materials. I am thus satisfied that this study provides an accurate, objective, yet sociologically empathetic evaluation of the very complex process of ideological change in the Islamic Republic of Iran.

A note on transliterations: Although transliterations from Persian and Arabic have been standardized, I have retained the spellings of several proper names as they have been commonly rendered in the British or American media. These include Arab proper names such as Mohammad Aduh and Saddam Hussein, as well as Iranian proper names such as Abdolkarim Soroush.

1 Remapping Charisma

> We propose . . . the development of a non-functionalist conception
> of society as a potentially contradictory institutional system. An
> adequate social theory must work at three levels of analysis—individuals
> competing and negotiating, organizations in conflict and coordination,
> and institutions in contradiction and interdependency.[1]
>
> —Roger Friedland and Robert Alford

The Revolution: Contending Paradigms

The notion that modern societies are beset by institutional and symbolic
contradictions is hardly new. From Karl Marx to Karl Deutsch, this
theme has informed nearly all of Western social science. What *is* new is
the decidedly postmodern sensibility that some scholars have brought to
this subject. Eschewing all linear conceptions of social change, Friedland
and Alford argue that Western political systems are constituted by
multiple and equally compelling "logics," each of which is grounded in
its own authority system, has an institutional and symbolic foundation,
and coexists in tension with the others. Moreover, they assert, because
Western social science has been "hobbled" by a long-standing "material-
ideal dualism," it cannot fully grasp the organic link between the "transrational" world of organized symbols and collective rituals, and the
rational world of individual choice and symbolic manipulation. Since
each perspective "has places it cannot see, territory it cannot map,"[2] they
invite us to design new conceptual maps that highlight how rational and
transrational forces create "contradictory institutional systems." This

book takes up that challenge, but with respect to a land far different from the world that Friedland and Alford have in mind.

On the face of it, the Islamic Republic of Iran does not seem an appropriate laboratory for investigating the phenomenon of multiple political logics; a state ruled by a messianic ideology and charismatic Supreme Ruler hardly invites this kind of analysis. Yet if we have learned anything from the collapse of communist states in Eastern Europe, or from the cracking of authoritarian juntas in Latin America, it is that even the most monolithic political orders are subject—in their own *distinctive* ways—to the destabilizing effects of contradictory institutional and ideological logics.[3] I emphasize the word *distinctive* because history teaches that no universal path exists from authoritarianism to something else. Because each country's past bequeaths a singular bundle of competing political, social, and ideological legacies, the struggle to redefine or transcend these legacies unfolds in a tempest of conflicting movements and ideologies, whose ultimate resolution can sometimes elude their most determined protagonists.[4]

Such indeterminacy does not easily coexist with the logic of comparative political analysis.[5] By its very nature, the quest to identify the broader verities of political change requires a simplified view of the authoritarian experience. Yet the more we know, the more difficult deductive analysis becomes. Consider the history of Soviet studies. The totalitarian model held sway for many years, only to be followed by a brief detour down the more optimistic road of transition studies.[6] The latter's focus on the rational dynamics of pact making and elite negotiation proved deficient on several counts, not least of which was its failure to integrate cultural and historical conditions into its analysis.[7] Post-Soviet studies thus moved toward the field of historical-institutionalism, an eclectic discipline that highlights the particular ways in which institutional and ideological paths or legacies structure political and social change.[8] Focusing on the authoritarian past rather than on an imagined democratic future, scholars demonstrated that the Communist Party had institutionalized *competing* notions of authority by promoting ethnoreligious identities in some quarters, reinforcing Marxist-Leninist mentalities in others, and elsewhere creating pockets of legal-rational civil society.[9]

For students of the Islamic Republic of Iran, this story has a familiar ring. In the wake of a revolution whose messianism resounded around the globe, some scholars found the totalitarian or mass society theory that had once guided Soviet studies to be a useful lens through which to view Iran's revolution. Arguing that rapid modernization had produced a "symbolic crisis," they held that the resulting thirst for utopia was quenched by a neototalitarian party whose charismatic leader mobilized the alienated urban classes in a Manichaean struggle with domestic and foreign enemies (i.e., the "Great Satan").[10] But as evidence of dissension within Iran's ruling clergy mounted, and as rational choice theory took center stage in the social sciences, the mass society approach gave way—as it had, briefly, in post-Soviet studies—to an instrumentalist one. Advocates of this approach held that the politics of the Islamic Republic of Iran followed a rational and even predictable pattern. Clerical power struggles were fueled by competing material interests rather than by religion. While a populist Shi'ite ideology that celebrated the "natural" unity of the Muslim community initially obscured these divisions, war and economic crisis eventually forced the regime to initiate the very market reforms long favored by conservative clerics. Khomeini and his allies thus began to distance themselves from the populist-religious imagery they previously had used to hide their capitalist project.[11]

The question facing scholars of Iran is whether this recent shift from a symbolic theory of mass society to an instrumentalist account of social forces and strategic action will prove as analytically limiting as it has in other fields. Must we choose between two contending paradigms, or should we perhaps take a cue from our colleagues in post-Soviet studies and move toward a more institutionalist approach? I believe the answer to this question is yes in that we must transcend rather than submit to the constraints of the symbolic-instrumentalist dichotomy. To make this case, I would like to briefly discuss how the two competing accounts of charismatic authority have framed, and in some ways distorted, our understanding of Iran's revolution in general and its charismatic foundations in particular.[12] To illustrate, I will juxtapose two citations. Consider the following by Ervand Abrahamian:

> The slippery label fundamentalism has been thrown at Khomeini so often that it has stuck—so much that his own supporters . . . have proudly coined a new word, *bonyadegar* . . . translating literally the English term "fundamentalist." . . . *Khomeinism*, in contrast, is . . . concerned with sociopolitical issues. . . . [It is a form of] . . . Third World populism . . . a movement of the . . . middle class that mobilizes the lower classes. . . . Populist movements use charismatic figures and symbols . . . that have potent value in the mass culture [to attack] the status quo . . . [while] . . . stopping short of threatening the petty bourgeoisie and the whole principle of private property.[13]

Abrahamian's approach, to which I refer as *structural instrumentalism,* does *not* deny the importance of identity, culture, or even irrational forces. But it adheres to the canon of instrumentalist analysis by arguing that cultural symbols were used by elites, who *constructed* a charismatic ideology to conceal the conflicting interests of a heterogenous ruling coalition. Grafting rationalist accounts of politics onto neo-Marxist theories of ideology, this approach reduces charisma to a deliberate ideological construct. Now consider, in contrast, this citation from Hamid Dabashi:

> There is the innate . . . human need for permanent re-enchantment. . . . What would be the direction of "creative effervescence" other than towards a constant . . . upgrading of the most essential symbolics of religious culture. . . . This radical desire for permanent change is itself a more mundane expression of . . . the irresistible longing for permanent rebirth. . . . Coming-into-a-new-being . . . is what a social revolution promises. The delivery is immaterial. . . . The cult of Khomeini feeds on fertile Persian imagination beyond the finality of the revolutionary sage.[14]

Dabashi's evaluation is informed by an approach that I call "symbolic utopianism." According to this school of thought, political communities, states, or systems are welded together by culturally resonant symbols or rituals that explain an otherwise meaningless existence. When these symbols lose their appeal, masses and leaders alike break with the routines of everyday life by plunging into transcendent rituals, symbols, and experiences that express society's communal vitality. These experiences may be reawakened or personified by a charismatic leader, whose *genuine* belief in his divinity, coupled with his struggle to reaffirm that divinity through bold acts and utopian ideas, "reenchants" the soul of society, thus paving the way for a new legitimacy structure.

Each paradigm asks some questions and ignores others.[15] And since there always are more facts to absorb than questions to pose, each paradigm squeezes facts into molds that obscure more than they clarify. For example, while Abrahamian acknowledges the "potent value" of religious symbols for Iran's "mass culture," he insists that the term *fundamentalism* is irrelevant because the revolution was determined by sociopolitical factors. Yet it is hard to imagine how the clerics' manipulation of religious symbols would have been possible unless those symbols partly shaped the collective conscience of society. As Dabashi argues, cultural symbols embedded in the "fertile imagination" of Iranian society pushed both secular and religious elites toward a utopian project. But Dabashi's adherence to a symbolic paradigm runs into similar problems. Echoing Emile Durkheim, he highlights the emotional forces that drove the quest for "effervescence;" but his claim that the "delivery was immaterial"—that Iran's revolution was ultimately propelled by a transrational ethos—understates how closely this quest for spiritual reawakening was woven with the struggle to rationalize material interests.

Such dichotomous views of Iran's revolution—mass irrationality expressed through culturally "authentic" transrational rituals, or elite use of symbols for rational purposes—suggest how far we are from mapping the kinds of contradictions about which Friedland and Alford have written. Shouting across conceptual barriers, "each theory empirically observes the other levels of analysis, but it does not theorize their emergent properties."[16] As a result, our understanding of Iran's revolution suffers from two shortcomings. First, we do not sufficiently appreciate its most enduring trait, which is *the twin valorization of a zealous quest for utopia alongside the pragmatic struggle for political order.* Second, as Michael Fischer has observed, we cannot fully grasp the "dynamic instabilities" that have ensued from this wedding of what I call "contending authorities."[17]

Tracing the genesis of this complex phenomenon requires nothing less than a "political anthropology" of the state and its constituent parts. Putting aside the dichotomized view of structure versus agency that has bedeviled the social sciences, this kind of inquiry considers how a historically specific constellation of social, institutional, and symbolic forces generates a given set of authority structures—and how, in turn, political leaders compete to shed, transcend, or reshape this ideological-structural legacy.[18] Although this kind of analysis is always about a particular place and period, it can, by highlighting the dance of structure and agency that simultaneously invites and limits political change, teach us broader fundamental lessons about the dynamic interconnection among history, culture, and political action.

My goal in this chapter is to prepare the theoretical ground for this inquiry by accomplishing two things. First, I seek to recapture the theoretical nuances that have been obscured by the simplifying logic of dominant accounts of charisma. The challenge is not to jettison symbolic and instrumentalist paradigms, but rather to carefully rediscover their hidden subtleties and affinities. My second goal is to redraw these affinities, to create a new conceptual map highlighting the multifaceted nature of revolutionary charisma in an era of globalization. We will now turn to the first task at hand.

Rediscovering the First Face of Charisma: Symbolic Utopianism

Weber, Durkheim, Mannheim, and Shils

To tease out the theoretical insights that animate the paradigm of symbolic utopianism, we must pay close attention to the way in which scholars of modern mass society such as Karl Mannheim and William Kornhauser, as well as students of Islamic fundamentalism, reworked the theories of Max Weber and Emile Durkheim into a paradigm of utopian movements. The crucial link between these scholars has been obscured by the tendency to apply Weber's concept of charisma "to virtually every situation in which the popularity of a political or any public personality is involved."[19] While acknowledging these psychological traits, Weber places them in an integrated theory that explains how sociosymbolic crises create an irrational need for charismatic experience, and how this quest unintentionally promotes *revolutionary* change. This theory begins with the assumption that people are driven by a desire to justify their social deprivations in an existentially meaningless world. Religion offered such justifications. As Weber puts it, behind every religion "lies a stand towards something in the actual world which is experienced as specifically 'senseless.' "[20] Religious thinkers addressed this void by forging concepts of redemption that "expressed a systematic . . . 'image of the world,' "[21] thus "rationalizing" religion for the wider society.

Weber's account is quintessentially systemic and functional. He argues that the effort to explain the suffering of humanity *inadvertently* undermines political order: the more that intellectuals translated "otherworldly" images of religion into organized rituals, laws, and institutions, the more religion lost the "pure animist and magical" character through which humanity experienced the divine.[22] By denuding religion of its mystical elements, rationalized religion deprived humanity of the mysteries that made life worth living. When such spiritual "disenchantment" occurred in "moments of distress—whether psychic, physical, economic, ethical, religious, or political,"[23] society could be enveloped by a need for "otherworldly" experience or "re-enchantment." "All *extra*ordinary needs," Weber writes, "which *transcend* the sphere of everyday economic routines, have always been satisfied . . . on a *charismatic* basis. The further we go back into history, the more strongly this statement holds" (1111).

This remark reminds us that for Weber, pure charisma was a feature of *ancient societies*, particularly of small religious communities in which leaders and disciples contributed to the quest for charismatic experience. In ancient societies, charismatic leaders literally exuded the divine force of charisma: they and their followers *genuinely* believed that the former were "the bearers of specific gifts of body and mind that were considered 'supernatural' (in the sense that not everybody had access to them)" (1112). Disciples absorbed and multiplied their leader's personal charisma. But, Weber adds, this dynamic only occurred when the leader's charisma filled a *preexisting* emotional void; in other words, when conditions had already predisposed people toward charisma's charms. The resulting "charismatic bond" is based on unconditional and total obedience: "Where charisma is *genuine* . . . [its] basis lies . . . in the conception that it is the duty of those subject to charismatic authority to recognize its authenticity. . . . Psychologically, this recognition is a matter of complete personal devotion to the possessor of the quality" (242; italics mine).

Because it evokes and demands blind love, charisma is hostile to all mundane political or economic calculations that might block its cathartic magic. As Weber puts it, since "charisma lives in, not of, this world . . . [i]n contrast to all patriarchal forms of domination, it is opposed to all systematic economic activities. . . . For charisma is by nature not a continuous institution, but in its pure type the very opposite" (1113). This means that the charismatic leader spurns tradition as much, if not more, than doctrines based on rational-legal authority. "Genuine charismatic justice does not refer to rules; in its pure type, it . . . maintains its autonomy toward the sacredness of tradition as much as toward rationalist deductions from abstract norms" (1115). Freed from all constraints, the charismatic leader is a revolutionary prophet *who creates his own truths and revelations.*

While charisma sustains itself by tapping into a desire for other-worldly experience, Weber argues that its irrational effects cannot be sustained indefinitely. Eventually, it must be "routinized" in permanent institutions and doctrines. Three factors destabilize charisma. The first of these is the innately unstable nature of charisma itself. As Weber explains it, "a leader . . . *retains* [his charismatic authority] . . . solely by proving his power in practice. He must work miracles if he wants to be a prophet. . . . Most of all, his divine mission must prove itself by bringing well-being to his faithful followers" (1114). Insisting that his direct access to the divine merits absolute obedience, yet forced to take actions that make this allegiance conditional, the leader unintentionally betrays the mundane sources of his authority. Second, Weber holds that charisma loses it magic when the issue of succession demands the selection of a new leader who lacks the supernatural aura of the charismatic hero. This often occurs in tandem with a third process: the subsiding of the crisis that originally spawned the need for "otherworldly" experience. When this occurs, "the tide that lifted a charismatically led group . . . flows back into the channels of workaday routines" (1121). Focusing on the pragmatic needs of everyday existence, and especially on the need to justify their social and political interests, disciples develop a "desire to transform charisma . . . from a unique, transitory form of grace . . . into a permanent possession of every day" (1121). Because this task requires replacing the supernatural authority of the revolutionary leader with a "permanent" *institution and legitimacy formula*, routinization is almost always completed *after* the charismatic leader passes away. At this point charisma is reduced to "a mere component of a concrete historical structure," a "dogma, doctrine, theory, regulation, law or petrified tradition" (1121–22).

Weber doubted that the above cycle would occur in modern societies. As he puts it, "the prophet for whom so many of our younger generation yearns simply does not exist."[24] There seem to be two reasons for his drawing this conclusion. First, Weber assumed that the cumulative process of scientific rationalization undermines the *need* of humanity for "pure charisma." Second, by focusing on the individual effort to justify suffering through divine redemption, Weber underestimated the role that all *collective symbolic systems*—whether modern or traditional—play in creating the means through which societies reaffirm their existence. If the need for otherworldly experience is *unchanging*, and if this need can be met by all symbolic systems, should we not conclude that the birth and routinization of pure charisma might also take place in modern societies?

By answering this question in the affirmative, Emile Durkheim furnished the sociological underpinnings for the analysis of modern charismatic movements. Not only does he assume that the need for "otherworldly" experience is essential to human beings; but, in contrast with Weber's focus on the individual's effort to rationalize his or her suffering, he also argues that each society's *preexisting "conscience collective"* provided the symbolic means through which humans "idealize" an alternative social world. The individual, Durkheim argues, internalized this collective vision *unconsciously*, by participating in shared rituals and mass celebrations, all of which create a "state of effervescence which changes the conditions of psychic activity. Vital energies are over-excited, passions more active. . . . Man . . . feels himself transformed. . . . The real world . . . has been replaced by . . . an ideal world."[25] Yet if the magical experience of "effervescence" has much in common with the dynamics of "re-enchantment," Durkheim's analysis of the former differs from the latter in two significant ways. First, he believed that the rapid modernization would increase people's *need* for spiritual re-enchantment. For by weakening the spiritual bonds of society, the "division of labor" into specialized fields overwhelmed individuals with intolerable feelings of moral isolation or "anomie." "There are periods in history," he writes, "when under the influence of some great collective shock, social interactions have become much more frequent. . . . Men look for each other and assemble" and thus experience that "general effervescence . . . which is characteristic of revolutionary . . . epochs."[26] Second, Durkheim holds that many kinds of "mythologies and theologies"[27]—including secular rituals such as the French Revolution—could serve as vehicles for collective effervescence and thus collective action.[28] While affirming that great leaders may advance this process by giving human form to the transrational aspirations of society, he argues that the symbolic and even physical intensity of the collective ritual itself matters most.

Seizing upon Durkheim's structural analysis of modern rituals, Mannheim forged a theory highlighting the organic link between modernization crises and "utopian" mass movements. Echoing Durkheim, he argues that as science and education exposed the man-made foundations of all beliefs, the individual experienced a completely "novel" condition: unable to "bear up under such severe inner crises as scepticism," he was forced to live "life in terms of an inner balance which must be ever won anew."[29] The majority were not up to this task. Unable to contend with a "realm of experience [in which] a discrepancy becomes apparent between the traditional modes of thought and the novel objects of experiences" (101), most people strive to transform the most modern of ideas—be they socialism, liberalism, or conservatism—into vehicles of utopian or ritual experience. Mannheim argues that this process was first manifested in the "orgiastic chiliasm of the Anabaptists" (211). By fusing the idea of collective redemption with the longings of underprivileged classes, chiliasm infused a messianic-revolutionary spirit into religion. "The . . . turning-point in modern history was . . . the moment in which 'Chiliasm' joined forces with the active demands of the oppressed strata of society. The very idea of the dawn of a millennial kingdom on earth always contained a revolutionizing tendency" (211–12).

This analysis echoes Weber's account of the charismatic prophet. Just as the prophet makes his own laws, while the chiliast creates his own reality by collapsing *historical and mythical time*: thus "he is not . . . concerned with the millennium . . . to come: what is important . . . is that it happened here and now, and that it arose . . . as a sudden swing over into another kind of existence . . . as a longed-for realization . . .

in this world" (216–17). Yet if this quest to collapse present and future time unwittingly sets the stage for revolutionary change, Mannheim argues that modernization *strengthens* this quest for utopia. Although doctrines such as socialism and liberalism may be outwardly rational in comparison to chiliasm, Mannheim suggests that in an age of mass politics, even the notion of democracy can become infused with a utopian-revolutionary spirit. This process occurs because mass politics creates a fragmented society in which no single worldview triumphs. Absent one dominant framework, each class insists that its utopia represents absolute truth, while dismissing its opponents' ideas as mere ideologies serving particular interests. "Free-floating intellectuals" encourage such ideological battles. Products of educational systems that distance them from any one class, they fanatically embrace the utopias of other classes precisely because they lack organic ties to any one weltanschauung.[30] In Mannheim's sociology—as in the work of Edward Shils, who rendered Mannheim's language accessible to a wider audience—modern intellectuals are the leading proponents of utopian ideas (or "charismatic ideologies," to use Shils's language).[31] Thus they are not legitimators of any particular interest. Instead, like Weber's charismatic prophet, modern intellectuals are the revolutionary creators of new realities that burst "the bonds of the existing order."[32]

From Mass Society to Symbolic Utopianism: The Paradigm Emerges

William Kornhauser synthesized the ideas of Weber, Durkheim, Mannheim, Shils, and others to produce the first master theory of "mass society." Like Durkheim, Kornhauser assumes that human nature is molded by participation in class, group, or associational life. Elites and masses operate "rationally" so long as their worldviews emerge from the day-to-day realities of their respective associational lives. But during periods of rapid modernization, a dangerous condition emerges in which "elites are unprotected from mass pressures and masses are unprotected from elite pressures."[33] By depriving *all members of society* of the "few points at which" social life can be "checked by personal experience and the experience of others" (37), this dynamic gives elites and masses alike a "feeling of resentment against the present and hope for something completely new in the future" (48). This utopian flame is lit by two forces, the first of which is the cathartic experience that mass movements themselves provide. By giving the alienated a chance to "substitute external identities for inner ones, to replace an unwanted or unknown self with a collective image" (112), these movements create the ritualistic means through which individuals move from anomie to mass activism. The second such force is constituted by the millennial ideologies of alienated intellectuals. Echoing Mannheim and Shils, Kornhauser argues that because "intellectuals . . . live for and off symbols . . . they are least able to suffer a vacuum in the symbolic sphere; at the same time, they . . . know how to create the symbols to fill" this vacuum (184–85). The purpose of these symbols is *not* to rationalize material interests. Rather, intellectuals' "remoteness from the day-to-day interests of people" "breeds resentment against the whole structure of society," thus giving "free reign to . . . messianic tendencies" (191–92). An educated but alienated public then absorbs the intellectuals' appeals in a mutually constitutive dynamic that engulfs elites and masses in *populism.* This term carries none of the Marxist baggage that was later attached to it. For Kornhauser, populist ideas serve an *existential* function. By making "the uniformity of opinion among large numbers of people" the "supreme standard, superordinate to traditional values, professional standards, and institutional autonomy," they give alienated people "directives on how to feel" about themselves (109). Alienated intellectuals spontaneously voice this *cris de coeur.* They are the modern-day equivalent of charismatic leaders, while their followers are the modern-day equivalent of charismatic disciples.

The systemic nature of utopianism places the modern populist in a vexing position. While leaders articulate populist longings, they share their followers' quest for catharsis. Yet their legitimacy cannot rest forever on such irrational appeals. How then can leaders meet the *practical* needs of their followers while living a revolutionary ethos? Citing Weber, Kornhauser writes that "[a]s a form of charismatic leadership," totalitarian cadres in mass movements are "outside the realm of everyday routine" and "foreign to all rules" (35). Thus, he deduces, these movements retain their utopian quality *so long as they are not captured by the state* (123). Yet while totalitarian states seek to hinder mass movements, the latter's emergence is a *precondition* for creating totalitarian orders. But Kornhauser has little to say about how this paradoxical transition from movement to state occurs.

Strange as it may seem, this failure to theorize the process of symbolic rationalization is a product of Kornhauser's analytical eloquence. His reading of Weber, Durkheim, and Mannheim is highly structuralist in that Kornhauser's socioinstitutional analysis of the collapse of group life transcends differences of culture, religion, or custom. But it lacks a feel for the internal logic of collective symbols and action that animates the work of Durkheim, Mannheim, and Weber. Thus despite Kornhauser's focus on the role that intellectuals play in creating populist ideology, he treats the cultures of which they are a part as a "black box." Are symbol systems merely vessels for the universal experience of alienation, or do some articulate this angst better than others, thus offering a *culturally specific* means through which charisma creates both a revolutionary and re-legitimating logic?

Despite his crypto-Marxism, Kornhauser inadvertently anticipated this sticking point in his analysis of the distinctive imprint that subcultures of socially and physically isolated classes or social groups give to the universal experience of alienation. For example, he holds that a "glorification of the rural past" born of "agrarian antagonism to symbols of urban preeminence" colored the ideologies of national socialism and fascism.[34] But he does not take this distinction between particular and universal consciousness to its logical conclusion by asking whether some symbolic systems are more likely to spark charismatic movements than others. This very question later animated students of Islamic fundamentalism such as Manfred Halpern. Highlighting the *interaction* of socioinstitutional dislocation and cultural alienation, Halpern argues that

> neo-Islamic totalitarianism appeals to a particular surplus in the population: the peasant . . . no longer with any land; workers . . . replaced or easily replaceable; . . . students without jobs; *ulema* [Islamic scholars] . . . above all . . . white collar workers and members of the lower middle class who resent the monopoly of power and wealth of those who dominate the state. . . . Neo-Islamic totalitarian movements . . . offer the individual the chance . . . to find salvation, by merging his fate entirely with that of a group striving to resurrect an idealized past.[35]

Note that while the desire for redemption was sparked by structural conditions common to all mass movements, in Halpern's view the Muslim Brethren's "chiliastic, reformist, and uprooted elements" were impelled by a symbolic logic, one that "retained sufism's striving for the millennium, and many of its organizational forms."[36] This structural-symbolic approach was both anticipated and later echoed by other scholars of Islamic fundamentalism, particularly those who studied extremist movements in Iran and Egypt.[37] Such was its enduring attraction that by the late eighties, elements of this paradigm entered the comparative framework informing the *Fundamentalism Project* of the American Academy of Arts and Sciences.[38] These and other studies of revivalism completed the paradigm of symbolic utopianism by demonstrating that "pure charisma" occurs only rarely—when there is what Weber calls an "elective affinity," or natural fit, between structural and cultural-symbolic forces.

The Second Face: Structural Instrumentalism and Manufactured Charisma

Elites, Ruling Formulas, and Myths

In contrast with symbolic explanations, structural instrumentalism holds that modernization engenders an expanding cognitive gap between the ways in which leaders and followers perceive authority in general, and charisma in particular. But while modernization invites the elite's manipulation of mass disenchantment for rational purposes, this project is as likely to sow anarchy as it is to create order. Whether modernization is ultimately creative or destructive depends partly on the ability of elites to "manufacture" forms of charisma that legitimate authority, be it traditional or modern.

We can trace the modern roots of instrumentalist theory to Gaetano Mosca,[39] who argued that the shared symbols of all societies—whether based on notions of a transcendent God or on modern ideas of democracy—were man-made "political formulas." Yet, he insists, the world's "great superstitions" were not "mere quackeries aptly invented to trick the masses into obedience." Instead, "they answer a real need in man's social nature; and this need, so universally felt, of governing and knowing that one is governed . . . on the basis of a moral principle, has . . . a *practical* and real importance."[40] These two themes—the *practical utility* of political myths and their *differential* understanding by leaders and the masses—are central to elite theory. From Mosca onward, elite theorists have argued that the masses' belief in transcendent truths "contributes powerfully to consolidating political organization and unifying peoples."[41] However, as Mosca's rationalist view of myths suggests, political order is not inevitable; it depends on the ability of elites to grasp the inner logic of the masses' worldview and employ it to create political order.[42] The third tenet of elite theory holds that by bringing the uneducated masses into the political arena, modernization widens the cognitive gap between leaders and followers. This process generates contradictory consequences: while an expanded franchise requires increasingly rational explanations of politics, democracy encourages elites to appeal to the mentality of the "mob." Highlighting this discordant dynamic, George Sorel warns that democracy invites "the pernicious influence of the demagogues." This is to be prevented by propagating "political myths," the most progressive of which was the "proletarian general strike: it awakes in the depth of the soul a sentiment of the sublime proportional to the conditions of a gigantic struggle . . . and thus protects the workers from the quackery of ambitious leaders."[43]

Yet if mass politics encourages elite demagoguery, theorists of "manufactured charisma" insist that modernization inhibits the creation of a genuine charismatic bond between leaders and followers. This bond is obstructed not merely by the cognitive gap mentioned earlier. Joseph Bensman and Michael Givant argue that it is also blocked by the growing physical gap between leaders and followers. While in small traditional societies they shared the emotionally intense experience of charisma, in modern societies leaders and followers are separated by thousands of miles.[44] Under such conditions, projecting "an image of a direct, warm, or exciting . . . 'human' persona" requires the manipulation of mass communications to "convey a sense of immediacy that appears to negate the very media that require its use."[45] This planned creation of an otherwise spurious bond is the very antithesis of pure charisma—which, as Bensman and Givant remind us, entails "the direct imputation of . . . the divine gift of grace . . . without the planned intervention of rational political managers. . . . The pure charismatic leader does not worry about his image, for his image is, to him, his reality."[46] But modern leaders *must* worry about their image. To transform whatever personal charisma they may have into a *social force*, they must overcome the physical chasm between themselves and their followers by "manufacturing" charisma.[47]

Bensman and Givant hold that this instrumentalist dynamic is especially marked in developing societies, where uneven advancement produces a culturally explosive chasm between elites and masses. Thus to ensure social cohesion, "highly sophisticated, European trained political leaders adopt the masks of charismatic leadership in order to create a national consciousness among a populace."[48] Such leaders deliberately "create the appearance of irrationality in societies where personal, irrational forms and symbols are the only meaningful styles of communication."[49] Pursuing this argument, Bensman and Givant define "modern rational charisma" as a "set of techniques . . . used by rational leaders . . . to both transcend and veil the use of rationality in political action."[50] This effort to produce "irrational legitimacy," to use Ronald Glassman's evocative term, can be risky, since the elite's effort to "alleviate the feeling of despair" through "irrational solutions" can unleash forces beyond their control.[51] Whether the use of manufactured charisma provokes order or chaos depends in part on the organizational and ideological skills of elites themselves.

Three Variants of Structural Instrumentalism

By suggesting that routinization is not preordained by some historical or systemic logic, the preceding accounts of manufactured charisma place human agency at the center of analysis. Still, these accounts fail to shed much light on two mysteries: *why* do elites use charisma, and what is the link between elite actions and the social interests of society's constituent groups? On these two questions there has been little consensus. Instead, structural instrumentalist theories of charisma have evolved along three trajectories, the third of which, national or authoritarian populism, offers the most compelling answers.

Let us begin with rational-choice accounts of ethnoreligious identity. Although not explicitly concerned with charisma, they emphasize the elite's use of culture or religion to promote or legitimate collective action. Such action is difficult to produce because most people prefer to let others pay the costs of producing public goods. This "free rider" problem is especially marked in large groups, where barriers to communication discourage individuals from cooperating.[52] The manipulation of ethnic, religious, or linguistic symbols is one strategy used to overcome these barriers. In its purist form, rational choice theory argues that ethnoreligious elites are "political entrepreneurs" who provide material or symbolic incentives to promote cooperation.[53] Having no essential loyalty to any one identity, they adopt those cultural symbols that provide the most effective language for inspiring collective action. As a result, elites often send conflicting messages. As Nikki Keddie argues in the case of Seyyed Jamal al-Din al-Afghani, this nineteenth-century Islamic reformer used a secular language when addressing the modern intelligentsia, and a religious language when speaking to the masses or the clergy.[54]

This strategy can either strengthen or destabilize society. If elites have a shallow grasp of mass culture, their conflicting ideas are easily exposed, thus alienating both traditional and modern followers. But when they understand their followers' culture, or have the rhetorical skills to obscure conflicting messages, this same strategy can promote forms of collective action that otherwise might not exist. In short, sophisticated rational-choice accounts acknowledge that symbols are not *infinitely* malleable. As Paul Brass notes, "the values and institutions of a persisting cultural group will suggest what appeals and symbols will be effective and what will not be."[55] This said, rational choice theory suffers from an oversimplified view of the motivations behind elite action. Assuming that elites are motivated by a crass desire for power, the theory attributes a set of universal preferences without considering how and in what ways elite motivations may be conditioned by the local culture or symbolic system.

Clifford Geertz offered a more dynamic view of elite and mass interaction. While he has been described as the father of a "primordialist" theory that ascribes ideologies of developing nations to the innate power of deeply embedded identities, Geertz builds a bridge between rationalist and symbolic approaches. Thus he *begins* with the Durkheimian proposition that culture provides the "cognitive road maps" by which individuals find their place in society. These maps are *manifestly* religious but *latently* political: they prescribe moral behaviors that inadvertently legitimate political order. Inevitably, however, those who have unconsciously internalized the ordering power of traditional symbols face modernity's perplexing message that religion is a man-made construct. With his cognitive universe profoundly shaken, the average person reacts by investing cultural symbols with new, explicitly political meanings. Thus "the function of ideology is to make an autonomous politics possible by providing the authoritative concepts that render it meaningful, the suasive images by means of which it can be sensibly grasped."[56] Yet while Geertz accounts for the *systemic politicization* of religion in Durkheimian terms, he tries to explain the consequences of this process in *instrumentalist* terms. Like Mosca, Bensman, and Givant, he argues that elites and their followers perceive and respond to the disenchantments of rapid modernization differently. The masses suffer a severe crisis of symbolic or "cultural strain" (219, 221). In contrast, elites provide "ideological guidance," the central feature of which is the authoritative reworking of cultural symbols into a new "compelling image of social reality" (229). But as his analysis of Indonesia's President Sukarno reminds us, even a telegenic leader may lack the skills for providing ideological guidance. Where these gifts are wanting, elites may "drift to revivalistic irrationalism and unbridled fantasy" (229)— in short, they may succumb to utopianism. By thus highlighting the fragile interplay of elite and mass logics, Geertz reaffirms one of the key insights of instrumentalist theory. What he does not do, however, is offer a sufficiently clear account of elite motivations. Instead, as Leonard Binder observes, Geertz remains wedded to a functionalist logic that assumes—without explaining why—that the inevitable *role* of leaders is (or should be) to reassert the smooth functioning of the political system itself.[57]

The variants of instrumentalist theory that have most influenced the study of modern charisma are neo-Marxist accounts of national or authoritarian populism. These accounts draw on elite, rational choice, and symbolic theory to provide a comprehensive, systematic explanation of the *interaction* of elite interest, social class, and mass culture. They do so by addressing one of the central mysteries of Marx's writings: how do leaders transform their subjective grasp of class consciousness into organized movements and ideologies? Antonio Gramsci addressed this question by grafting elite theory onto Marxist analysis. Adopting the elitist logic of the Machiavellians, he argues that acting through political parties, leaders forge ideological "hegemony" within their own social classes, and between dominant and subordinate classes as well. This is not a matter of promoting "false consciousness," a term Gramsci spurned. Hegemony entails a conscious effort to legitimate organized support. Like Mosca, Gramsci argues that to be effective, elites must "organically" reflect the culture of their constituents. Conversely, "arbitrary" leaders who impose themselves on an alien constituency cannot achieve genuine hegemony.[58] Gramsci holds that this *failure* to produce hegemony opens the door to charismatic leadership: "At a certain point in their historical lives, social classes become detached from their traditional parties. . . . When such crises occur . . . the field is open for violent solutions, for the activities of unknown forces, represented by charismatic 'men of destiny.' "[59] These leaders bear little resemblance to Weber's charismatic hero. While the latter shares his followers' irrationality, Gramsci maintains that the charismatic leader is a rational actor: he "changes men and programs and, with greater speed than is achieved by the subordinate classes, reabsorbs the control that was slipping from its grasp."[60] Charisma is thus an ideological surrogate for re-traditionalization. Arising during those historical junctures when "no group, neither the conservatives nor the progressives, has the strength for victory," it legitimates "a static equilibrium."[61]

Gramsci's analysis of hegemonic crises inspired a wide range of neo-Marxist accounts of authoritarian or national populism. Derived from studies of Latin America, these theories hold that authoritarian populism emerges when a precarious balance between a rising urban bourgeoisie and the ruling rural oligarchy obliges the latter to ally with the subordinate urban petty bourgeoisie. This alliance cannot be legitimated merely by recourse to rational-modern ideology. As Gino Germani puts it, "democratization variously affected the politicization of both the masses and the elites." While the former's worldview was marked by "the dominance of tradition . . . connected to preindustrial life forms," the elite's perspective was shaped by an "extreme Machiavellianism" that saw "the affirmation of tradition . . . [as] essential for securing social stability."[62] This dynamic created a paradoxical situation: on the one hand, as leaders manipulated mass fantasies, "a gap was created between the aims of the elite and those of the masses." On the other hand, the ensuing "ideological action tended to reinforce and to fuse with cultural or traditional authoritarianism," thus undermining the elite's ability to *unilaterally* manipulate popular symbols. Caught in this structural bind, charismatic leaders are both empowered and constrained. By cultivating a persona that reflects the longings of the masses, they not only engage the loyalty of the people, but also obscure the self-serving nature of their social project. Peron's intuition, flexibility, and political pragmatism, Germani argues, "together with his qualities as a charismatic leader (with peculiarities especially suited to stimulate and express the Creole spontaneity) allowed him to control and profit from these contrasting elements."[63] But this manipulation of different voices also assures that the populist leader, far from being the Godlike superman, is full of ambiguity and contradiction. While such ambiguity has tactical value, the projection of irrational messages to the masses and rational ideology to the elite risks disillusioning both. Germani sums up this dilemma in his analysis of Peron:

> The military and the available masses were necessary for his ascent to power. This contradiction . . . inherent in the movement's own constitution, had wide-ranging consequences for the regime's organization, its political policy, its public image, and even the internal heterogeneity and the intrinsic ambiguity of Peronism which has survived until today.[64]

When does the contradictory nature of modern charisma support order, and when does it undermine it? Presumably, the answer to this question partly lies in the rhetorical skills of elites and their grasp of popular culture versus their ability to forge a ruling apparatus possessing the unity and organizational capacity to control mass political organizations. Seen through this dynamic lens, the rationalization of charisma depends as much on socioeconomic and institutional forces as it does on the ideological talents of the ruling elite.

The Inescapable Logic of Modernization Theory?

Are we left then with two opposing concepts of utopian leaders and movements? The points of divergence are clear: while both the symbolic and instrumentalist paradigms suggest that charismatic movements stem from rapid modernization, symbolic accounts argue that charisma emerges from a crisis of cultural disorientation and sociopolitical dislocation that systemically (and unintentionally) transforms the consciousness of elites and masses alike. In contrast, instrumentalist approaches maintain that mass alienation becomes a social force when elites—by virtue of the cognitive gap that separates them from the masses—manipulate cultural alienation to re-create and/or sustain political order.

This said, the above review of each paradigm suggests several important points of theoretical convergence. For example, while symbolic theories trace pure charisma to the structural effects of rapid modernization, its most nuanced variants acknowledge the "pushing effect" of material interests by arguing that the practical exigencies of daily life push elites toward an instrumentalist view of charisma. Where such theories fall short is in conceptualizing this shift from mass irrationality to new forms of legitimacy. Similarly, while structural theories highlight the rationalizing logic of elites, its most comprehensive and dynamic variant acknowledges the "pulling effect" that mass cultural alienation can have on a leader's efforts to use charisma in ways that justify the economic interests of his social class. But such theories offer a rudimentary account of why certain symbolic systems invite charismatic crises in the first place. In short, each theory incorporates some dimension of the other. Where they part company is in their divergent conceptions of the rationalities shaping elite and mass responses to rapid social and cultural change.

Such conceptual overlapping suggests a simple solution: rather than assume that elite and mass reactions to crises of modernization must either converge or diverge, we might view their responses as part of a linear *dialectic* through which political consciousness—particularly that of the elite—changes. Initially, elites and masses *both* respond to the alienating effects of rapid modernization by embracing culturally inspired utopias. Later, the sobering slap of material, political, or state interests awakens the elites from their utopian stupor, renewing an instrumentalist rationality that sets them apart from the masses. Seen through this lens, symbolic and instrumentalist paradigms are two sides of the same coin. We can employ Weber, Durkheim, Mannheim, Kornhauser, and others to explain the crisis of alienation that spawns charismatic leaders and movements. Turning to Marx, Gramsci, Brass, Bensman, Givant, Germani, and others, we can then explain the subsequent process by which elites transform pure charisma into ideologies and institutions that legitimate the interests of a particular class or social group.

Still, the problem with this approach is its insistence on viewing change in dialectical terms. Far from capturing the chaotic, nonlinear struggle of competing authority systems that has marked our postmodern era, this familiar approach remains embedded in the fundamental premises of Western modernization theory, *whether presented in culturalist or instrumentalist forms:* namely, that the instrumentalization of charisma will eventually reestablish *one dominant and stable form of legitimacy,* be it based on tradition and custom or modern, rational-legal authority. This is not to say that charisma disappears completely.

Rather, as Weber's own analysis of routinization suggests, instrumentalized charisma may become an ideological, but *subordinate,* prop for tradition (as it does in monarchies) or for modernity (as it does in some democracies). Joined at the hip of modernization theory, both symbolic and instrumentalist accounts of authority in general, and of charisma in particular, suggest that leaders can be genuinely charismatic, or they can manipulate the masses' utopian longings to legitimate their rule; *however, they cannot serve both logics equally.* To grasp this contradictory dynamic, we need a multifaceted map of authority systems that transcends all teleological conceptions of modernization—including those that animated Weber's sociology of charisma.

Revolutionary Charisma in a Globalizing Age

Conceptual maps are inductive, heuristic tools. They offer a framework that points analysis in a certain direction without imposing rigid assumptions about outcomes. By their very nature, these maps must be periodically revised to keep pace with the changing social landscape. This process of remapping does not mean abandoning the old conceptual signposts; rather, it requires *relinking* these posts in a way that more effectively tracks new social and political realities. The dialectical map of charisma described earlier had its moment: it pointed forward, beckoning us to focus on a "natural" move from transrational to rational authority. I would like to suggest, however, that over the last half century, profound social, intellectual, economic, and technological changes have altered the relationship between transrational and rationalist logics, so that a revised map of authority systems is needed.

For the leaders of Iran's revolution, these changes came at an inconvenient moment.[65] Many had been championing a messianic ideology that promised to liberate the entire world from the shackles of materialism and injustice. However, they operated in a social, economic, and political context that thwarted such grandiose aspirations. Indeed, Iran's revolution followed a pattern of political change that had far more in common with the multifaceted political orders in Third World states of the midtwentieth century than with the monolithic systems birthed by the "great revolutions" of the previous era. This ideological heterogeneity was expressed in new institutional and ideological forms that belied easy classification. Part charismatic, part legal-rational, part traditional, these authority systems were not the products of any linear developmental logic.

Said Arjomand has traced the above changes to the "increasing . . . conflict among the heterogenous principles of order"[66] that has marked the modern era. He argues that the global diffusion of competing notions of constitutionalism has made philosophical eclecticism the order of the day. While his focus on constitutional principles hits the mark, I would argue that this development is a product of a much wider set of processes, the roots of which can be traced to the *increasing* globalization of economic, cultural, and political life. I emphasize the word *increasing* because globalization is a twentieth-century phenomenon, the pace of which began to accelerate during the post–World War II years. Indeed, it can be argued that India's Mahatma Gandhi was the first great charismatic leader to personify globalization's beguiling effects. As revealed in the biography by Susanne and Lloyd Rudolph, Ghandi spontaneously experienced *and* deliberately manufactured charismatic authority. A product of both East and West, his vision of politics was molded by the notion of instrumentalism and legal-rational authority as much as it was forged by a charismatic sensibility that bore the imprint of his upbringing and his native culture. His struggle to reconcile Gandhi the politician versus Gandhi the ideologist[67] anticipated a world in which political leaders assimilate *contending* notions of authority through the course of their life experiences.

The following map of contending authorities connects the four conceptual guideposts that I believe distinguish charismatic leaders and ideologies in our postmodern age: (1) multiple biographies; (2) the layering of multiple, imagined worlds; (3) dissonant institutionalization; and (4) complex routinization. While these heuristic guidelines may be applied to any number of countries or regions, I will briefly indicate how each has operated in the particular case of the Islamic Republic of Iran. In doing so I offer the reader a taste of what is to come: a journey through the birth and development of a system of contending authorities whose paradoxical consequences continue to shape the politics and ideological struggles of the Islamic Republic.

Multiple Biographies

The notion of multiple biographies begins with the premise that there is no a priori reason to assume that elite consciousness must be dominated by either cultural alienation or rational calculation. Rather, leaders may consciously or unconsciously absorb experiences, messages, and symbols that imbue them with *contending* concepts of authority. Although the phenomenon of multiple biographies is not entirely new, it is a product of the competing cultural, social, and political forces that have shaped the consciousness of charismatic Third World leaders in the postmodern age. Whether we are talking about Ayatollah Khomeini, Rashid Ghannouchi, or Sheykh Fadlallah, most Islamist leaders today do not fit the one-dimensional mold of the "true believer."[68] They may see themselves, to use Eric Hoffer's evocative language, as "part of something that stretches endlessly backward and forward—something eternal."[69] But in a world of globalized communications, this quest for utopia has been transformed by a cacophony of rationalities.[70]

The phenomenon of multiple biographies should be distinguished from two other approaches to the study of biography and political leadership. First, it should not be confused with psychoanalytic accounts of multiple personalities or other "dysfunctional" forms of leadership. Employing Freudian theories, Harold Lasswell and others argue that the "pathologies" of extremist leaders are rooted in the process by which they unconsciously "project" the narcissistic injuries or emotional repressions of youth onto the public field.[71] While it is certainly possible that the burning desire for spiritual transcendence that typifies the modern (or postmodern) charismatic prophet may have roots in the formative trials and tribulations of childhood, the notion that such experience *must* trump all, that it is so "over-determining" that it must produce a fundamentally irrational personality, is not compelling. This said, the concept of multiple biographies retains the key assumption that the formative episodes of youth may infuse a leader with an enduring desire to experience transcendent or spiritual forces. Thus the biography of a leader often begins with an analysis of the particular events that may have given rise to an enduring desire for transrational experience. From that point onward, it is an empirical question as to what other commitments attach themselves to the quest for spiritual effervescence.

Second, the concept of multiple biographies includes—but also transcends—the familiar postmodern approach that locates the *political importance* of biography not in the "facts," but in the struggle of disciples to selectively reinterpret the illusive details of their leader's life history. As Michael Fischer astutely notes, this is only *one* of several "levels of understanding" from which the life history of a charismatic leader can be evaluated. It is certainly true that "Khomeini's life . . . is itself a revolutionary instrument . . . to be utilized. The facts of the matter are vague and contradictory, and largely irrelevant." But, he asks, doesn't biography also inform "from multiple angles, portraits in the round, or wider social relations and cultural forms refracted through one living?"[72] These "refractions" are not merely objective. Biographies may seem vague not only to those who interpret and use them: as Fischer observes, when leaders assimilate diverse values and notions of authority, their *own* self-understanding may be multidimensional or even contradictory.

This revealing analysis is full of political and social implications. Charismatic leaders who absorb multiples visions of authority bear little resemblance to the political opportunist described earlier in the instrumentalist accounts of leadership. They do not rationally forge alternative messages for different constituencies. Instead, because these leaders are *genuinely* attracted to competing ideals and norms, they consciously or unconsciously direct a confusing array of signals to their disciples and the wider populace. This contradictory dynamic can have paradoxical consequences for the institutional and ideological development of the state: not only does it mean that the leader's own deep ambivalences will be reflected in the institutions and doctrines of the state; but, as I describe below, it also makes it highly likely that after he dies, the struggle to routinize the leader's ideological legacy will encounter a myriad of difficulties, opportunities, and contradictions.

In the case of Khomeini, we shall see in chapter 2 that the personal deprivations of youth, together with his education in Islamic mysticism, marked him with an enduring desire for—and ability to express—charismatic experience. Yet Khomeini could not have anticipated the countervailing notions of authority that he would absorb over the next seven decades. If the political behavior that ensued from this multiple biography was erratic and sometimes confused, this reflected the different visions of authority that shaped Khomeini's political imagination.

The Layering of Multiple, Imagined Worlds

In contrast with the phenomenon of multiple biographies, which focuses on the individual, "multiple, imagined worlds" refers to the *shared* heterogenous worldview that specific social groups collectively absorb when the social, cultural, and political dynamics of globalization expose them to multiple visions of political community. These groups tend to be composed of intellectuals—in other words, men and women who make their living from the study, consumption, or creation of secular or religious knowledge. We have already noted that symbolic and instrumentalist theories of charisma focus on the intellectuals' role in spontaneously exuding or instrumentally manipulating the populace's quest for "re-enchantment." We have also noted that these two dynamics can be viewed dialectically. As Geertz and others note, mass alienation may be a *precondition* for the rational manipulation of symbols by an intellectual or political elite. However, there is no a priori reason to expect that rapid modernization will engender this neat transition from transrational to rational elite consciousness. The conventional literature on the "alienation" of Third World intellectuals assumed that this dialectic stemmed from *sequential socialization.* Moving from the rural world to the modern metropolis, the members of a rising intelligentsia would either learn how to adjust the traditional ethos of the village to the rational exigencies of the modern city, or they would be overwhelmed by anomie when such efforts at compartmentalization become unbearable.[73] While this dichotomizing logic still operates today, in recent years many "knowledge communities" in developing nations have been exposed to processes of *concurrent socialization* that have blurred the geographical, institutional, cultural, and cognitive boundaries between the traditional and modern world.[74] I have in mind a diverse range of social, cultural, political, and economic forces that communicate multiple but *shared* rationalities to a given intellectual community. Rather than experience these visions as either separate or opposed realities, the members of this community absorb them as *multiple layers* of one complex and elusive collective reality.

Economic, political, and cultural globalization has been the central force behind this blending of conventional identities and rationalities. Radio transmissions, tapes, newspapers, global satellite television, human travels to and from the Third World diaspora communities in the West, and the recent expansion of the Internet—all this has allowed people from a myriad of social classes and groups to access different representations of authority.[75] The result, writes Arjun Appadurai, has been a transformation in the very way that some social groups *imagine* political communities:

> The image, the imagined, the imaginary—these are all terms which direct us to something . . . new in global cultural processes: *the imagination as a social practice.* No longer mere fantasy (opium for the masses) . . . no longer simple escape (from a world defined principally by more concrete purposes . . .), no longer elite pastime (thus not relevant to the lives of ordinary people) and no longer mere contemplation (irrelevant for new forms of desire and subjectivity), the imagination has become . . . sites of agency ("individuals") and globally defined fields of possibility.[76]

Note that Appadurai implies something quite different from Benedict Anderson's "imagined communities." The latter is a metaphor for the creation of *distinct* and often antagonistic *national* identities.[77] In contrast, Appadurai's postmodern sensibility suggests that nationalist identities are continuously confronting and absorbing contending visions of community. Hence he speaks of "multiple worlds . . . constituted by the historically situated imaginations of persons and groups spread around the globe."[78]

Because the process described above has not affected all groups equally, it would be useful to distinguish between *primary* and *secondary* exposure to multiple imaginations. The former obtains in professions that bring people into daily contact with global intellectual and social trends. The modern knowledge professions such as journalism, academia, and science provide the most fertile grounds for multidimensional imaginations. Still, we must avoid the straitjacket of modern/ traditional dichotomizing. Where "traditional" institutions, such as religious seminaries, have been exposed to the contending rationalities of a globalizing world, primary exposure to multiple imaginations might also ensue. In contrast, in those arenas where direct contact with globalizing forces (whether "modern" or "traditional") is impeded by institutional forces or is mediated by other actors, *secondary* exposure to multiple imaginations will ensue.[79]

Chapter 3 explores the significance of multiple shared imaginations in Iran's revolution. We shall see that the modernizing and largely state-dependent intelligentsia was the primary absorber of multiple imaginations. 'Ali Shari'ati and other intellectuals developed a highly contradictory and implicitly relativistic consciousness. While their exposure to Shi'ism's messianic-mystical qualities imbued these thinkers with deep longings for charismatic experience, their exposure to existentialist and Marxist thought gave them a keen appreciation of the malleability and utility of religion. Shari'ati tried to unite these two logics by forging a revolutionary ideology that promised the people deliverance from social and cultural alienation. Khomeini distrusted Shari'ati and other "Islamic Leftists," as I call them. But due to the increasingly porous walls between seminary and university, he and his clerical allies imbibed the blend of utopian longing and revolutionary instrumentalism that Shari'ati articulated. Such secondary exposure to multiple imaginations helped set the stage for the institutionalization of contending authorities in the ideology of Khomeini, and in the very heart of the Islamic Republic's ruling institutions and guiding doctrine.

Dissonant Institutionalization

Dissonant institutionalization occurs when competing images of political community and the symbolic systems legitimating them are reproduced in the formal and informal institutions of state and society, and in the political rhetoric or ideology of the ruling elite. I use the term *dissonant*[80] to distinguish this phenomenon from the more harmonic understanding of "dominant ideology" first outlined by Marx, developed by neo-Marxist scholars such as Gramsci, and later integrated into mainstream sociological studies by scholars such as Clifford Geertz and Theda Skocpol.[81] In recent years scholars working in the field of "new institutionalism" have noted that even an authoritarian state that aspires to hegemony might be compelled by an array of political, social, and cultural forces to institutionalize competing ideological "scripts."[82] We have already seen that Arjomand emphasizes the role that constitutions and the diffusion of constitutional principles play in this process. However, constitutions are only the tip of a very large institutional iceberg. Competing scripts can be regularized in a wide array of state-controlled institutions such as schools and universities, the official media, and parliaments. Moreover, inasmuch as charismatic leaders and/or their disciples absorb contending visions of authority, we would expect that dissonant institutionalization would be manifest in these leaders' writings, pronouncements, and speeches.

Where competing scripts are institutionalized, the organizations and elite factions that constitute the state are likely to mirror such ideological eclecticism, and thus develop in diverse or opposing directions. This dynamic differs from the one suggested by the concept of "path dependency." The latter describes a process by which the cumulative effect of institutional development is to push the state, its cadres, and organizations into an increasingly predetermined line.[83] But where dissonant institutionalization prevails, the appearance of one "path" can hide alternative paths, each of which maintains a measure of autonomy from the other.

The institutionalization of multiple paths creates constraints as well as opportunities. In the short term a *controlled measure* of ideological competition may enhance a leader's authority by giving him the means to arbitrate and thus limit conflicts within the regime.[84] But in the long term, the accommodation of contending ideologies within state institutions or the leadership can prove constraining. After all, however monolithic it may appear, a state subject to dissonant institutionalization actually lacks complete hegemony. Because its authority is *not* based on a "symbol system [that] will provide a clue . . . to what is so commonsensical that attempts to change it seem pointless,"[85] such a state can become vulnerable to efforts by competing social forces to radically redefine its ideological foundations. To make matter worse, while charismatic rulers may initially rely on their personal magnetism to hide such disputes, their own absorption of multiple identities may only justify or invite ideological conflict. In short, we are talking about a state that is profoundly vulnerable over time to legitimacy crises. To preclude such instability, ruling elites must eventually forge a more coherent legitimacy formula, one that is not dependent on the leader. For reasons I shall discuss below, a legacy of dissonant institutionalization greatly complicates this routinization process.

The case of the Islamic Republic of Iran displays many of these paradoxical dynamics. As we shall see in chapter 5, dissonant institutionalization became the defining feature of the Islamic Republic of Iran. Its effects were manifest not only in the 1979 Constitution, which accommodated charismatic, traditional; and legal-rational authorities in one document, but also in the eclectic ideology of Khomeini himself. His attempts to address these divisions were hampered by his competing commitments. Throughout the ten years of his rule, he was devoted to divergent views of political community: Khomeini wanted charismatic revolutionary action, the controlling authority of Islamic law, and the benefits of a rational utilitarianism that valued state interests above all else. These multiple commitments were mirrored in the ideological factionalization of the ruling elite. If conservative and radical clerics could each claim a piece of the revolutionary pie, this was because their leader made such contending ideological claims seem perfectly normal.

Complex Routinization and the Struggle over a Multiple Legacy

By creating multiple paths, dissonant institutionalization sets the stage for complex routinization. This concept refers to a nonlinear dynamic whereby *political struggles* within the state can either *obstruct or advance* the transformation of revolutionary organizations and ideology into enduring institutions, laws, and doctrines that legitimate the interests of the ruling elite. I emphasize *political struggles* to distinguish complex routinization from dissonant institutionalization. The latter refers to a systemic dynamic by which competing visions of authority become a regularized feature of politics. In contrast, *complex routinization* refers to the political strategies and ideological discourses elites use to address the destabilizing *consequences* of ideological dissonance—in other words, their calculated efforts to construct a more coherent basis for sustaining political power and legitimating their respective social interests.

The role of agency, choice, and deliberation is thus central to complex routinization, although the decisions and choices elites make reflect the multifaceted legacy of dissonant institutionalization.

To better appreciate the zigzag dynamic of complex routinization, it is useful to contrast this phenomenon with the linear dynamic envisioned in symbolic and instrumentalist theories. We have reviewed Weber's argument that pure charisma is unstable: when a crisis subsides, the charismatic leader is compelled to "prove" his authority in a manner that reveals its mundane foundations. While this process undercuts the irrational bases of his authority, a charismatic revolutionary cannot be the *primary* vehicle of routinization. Instead, the manufacture of charisma *is driven and almost always completed* by his disciples: deeply committed to him, yet compelled to defend concrete interests, they transfer his magical aura to traditional institutions and ideologies that can carry out these rationalizing functions. Instrumentalist theory suggests that this dialectic is completed when skilled elites use the available symbolic resources and organizational networks to rework the utopian quest for charisma into a new ideology of political order.

I would suggest that neither phase in this dialectic ensues where dissonant institutionalization defines the political landscape. This is because dissonant institutionalization imbues both charismatic leaders *and* their disciples with contradictory goals and desires. As noted, where multiple biographies shape charismatic leaders' consciousness, they may be as devoted to the idea of revolutionary action as they are attached to the instrumentalist principle of legitimating political order. Pushed by opposite commitments, they are just as likely to resist routinization as they are to initiate it. Confronted by a leader's failure to make a clear choice, advocates of routinization may find that their efforts both to institutionalize power, and to create an enduring economic system that serves the particular interests of a given group, will be undermined one day and advanced the next. This unpredictable dynamic does not fade once the leader passes from the scene. On the contrary, because his followers ascribe a divine or transcendent quality to his speeches, writings, and utterances, the struggle to routinize his charisma is bound to pivot on what he *supposedly* said or wrote. This phenomenon embraces yet transcends the "disintegrative legacies of . . . charisma" of which Ahmad Ashraf has written.[86] The ideological legacies of all leaders invite and even demand competing rationalizations. What must be emphasized is how open and *indeterminate* this process becomes when the charismatic leaders leave a demonstrably multidimensional legacy. When this occurs, the struggle to "transform the institutional relations of society by exploiting . . . contradictions"[87] will be prolonged, chaotic, and multidirectional. Since each group can make an *equally plausible* case that its vision of politics is an authentic expression of the founding father's wishes, the ideological field is open to twists and turns, none of which can be easily predicted, even by the players themselves.

Chapters 6, 7, and 8 trace the *particular* dimensions of complex routinization in Iran. I emphasize *particular* because the political and ideological dynamic ensuing from dissonant institutionalization is always a function of the specific array of contradictions and tensions that has taken root in the institutions and ideologies of a given state. In Iran, the routinization struggle was—and indeed remains—marked by constant surprises, perplexing shifts, and unintended outcomes. It began with Khomeini's own erratic attempts to institutionalize the revolution. As we shall see in chapter 6, Khomeini at times espoused a quintessentially charismatic view of economics, insisting that the revolution had nothing to do with such mundane matters as prices, housing, or production. This attitude was clearly evident during the eight-year war with Iraq, which Khomeini viewed as the last bastion of mass charismatic experience. But when his celebration of the mystical benefits of martyrdom threatened the very viability of the Islamic Republic, he refocused his attention on the task of routinization. In January 1988 Khomeini endorsed a utilitarian vision of authority that subordinated the religious dictates of Shi'ism to what he called the "interests" of the state and/or government; endorsed the call to revise the Constitution; and finally accepted a cease-fire with Iraq, an act he equated with drinking from a "poisonous chalice."

Such contradictory behavior invited a fierce battle over Khomeini's legacy. We shall see in chapter 6 that this battle began while Khomeini was still alive. However, as illustrated in chapter 7, the struggle over his legacy became the *central feature* of the political game following his death in June 1989. Iranians were still in mourning when *Majles* Speaker 'Ali Akbar Hashemi Rafsanjani invoked Khomeini's edicts to introduce constitutional reforms reducing the charismatic authority of the *faqih* by separating the position of *rahbar*, or leader, from that of religious guide, or *marja'*. Elected president in July 1989, Rafsanjani formed an alliance with the *faqih*, Supreme Leader Khamene'i. The two men then invoked Khomeini's words to rationalize a reform program that blended market liberalization with authoritarian rule. When radical deputies objected to this program, they were purged from the *Majles* in 1992. Paradoxically, as chapter 8 shows, this assault on the "children of the revolution" encouraged a new alliance of intellectuals and political activists. Led by clerics such as Khatami and lay Islamic Leftists such as Abdolkarim Soroush, these and other reformers invoked Khomeini's legacy to legitimate a more pluralistic and less xenophobic vision of Islamic community.

This vision found a vast audience among Iran's disillusioned young people, many of whom followed cultural and social trends in the West. It was this happy coincidence between the reformist ideas espoused by Khatami and his allies, and the desire for change among the young-adult population, that set the stage for Khatami's election in May 1997. Yet, as we shall see in the conclusion, the struggle that Khatami and his allies subsequently waged to reform the ideology and ruling organizations of the Islamic Republic demonstrated the continued and often negative effects of dissonant institutionalization. Now that we have entered the new millennium, it seems that the phenomena of contending authorities and complex routinization have proved to be resilient not only in the Islamic Republic but also in many other quarters of the Islamic world.

2 Ascetic Mysticism and the Roots of Khomeini's Charisma

> Allah is the light of the heavens and the earth; the parable of His light
> Is as if there were a niche, and within it a lamp . . . enclosed in glass
> The glass as it were a brilliant star lit from a blessed tree
> An olive, neither of the East nor of the West
> Whose oil well-nigh luminous, though fire scarce touched it
> Light upon Light! Allah doth set forth parables for men:
> And Allah doth know all things.
> —Qur'an 24:35

From Singular to Multiple Biography

This chapter traces the cultural, political, social, and psychological forces that gave birth to Ayatollah Ruhollah al-Musavi Khomeini's charismatic authority. Highlighting his early exposure to personal asceticism and Islamic mysticism, it argues that these two traditions articulated Khomeini's profound disillusionment with everyday existence after experiencing various injustices and indignities. The resulting charismatic sensibility—his ceaseless desire to experience directly what the Qur'an refers to as the "Light of the Heavens"—remained with Khomeini throughout his life, illuminating a path that took him from his career as a teacher to his position as Imam (leader of the *umma*, or Muslim community) of the first and only successful charismatic revolution the modern Islamic world has ever experienced.

On the face of it, this classic tale of charismatic leadership fully accords with conventional accounts of Khomeini's life in general, and his personal charisma in particular. One way or another, these biographies portray Khomeini as a revolutionary zealot. Farhang Rajaee minces no words in adopting this position. "The concept of *raison d'état,*" he insists, "at least in theory, plays no part in Khomeini's thought. Instead, the doctrine of the *raison d'ideologies* might be used to explain Khomeini's view of state."[1] This thesis is amplified in biographies published by the Ayatollah's allies *and* his detractors, in which Khomeini is portrayed as a charismatic ideologue who from a young age was determined to follow a revolutionary path.[2] How do such messianic portrayals fit into a study whose purpose is to portray the phenomenon of multiple biographies? The answer is that these accounts, with their *raison d'ideologies* viewpoint, capture an essential feature of Khomeini's biography. However, they err by implicitly endorsing a basic assumption of symbolic theory, namely that the irrational pull of pure charisma cannot coexist with other forms of authority such as *raison d'état.* The concept of multiple biographies argues that such accommodation is not only possible but likely—particularly where the *formative experiences of youth* imbue a leader with a powerful capacity for feeling and expressing charisma. Thus "stamped," the charismatic impulse can endure for a lifetime, pulling a leader in one direction as other ideals push him along opposing paths. Even the most nonlinear history of charismatic leadership can have a *point of inception,* a point of origin that bears scrutiny. To analyze this point we must identify those forces that give birth to the charismatic impulse.

The Individual and Social Roots of Pure Charisma

This chapter uses the term *pure charisma* in a manner that tracks the two dimensions of the phenomenon that Max Weber emphasized. The first is that "highly individual quality" or "specifics of body and mind" by virtue of which such leaders believe they are the repository of "supernatural" powers.[3] This transrational dimension flows from the very core of the leaders' physical and spiritual being, "qualitatively delimited from within, not by an external order."[4] Amplifying on this intrinsic quality, Weber suggests that charismatic leadership combines the most powerful attributes of two kinds of religious prophets. Like the "emissary" prophet, the charismatic leader practices a form of "active asceticism, or God-willed *action* nourished by the sentiment of being God's 'tool' "[5] By "active asceticism," Weber means the hard work and self sacrifice that leaders undertake *in this world* to earn God's salvation in the next. This quest is aimed at a particular constituency and thus is innately social. At the same time, like the "exemplary prophet," the charismatic leader undertakes individual religious practices that produce "mystic, orgiastic experiences and extraordinary psychic states." Intensely personal, these practices imbue the individual with the sense that he is directly experiencing the divine. However, in contrast with those of the exemplary prophet, such mystical encounters do not create a "deep abyss" that separates "the way of life of the laymen from that of the community of virtuosos."[6] Instead, the divine aura that accompanies these orgiastic practices can inspire people to embrace an exemplary prophet's activist asceticism. Thus charismatic leadership fuses aspects of exemplary and emissary prophethood to create a unique and powerful being.

The innate qualities that distinguish the charismatic prophet do not create a charismatic following by themselves. Weber holds that a leader's personal qualities become a *social force* when they are "directed to a local, ethnic, social, political, . . . group."[7] Psychologically speaking, the "complete devotion" of followers arises "out of enthusiasm, or of despair and hope,"[8] or from "extraordinary psychic . . . states . . . produced by extraordinary events."[9] While Weber further attributes such events to collective distress stemming from "disenchantment" with the rationalized symbols of everyday life, we noted in chapter 1 that Emile Durkheim's structural analysis of the *conscience collective* reminds us that the *potential* for a charismatic response is conditioned by society's preexisting symbolic system. Durkheim's sociology implies that some societies are more prone to charismatic responses than others. The following analysis highlights the interaction of these personal and social forces. On the individual level, we will identify the psychological, cultural, and social factors that imbued the young Khomeini with a deeply personal desire for a transcendent or messianic experience. At the societal level, we will consider the social *and* symbolic factors that encouraged his followers to embrace this quest for transcendent activism. In short, we will ask how Khomeini's charismatic aura tapped into his students' deepest yearnings for an "effervescent" vision of Twelver Shi'ism.[10]

An "Orphan's" Story

In late winter 1903, a religious scholar named Seyyed Mostafa was killed by assassins dispatched by an absentee landlord—at least this is the version of events passed on by his family for generations.[11] The historical accuracy of this account is less important than its symbolic meaning. The idea that Mostafa was "murdered by bandits of the Qajar Dynasty"[12] had a profound effect on his son, Ruhollah Khomeini. As Ruhollah was born only six months before his father was killed, Mostafa's very absence must have magnified the mythical nature of his death: after all, as Khomeini would soon learn, his father's supposed martyrdom echoed the tradition of selfless abnegation and moral courage that his family had sustained for three generations.

Khomeini's father came from a long line of Seyyeds—men claiming descent from the Prophet Mohammad himself. In the late eighteenth century, Mostafa's grandfather moved his family from northeastern Iran to India, where one portion of family settled in Lucknow and the other in Kintur. His son left Kintur for the Iraqi Holy City of Najaf in the early nineteenth century, and in 1849 settled in the small Iranian town of Khomein, where Mostafa was born. Like his father and grandfather before him, Seyyed Mostafa became a religious scholar. He began advanced studies in Esfahan, where he was a pupil of Mir Mohammad Taqi Modarresi, father of Seyyed Hasan Modarresi, a prominent opponent of Reza Shah Pahlavi in the 1930s. Mostafa trained to be a cleric in Najaf, then the holy capital of Shi'ite Islam. He studied under Mirza Hassan Shirazi, the famous cleric whose *fatva*, or religious edict, marked the beginning of the boycott waged against the British tobacco monopoly in 1892. Upon Shirazi's death in 1894, Mostafa returned to Khomein, some two hundred miles southwest of Tehran. There he raised six children, of whom Ruhollah Khomeini—named after the town in which he was born—was the youngest.

Although few details of Khomeini's boyhood are known, the early roots of his active asceticism seem to lie within several personal tragedies he experienced. As noted, the first of these was the murder of his father. Whatever the circumstances of his death, Mostafa did have a wide following among clerics, a fact attested to by the many memorial services held for him in cities as far apart as Najaf, Esfahan, Tehran, Khomein, Arak, and Golpayegan.[13] In the ensuing years the idea that Mostafa was martyred defending the rights of the Shi'ite community was apparently impressed upon Ruhollah by his mother, Hajieh Agha Khanum. A self-willed and independent woman, remarkable for her time, she repeatedly journeyed to Arak to demand the arrest of the assassins. When one of the suspected killers was finally apprehended, Hajieh, accompanied by her two oldest sons, Morteza and Nurreddin, as well as her sister-in-law Sahebeh Khanum, traveled to Tehran. There the entire family lobbied the acting prime minister to impose justice. The accused was duly beheaded, and the family returned to Khomein.[14]

For Khomeini, this marked a turning point in his life. Although he had been denied a father—a devastating blow that he apparently never put behind him—his family's relentless pursuit of his father's killers taught him that self-sacrifice and suffering can serve a higher purpose by defeating evil and bringing justice to *this world*. The seeds of "active asceticism" were thus planted in the young Khomeini's mind. In the years that followed, other events would reinforce this harsh image of the world. Although his father had been prosperous, and the town of Khomein by no means poor, local bandits conducted frequent and bloody raids. In this "bleak, somewhat hair-raising environment," Khomeini soon emerged as a self-sufficient, tough little boy.[15] Raised by his mother and particularly by his paternal aunt Sahebeh,[16] tragedy soon struck again: in 1917, at barely fifteen years of age, he suffered the death of his aunt and then his mother during a cholera epidemic.

The Suffering of the Imams: Shi'ism as a Personal and Mythical Biography

It is difficult to imagine that the ascetic sensibility arising from these losses would have had such a lasting impact on Khomeini had it not been for the way his life echoed the founding myths and symbols of Twelver Shi'ism. Placed in a *maktab*, or "place of writing," Khomeini soon memorized the long passages from the Qur'an and *hadith* (stories) of the Prophet and his Shi'ite successors that together constituted the symbolic universe of Twelver Shi'ism. At the center of this universe was one key idea: that the righteous few suffer the injustices of the evil many. This Manichaean worldview had its roots in a seventh-century dispute over who was to succeed the Prophet as Caliph, or leader, of the Muslims. The Sunnis held that Abu Bakr, by virtue of the political and moral consensus of the community's leaders, was next in line. The minority, who later became known as Shi'ites, spurned this rational test, insisting that 'Ali had an absolute right to the Caliphate because, as first cousin and son-in-law of the Prophet, he had inherited the Prophet's divine or infallible (*ma'sum*) knowledge of God's revelation. In effect, the Shi'ites held that the right to be leader of the *umma*, or Islamic community, derived from charismatic authority.

Although in A.D. 644 'Ali was chosen as Caliph, he later relinquished the title; this act of statesmanship cost him his life at the hands of assassins who accused him of betraying the cause. His son Hoseyn then claimed the Caliphate, but was killed by the Sunni Umayyad Caliph Yazid on the desert of Karbala, in present-day Iraq. In the ensuing centuries Twelver Shi'ites asserted that because the ten male descendants of Hoseyn had inherited a divine or supernatural knowledge of the Qur'an, they were the only legitimate leaders, or Imams, of Muslims. Since the

Twelfth Imam was said to be in hiding or "occultation," Shi'ites further argued that the creation of a fully legitimate Islamic state had to await his return. In the interim the legal scholars, or *mojtaheds*, became the defenders of a persecuted minority who suffered at the hands of innately unjust rulers.[17] While these scholars were *not* viewed as bearers of the Imam's infallible authority, their knowledge of the law endowed them with considerable moral and judicial authority in their communities. Thus in contrast with the Imams, the *mojtaheds'* central position in the Shi'ite community was based, first and foremost, on traditional rather than charismatic authority.

Whether Khomeini grasped this distinction between tradition and charisma is a different matter. Listening to his teachers recount the epic stories of Shi'ism, he must have noticed parallels between the lives of his relatives and the those of the charismatic Imams. Poisoned or otherwise murdered by their enemies, the Imams left a legacy of martyrdom that Khomeini's father—himself a descendent of the Seventh Imam— had emulated. More decisively perhaps, Khomeini's story seems to echo the very lives of Islam's divine Messengers. He was born on the twenty-fourth of "Jumad, a most auspicious date—the birthday of Fatima, the daughter of the Prophet Muhammad."[18] What is more, his very name, "Ruh-Allah," recalled the holy spirit, or *ruh*, which— as one Shi'ite text about the Imams puts it—was "present with the Messenger of God . . . and . . . now with the Imams."[19] More than this, Khomeini's orphanhood echoed the early tribulations of 'Ali and the Twelfth Imam: both of whom supposedly lost their parents at a young age.[20] Deprived of parental love, they replaced this most direct and warm of human connections with the more abstract embrace of a Shi'ite community. This too was Khomeini's story: abandoned by cruel fate, he absorbed a "vocabulary and feeling of being wronged"[21] that drove him to embrace—in the grandiose manner typical of charismatic leaders— the "family" he had always been denied.

Mysticism, the "Self," and Human "Perfection"

In the three years following the deaths of his mother and aunt, Khomeini pursued Arabic and Persian studies with his elder brother Seyyed Morteza. A cleric who was later known as Ayatollah Pasandideh, Morteza apparently did not compensate for the absence of a father. On the contrary, although he was Khomeini's teacher, he seemed to have deferred to him, later recalling, "I was older than Ruhollah but he was always wiser."[22] Nevertheless, these studies prepared Khomeini for the next step. At the age of seventeen he left for Arak, a town some thirty miles south of Khomein. There he joined Ayatollah Abdolkarim Ha'eri-Yazdi, a leading cleric who ran a religious school, or *madreseh*.[23]

By 1920, the year that Khomeini moved to Arak, a series of tumul-tuous events had swept through Iran, leaving in its wake an unstable political and social environment that would dramatically affect Khome-ini's fortunes and political sensibility. The previous decade had seen the rise and fall of the 1905–11 Constitutional Movement. While sharp divisions among leading clerics had undermined this drive for reform, British and Russian imperialism played a decisive role in its collapse. Two central events marked this period: the August 1907 Anglo-Russian Convention, which divided Iran into three zones (Russian in the north, British in the southeast, and a "neutral sphere" along the Persian coast); and the dissolving of the Second *Majles*, or Parliament, in December 1911. The Russians, with British acquiescence, not only backed the Bakhtiyari tribal leaders who toppled Iran's first constitutional govern-ment, but also occupied northern Iran. One year later, Russian troops bombed the shrine of the Eighth Shi'ite Imam Reza, the most hallowed religious site in Iran. With the last Qajar monarch, Ahmad Shah, weak-ened by foreign intervention, the scene was set for the February 1921 coup d'état of Reza Khan, father of Mohammad Reza Shah and founder of the Pahlavi dynasty. Having installed himself as minister of war, in 1925 Reza Khan toppled the monarchy and then manipulated a hastily convened Constituent Assembly into proclaiming him Shah of Iran.

These troubling events strengthened Sheykh Ha'eri-Yazdi's deter-mination to construct an ethical wall between the corrupt world of political intrigue represented by Tehran, and the sublime life of schol-arship and moral rectitude exemplified by his *madreseh*. For this pur-pose he moved to Qom in 1921. Although an early center of Shi'ism which boasted the shrine of Ma'sumeh, the sister of Imam Reza, the Eighth Shi'ite Imam, Qom was also a city whose "entire population" seemed to consist of "the blind, the lame, the hunchbacked, the sick and the mentally infirm."[24] It thus offered Ha'eri-Yazdi a perfect locale for building a new center of Shi'ite learning. Ruhollah Khomeini soon followed, quickly becoming one of Ha'eri-Yazdi's prize students. In the ensuing three decades, Khomeini's *personal* charisma would fully blossom. As Weber would predict, this transformation was *not* propelled by exposure to religious traditionalism. Although Khomeini studied conventional topics such as *feqh* (law), it was his exposure to the esoteric and highly controversial world of Islamic mysticism that imbued him with a charismatic aura and sensibility.

Islamic mysticism is a form of religious practice in which the individual supplements the intellectual *knowledge* of God's laws gained through the study of holy texts, with an emotional *experience* achieved by spiritual contact with God's cosmic presence. Asceticism has always been an indispensable aspect of such experiences. By denying all but the most basic needs—sometimes to the point of physical suffering—and by engaging in simple but passionate forms of prayer that can produce trancelike effects, the mystic, or Sufi ("he who wears the woolen hair shirt") loses his "self" in the "Essence" of God, the most pure form of which is light itself.

Khomeini was clearly predisposed to this mystical life when he began his studies in Qom. By then, he had not only imbibed an ascetic ethos that resonated with both his personal history and the history of Shi'ism, but also witnessed the suffering of a country whose leaders were engulfed in the kinds of self-indulgent political intrigue that drove many young men to the refuge of Ha'eri-Yazdi's seminary. Thus it was not long before Khomeini embraced the spiritual principles of Shi'ite mysticism, or *'erfan*. Several men taught him *'erfan,* among them the eminent scholar Mirza Mohammad 'Ali Shahabi (d. 1950) and the more controversial Mirza Javad Aqa Maleki Tabrizi (d. 1925). Both scholars "linked the future ayatollah to the long tradition of learning in Iranian Islam . . . dating back to the teachings of such seminal figures . . . as Mir Damad (d. 1630) and Molla Sadra (d. 1640), who had drawn their inspiration from eminent predecessors, such as Heydar Amoli (d. 1358), Ibn 'Arabi, and Yahya al-Sohrawardi."[25]

Of these mystics, Molla Sadra—and by association Ibn Arabi, who was Sadra's indirect disciple—had the most enduring impact on Khomeini. In his book *Kitab al-Asfar* (Book of journeys), Sadra develops Ibn Arabi's notion of a journey of purification, at the end of which the individual reaches a "transcendent state . . . [or] 'opening' through which direct knowledge of God and the unseen is achieved."[26] This state *cannot* be achieved by most people. Arabi holds that the "opening" was a *gift from God* bestowed only on those rare individuals who reached a state of complete or total being.[27] This "perfect man" *(al-insan al-kamil)* emerges after a four-stage spiritual journey, during which he moves further away from his self and the worldly attributes of God, and closer to his divine essence. Having reached God and then returned to the world and his self, he finally enters the last stage—that of wandering from person to person, "bestowing on his community a new dispensation of spiritual and moral order."[28]

This messianic vision seems to have had a momentous effect on Khomeini. Inspired by *Kitab al-Asfar*, which was the first mystical work that he read under Shahabi's tutelage,[29] Khomeini developed his own version of Sadra's four-part spiritual journey in his 1928 commentary on a popular Shi'ite litany, *Sharh-e Do'ay-ye Sahar* (Commentary on "The Morning Prayer"), and his 1930 *Misbah al-Hidaya ila al-Khalifa wa al-Waliya* (Lamp [lighting] the right way to vice-regency and sainthood). In *Sharh* Khomeini adds a messianic intensity to the notion of a four-part journey which went beyond that suggested by his hero Molla Sadra. In Khomeini's version, on the final journey, "the Perfect Man . . . God's great sign, created in God's image,"[30] returns to earth in order to establish *velayat*—the deputyship or vice-regency of God as carried out by the Perfect Man:

> The more perfect is God's manifestation in the mirror of His Essence, the more clearly it points to what is hidden in the world of the Unseen. This World . . . free from the darkness of substratum, far removed from the contamination of matter . . . is nothing but God's most perfect worlds. . . . The Perfect Man, being the all-encompassing entity . . . constitutes God's most perfect world. Furthermore, his is the divine book. . . . A report, dating back to our Lord, Commander of the Faithful . . . says: "Don't you know that you are a small body, while in you the entire great world is folded up! You are a Manifest Book through the letters of which the hidden secret has become explicit."[31]

The key part of the preceding statement comes near the end. Citing a "report," or *hadith*, from 'Ali—the First Imam of the Shi'ites and "Commander of the Faithful"—Khomeini suggests that the human race is a microcosm of God's universe, a "small body" in which is "folded up" both the outward manifestations of God along with his divine attributes. The average person cannot access these possibilities for perfection because he is *not* removed from the "contamination of matter" that diverts his spirit from God. The notion that earthly existence exposed humanity to unrelenting evil stayed with Khomeini throughout his life. The realization of our perfection, he came to believe, is thwarted by our weakness for earthly pleasures. Thus the only solution is for us to transcend the "self."

Khomeini seems to have acquired this notion of "self"-transcendence from Ibn 'Arabi, who in his doctrine of *wujudiyya*, or absolute existence, had envisioned the mystic's primary goal as "passing away from self (*fana*) culminating in a complete comprehension of Divine Unity and rejecting any notion of 'otherness.' " (647). Although this doctrine clearly had influenced him, Khomeini points 'Arabi's doctrine in new directions. The latter had argued that only God could grant divine transcendence: "For all power to act . . . is from Him," 'Arabi writes (n. 64). In keeping with this idea, the Shi'ite doctrine of the Imamate holds that only the Imams had been granted the power to know God's Essence. However, in his *Misbah al-Hidaya*, published in 1930, Khomeini suggests a broader field of charismatic transformation. As Knysh keenly observes, in this work Khomeini distinguishes between two types of "vicegerency": a "timeless archetypal vicegerency," which he asserts is constituted by the "spirit of Mohammedan successorship, its master, its root, and its principle"; and an individual or "historical" "externalization" of this timeless vicegerency, as realized in the concrete *missions of all divine prophets and saints* (645–66).[32] Khomeini suggests that even a mortal—if exceptional—person could *achieve* divine transcendence. "Anyone," he writes, "who has the quality of Perfect Man . . . is a caliph in this world."[33] Thus it is now the *journey or act* of mystical transformation that counts: for the rare but flesh-and-blood individual, this journey offers a chance to "become identical with the universal Body" and thus *earn the right* to become God's divine deputy on earth.[34]

Nothing in what Khomeini wrote during his first decades in Qom suggests that he conceived of himself as this worldly viceregent. Nor should we conclude that Khomeini had already forged the foundations for his revolutionary doctrine of *velayat-e faqih*, or the "Rule of the Jurist." Nevertheless, given his passionate embrace of active asceticism as a young man, and his elaboration in Qom of a mystical doctrine that linked charismatic transcendence to prophetic action or "missions," it would be fair to conclude that by the early thirties, Khomeini already felt himself possessed by a holy *ruh* that merited the respect if not allegiance of those around him.

Chiliasm and the Cultural Preconditions of Charisma

That Khomeini possessed this quality certainly was the firm belief of his closest disciples. During the twenties and thirties Khomeini radiated charisma and thus inspired a devoted following. Two factors helped to create this charismatic bond. First, Khomeini illuminated a "this-worldly" path of action promising spiritual wholeness to those suffering from the alienating effects of modernization. Second, he articulated this "mystical activism" in terms that resonated with the latent charisma of Persian and Shi'ite culture. Tapping into this symbolic vein, he offered a solution to moral degeneration and cultural alienation that was consonant with a widely shared symbolic system.

The symbolic foundation of Khomeini's charisma suggests something of a paradox, given that in its most traditional form, Shi'ism was opposed to political activism. For centuries, many clerics argued that the doctrine of the Imamate justified political quietism inasmuch as any effort to establish an Islamic state in the absence of the Twelfth Imam constituted a form of *shirk*—the sin of taking on the attributes of God and his Holy Imams. When taken to extremes, this view could justify suffering, since, as Hamid Algar notes, "from a . . . traditional perspective, the profusion of tyranny is a sign of the imminence of the return of the Twelfth Imam, and thus a 'preparation' for his coming."[35] However, this paradox was never as sharply defined as it seemed. *Political quietism was not the same as moral silence.* Even advocates of quietism agreed that the leading clerics had a duty to provide ethical and legal guidance to any Shi'ite community living under a government that was not considered fully legitimate. During the nineteenth century this view gained credence as proponents of *Usuli* Shi'ism advanced the idea that Shi'ites should choose a prominent scholar, or *marja'-e-taqlid* ("source of imitation"), after whom they could pattern the moral and legal dimensions of their daily lives. Sometimes this practice led to the emergence of one leading *marja'-e motlaq* (absolute *marja'*) whose interpretation of the law could take precedence over that of other *maraje'*. The latter's authority was principally traditional, in the sense that it derived from the knowledge of law. Thus it was always open to rational reevaluation. However, the rare *marja'* who could also shepherd his flock with personal fervor might also attain a *measure* of charismatic authority. In this sense, even the traditional notion of clerics as "moral guides" echoed what Dabashi has called the "permanently charismatic feature of Shi'ism."[36]

In part, this charismatic trait can be traced to the doctrine of the Imamate itself. The notion that the "Hidden Imam" will eventually reappear and restore justice to the world occupies a central place in the collective conscience of Iranian society. While this chiliastic feeling does not prescribe any particular form of political activism—indeed, as noted, it could be interpreted to justify an extreme form of quietism—it nevertheless instilled, in the words of the modern Iranian essayist Jalal Al-e Ahmad, a sense that "because no ephemeral government has come through on the least of its promises . . . all religious structures . . . are filled with signs . . . of the advent of the promised messiah."[37]

Iranian-Shi'ite culture expressed this messianic sensibility in three symbolic structures that incorporated yet transcended Shi'ite Islam: the concept of light mysticism, nonreligious Persian poetry, and the Shi'ite passion play, or *ta'ziya*. The first of these forms can be traced to the Qur'an. As Roy Mottahedeh has noted, Sufi mysticism grew out of an ascetic sensibility that was "encouraged by the Koran. . . . Asceticism was . . . an instrument for the constant 'mindfulness' of God that the Koran repeatedly enjoins. . . . A few of the early Muslim ascetics . . . wanted to collapse eschatology, the doctrine of final things, and experience in this life the 'meeting of God' that the Koran promised in the hereafter" (145). The Qur'an speaks of this "meeting" in mystical terms: as suggested by the *sura* (section of the Qur'an) partially cited at the outset of this chapter, the Qur'an uses light as an inspiring metaphor for approaching God. But the tradition of light mysticism dates to Zoroastrianism, a pre-Islamic faith that in its early form espoused a dualistic vision in which Light and Darkness are at war. This vision was echoed by the ancients: Plato offered a philosophical rendering of it in his famous description of the "cave," a setting where humans see the "shadows" of an essential truth that remains beyond their reach. His philosophy later inspired Sunni and Shi'ite mystics alike; in their "divine" rendering of Plato, light itself becomes the purest manifestation of God (153).

Beyond the Qur'an and the Persian tradition of light mysticism, the charismatic sensibility that is so central to Iranian-Shi'ite culture was also popularized through the recitation of Persian poetry and the performance of *ta'ziya*, many of which incorporate this poetic tradition. Performed during the month of Muharram, which marks the martyrdom of Hoseyn at the hands of the illegitimate Sunni Caliph Yazid, these passion plays allow the audience to "relive" Hoseyn's dramatic confrontation with evil and his subsequent martyrdom. They communicate the idea of the charismatic hero in a manner that is readily grasped by an illiterate or uneducated public. Persian poetry also echoes the myth of the Iranian hero, but does so in a language that predates Islam. Epic poetry, of which Ferdowsi's *The Book of Kings* is the most well-known example, celebrates the pre-Islamic struggle of both Iranian kings and nonroyals against their "evil" (non-Iranian) enemies, while lyric poetry incorporates the gnosticism of the third-century Iranian prophet Mani, who preached a "dualistic religion in which the material world was evil and revealed knowledge was a method for releasing the soul from its imprisonment in matter" (159). The great advantage of this symbolic medium is that it can articulate charismatic ideas in transrational terms: as with music, one doesn't need to read notes to be inspired by beautiful sounds.

The aforementioned three symbolic structures defined the cognitive road map of Iranian Shi'ites during the first half of the twentieth century. Many of the young *talabeh*s (students of religion) who came to Qom during this crucial period thirsted for a transcendent religious experience. Their need for "effervescence," as Durkheim would call it, was intensified by the culturally disorienting effects of Reza Shah's modernization program. Inspired by Turkey's autocratic modernizer, Kemal Attatürk, this program sought to link Iran's cultural, economic, and political fate to the West. Although its effects were not as far reaching as those ensuing from the modernization program of the sixties and seventies, they produced a sense of symbolic threat within the spiritually charged world of Qom's religious seminaries.[38]

Mystical Activism

While Iranian-Shi'ite culture carried within its symbolic folds a *propensity* for charismatic chiliasm, a propensity that was also fed by the Shah's policies, realizing this capacity required "charismatic figures of authority [who] can read to a receptive audience the mobilizing content of an otherwise opaque semantic."[39] Khomeini's embracing mystical activism enabled him to "read" Shi'ism's charismatic potential to a "receptive audience." This activist bent was reinforced by the periodic assaults on the clerical establishment that took place during the twenties and thirties. Khomeini was undoubtedly dismayed by the failure of his teachers and colleagues to respond to such attacks: Ha'eri-Yazdi, the very scholar who introduced him to the world of the Islamic seminary, remained silent when the British expelled Shi'ite leaders from Iraq in 1923; did not back Esfahan clerics when they rose against the government a year later; and failed to protest when Ayatollah Mohammad Taqi Bafqi was exiled by the royal court in 1929. Khomeini's immersion in Shi'ite mysticism pointed him in a different direction: as his Tehran biographers put it, "*irfan* . . . never implied social withdrawal or political quietism, but rather the building up of a fund of energy that finds its natural expression on the socio-political plain."[40]

Khomeini both personified and articulated this ethic. Adopting the "ascetic practices associated with the early stages of the Sufi path: renunciation of worldly delights and desires, self-imposed poverty, [and] scrupulous discernment of the 'lawful' and the 'forbidden,' "[41] he demonstrated a desire to "talk with God" that often shocked his closest associates.[42] He also read and composed Persian poetry—a beloved avocation since his youth. Such was his devotion to this icon of Iranian culture that a poet who met Khomeini in the early sixties recalls, "We recited poetry for four hours. Every first line I recited from any poet, he recited the second."[43]

While ascetic practices and mystical poetry articulated the charismatic sensibility of Iranian culture, Khomeini's writings and lectures gave this transrational orientation a more systematic, worldly expression. Following the latently activist example of his teacher Shahabi, he translated the esoteric mysteries of Shi'ism into a language that his most motivated students could grasp and apply to their daily lives. His novel reinterpretation of Ibn 'Arabi and Molla Sadra (discussed above) facilitated this objective. The notion of spiritual "migration," by which humanity narrows the gap between its material existence and God's universal "Essence," had social and even political overtones: it implied that by purifying one's soul of egoism and corruption, an individual could morally defy the secularizing doctrine of Reza Shah.

Equally important was the way Khomeini linked this novel version of Shi'ite mysticism to conventional subjects such as law. This point cannot be emphasized strongly enough. Although mysticism had deep roots in both pre-Iranian and Shi'ite culture, the traditional clergy were suspicious of it. They feared that a charismatic *marja'* who mobilized followers by exuding the mysteries of *'erfan* might be embraced as a divine figure or new "Imam." While lamenting the fact that "some of the ulema [Islamic scholars] should . . . deprive themselves of the benefits to be gained from studying *irfan*,"[44] Khomeini understood that to make mysticism relevant to his followers, he had to demonstrate that "there was no intrinsic contradiction between *irfan* . . . and a strict adherence to the *Shari'a* [sacred law of Islam]."[45] Toward this end, he offered an unconventional curriculum that, by the early forties, brought together the study of mysticism, philosophy, ethics, and Islamic law. Few scholars of his age could compete with this eclectic synthesis.

Ethics figured prominently in this program. Khomeini began teaching this subject in response to the secularizing policies of Reza Shah, manifested brutally in 1935 when the Shah's troops massacred *madreseh* students in Mashhad who had been protesting the arrest of two clerics. Although Khomeini didn't witness the violence, he was shaken by the sight of one of the shackled clerics who, he recalled, was "sitting under guard at the side of the road, with his turban removed."[46] Beyond these events, Khomeini feared that Reza Shah's secularizing policies were producing the results to which he so fervently objected: The people, he later wrote, "were selfish, feeble and sluggish, and thus "unable to resist the dictatorship of Reza Shah."[47]

To address this "selfishness," Khomeini needed a venue from which to reach the public extending beyond his formal classes. For this he chose Qom's Feyziyeh Seminary. Located next to the Shrine of Masumeh, it promised a large audience of locals as well as visiting pilgrims— particularly on Thursdays and Fridays, when many people traveled from as far away as Tehran just to hear Khomeini speak.[48] In little time,

Khomeini's message achieved the impact he sought: while the average Iranian might not have grasped the esoteric mysteries of mystical Islam, Khomeini's "fire and brimstone" sermons on Islamic ethics inspired the crowds. Standing before them in his flowing robes and black turban, his severe aloofness variously inspired admiration, awe, and fear from those around him. Such was the effect of his preaching that by the early fifties both the authorities and his fellow clerics forced Khomeini to abandon it briefly.[49] However, by then the inner-directed aspects of his charisma had found the receptive audience without which his personal allure would have remained as but one aspect of individual character.

We can divide this audience into two concentric rings. The outer ring consisted of a large following of *talabeh* and clerics from Qom and other Iranian cities and towns. While not disciples in the conventional sense, they were drawn to Khomeini's charismatic persona and message, particularly as it was revealed in his sermons on ethics. The inner circle consisted of his direct disciples: several dozen students who regularly studied with him. Sociologically speaking, they constituted the "charismatic community" out of which Khomeini would mold an ideological vanguard some four decades later. Among them were Ayatollahs Morteza Motahhari, Hoseyn 'Ali Montazeri, and Javadi Amoli. As students of mystical Islam, they were inspired by what one follower of Khomeini has called his "personal motto": "Oh God, grant me total separation from other-than-You and attachment to You, and brighten the vision of our hearts with the light of looking upon You, so that they may pierce the veils of light and attain the fountainhead of magnificence, and our spirits may be suspended from the splendor of Your sanctity."[50]

Summary: The Road from Charismatic Teacher to Charismatic Revolutionary

While the fusion of personal and collective charisma transformed Khomeini into a charismatic figure during the thirties and forties, at this juncture in our story he and his disciples did not constitute the charismatic utopian *movement* of which Karl Mannheim and William Kornhauser later wrote. Khomeini's first years in Qom remind us that "pure charisma" often emerges as a subculture—a microcosm reflecting the shared symbols of society and the personal power of a leader, but without transforming the interaction of these two forces into a mass phenomenon. That is not to say that this subculture was unimportant— far from it. The forging of Khomeini's charisma was a necessary but

insufficient precondition for the explosion that led to the fall of Shah Mohammad Reza Pahlavi forty years later. But we should not deduce from
this that Khomeini desired this momentous event. Although his heart
burned for messianic deliverance, there was a huge theoretical, intellectual, and experiential jump from his mystical notion of vice-regency
to the political or ideological rendering of this doctrine that Khomeini
advocated on the eve of the 1979 Islamic Revolution. This transformation
would take several decades to unfold. From the mystical-charismatic
teacher who emerged in the thirties to the revolutionary Imam who led
Iranians to victory in the seventies, there remained a long journey, upon
which Khomeini was just embarking.

3 Absorbing the Multiple Imaginations of the Islamic Left: From Shari'ati to Khomeini

> Total consistency is tantamount to fanaticism, while inconsistency is the source of tolerance.[1]
> —Lezek Kolakowski

Power and Interests

Hannah Arendt maintained more than thirty years ago that the authority of charismatic revolutionaries derives from the irrational way they make the world *appear* coherent: "Totalitarian movements," she writes, "conjure up a lying world of consistency . . . in which . . . uprooted masses can feel at home and are spared the never-ending shocks [of] . . . real life."[2] This judgment is not far from that offered by the Polish philosopher Lezek Kolakowski: by *inconsistency* he means an ethos that celebrates the endless play of competing truths. Spurning this pluralistic ethic, the quintessential charismatic leader strives to conjure up a new reality, one in which everything seems to be whole and complete.

From his seat in Qom's Feyziyeh Seminary, Khomeini articulated this need for wholeness. That he did so in a novel manner never detracted from his charisma: on the contrary, his immersion in ascetic mysticism taught him that direct experience of the Absolute was attainable. This chapter explores Khomeini's assimilation of a very different view of authority. Subordinating the first principles of religion to the mundane goal of creating and maintaining power, this pragmatic ethos envisioned Islam as a *useful tool* for politically unifying Muslims. Placing Islam in the service of the Muslim community's temporal needs, it suggested that the "truths" of Islam were to be determined by changing social and political *interests*, rather than by timeless religious verities.

Following the conceptual framework set out in chapter 1, my analysis of Khomeini's absorption of utilitarian Islamism transcends instrumentalist and symbolic accounts of charisma. Symbolic theorists acknowledge that the rationalization of religion sets the stage for the emergence of pure charisma, but they would insist that this process unfolds sequentially. Thus Hamid Dabashi argues that the instrumentalization of Islam by intellectuals such as Jalal Al-e Ahmad and 'Ali Shari'ati constituted a vital but *distinct phase in a dialectic of alienation* whose ultimate realization could only be achieved by a charismatic clerical elite. Like Molière's *Bourgeois Gentilhomme*, these clerics were unaware of the very instrumentalist language they were speaking. In Dabashi's view, Shari'ati prophesied "a universal revolt of the glorified masses" that Khomeini fulfilled *"almost unknowingly."*[3] Structural instrumentalists dismiss this sociology of unintended consequences. Abrahamian argues that Khomeini and his clerical allies appropriated the revolutionary ideology of the Islamic Left to rationalize a preconceived economic project. Thus they never unknowingly transmitted the Islamic instrumentalism of Shari'ati and his colleagues; on the contrary, the clerics deliberately, if begrudgingly, repackaged it in a bid to legitimate their rule.[4]

Both accounts rest on the erroneous premise that the actions of charismatic leaders are based on *one dominant concept of authority*. This chapter suggests a different dynamic, one through which Khomeini and his allies accommodated an instrumentalist ethos to the transrational logic of charisma. To probe this dynamic, I highlight the *secondary process* through which Khomeini absorbed the "multiple imaginations" of the Islamic Left. This process was filled with paradoxes. Despite the nativist tone of their rhetoric, Islamic Leftists championed an essentially Western political vision. Moreover, although they did so in absolutist terms, they were *au fond* the transmitters of a relativist notion of religion. Khomeini decried such instrumentalism, insisting that Islam was not about economics. But he could not help absorbing the core message of the Islamic Left, namely that religious truths are *made*—and unmade—by people and for people.

While this chapter emphasizes the rationalizing message of the Islamic Left, the latter's vision was not devoid of utopianism: inspired by a mystical messianism integral to Shi'ism, many radicals envisioned a rebirth of collective being that would eradicate the "disease" of alienation they called "Weststruckness." Of course, it was this demonization of the West that made the Islamic Left's vision so appealing to conservative clerics. It was only much later, when several Islamic Leftists began to push their rationalism in a more pluralistic and less xenophobic direction, that many within the clerical establishment began to distrust their radical partners. But this is getting ahead of ourselves; we will now rejoin our story. I begin by reviewing the events that raised Khomeini's political consciousness during the forties and fifties. Here I discuss his absorption of a traditional—but latently political—Shi'ism that envisioned clerics as moral guides. I then discuss the roots of Khomeini's utilitarianism. I begin by noting the impact that the Sunni-Islamist notion of *maslahat*, or "interest," apparently had on him. Then I trace the impact of the Islamic Left. Applying the tools of structural-instrumentalism, I analyze the social and cultural forces that spawned an alienated class of "new intellectuals," and then highlight the multiple imaginations of four thinkers: Jalal Al-e Ahmad, 'Ali Shari'ati, Mehdi Bazargan, and Seyyed Mahmud Taleqani. Finally, I explore the secondary process of ideological diffusion and absorption through which Khomeini and his allies assimilated the Islamic Left's revolutionary instrumentalism during the sixties and early seventies.

1941: Clerics as Guardians of the Community

During the forties and fifties, Khomeini's understanding of authority became more political and pragmatic. This development was not totally at variance with his charismatic orientation, for his mysticism was infused with an activist impulse that revealed itself in ethical terms. However, at its core this activism was embedded in a utopian vision that suggested no concrete political form. In contrast, the vision of authority that Khomeini began to develop in the forties, while hardly unambiguous, suggested a more practical set of concerns.

This transition from mystical to political activism was prompted by a fear that under Reza Shah Pahlavi, the clerics' role as guardians of the community's moral integrity was being weakened. We have noted that this role was largely based on traditional rather than charismatic authority: the *mojtahed*, or interpreter of the law, uses his training in *feqh* (law) to rationally interpret the law, hence the term *faqih* (or jurist). Thus from a traditionalist perspective, if *velayat-e faqih*, or "Rule of the Jurist," exists at all, it does so in a clearly circumscribed sense: a *faqih* addresses legal matters pending the return of the Twelfth Imam (leader of the *umma*, or Muslim community), but he neither gets directly involved in politics nor exercises *executive* authority. Still, the boundary between legal and political authority was malleable. As a result, when traditionalist clerics such as Sheykh Fazlollah Nuri demanded the inclusion of an article in the 1906 Constitution that would provide for a clerical committee to oversee laws passed by the *Majles* (Parliament), they implied that even from a traditionalist perspective, the clerics' legal and moral authority had political implications.[5]

While Khomeini's training as a *mojtahed* had imparted to him this traditionalist view of the link between Shi'ism and politics, by the late thirties he began to worry that the Shah's policies were weakening the clerics' ability—even their desire—to serve as moral guides. These fears were fed by a fallen cleric and historian, Ahmad Kasravi, whose claims that the clerics were backward had been well received in some circles. Consequently, when one of Kasravi's supporters published a virulent assault on the clerics, Khomeini produced a line-by-line refutation. *Kashf al-Asrar* (Discovery of secrets)—completed several months after Reza Shah abdicated the throne, and published anonymously in 1943—suggests that Khomeini had now come to believe that the clerics should not only guide the people, but also perhaps become more directly involved in politics.

This evolution in Khomeini's thinking was reflected in his demand that Article 2 of the 1906 Constitution (providing for clerical supervision of the *Majles* yet was never applied) finally be enforced. Echoing the traditionalist position, Khomeini distinguished between the divine rule *(hokumat)* of God and the legal guardianship *(velayat)* that clerics exercise over mundane government. Therefore, he could assert that although "no one except God has the right to rule over anyone," and although "by reason the right to legislate belongs solely to God who creates rule *(hokumat)* for man," guardianship over man's moral conduct required that the clerics *supervise the law:*

> If we say that the government *(hokumat)* and guardianship *(velayat)* is today the task of the *foqaha* (religious jurists), we do not mean that the *faqih* (jurist) should be the Shah, the minister, the soldier or even the dustman. Rather, we mean that a *majlis* that is . . . [run] according to European laws . . . is not appropriate for a state . . . whose laws are Holy. . . . But if this *majles* is made up of believing *mojtahids* [interpreters of the law] who know the divine laws and . . . if they elect a righteous sultan who will not deviate from the divine laws . . . or if the *majles* . . . is under the supervision of the believing *fuqaha*, then this arrangement will not conflict with the law.[6]

In this statement Khomeini reduces government to a mechanistic function that several types of institutions or leaders could perform—Sultans, ministers, soldiers, or even street sweepers—*so long as their actions were guided by the clerics.* But note that he leaves the vehicle of such guidance unclear. The *Majles* might consist of clerics, or of politicians supervised by the former. Elsewhere in *Kashf* he endorses the notion of monarchical rule, and even approves of clerical support for a dictatorship, providing that two conditions obtained: first, that the leader was appointed by a clerical council: and second, that he secured political and social order "in the interests *(maslahat)* of the nation and its people."[7] How do we explain these conflicting conceptions of clerical guidance? The answer lies in the functionalist view of politics that informs the extract above. Like other traditionalists, Khomeini believed that good politics comes from good laws. Moreover, his concern with the problem of political order suggests that by 1943 he already was beginning to assimilate a more utilitarian, interest-based ethos. In short, he believed that so long as clerics made rulers uphold the law and maintain order, any number of governing institutions were possible. However, the implicit corollary of this position was that when the existing institutions failed to ensure that rulers executed these responsibilities, the clerics' duty was to redefine their relationship with the state.[8] While it would appear that Khomeini was unsure of how far this process should go, by the forties he certainly seemed open to altering this relationship. In this spirit, he insisted that because Reza Shah had created a government "at bayonet point,"[9] all orders issued by his government were worthless.

The Forties and Early Fifties: Nationalism and Sunni Realism

The election in 1944 of a fiery politician named Mohammad Mosaddeq to Iran's Parliament, and his nationalization in 1951 of the Anglo-Iranian Oil Company, transformed Iran's politics in ways that had a profound impact on Khomeini. Although they brought Iran to the brink of bankruptcy, Prime Minister Mosaddeq's actions were applauded by his countrymen. Fearing civil insurrection, the Shah, Mohammad Reza Pahlavi, dismissed him. When Mosaddeq rejected the command, the Shah fled Tehran.[10] Backed by the British, the United States sponsored a coup d'état against Mosaddeq in 1953, an act that allowed the Shah to return to Tehran.[11] Henceforth most Iranians believed that the new Shah was merely an instrument of Western imperialism. By turning

Mosaddeq into a hero, the coup engendered support for nationalist ideology at the expense of Islam. Activist clerics such as Ayatollah Seyyed Abdolqasem Kashani—who had been a member of Mosaddeq's National Front—an alliance of largely secular, nationalist forces chiefly drawn from the intelligentsia and professional middle classes—until he broke with it in 1952[12]—responded by trying to absorb nationalist and populist themes into Islamic ideology.

Although Khomeini was "conspicuously absent from politics in the turbulent years from 1951–1953,"[13] he was affected by the events and ideas emerging from this crucial period. Among the most important of these was the rise, in 1946, of Grand Ayatollah Mohammad Hoseyn Borujerdi to the position of leading *marja'-e taqlid,* or "source of imitation." Although he banned clerics from participating in politics and tried to maintain cordial relations with the new Shah, Borujerdi was hardly a conventional quietist. Instead, he set about reforming the clerical establishment by centralizing its financial, administrative, and teaching institutions.[14] By 1953 Khomeini emerged as a loyal supporter of Borujerdi,[15] yet at the same time partly defied his master's ban on politics by meeting with Ayatollah Kashani, whose political views of Shi'ism Khomeini found inspiring.

These developments took place at a crucial moment for the entire Middle East. From Tehran to Algiers, clashes between nationalist leaders and discredited regimes were matched by the successful efforts of Islamic groups to appropriate nationalist and socialist themes. Although Borujerdi did not advocate the ideologization of Islam, the *talabehs* (students of religion) of Qom were certainly affected by this trend. Borujerdi seems to have contributed to this development by dispatching emissaries to the Arab world, promoting closer ties between Shi'ite and Sunni theologians, and encouraging students of religion to take a more active interest in their country's day-to-day affairs.[16]

This changing political and religious atmosphere exposed elements within Iran's clerical establishment to the pragmatic logic of "Sunni realism," a term Hamid Enayat coined to describe the belief that the "supreme value in politics [is] . . . not justice but security—a state of mind which set[s] a high premium on the ability to rule and maintain 'law and order' rather than on piety."[17] Although inspired by the twelfth-century theory of the Caliphate, in the modern era a new generation of Islamic reformers gave this vision a distinctly utilitarian twist. Warning of the threat posed to the *umma* (Islamic community) by Western imperialism, Seyyed Jamal al-Din al-Afghani, Mohammad Rashid Rida, and Hasan al-Banna, the leader of Egypt's Muslim Brethren—a mass-based

Islamic fundamentalist movement—argued that a powerful state was necessary to unify Muslims.[18] This emphasis on the exigencies of state rule, as Sami Zubaida notes, was inspired by Western notions of mass politics and popular sovereignty.[19] The Brethren soaked up the inner logic of Western nationalism because it pointed the way to collective political power. Inspired by Rashid Rida's neopositivist conception of Islamic law,[20] the Brethren's theoretician Mohammad Ghazzali went so far as to argue that Islamic law should be based on *maslahat*, a term best translated as "expedient interests" or "public welfare."[21] Implicit in this notion was the idea that such interests could take precedence over the timeless dictates of *Shari'ah* (sacred law of Islam), particularly when the unity and order of the *umma* were threatened from within or without.

It should be noted that *maslahat* is *not* part of Shi'ite jurisprudence. While Shi'ite theologians have advanced other concepts calling for pragmatism and rationalism in interpreting the *Shari'ah* such as *tabdil* ("substituting something better") and *ejtehad* ("open interpretation"), before the 1979 revolution most had rejected *maslahat* as a dangerous innovation *(bed'at)*.[22] How then to explain Khomeini's use of the term in *Kashf*—decades before the revolution?[23] One possibility is that he had imbibed the logic of Sunni realism during the forties, if not before. Certainly there is some circumstantial evidence to this effect. It is reported that during a brief stay in Najaf in 1937, he read the pamphlets of Brethren leader Hasan al-Banna and met with members of the movement.[24] Khomeini's encounters with Mohammad Navvab-Safavi, an admirer of the Brethren and leader of Iran's Devotees of Islam (*Fada'iyan-e Islam*, a radical Shi'ite revivalist group that had ties to the Muslim Brethren), may also have influenced him.[25] Finally, his increasing utilitarianism may reflect the ideas of Seyyed Abu al-'Ala Mawdudi. The founder of the Sunni-Muslim *Jama'at-i Islami* in India, Mawdudi advocated a "theo-democracy," an idea partly inspired by the mass "election" of totalitarian movements in Europe.[26] Whether such definitive linkages to Khomeini's beliefs can be established is less important than the fact that by the fifties, the Brethren's utilitarian Islamism was setting the ideological tone for the Islamic world: their emissaries carried an inspiring message of Islamic unity and power to Iran at the very moment that Iranian representatives dispatched by Borujerdi were arriving in the Arab world. In this atmosphere of ideological cross-fertilization—doubly charged by the 1944–48 Arab–Israeli War—it seems very likely that Khomeini already was absorbing an interest-based ethos that would later come to play a major role in his political vision, and in the multifaceted ideology of the Islamic Republic.

The Multiple and Shared Imaginations of the Islamic Left

If the advocates of Sunni realism demonstrated the practical ends to which state power could be deployed, Iran's Islamic Left emphasized the political utility of Shi'ite symbols. In comparison with the Sunni realists, the greater influence of the Islamic Left is easy to explain: these were native sons who advocated what they claimed was a distinctly Shi'ite vision. Yet, paradoxically, it was through their exposure to the Western ideas that Shari'ati and other Islamic Leftists assimilated the notion of *using* culture for revolutionary purposes.

Although other scholars prefer the term *modernist* or *Islamic Republican,* I employ the term *Islamic Left* because it emphasizes the central role of Marxist ideology in shaping the vision of Iran's new intellectuals. With the exception of Taleqani, the leaders of the Islamic Left shared a vision of Islam that came from *outside* the religious establishment.[27] While many had received a traditional education during their youth, and many had close ties to the urban *bazaar* (the merchant middle class) and its clerical supporters, the journalists, novelists, literary critics, and academics who constituted this rising intellectual elite absorbed a positivist view of authority in secular Iranian schools or Western-oriented institutions, and/or in the West itself.

These modernizing intellectuals were dependent on the state's financial largesse, which grew at an alarming rate especially during the sixties and seventies. Fueled by oil income, the state expanded university education, so that admissions rose from 5,781 in 1960–61 to 28,500 in 1978–79.[28] New graduates were employed in state universities, the National Iranian Oil Company, or Iranian National Radio and Television. But far from producing a new cadre of mandarins, such dependence created resentment. As appendages of a modernizing autocracy that wanted their skills without the encumbrance of real participation or loyalty, most of these elites viewed the state with distrust and cynicism.[29] This was particularly true of intellectuals. They endured what one Iranian writer has called a profound "sense of guilt . . . about their cooperation with the state, so much so that opposition to the state became a value in itself."[30] Opposing such a state presents manifold challenges, not least of which is securing an audience outside its ambit. The solution many intellectuals adopted will be familiar to students of what Harold Lasswell once called "coercive elites."[31] As Boroujerdi notes,

> The self-sacrificing militants, the nonconformist students, and the dissident faculty all counterbalanced their isolation from the ordinary masses with

a populist approach to political struggle. They attempted to reflect the demands of "the masses" while not . . . succumbing to the latter's world view. Toward that end, they resorted to an imitation of the language and demeanor of the masses as a way of building ties to them.[32]

While not unique to Iran, this pattern was distinguished from similar cases of Third World populism by its anti-Western discourse. We can attribute this resentment to a complex sociocultural dynamic, the theoretical contours of which were outlined in chapter 1: *the differential effect of rapid modernization on the consciousness of elites and masses.* For Iran's lower middle classes, rooted in the traditional culture, the introduction of new symbols and values created a "symbolic crisis." Although rapid urbanization was partly responsible for this predicament, the rapid and *uneven* expansion of state education was the chief culprit. Between 1961 and 1979, the number of high school graduates jumped from 15,924 to 235,000. This meant that young people from traditional backgrounds underwent a disorienting process of social mobilization. While some of these youths entered the universities, the majority did not, owing to insufficient space: during the same period that high school enrollment skyrocketed, university admissions rose from only 5,781 to 28,500. With the percentage of high school graduates admitted to university falling from 36 percent to 12 percent,[33] a large pool of young people were on what David Menashri calls a "bridge to nowhere."[34] What is more, their malaise was often shared by those who did make it into university: as more *howzeh* (Islamic high school) students pursued higher education, their efforts to accommodate their traditional upbringing to the demands of a modern university produced a constituency that was primed to receive a new charismatic message.

As the products of a socialization process different from that which had shaped the consciousness of the newly mobilized urban masses, Iran's new intellectuals were ready to manufacture this message. Whereas the exposure of the masses to Western ideas was limited, the upbringing, education, and overseas travel of Iran's leading intellectuals exposed them to the positivist foundations of Western political thought. In short, these intellectuals were exposed to the globalizing process that imparted what was called "a multiple and shared imagination" in chapter 1; in other words, a shared vision of authority in which contending notions of political community coexisted in an uneasy partnership. That many expressed this relativist sensibility in absolutist terms is not as ironic as it seems: the intelligentsia imbibed the double message of Marxist (and especially Gramscian) ideology, namely that while all political ideas are man-made, some express universal truths. From here it was a short jump to the "Third Worldist" ideologies of the sixties, which held that liberation from imperialism required the politicization of native identity. Armed with this idea, Al-e Ahmad, Shari'ati, and others concluded that to capture the imagination of the masses, they had to *create* a culturally "authentic" Islamic radicalism.

Biographical Snapshots of the Islamic Left: Absolutism and Multiple Imaginations

Though hardly revolutionaries, professors Seyyed Fakhr Fakhreddin Shadman (1907–67) and Ahmad Fardid (1912–94) unwittingly set the stage for the Islamic Left's nativism by arguing that modernization had rendered Iranian society vulnerable to the temptations of an alien and culturally decadent West.[35] That they had fashioned this critique in terms adopted during their studies in France, Germany, or England did not stop them from advocating a rediscovery of the moral "essence" of Shi'ite-Iranian civilization. "Employing Heidegger's premise that during each historical era a truth arises that obscures competing truths," Shadman argued that the abandonment of *Gharbzadegi* (Weststruckness) was a first step toward reasserting Iran's spiritual identity and political unity.[36] Inspired by this idea, **Jalal Al-e Ahmad** (1923–69) transformed the concept of *Gharbzadegi* into the rallying cry of a generation.

Paradoxically, Al-e Ahmad's advocacy of nativist thinking can be traced to his early rejection of Shi'ism. The son of a cleric, he wore the religious habit throughout his youth, but eventually disappointed his father, who had hoped he would pursue a religious vocation. This break occurred after Al-e Ahmad spent several months studying in Najaf. As Al-e Ahmad tells the story, having seen in his future "a snare in the shape of a cloak and *aba* [an outer garment traditionally worn by the Shi'ite clergy]," he rushed back to Iran, "turning my back on both my father and brother."[37] He then enrolled in Tehran's secular Teacher's College, graduated in 1946, and subsequently embarked on a doctoral program in Persian literature at Tehran University. By this time his rejection of clericalism seems complete: adopting the utilitarianism of Iran's most famous anticlerical intellectual, Ahmad Kasravi, Al-e Ahmad joined the communist Tudeh Party and soon emerged as its most articulate spokesman. But after the party militated for granting the Soviet Union oil concessions, he defected along with several other prominent Iranian communists. Al-e Ahmad then backed the creation of several other small parties, including the Third Force, which advocated a mixture of nationalism and Marxism. Following the 1953 coup, he cut all ties to political parties and then embarked on a career in journalism and literature.

In the ensuing years, Al-e Ahmad was pulled in multiple directions. During the midfifties he toured rural Iran, where his encounter with village life gave him, in Dabashi's words, "a realistic understanding of the diversified masses of people and their valid . . . cultural frames of reference."[38] However, it was the West that commanded his attention. In the summer of 1957 he traveled with his wife to France and England. Intrigued with this experience, he returned alone to Europe in 1962 and toured France, Switzerland, Holland, and England. Al-e Ahmad, we are told, was both "attracted and repelled by the allure of the liberal mind"—fascinated by its intrinsic openness to different ideas and experiences, and disgusted by its failure to adhere to any single moral standard.[39] The following year he spent several weeks in Israel, mainly touring kibbutzim. In an analysis foreshadowing his instrumentalist vision of religion, he writes that "as an Eastern state, Israel is a model, [better] than any other . . . of how to deal with the West. How to extract from its industries by the spiritual power of a [mass] martyrdom, how to . . . spend the capital thus obtained to advance the country."[40] In 1964 he made the pilgrimage to Mecca, an experience that apparently rekindled a latent spirituality, yet hardly reconverted him. One year later Al-e Ahmad attended a Harvard International Summer Seminar hosted by Henry Kissinger, during which he not only traded insights with Robert Coles, David Reisman, Norman Mailer, and Ralph Ellison, but also was compelled to play baseball with one of his "typical" American family hosts.[41]

These and other travels—including a trip to the Soviet Union—were not the sole vehicle through which Al-e Ahmad developed a multiple imagination. His literary travels took him through the existential lands of Martin Heidegger, André Gide, Albert Camus, and Jean-Paul Sartre. Such was his attraction to these thinkers that he set about the task of translating many of these works into Persian. Sartre's notion of the politically *engagé* intellectual had an enormous impact on him, as did Heidegger's critique of the alienating effects of technology. Having been introduced to Heidegger's ideas by Ahmad Fardid, Al-e Ahmad developed his own stinging critique of Western technology, and by implication, of Western "civilization" itself. Insisting that machines were, as Boroujerdi puts it, a veritable "mode of thought" of Western domination,[42] he posited the argument—which Khomeini would later repeat almost verbatim—that the decline of traditional industries such as carpet weaving heralded the West's economic and existential victories over the East.

A fusion of Marxist and existentialist thought, this familiar Third World diagnosis of cultural and economic dependency also suggested a very Western cure: the harnessing, by intellectuals in these countries, of the "people's" identity. While Al-e Ahmad never posited a systematic Shi'ite version of this cure, his knowledge of rural Shi'ism and Persian epic poetry taught him that Shi'ite myths were, in his words, "the most real of realities."[43] Armed with this insight, he concluded that intellectuals should forge an alliance with the "doctors" most qualified to speak for society: the clerics.[44] (Thus in a visit he paid to Khomeini prior to his exile from Iran in 1964, Al-e Ahmad is said to have told the Ayatollah that "if we continue to join hands we will defeat the government."[45]) In 1962 he summed up his message in his *Gharbzadegi*, or "Weststruckness." The monograph caused an overnight sensation by suggesting that the West's "unavoidable onslaught" had "reduced . . . our government, our culture, and our everyday lives into some semblance of a machine." The resulting "illness" left "west-stricken man . . . no place to stand. His is a dust particle floating in space. He has severed his ties with the essence of society."[46] This fearless attack on Western technology, its call for intellectual, cultural, technological, and political independence— and, by implication, its indictment of the Shah's regime—made it the rallying cry of an entire generation.

'Ali Shari'ati (1933–77) met Al-e Ahmad in Mashhad one year before Ahmad's death in 1969. Although they had much in common, the forces that shaped their young lives were quite different. Rather than reject religion, Shari'ati assimilated his father's rationalist vision of Islam. Mohammad-Taqi Shari'ati was a preacher who believed that Islam was a social and political doctrine.[47] Having founded the Center for the Propagation of Islamic Truth, an organization he created to combat the influence of the Tudeh Party, Mohammad-Taqi encouraged his son to read extensively. Plunging himself into his father's library, Shari'ati devoured works of literature, poetry, and philosophy from the West and East alike. While this literary feast at first caused him to doubt the very existence of God, his exposure to Shi'ite mysticism during his high-school years imbued Shari'ati with a lifelong attachment to the charismatic notion of personal and collective spiritual transcendence arising from asceticism and self-sacrifice.[48] After graduating Mashhad's Teacher Training College in 1952, he became an elementary-school teacher. But he was not satisfied to be a mere educator: having absorbed a revolutionary vision of Shi'ism, he joined a succession of small populist Islamic parties, beginning with the Movement of God Worshiping Socialists. After the 1953 coup, Shari'ati joined the National Resistance Movement, a Mosaddeqist organization that blended nationalism, socialism, and

Islam.[49] One year later he entered the Faculty of Letters at Mashhad, where in 1960 he earned a bachelor's degree in French and Arabic. Having married and graduated, he went on to Paris, where he pursued a *doctorat d'université* in letters at the Sorbonne.

The ensuing five years transformed Shari'ati into the master ideologue of Shi'ite radicalism. In retrospect this development seems preordained. Paris was then the international hub of "Third Worldism," an intellectual crucible in which revolutionaries from every corner of the globe sought to link their traditional sensibilities to the peculiar blend of Marxist existentialism represented by Sartre and other *intellectuels engagés*. Although Shari'ati despised the hedonism of French society, he soaked up the diverse intellectual currents of the *Quartier Latin*, thus producing a multifaceted vision that was as intellectually contradictory as it was morally and politically uplifting. Inspired by the positivist sociology of Jacques Berque, Shari'ati viewed religion as a product of human will and action. "In order to know religion," he writes, "we should follow the same road as that taken by nonreligious or even antireligious scientists. . . . I speak with the same language, which in the name of science, sociology, economics, philosophy of history, and anthropology, renounces religion or negates its metaphysical roots."[50] Yet as this statement suggests, Shari'ati's view of religion did not rest on positivism alone. During his years in Paris, he absorbed the existentialism of Sartre, the phenomenology of Edmund Husserl, and the violent nativism of Frantz Fanon. Out of this ideological mixture he forged a voluntaristic vision of Islam that, as Dabashi notes, made the individual "totally responsible for what he is and what he does, completely divorced from any historical, sacred and securing order."[51]

Nonetheless, Shari'ati refused the nihilism of existentialist thought. In a manner at variance with his stated belief that "in action . . . truth manifests itself,"[52] he concludes that ultimate "truth" would be realized by a revolutionary vanguard that expressed *the transcendent logic of a communal history*. Inspired by revolutionary parties such as Algeria's National Liberation Front, he argues that intellectuals should "communicate the objective abject conditions of the masses to the masses, until they attained a level of consciousness that would lead them to revolt."[53] This process required, as Ali Rahnema notes, "a deep understanding of . . . [the masses'] belief system," or, to put it more succinctly, a *transformation* of that belief system into a political ideology.[54] Of course, Shari'ati did not describe this process as a "transformation." Instead, he held that intellectuals should "rediscover" the *original* revolutionary meaning of Shi'ite concepts, which the traditional clergy obscured. Thus he argued that the terms *Imamat* and *velayat* did not mean the passive acceptance of the status quo pending the return of the Twelfth Imam; rather, they stood for the creation of a revolutionary *Hezbollah*, or Party of God—a "total" political party whose mission was to mobilize "the masses of society" and thus realize "the hopes of the disinherited classes."[55] These hopes were a given: his instrumentalism notwithstanding, in Shari'ati's mind, the ruling party, the Imam, and most important the *umma* were all vehicles through which *the* transcendent force of history—the people—expressed God's grand design:

> The people addressed in every school of thought and religion are the fundamental and effective factors of change. . . . In all the various parts of the Koran, the people *(al-nas)* themselves are addressed. The Prophet is sent on a mission to the people. He speaks to the people . . . the People are responsible for society and history. . . . The word, people, is a valuable word. The only word that is close to it, is mass *(tudeh)*. In sociology, mass means the body of the people without any regard to class distinction.[56]

After returning to Iran in 1965, Shari'ati began to forge his politicized concept of Shi'ism, first as a professor at Mashhad University and then from 1967 through 1972 as a popular lecturer in Tehran's *Hoseyniyeh-ye Ershad* (discussed later in this chapter). In 1973 he published his major work, *Eslamshenasi*, or "Islamology." Based on his lectures, the book's declared purpose was to create a new group of Muslim intellectuals whose task would be to create a formal "Islamic ideology," or *maktab*. A term intended to echo the traditional concept of a *mazhab*, or "school of legal thought," in Shari'ati's instrumentalized lexicon the term *maktab* reflected its Marxist-existentialist roots: "A *maktab*," he writes, "is a harmonious . . . set of philosophical perspectives, religious beliefs, ethical principles and methods of action which . . . [taken together] . . . constitutes an active, meaningful, goal oriented body which is alive . . . [all of whose] various organs are fed by the same blood and . . . the same spirit."[57]

Devoured by thousands of young Iranians, *Eslamshenasi* defined for an entire generation the two most compelling facets of Shari'ati's thinking: his instrumental rationalism and his messianic charisma. The former resided in the very notion of creating an ideology. As Dabashi notes, "To launch a revolution, Shariati needed rational creatures, enchanted with his revolutionary terms of identity."[58] Shari'ati openly declared his belief that the lay intelligentsia was the only legitimate agent for this ideology. In contrast with Al-e Ahmad, he not only spurned the clergy, but also argued that the connection between the seminary and the *bazaar* was the very "source of misery for Islam."[59] Indeed, in Ali Rahnema's words, he went so far as to call for the "Muslim intellectual [to embrace] an Islamic Protestantism similar to that of Christianity in the Middle East . . . [thus] giving birth to new thoughts and new movements."[60] On the other hand, Shari'ati's ideology was tinged with messianic expectations. A devotee of mysticism, his vision of a total return to the "self" (*bazgasht*)—while inspired by existentialism—articulated the charismatic core of Shi'ite culture.[61] Between these two opposing poles of instrumentalist rationalization and the transcendental transformation of history stood the unifying notion of the people. Shari'ati despised liberal democracy, but embraced the Marxist-Leninist notion of mass representation and popular sovereignty—as directed, of course, by a revolutionary party that knew the truths of Shi'ism as defined by Shari'ati himself.[62]

Although **Mehdi Bazargan** (1907–97) and Shari'ati were allies, the former championed a relatively more liberal Islamism. Born in Tehran, as a boy he imbibed the religious fervor of his father, a merchant from Azerbaijan who had close ties to religious circles.[63] After receiving a traditional Islamic education, Bazargan attended one of Iran's first modern high schools while also pursuing Qur'anic studies and philosophy. In 1928 he won a scholarship from Reza Shah's government to study in France. After pursuing studies in Nantes, he moved to Paris in 1930, where he completed an advanced degree in engineering at the elite École Centrale. Five years later, he returned to Iran, where he embarked upon a remarkable intellectual and political career.

That career was partly inspired by a liberal sensibility that had gelled during his years in France. In contrast with Al-e Ahmad and Shari'ati, whose antagonism to Western technology was partly shaped by the neomarxist Third Worldism of the 1960s, Bazargan's more positive view of the West reflected his appreciation of the universalist, democratic, and procapitalist utilitarianism that animated French society in the 1930s. "There are," he writes, "significant resemblances between machines and democracy. In a machine, all the various components . . . work together according to a plan. Similarly, in a society that wants to progress, all . . . must cooperate . . . toward the common good."[64] Imbued with this pragmatic ethos, in 1937 he joined the Faculty of Engineering of Tehran University, founded a small business, and in 1940 became director of the Construction Bureau of Bank Melli (the National Bank of Iran). Two years later he joined forces with an activist cleric named Seyyed Mahmud Taleqani (1910–79). The director of the Islamic Society, Taleqani believed that the greatest challenge facing Iran was, as he put it, the "rapid spread of Marxist and materialist principles and the founding of the Tudeh party."[65] Bazargan shared these concerns. Having witnessed the rise of the Tudeh Party at Tehran University, he began attending Taleqani's Qur'an interpretation sessions in an effort to deepen his understanding of the congruence between Islam and the modern sciences. These classes encouraged Bazargan to become more politically active, so in 1951 he accepted Prime Minister Mossaddeq's request to chair the board of directors of the National Iranian Oil Company. Mossaddeq's ouster in 1953 induced Bazargan to join the National Resistance Movement and then its successor, the Second National Front. Out of the latter emerged in 1961 the Iran Freedom Movement (IFM), a heterogenous collection of mostly lay intellectuals who espoused one version of Islamic Leftist ideology or another.[66] Assuming the leadership of the IFM, Bazargan and Taleqani became the spokesmen for the Islamic Left until Shari'ati returned to Iran in 1965.

Bazargan defined the IFM's mission in "Islamic" language that barely concealed its Western and particularly French inspiration. "Our entry into politics," he declares, "was prompted by our national duty *and* religious obligations. . . . Serving the people [is] . . . an act of worship. . . . We . . . Muslims . . . believed in the principles of justice, equality . . . *before* they were proclaimed by the French revolution and the Charter of the United Nations."[67] Proceeding from this populist stance, Bazargan posited—along with Taleqani—an evolutionary view of history that envisioned an advance from nationalism, liberalism, capitalism, and communism to a new form of Shi'ism. Viewed teleologically, every Islamic symbol had to be reinterpreted—or, to be more specific, redefined—to manifest this march toward freedom and equality. For this purpose, Bazargan established what Dabashi calls a "utilitarian function" for interpreting events such as the *hajj* pilgrimage. "The Shi'ia Imams," Bazargan argues, "on many occasions took advantage of the *hajj*. . . . Mecca has repeatedly . . . been used to propagate, incite and mobilize revolutionary movements."[68] Yet while defining Islam as a political "ideology," his rendering of this term is more pluralistic than Shari'ati's. "Our operative definition of this word," he writes, "is the same current meaning as used by political parties and intellectuals . . . [a] constellation of beliefs . . . which . . . a person or group . . . [adopts as] . . . an instrument for . . . designating the path and method for social struggle."[69] Similarly, while endorsing the idea of clerical leadership, Bazargan rejected the notion that one single "Party of 'Ali" should rule. In utilitarian terms that President 'Ali Akbar Hashemi Rafsanjani would echo many years later, he insists that "government has to be combined with legitimacy, justice, and piety, and [thus] . . . have permission, from the Imam and the *ommat* (the Shi'ite community)."[70]

Although **Seyyed Mahmud Taleqani** (1910–79) was a cleric, he was closer to the lay Islamic Left. That said, his vision of Islam was far more radical than that espoused by Bazargan. The son of a prominent cleric, Taleqani lacked his colleague's direct experiences of European society and ideas; unlike Bazargan, he gained his knowledge of the West by reading Iranian-produced studies reflecting the revolutionary ideas of continental Europe.[71] Thus while a profound knowledge of Shi'ism infused his interpretations of Islam, his *social and political* readings of the faith were inspired by Marx's teleological conception of history and scientific faith in humanity's power to realize collectively the social nature of the individual. This view was much closer to Shari'ati's revolutionary Shi'ism than to Bazargan's liberalism. Still, both he and Bazargan believed that some form of divinely inspired clerical guardianship could be wedded to the rationalizing force of mass politics. Taleqani summarizes this marriage by holding that while "the social issues are in the hands of just and pious religious authorities, . . . [the] people . . . [elect] and designate [the leader]." Thus, he insists, "constitutionalism, democracy and socialism" were all "successive steps" toward the ultimate ideal of Islam.[72]

Diffusing Multiple Shared Imaginations: The Intertwining of Seminary and University

During the sixties and early seventies, some of the populist ideas advanced by Iran's Islamic Left began appearing in Khomeini's speeches, letters, and declarations. While adherents of structural instrumentalism see this trend as part of a calculated effort by Khomeini and his allies to camouflage economic interest, I attribute it to a broader—and less conspiratorial—interplay of forces. Khomeini did not merely "appropriate" the ideas of the Islamic Left at an opportune moment; instead, through a protracted process of ideological diffusion and absorption that unfolded in tandem with his evolving biography, he indirectly imbibed these ideas in a manner often more unconscious than calculated. As a result, Khomeini developed *genuinely* contradictory visions of authority.

This ideological process was sparked by the overlapping of two contending subcultures: the seminary-based subculture of the clerics, and that of the university-based lay Islamic Left. We have already noted Borujerdi's role in rationalizing clerical institutions: by 1976 there were more than 23,000 clerics.[73] Meanwhile, the university subculture expanded at a faster rate. Although Iran had only 1,814 university students in 1941, 65,000 students were attending 17 universities by 1975. Factoring colleges into the equation, the total number of students in higher education climbed from 7,463 in 1951 to 151,905 in 1975.[74] Under such conditions the number of university students from traditional, rural, and thus religious backgrounds grew more rapidly than those from a more modern background. This trend was supported by the clerical elite, which under Boroujerdi's guidance encouraged *howzeh* graduates to pursue higher education.[75] More important was the increasing number of clerics obtaining positions in theology and philosophy departments at Iran's leading universities. By teaching in these secular arenas, Ayatollahs Morteza Motahari, Mohammad Beheshti, Mohammad-Javad Bahonar, and Mohammad Mofatteh—*all former disciples of Khomeini*—encouraged a slow exodus of seminary students to various theology faculties, thus creating islands of advanced religious training within *state* institutions.[76]

Similarly, we must also note the emergence of hybrid intellectual institutions that brought together politically oriented clerics and lay intellectuals. This was not a completely new development: by the early fifties, activist clerics such as Bahonar, Beheshti, and Mofatteh had already joined secular organizations such as Iran's Teachers Association in order to counter the influence of the Tudeh Party.[77] This interaction increased after Borujerdi's death in March 1961. Not only did his passing pose the challenge of choosing a new leading *marja'* (religious guide); but, in the absence of a suitable candidate, it also compelled lay and clerical thinkers to review the very principle of the *marja'iyyat*. Such a review took place during the 1962 Congress of Islamic Societies. Setting the tone, Bazargan argued for the creation of an "Islamic Society for the Social Sciences" charged with producing an enlightened Islam. Led by clerics and lay thinkers, the society would guide politics by remaining *separate* from it; politics would ensue through *showra* (consultation) and democracy, it being "the duty of every Muslim to . . . intervene in politics." This "manifesto," as Sharough Akhavi dubbed it,[78] was well received by a group of reformist clerics who had been meeting in Tehran since 1960 under the auspices of Professor Motahari's "Monthly Lectures." While Khomeini played no role in these meetings, Beheshti, Motahari, Taleqani, and Bazargan did. Shortly after Borujerdi's death, these and other religious activists issued a volume of essays in which they made two significant recommendations. First, they called for an autonomous consultative clerical committee, or *showra-ye fatva*, to replace the institution of the *marja'-e motlaq*. Fearing that this institution "invited comparison to the role of the Imam in a disturbing manner," they recommended that the new committee consist of "specialized" clerics who would "issue joint opinions on questions of the moment."[79] Second, several reformists argued that the Qur'anic injunction *al-amr bi al-ma'ruf wa al-nahy 'an al-munkar* (enjoin the good and forbid evil) should henceforth be *the* principle for expressing the public will. As one cleric puts it, this populist rendering of a basic Islamic precept was to become "the foundation for the reform of society."[80]

1963: Khomeini Confronts "Yazid"

The aforementioned authors did not consider how these two objectives would be reconciled. How would a permanent council of "specialized" clerics operate alongside a system of mass participation through which the people would "enjoin the good"? Whatever the theoretical difficulties implied by this project, the fact that the clerical reformers proposed it suggests the extent to which the positivist notions of authority championed by Bazargan had been assimilated by a small, but important group of activist clerics. This said, during the early sixties their influence was confined. The activist clerics were persecuted by the Shah Mohammad Reza Pahlavi's regime, and more important, most members of the clerical establishment distrusted a reform program promoting a substantial level of authority for the masses. Thus during the early sixties the drive to reform Shi'ism rested, for a brief moment, with Bazargan and the IFM.

However, 1963 signaled the beginning of a sea change in the correlation of ideological and political forces. Slowly the balance of power shifted from the Islamic Left and its middle-class constituency to Khomeini, the activist clerics, and their lower-middle-class followers within the bazaar, the student population, and the shantytowns of southern Tehran. The inauguration of the White Revolution helped set this process in motion. Among other things, the program called for land reform, the enfranchisement of women, and the creation of a literacy corps. Affirmed by a national plebiscite, but without recourse to constitutional procedures (the Parliament was suspended in May 1961), this classic case of authoritarian modernization offered Bazargan an ideal occasion for urging genuine democratic consultation. In an effort to silence his protests, the Shah imprisoned Bazargan and Taleqani. With Bazargan and his allies removed, the leadership of the IFM fell to lower-ranking activists, many of whom were from traditional backgrounds and thus sympathetic to the reformist clerics.[81] As fate would have it, this shift in power occurred during the very year in which Khomeini rose to national prominence.

Khomeini's decision to challenge the Shah stemmed from the death of Borujerdi and Khomeini's growing conviction that, in his words,

"The son of Reza Khan . . . has embarked on the destruction of Islam in Iran."[82] Prompted by such fears, in the fall of 1962 he denounced a new local election law because it failed to stipulate that only Muslims could run for provincial and city councils. However, it was the Shah's White Revolution one year later that catapulted Khomeini to fame. Aware that most high-ranking clerics were afraid to denounce the Shah, he issued a *fatva* (religious edict) in which he commanded Iranians to disregard the pre-Islamic Persian New Year of Nowruz.[83] The regime responded by encouraging a mob to attack students outside Khomeini's Feyziyeh Seminary, leading to the death of several *talabeh*s. Khomeini denounced the government, asserting that its strategy was to "bring about the total effacement of the ordinances of Islam."[84] The Shah retaliated by mounting a public campaign to vilify the clergy, inciting violent protests. Unfortunately for the Shah, the protests fell on 3 June 1963, the holy day of *'Ashura,* which marks the anniversary of Imam Hoseyn's martyrdom at the hands of the Sunni Caliph Yazid. Seizing the moment, Khomeini prepared to make his way from his home to Feyziyeh Seminary. Anticipating this move, the Shah stationed security forces throughout Qom, thus provoking fears of a widespread bloodbath. Khomeini then took the decisive action that almost instantaneously established him as a national charismatic leader. As one eyewitness of the ensuing events records,

> At this juncture, by announcing that: "Even if blood became knee-deep in the city, it will not stop me from going to Faizieye School," Ayatollah Khomeini broke the state of indecision and fear. Following the announcement, shouts of 'Lord is great' were heard from the residence of the Ayatollah. Some two hundred volunteers signed their last will and testament and surrounded the Ayatollah's house. Under [their] . . . protection, the Ayatollah was . . . put in a convertible . . . and the procession headed [towards] . . . the Shrine of Massoumeh. As the crowd approached the shrine, the armed soldiers suddenly retreated and left the city altogether.[85]

Emboldened by this seemingly miraculous event, Khomeini gave a fiery sermon in which he not only drew an explicit parallel between the Shah and the Sunni Caliph Yazid, but also assailed the former in language that played into the prejudices of the crowd: "I advise you wretched, miserable 45-year old man to stop and ponder a little. These people prefer to brand you as Jew, in which case I am required to declare you an infidel. Then you will be kicked out of the country."[86] Enraged by this inflammatory attack, the Shah had Khomeini arrested. This act led to riots in which the Shah's security forces killed some one hundred people in three days of protests.

These violent measures only served to heighten the apocalyptic expectations of Khomeini's followers. Having witnessed or heard of his fearless defiance of the Shah's troops, these youths began to view Khomeini as a kind of modern-day Hoseyn. Indeed, in the mythology of the Islamic Revolution, this "Second *'Ashura*" marked the start of a sixteen-year battle to destroy the new "Yazid." The Shah played into this mythology by dragging out the confrontation with Khomeini. After arresting him, the Shah released him weeks later, which only encouraged Khomeini to escalate his attacks on the new "Yazid." Finally, the Shah expelled Khomeini to Turkey in November 1964. A little less than one year later, in October 1965, Khomeini was exiled to the Holy City of Najaf in southern Iraq.

1964–72: Absorbing the Revolutionary Instrumentalism of the Islamic Left

Although the 1963 crisis created the emotional crucible out of which Khomeini's charisma found a national following, the same crisis created conditions that accelerated his absorption of the Islamic Left's ideas. That process had begun at least as early as 1962, when Khomeini organized a memorial service in Qom for Al-e Ahmad's father. Khomeini, we are told, informed Al-e Ahmad that he had read *Weststruckness* and admired it—a report that seems credible given Khomeini's use of the term in the ensuing years.[87] However, there were other paths, direct and indirect, through which Khomeini assimilated the ideas of the Islamic Left during his years in Iraq. Among them we should mention the role played by Ayatollahs Motahari, Beheshti, and Bahonar. We have seen that during the sixties, these men participated in associations that brought Islamic Leftists and clerics together. After Khomeini was expelled from Iran, all three—as well as Seyyed 'Ali Khamene'i, Hossein 'Ali Montazeri, and 'Ali Akbar Hashemi Rafsanjani—became his representatives in Iran and primary conduits through which the ideas of the Islamic Left reached him. Motahari was the most important member of this group. His relationship with Khomeini dated to 1945, when they read mystical texts together. In the following two decades he became a leading theologian and philosopher in his own right, as well as Khomeini's sole representative in charge of collecting taxes during his exile in Iraq and then Paris (1965–79).[88]

Khomeini's disciples were not the only channels of influence. During the late sixties the emergence of a more radical generation of Islamic

Leftists intensified the exchange of ideas between clerics and lay thinkers. Filling the vacuum left by Bazargan and other imprisoned IFM leaders, this new vanguard was led by 'Ali Shari'ati. In 1965 he returned to Iran and with Ayatollah Motahari transformed a popular intellectual institution, the *Hoseyniyeh Ershad* Institute, into the leading venue of dialogue between radical clerics and the Islamic Left. Instead of locating the institute in Tehran's traditional south, it was placed in the more modern and prosperous north, smack in the middle of the constituency over which the two groups were contending for influence.[89] With his classes attracting as many as five thousand students and his books reaching two million by the midseventies, by 1972 Shari'ati's ideological Shi'ism became the common discourse through which lay intellectuals and radical clerics debated Iran's future.

Shari'ati's ideas were embraced with particular zeal by the *Sazman-e Mojahedin-e Khalq-e Iran* (Organization of the Iranian People's Holy Warriors). Founded in 1965, the group's revolutionary-socialist brand of Shi'ism soon attracted many university students. Taleqani's relations with some leaders of *Mojahedin* helped channel the latter's ideas to the radical clergy.[90] The imprisonment of *Mojahedin* activists along with members of the Tudeh party had a similar effect. Despite torture and other brutalities, some prisoners managed to discuss, read, and write about politics. As Arjomand notes, from their discussions with *Mojahedin* and Tudeh activists, militant clerics became better acquainted with "the art of constructing an ideology" and thus were better equipped to seize the initiative from their leftist competitors.[91]

Similar discussions took place with greater intensity outside Iran. Beyond the reach of the Shah's secret police, Iranian students in American and European universities vigorously debated the ideas of Shari'ati, Taleqani, and other Islamic Leftists. These debates filtered up to Khomeini via a global network of Muslim Student Associations (MSAs), many of whose leaders formed the new vanguard of the IFM. Almost all of these men, such as Ebrahim Yazdi (b. 1931), Mostafa Chamran (1933–81), 'Abbas Amir-Entezam (b. 1933), and Sadeq Qotbzadeh (1936–82), had received their graduate degrees from U.S. institutions. Advocates of Shari'ati's *Islamology,* they relayed the students' concerns to Khomeini and transmitted his pronouncements to these followers. Here Yazdi played a key role. As Khomeini's personally designated representative in the United States, he disseminated religious publications notably lacking "any articles extolling democracy, tolerance and moderation."[92] A similar pattern obtained in Europe. There, in addition to the role played by Qotbzadeh, we must note the activities of Dr. Abolhasan Bani-Sadr. A Paris-based economist (and the first president of Iran) who advocated a utopian version of Islamic Leftism, he served as a link between Iranian student groups and Khomeini.

Dabashi argues that these students' "collective correspondence with Khomeini became a crucial aspect of their coming to political consciousness."[93] Their attraction to radical Shi'ism is explained, at least in part, by their paradoxical relationship with their host countries. Many of these students—some thirty thousand by 1961—chose to study overseas because there was insufficient space in Iranian colleges. In sharp contrast with the experience of Bazargan and even Shari'ati, many of these young people "tended to shut themselves off completely from their environment . . . and [made] no attempt to understand the West on its own terms."[94] Yet their relationship with the clerics was not one-sided. The students' zealous advocacy of Shari'ati's populist Islam, particularly as it was articulated by Yazdi and other Islamic Leftist leaders in the United States and Europe, helped transmit the Islamic Left's Third Worldist utilitarianism to Khomeini, and also to his clerical allies, who maintained contact with the MSAs throughout the late sixties and seventies.

Traces of the Islamic Left's thinking can be found in Khomeini's speeches and pronouncements at least as far back as 1963, the year he confronted the Shah. For example, in early spring of that year Khomeini lambasts Prime Minister Alam: "I will expose all your actions which are against the country's interests." As Moin notes, the term "'Iran's interests and glory' now entered the new political vocabulary of the clergy . . . widening the appearance of Khomeini among lay political activists."[95] Khomeini used populist and utilitarian ideas even more frequently the following year. For example, in October 1964 he declares that the *Majles* had acted as a "servant" of the United States by granting that country capitulatory rights. While attributing this situation to the Shah's failure to implement Article 2 of the Constitution (giving the *mojtaheds* [legal scholars] a supervisory role in the *Majles*), Khomeini not only repeats an accusation that he had made years earlier—namely that the "Majlis [was] elected at bayonet-point"—he also openly bemoans a *Majles* whose deputies, he complains, were not *elected* by the "Iranian nation."[96]

By citing this declaration, I am not suggesting that Khomeini had wholly embraced the radical "republicanism" of the Islamic Left; far from it. What he seemed to find most appealing was the pragmatic idea that the paramount task of the "Iranian nation"—indeed the entire Islamic world—was to confront the West by using whatever political institutions and ideas *most effectively served this end.* Evincing this pragmatism, Khomeini declares that the safeguarding of the Islamic community was *not* the sole prerogative of the *ulama* (scholars of Islam); rather, he holds that "those who bear the utmost responsibility are the Islamic governments, Islamic presidents and kings."[97] From this utilitarian vantage point, Khomeini further deduced that government must flow from the people, or at the very least reflect their aspirations. Thus by 1967, in an open letter to Prime Minister Hoveyda, Khomeini condemns the official for refusing "to let the people freely choose their representatives."[98] Four years later Khomeini calls upon Muslim governments to confront the "foul claws of imperialism," to "listen to the people explain their problems . . . and [to] neglect no measure necessary for the solution of those problems."[99] By late 1971 this populist drift leads Khomeini to conclude that a monarchy is morally and institutionally incapable of addressing such "problems." "Islam," he declares, "is fundamentally opposed to the whole notion of monarchy . . . [which is] one of the most shameful . . . *reactionary* manifestations."[100] The following year, in a message to Muslim students in North America," he speaks to his followers in Third Worldist terms they could readily grasp. "Imperialism," he warns,

> of the left and . . . the right have joined hands . . . to annihilate the Muslim people . . . (and) . . . plunder their abundant capital and natural resources. . . . Devote greater attention to planning the foundations of an Islamic state. . . . With God's aid, it may then be possible to create the foundation for the independence and freedom of Iran and to put and end to the oppression of the tyrannical regime and the servants of imperialism.[101]

Summary: An Amalgam of Visions

Khomeini's absorption of Sunni Realism and later the Islamic Left's revolutionary instrumentalism did not ensue from a calculated plan by which radical clerics selectively integrated the Left's ideas into a preconceived project. Rather, during a process that took at least a decade to unfold, the institutional and ideological boundaries between seminary and university became increasingly blurred, thus enabling the political visions of the Islamic Left and militant clergy to seek each other out. Here, in embryonic form, we see the fusing of elite and masses that Kornhauser argued is central to the creation of both mass movements and charismatic or "populist" ideologies.

Given these early stirrings of mass society, it is certainly tempting to think about Shari'ati and his colleagues along the lines suggested by Kornhauser, Mannheim, and Shils: did Shari'ati not speak for an alienated intellectual elite whose relativist notion of truth set the stage for their fanatical embrace of a revolution against the "machine" (as Al-e

Ahmad imagined it) of Westernization? And was he not the modern-day equivalent of a charismatic leader? While his messianism might support this thesis, the most striking feature of Shari'ati's thinking was its *implicit* instrumentalism. Yet, paradoxically, if the idea of *creating* a new Islam inspired his followers, in the long run this notion benefited the clerics most. One reason Khomeini prevailed was that the populist notions of politics that he had absorbed were articulated by a turbaned elite that grasped and spoke a language that Shari'ati and company could never claim as their own. Long before Shari'ati came to prominence, Khomeini had established his credentials as a charismatic mystic who, with a small coterie of devoted students, was following in the footsteps of the holy Prophets, the Imams, and their clerical heirs.

Perhaps Shari'ati should have seen this coming. By 1972 his partner at the *Hoseyniyeh Ershad*, Ayatollah Motahari, had already broken with the master Islamic ideologue. Not surprisingly, one observer of these events tells us that Motahari "questioned all the basic concepts that Shariati put forward . . . [and] thought that Shariati was an instrumentalist, in the sense that he used religion as an instrument for his political and social objectives."[102] The irony was that by the time Shari'ati was forced out of the Ershad, Khomeini already had assimilated a utilitarian vision of authority. This may explain, in part, why he twice refused several clerics' demands that he condemn Shari'ati's writings. Acknowledging in early 1977 that he had read Shari'ati's books, he explained that he sent him a message that "it is now not the right *time* for these things."[103] Yet such tolerance had its limits. For Khomeini not only still adhered to the view that the clerics were the "guardians" of society, but also spurned the secular world and ideas that had shaped the multiple imaginations of Al-e Ahmad, Bazargan, and Shari'ati. That he did so reminds us that authority systems can persist, despite—or perhaps because of—their most profound contradictions.

4 The Rule of the Jurist: Genesis of a Revolutionary Doctrine

> If the Western philosophers consider the world . . . a mixture of conflicts and strife, it is possible to call [Khomeini] . . . the center of contradictions and the pivot of divergent tastes and feelings. The man who talks about . . . theosophy and mysticism . . . can simultaneously think about the establishment of an Islamic government, justice for the oppressed and implementation of Islamic law.[1]
>
> —A. Ferhi

The Multiple Roots of Islamic Government

Thus far we have traced the process by which Khomeini's world-view was shaped by three concepts of political authority. The first two emerged during the twenties and thirties. Molded by hardship and the loss of his father, and shaped by his subsequent immersion in mysticism and asceticism, Khomeini developed a *charismatic* sensibility that found an audience among a loyal following of clerics and students. During this same period, he also internalized a *traditional* but implicitly political vision of authority, best summed up in the notion that the clerics should act as moral guides for the community. Finally, in the forties, fifties, and sixties, Khomeini imbibed a *neoutilitarian* notion of politics in general, and ideology in particular. This instrumentalist vision—the first hints of which appeared in his book *Kasfh al-Asrar*—called for subordinating the givens of religion and divine law to the changing exigencies of power, legitimacy, and political unity.

Having explored Khomeini's assimilation of multiple images of authority, we must now consider how this dynamic helped produce the very doctrine for which he and his revolution stood: *velayat-e faqih,* or "Rule of the Jurist." We shall see that while this doctrine was largely an ideological innovation, its novelty derived not merely from the idea of one ruling *faqih,* or Supreme Leader, but also from its *eclectic* intellectual foundations. Drawing on traditional, charismatic, and utilitarian themes, Khomeini created a vision of Islamic rule that was influenced by his own multiple biography. After detailing this argument, this chapter will review the social, cultural, and political conditions that set the stage for Khomeini's emergence as the *faqih* in 1979. My object here is to highlight the striking way in which the "Rule of the Jurist" anticipated the Janus-faced nature of Iran's Islamic Revolution: a mass revolt that expressed a transrational quest for collective renewal, and a sociopolitical struggle for economic independence and social justice.

Velayat-e Faqih: From Moral Guide to Political Executive

During the late sixties Khomeini began to propound the idea that clerics should be the primary wielders of judicial, legislative, *and* executive power. Although this idea represented a radical departure from the juridically limited conception of *velayat* (vice-regency) to which he still adhered when he arrived in Najaf in 1965, it was consistent with a certain political logic to which Khomeini had given expression as far back as 1941. As we have seen, in *Kashf al-Asrar,* Khomeini had suggested that the clerics should restrict their activism to providing legal and moral guidance—*providing* that the state's rulers enforced Islamic law, respected the clerical establishment, and maintained social and political peace. Once these conditions no longer prevailed or were under threat, the clerics had a right to oppose the ruler or take other appropriate actions.

But what actions? Although the White Revolution of 1963 threatened the clerics' legal authority and financial independence, and although Khomeini claimed in 1963 that the Shah's actions endangered the "very existence of the religious class," during his confrontation with the Shah that year, he refrained from calling for the overthrow of the latter's government.[2] By the late sixties, however, Khomeini began to fear that the very existence of the Shah's government threatened the clerics' authority. Not only was the Shah pursuing secularizing policies; but, sitting in Najaf, Khomeini learned that the Shah also had launched a campaign to subordinate Shi'ism to a pre-Islamic Persian identity. This policy reached new heights during the October 1971 festivities, held in Shiraz and at the ruins of Persepolis and Pasargadae, to commemorate the twenty-five-hundredth anniversary of the founding of the Persian Empire. Fearing for the very survival of Iran's Islamic identity, Khomeini now concluded that the clerics should make the transition from moral guides to executive rulers.

Hamid Dabashi implies that this transition was driven by an innate cultural logic. The "development of this political doctrine [*velayat-i faqih*]," he writes, had been "in dormant process since the very inception of the Shi'i cause."[3] While I would not go so far as this, I would agree that Khomeini's interpretation of *velayat-e faqih* echoed what Dabashi calls the "permanently charismatic feature of Shi'ism."[4] It did so by intimating that a leading *marja'* (religious guide) could have something of the divine spark that illuminated the Imams. This implication, by the way, explains why the Grand Ayatollahs of Iran and Iraq all spurned Khomeini's notion of clerical rule. They believed that the people should experience Shi'ism's effervescence through prayer, ascetic practices, or lamentation sessions. But they would not countenance the idea that a mere mortal could inherit the divine *'esmat* (infallibility) of the Prophet Mohammad and the Twelve Imams, or invoke that infallibility to authorize the creation of an Islamic state.[5]

Despite such reservations, such was the charismatic allure of Shi'ism that few of the Shah's opponents could ignore its hold on the popular imagination. Indeed, as early as the midsixties, the most prominent members of the Islamic Left were already arguing that Islamic government required "permission" from a living *faqih* or Imam—providing that he acted with the support of the *umma* (Islamic community).[6] Whether this fact influenced Khomeini's thinking is hard to say. With the partial, if very telling, exception of Jalal Al-e Ahmad, Khomeini makes no references to his Iranian contemporaries, be they lay intellectuals or clerics. Nor does he refer to the Grand Ayatollahs of Najaf, all of whom rejected his radical reinterpretation of Shi'ism. (The only exception may have been Ayatollah Seyyed Mohammad Baqer al-Sadr, a leading Iraqi Shi'ite thinker whose writings on Islamic government may have influenced Khomeini.)[7] Such silence was undoubtedly useful. By largely relying on the Qur'an—and particularly on famous *hadith*s, or sayings attributed to the Prophet Mohammad and to the Twelve Imams (especially 'Ali and Hoseyn)—Khomeini implied that his theory of Islamic government was an authentic expression of Islam itself, while at the same time undercutting his potential ideological competitors.[8]

Islamic Government: A Functional-Utilitarian View of Infallibility

Such intimations of authenticity were unconvincing: *velayat-e faqih* is a revolutionary tapestry inspired by utilitarian, mystical, *and* traditional ideas. In constructing this fabric Khomeini faced a tricky problem: he championed the rule of one supreme *marja'* over an Islamic state without implying that the Twelfth Imam had returned to reveal the full meaning of the Prophet Mohammad's divine Message—or that someone with divine qualities similar to those of the Twelfth Imam had emerged. From a traditional vantage point both ideas were blasphemous. How could Khomeini argue for a *form* of charismatic rule without implying that this rule constituted a *divine* consummation of Mohammad's revelation? Khomeini's solution to this dilemma consisted of two parts. The first, outlined in his book *Islamic Government*, entailed a theoretical exercise by which Khomeini combined traditionalist and utilitarian, or "interest-based," arguments to advance a quintessentially political account of the authority exercised by the Prophet and the Imams. The second consisted of a mystical reinterpretation of *esmat* that implied that infallibility could be acquired through a form of active asceticism.

On one level *Islamic Government*—published in 1971 and based on a series of lectures that Khomeini gave in early 1970—offers a ringing defense of traditional Shi'ite orthodoxy. Denouncing the 1906 Constitution, which he correctly notes was "borrowed" from Belgian legal code, Khomeini asserts that henceforth the term *constitutionalism* should not be abused to "take advantage of" or "deceive the people."[9] Echoing Jalal Al-e Ahmad, he argues that Iranians who facilitate such deceptions are " 'Westernmaniacs' and . . . servants of imperialism" (38). Having staked out this take-it-or-leave-it position, Khomeini had to abandon his earlier support for Article 2 in the 1906 Constitution which called for a committee of clerics to supervise the law. Instead, he advanced the prototypical position of all "fundamentalists"—namely, that the "Glorious Koran and the *Sunna* . . . contain all the laws and ordinances that man needs in order to attain happiness and the perfection of his state" (44). Since "Law . . . is actually the ruler" (79), all Khomeini would concede is that "Islamic government . . . is constitutional in the sense that the rulers are subject to . . . *conditions that are set forth* in the Noble Koran and the Sunna of the Prophet" (55; italics mine).[10]

Yet Khomeini implicitly admits that the Qur'an and the Sunna could *not* by themselves provide for a comprehensive system of government. Laws must be *executed* by a person or institution, and they must be executed *for a purpose*. Addressing the latter, we should emphasize that Khomeini does *not* proffer the familiar orthodox rationale, according to which laws must be executed because they are God's will. Quite apart from the intrinsic authority of God's immutable Revelation, Khomeini employs deductive reasoning to reach a simple conclusion: laws and government exist to prevent people from transgressing "against the rights of others for the sake of their personal pleasure."[11] Although this statement echoes his enduring commitment to mystical asceticism, it anticipates a very utilitarian thesis. Government, Khomeini argues, was created to "prevent . . . anarchy and disorder." "Islam," he insists, "came . . . to establish order in society; leadership and government are for the sake of ordering the affairs of society." Using terms that he would repeat almost verbatim eighteen years later, Khomeini declares that the purpose of Islam is to create a system of public order that protects the interests of Muslims: "It is our duty to preserve Islam," he writes. "This duty is one of the most important obligations incumbent upon us; it is more necessary even than prayer and fasting" (42, 75). Pursuing this theme, he points out that because "God . . . entrusted [to Muhammad] . . . the task of government and command . . . in conformity with the *interests* of the Muslims, he arranges for the . . . mobilization of the army, and appoints . . . governors and judges" (78; italics mine). Reiterating this point in the last pages of *Islamic Government*, Khomeini maintains that the "ruling given by the late Mirza Hasan Shirazi (d. 1921) prohibiting the use of tobacco . . . was a governmental ruling, based on the interests of Islam and the Muslims and his determination of secondary conditions *(unvan-i sanavi)*" (124).[12]

This remarkable statement demonstrates the extent to which Khomeini's understanding of Islamic government departs from the traditional defense of Shi'ite orthodoxy that he mounts in the first pages of *Islamic Government*. As we have noted earlier, Shi'ite traditionalists disdained the notion of interests. They rightly feared that it could become a Pandora's box that, once opened, could reduce Islam to whatever mundane definition of *interest* prevailed at any given moment. Khomeini's attempt to justify its use by associating interests with "secondary conditions" was also a juridical stretch: in Shi'ite law secondary conditions are invoked in cases *of law* for which the "primary ordinances" of the *Shari'ah* (sacred law of Islam) do not provide a sufficient basis for reaching judgment. That Khomeini—almost as an afterthought—would claim that this narrow principle could be associated with the vast exigencies of a governmental ruling suggests the extent to which his understanding of Islam was conditioned by notions of power, expediency, and interest.[13]

The second question that Khomeini had to address concerns *who* is to exercise power or determine interests, given that the Twelfth Imam has not yet returned to complete Mohammad's revelation? To answer this question without appearing to violate the doctrine of the Imamate, Khomeini adopts a brash solution: again relying on deductive reasoning, he suggests that those who believe that the clerics should not rule because they are fallible human beings have misunderstood the doctrine of the Imamate. To begin with, Khomeini argues, it would be illogical to assume that God believed that his laws should be applied "only in the time of the Commander of the Faithful ['Ali], . . . and that afterwards, men became angels."[14] Since man was still evil, God surely wanted him to observe his laws. Beyond this appeal to logic, he holds that the Qur'an's "authorization" *suras* (passages),[15] and *hadith*, or "stories" attributed to the Prophet and the Imams, clearly indicate that both the Prophet and 'Ali intended religious scholars to exercise judicial and executive authority pending the return of the Twelfth Imam. To take just one example, Khomeini cites a *hadith* in which the Prophet tells 'Ali that he (Mohammad) should be succeeded by "those who come after me, transmit my traditions and practice, and teach them to the people."[16] Since only the *foqaha* (plural of *faqih*) are qualified to undertake such tasks, Khomeini reasons that the latter should inherit the authority of the Prophet and the Imams who followed him.

Yet, Khomeini stipulates, this does not mean that "the status of the *faqih* is identical to that of the Imams and the Prophet" (62, 64). "No one," he insists, "can attain the spiritual status of the Imams." Citing another *hadith*, Khomeini claims that the Imams and the Prophet "existed before the creation of the world in the form of lights situated beneath the divine throne; they were superior to other men even in the sperm from which they grew" (64). However, if no mere mortal could have the spiritual status of the Prophet and the Twelve Imams, Khomeini asserts in a remarkable passage that this "status" was "unconnected with the function as ruler." The "function" of rule, he argues, derived instead from "government powers" whose source is a "rational and *extrinsic* matter." In short, the critical thing about ruling is its function, namely the rational exercise of power. And since "superiority with respect to spiritual virtues does not confer increases in governmental power," it follows that "God has conferred upon government in the present age the same powers and authority that were held by the Most Noble Messenger and the Imams." A "duty" necessitated by reason rather than a "privilege" derived from spiritual status, government "devolves . . . upon one who possesses . . . knowledge and justice" and thus is no less incumbent on the clerics now than it was on their "functional" predecessors during the early years of Islam (62–64)!

This ingenious utilitarian distinction between intrinsic spiritual status and extrinsic political function notwithstanding, Khomeini admits one critical difference between the era of the Imams and that which followed. In the present day, "no single individual has been designated for the task" of rule (54–55). How then was the religious leader to be selected? In response to this question, Khomeini cites from the Qur'an and several *hadiths* to argue that the Ruling Jurist must have three qualities. He must know the law; he must be morally "just"; and he must be an "Imam." By "Imam," Khomeini hastens to add, he has in mind the "common" rather than "technical" Arabic meaning of *Imam*— in other words, a religious "leader" or "guide" rather than one of the Shi'ite Imams (82–83). When a man possessing these three attributes emerges, Khomeini writes, "he will possess the same authority as the Most Noble Messenger [the Prophet Muhammad] . . . and it will be the duty of the people to obey him" (62).

However, Khomeini did not explain how these three qualities were to be measured. On what basis would one ascertain whether a leader was "just," "moral," and "knowledgeable"? The subjective nature of the first two of these qualities hardly lent itself to "rational" measurement, while the latter trait—while rational—was also hard to measure objectively. Khomeini's assertion that the Ruling Jurist had to be chosen according to his "leadership" attributes provided no answer either. Khomeini used the term *imamat-i i'tibari*, or "extrinsic imamat," when speaking of the Imam's leadership, thus again implying that his authority was gained through action rather than endowed by divine powers (158 n. 93). Yet, how can a man who "possesses the same authority as the Noble Messenger" be chosen *without* some reference to the intangibles of personality or charisma? Khomeini did not squarely address this question in his *Islamic Government*. The position of Ruling Jurist was to somehow "fall" on a scholar who could demonstrate his achieving the level of *ejtehad*—in other words, a scholar who had acquired the *intellectual* capabilities to "discern the true practices of the Messenger of God" (64, 70). Such a *faqih*, he boldly states, "is the legatee of the Most Noble Messenger . . . and . . . during the Occultation of the Imam, he is the leader of the Muslims" (84).[17] If, on the other hand, such a person cannot be found, the task must "fall" on the *foqaha* as a group. Yet, however much this reasoning derived from rational argument, it invited the suspicion that the Ruling Jurist would have to be a man blessed with more than mere intellectual powers.

Two years later Khomeini tried to solve the puzzle that he had failed to resolve in his *Islamic Government*. In a series of lectures published under the title *The Struggle Against the Appetitive Soul, or The Supreme Jihad*, he offered a mystical reinterpretation of *'esmat* in which he implied that a certain kind of infallibility could be acquired through ascetic practices. In some ways, as we saw in chapter 2, Khomeini had anticipated this argument forty years earlier. Inspired by Ibn 'Arabi's idea of absolute existence, or *wujudiyya*, he had envisioned a series of mystical journeys through which a mortal—if exceptional—man may reach ever-higher levels of God's divine light. But he had not gone so far as to suggest that the "perfect man" was anything more than an archetypal figment of a mythical world. In *The Supreme Jihad*, this journey becomes a real possibility.

Khomeini gets to the rub of his argument by advancing the bold idea that the *Ma'sumin* ("Infallible Ones") were "not only created out of pure substances . . . they also . . . perceived themselves to be in the presence of God Almighty . . . as a result of their *ascetic exercises* and the acquisition of luminosity and noble virtues." Thus, there are two kinds of infallibility: one that is endowed by God, and one that "derives . . . from the perfection of faith . . . [and that is] the product of faith."[18] Because, in theory, all human beings can attain such faith, Khomeini *does not* equate the *Ma'sumin* with the Imams; instead, he speaks more generally of "God's servants, His Prophets, *awliya*, and angels."[19]

This inclusion of *awliya*, or "Friends of God," merits further comment. Although the term is used in various way in the Qur'an, it generally includes anyone who worships God and obeys his laws. Although such religiosity puts one "closer to God," the *awliya* are not endowed with the gift of grace.[20] But in the Islamic mystical tradition, the term has a different meaning. *Awliya* are saints—those who have approached God through ever-higher levels of mystical experience.[21] In *The Supreme Jihad* Khomeini uses the term in this sense, but also pushes it in new directions. He states that *all* the Prophets (and thus not merely Mohammad or the Imams), as well as the *awliya*, attained *'esmat* from the "perfection of faith"[22] that comes from total devotion to God. Man, he implies, can only reach this state of total faith by renouncing "the desire of his carnal self." Shorn of his "veils of darkness" and his "worship of the world,"[23] he is reborn before "an armed powerful [master]" and thus attains "infallibility."[24] Having forged this link between *'esmat* and ascetic self-denial, Khomeini exhorts his audience to cut "any tie or link binding you to this world in love. . . . This world, despite all its apparent splendor . . . is too worthless to be loved, particularly if one is deprived of what it has to offer."[25] Thus, if "you purify the intention with which you perform acts of worship, make your deeds truly righteous, rid your hearts of self-love, . . . lofty stations and elevated degrees await you."[26]

The Supreme Jihad completed the redefinition of *velayat* and *'esmat* that Khomeini had begun in *Islamic Government.* The duty to rule was not thrust on the clerics merely by rational knowledge or the need to determine interests. Instead, it could ensue from a form of mystical revelation that anyone could strive for, but only few among the clerics could attain. While this elitist focus seemed to contrast with the populist themes that Khomeini was expressing during this same period,[27] we would be mistaken to conclude that he was engaged in a strategy of rhetorical subterfuge by which he directed elitist ideas to the clerics and populist ones to the people. The traditional, utilitarian, and charismatic notions of clerical leadership advanced in *The Supreme Jihad* and *Islamic Government* addressed two levels of one vision. For Khomeini, there was no contradiction between the exigencies of clerical rule and the role that the people played in submitting to the *faqih's* authority. Thus in *Islamic Government* he not only holds that Iranians should "end all this plundering and usurpation of wealth" for which the "imperialists" were to blame, but also insists that "the people as a whole have a responsibility in this respect." He then hastens to add, however, that "the responsibility of the religious scholars is graver and more critical. . . . We must be in the forefront."[28] In short, Khomeini's eclectic thinking leads him to a "vanguard theory" of revolution. While it would be a stretch to suggest that Khomeini was to Shi'ite Islam what Lenin was to Marxism, it is not hard to find in these assertions an echo of 'Ali Shari'ati and other Islamic Leftists, all of whom believed that with the people's backing, the *faqih* should express history's transcendent truths. The problem was whether Khomeini would author his own prophecy, or whether instead some force would descend from the heavens and accomplish this task for him.

Iran's Twin Revolution: The Victory of Being over Interests, 1972–78

Khomeini may have hoped in 1972 that he would one day become the utilitarian-charismatic prophet described in *Islamic Government* and *The Supreme Jihad.* Indeed, as Baqer Moin notes, during the first half of the seventies, both books "were widely . . . distributed in Iran . . . often together."[29] But luck played an important role as well. Reflecting on the forces that set the stage for Khomeini's emergence as the Imam, one

Iranian scholar argues that "[m]odernization had a schismatic impact on the structure and cultural orientation of Iran's urban society. . . . The process gave rise to two ideologically antithetical . . . parts. These correspond to the 'secular' and 'theocratic' forces."[30] With the benefit of hindsight we must amend this judgment in two ways. First, these two "antithetical" forces were divided less by a secular–theocratic schism than by an instrumentalist–charismatic one. The intellectual vanguard of the new middle class viewed Shi'ism as a potent tool with which to rationally defend their political, social, and ideal interests. In contrast, the lower-middle class elements who migrated from the villages to the cities embraced messianic Shi'ism as a transrational, charismatic solution to mass alienation. Hence we are dealing with two different forms of rationality, not religion itself. Second, during the late seventies these two tracks converged. Pushed together by the disorienting effects of mass society, a "revolution of being" briefly overwhelmed a "revolution of interests." Khomeini's good fortune was that his eclectic vision of Islamic government articulated both revolutions, but without ceding the symbolic terrain to the middle-class intelligentsia and its intellectual vanguard.

It should be noted that the "revolution of interests" was also embraced by two other classes: the traditional *bazaaris* (the traditional merchant middle class) and industrial workers. Despite their structural proximity to the clerics, small merchants, producers, and traders remained passively loyal to the regime until the early seventies. But as they were undercut by the economy's growing dependency on oil exports and the industries that sprang up around this *rentier* sector, they turned against the regime. The final straw came in 1975–76, when *bazaaris* became the primary targets of the Shah's "anti-profiteering campaign," and saw their traditional guilds replaced by state-controlled institutions.[31] Workers in state-supported industries such as oil, government services, and construction were also hard hit by the economic downturn of the late seventies. But relative to other sectors, the industrial proletariat played a limited role in the revolution.[32] Comparing all three of the above groups, we find that middle-class intelligentsia—university students, professors, and writers—were the most outspoken critics of the regime. Emboldened by the Shah's brief liberalization policy in 1977, they reestablished a myriad of professional, academic, and intellectual organizations, thus providing the Islamic Left and the National Front a venue through which to press for one or another version of democracy, free expression, and the like.[33] As for the "revolution of being," while the radical clergy were its foremost advocates, their message was embraced by what Khomeini called the *mostaz'afin*, or "disinherited." Consisting mostly of rural migrants who worked in construction and various non-industrial sectors, this *lumpenproletariat* lacked enduring ties to formal interest groups, parties, and other means of empowerment. Crowded into the slums of Tehran and other cities, they were profoundly disoriented by the blatant corruption and ostentatious lifestyle of the ruling monarchy, and by the Shah's introduction of a pre-Islamic ideology for which they had little sympathy or innate understanding. Seeking solace in self-help groups and religious associations, they seized upon the notion of charismatic redemption advocated by the radical clerics and their followers in the seminaries and, to a lesser extent, the universities.

Although the revolutions of interest and being initially proceeded along separate tracks, by the late seventies the first was overtaken by the second. We have already noted that the roots of this process date to the late sixties. It was during this period that the overlapping of seminary and university subcultures began to blur the distinction between those forces seeking to use Shi'ite symbols as an ideological weapon in the struggle for political reform, and those viewing Shi'ism as an essential, transcendent reality. The arrest of Mehdi Bazargan and the subsequent rise of a new cadre of Islamic Leftists heightened support for Shari'ati's revolutionary Shi'ism among the high-school and university student population. Having adopted his charismatic message without fully grasping the political implications of his instrumentalism, these students constituted—often without knowing it—a pool of potential recruits for Khomeini's ideology of *velayat-e faqih.*

Yet by itself, this development does not explain what Said Arjomand calls the "abject surrender to the clerical party of . . . the feeble, middle-class based political factions."[34] Why in 1978 did the leaders of the middle class accede to Khomeini's emergence as Imam? The catalyst that facilitated this momentary triumph of being over interests was a crisis of "mass society." While not as profound as that which swept Germany during the forties, Iran's crisis was sufficiently disruptive to impel nearly all urban social groups to mobilize in their quest for charismatic experience and leadership.[35]

It will be recalled that the phenomenon of mass society springs from a double crisis: on one level it is a crisis of alienation resulting from the rapid introduction of new cultural symbols for which the population is unprepared; on another it ensues from conditions of institutional fragmentation making "elites . . . readily accessible to . . . non-elites and non-elites . . . readily available for mobilization by elites."[36] This structural dynamic produces a "populist" form of consciousness in which "the uniformity of opinion . . . becomes the supreme standard, superordinate to traditional values, professional standards, and institutional autonomy."[37] The resulting quest to experience charismatic transcendence is partly structured by the availability of utopian symbols in a given culture. Thus, while all societies are vulnerable to such crises, some lend themselves more than others to charismatic mass movements. Next I shall briefly trace this meshing of structural and symbolic forces that set the stage for Iran's revolution.

We have already mentioned the symbolic crisis that Shah Moham-mad Reza Pahlavi provoked by belittling indigenous Shi'ite traditions in favor of a pre-Islamic nationalist credo represented in the symbols of the Pahlavi monarchy. This campaign began with the crowning of the Shah in 1967, and then seemed to reach its zenith in 1971 with the lavish celebrations marking the twenty-five-hundredth anniversary of the founding of the Persian Empire. But the festivities at Persepolis and elsewhere—at which foreign dignitaries feasted on fowl, champagne, and caviar without the bothersome presence of common Iranians— were just the beginning. In 1975, with the onset of the oil boom and the resulting huge profits accruing to the state's coffers, the Shah's "imperial grandeur" attained new heights. From his perch upon the gilded "Peacock Throne," he tried to reshape the consciousness of the Iranian people in his own pre-Islamic, Persian image. He began by spon-soring international meetings at Persepolis and other cities to discuss the contributions of pre-Islamic religions to Iranian history. One year later, he decreed that the Iranian-Islamic calendar be replaced with the "Sal-e Shahanshahi, the . . . 'Year of the King of Kings,' based on the putative founding of the first Iranian kingdom."[38] Overnight, Iranians learned that it was no longer 1355, but 2535! The disorienting effects of this cam-paign were compounded by its close association with the United States. The Shah encouraged this perception by courting successive American administrations with an ardor that bordered on the neurotic. While the failure of these administrations to forcefully address the use of torture by the Shah's secret police contributed to anti-American sentiment, it was not the only or even crucial cause of it. The central factor was widespread cultural strain. Inundated by American arms, political support, material goods, and cultural products, Iranians from all walks of life soon sensed that Al-e Ahmad's *Weststruckness* was no longer the stuff of nightmares. With some six hundred thousand tourists visiting the country each year, and fifty thousand Americans residing in Iran on the eve of the 1978 revolution, many felt that their country was again under siege by an alien force bent on dividing their society.[39]

Yet this sentiment alone was not strong enough to produce the longing for charismatic experience that came to define the cognitive terrain of Iran's urban society. This aspiration, as Michael Fischer has noted, was produced *in part* by the "repression of other modes of political discourse."[40] By shutting down political parties, trade unions, and the like, the Shah not only eliminated the crucial "overlapping memberships among groups, each of which concerns only limited aspects of its members' lives, [thus restraining] each group from seeking total domination over its membership";[41] but also, more decisively, compelled nearly all urban groups—intellectuals, *bazaaris*, students, and the lowermiddle-class *mostaz'afin*—to seek refuge in mass arenas such as the religious seminaries, universities, mosques, and ultimately the *streets themselves*. Thus in 1978 Iran witnessed a series of violent protests, each of which brought more and more demonstrators into the streets and squares of Tehran and other cities. Under such conditions, the sense that Iranians belonged to one *umma*—to one community of being—began to take hold.

The final ingredient that sparked the storm of mass charisma—messianism—was embedded in Shi'ite culture. By articulating chiliastic expectations in ways that made them real and relevant to Iranians, Khomeini forged a charismatic bond with his followers. That he was able to do so, first from Iraq and then from his headquarters outside Paris beginning in September 1978, reminds us just how fully he understood and used the symbols of martyrdom and self-sacrifice that are central to Shi'ism. Mobilizing a network of several thousand students, Khomeini inundated mosques, universities, and streets with cassette tapes in which he asserted that Iranians were participating in a final battle to topple the "Yazid" and thus hasten the return of the Twelfth Imam.

This apocalyptic drama began to unfold in October 1977 with the sudden death of Khomeini's son, Mostafa. Although devastated by what he assumed was a SAVAK[42]-inspired assassination of the "light of my eyes," Khomeini did not publicly mourn Mostafa's death. His stoic defiance had its intended effect. At mourning sessions held throughout the country, Iranians of every background came together to grieve, in the words of an obituary published by Khomeini's father-in-law, for "the offspring of the Exalted Leader of All Shi'ites of the World."[43] The Shah's court retaliated by having the daily newspaper *Ettela'at* publish a defamatory article describing Khomeini as a British agent and a "mad Indian poet with homosexual tendencies."[44] Outraged, Khomeini's supporters took to the streets of Qom on 8 January 1978. Once again the Shah—as he had done fifteen years earlier—fueled messianic aspirations by turning young Iranians into martyrs. While the 9 September 1978 slaying of several hundred protestors in Tehran's Jaleh Square set the stage for this drama, it was the ensuing violent suppressions over the holy month of Muharram that created the "sudden swing over into another kind of existence" of which Karl Mannheim wrote in his analysis of utopianism.[45]

By killing protestors who were marking the martyrdom of Hoseyn with public displays of repentance, the Shah's troops gave a vital sense of reality to demonstrators' apocryphal chants: "For Yazid's sake, do not kill the son of the Prophet—fear God." When troops replied with more bullets, the bloodied protestors sensed that they were about to realize their prophetic struggle against tyranny: "There were three idol-breakers," they exclaimed, "Abraham, Mohammad and Ruhollah Khomeini."[46]

Millenarian Dreams and Prophetic Action: Khomeini Defines the Terrain, 1978

While more and more Iranians declared their leader a veritable Prophet, Khomeini articulated such millenarian dreams in terms echoing the contending notions of authority that had animated his essays on *Islamic Government* and *The Supreme Jihad*. During the momentous year of 1978, utilitarianism, traditionalism, and charismatic asceticism all found their way into his speeches and declarations, thus expressing a multifaceted vision that inspired Iranians from all walks of life. To take just one example of Khomeini's uncanny ability to articulate material and existential suffering, consider the speech he gave to commemorate the 9 January 1978 massacre of protestors in Qom. Boldly proclaiming that this event constituted the fulfillment of a divine prophecy, he proclaimed that "[i]n accordance with the prediction of the Prophet's family . . . that Qom would be a center of learning whence knowledge would be disseminated to all lands, we now see that it is not knowledge alone that is disseminated from Qom, *but knowledge and action together*." Turning the tables on traditionalist clerics who declared such action blasphemous because it preempted the return of the infallible "Image of the Age," Khomeini implied that the Qom protestors manifested the very same spark of divinity that had emanated from the *acts* of all Prophets:

> You . . . know well that Abraham, who . . . stood at the beginning of the line of the prophets, took up his axe to shatter all idols. . . . If he had been afraid, he would not have been a prophet. . . . Moses stood alone with his staff against the Pharaoh who was claiming divinity . . . [while] the Most Noble Messenger . . . and the Commander of the Faithful ruled, engaged in politics, and fought wars.[47]

In short, as he had previously suggested in his *The Supreme Jihad*, Khomeini implies that Iranians can experience charisma through action, not merely—to use Max Weber's term—as "gift of grace."

Beyond expressing and experiencing their closeness to God, Khomeini suggests that the protestors' deeds reveal the huge gulf between the Shah and his "imperialist" backers on the one side, and the "masses of people who are the faithful soldiers of Islam" on the other (213). Addressing this existential divide, Khomeini argues that because the masses are the natural vessels of Islamic identity, it follows that the Shah "is against whatever they attach value to." Thus the Shah "is against the Islamic calendar," a stand that Khomeini equates with being "against Islam itself . . . an affront to the Most Noble Messenger himself" (217–18). Turning to the plight of the *mostaz'afin* in particular, he decries the "pits, those holes in the ground where people live" in southern Tehran, while "those so-called friends of humanity [i.e. the United States] have appointed their agent to rule their country in order to prevent the poor from benefiting from its riches" (223–24). Invoking the populist ideas that he had imbibed over previous years, Khomeini insists that this moral and social gap will never narrow so long as the Shah fails to "pay some heed to the people's demands"—chief of which is that rulers "perform their true duties and move in the direction of Islam and the laws of Islam" (217). Completing this rousing message, Khomeini holds that the people's "demands" must ultimately be defended by a supreme cleric whose knowledge of the law *and* "closeness" to God endow him with supreme authority. Echoing themes from his *Islamic Government* as well as *The Supreme Jihad*, this vision of clerical leadership is at once charismatic and traditional:

> Those "holders of authority" who are mentioned right after God and the Messenger in the Koranic verse, "Obey God and obey the Messenger and the holders of authority from among you" (4:59) must also be close to God and the Messenger in their *practice*. They must be the shadow of God and the Messenger. Yes, the Islamic ruler is the shadow of God, but what is meant by a "shadow" is something that has no motion in of itself. Your shadow does not move by itself; *it moves only when you move*. Islam recognizes a person as the "shadow of God" who abandons all individual volition in the sense that he *acts* only in accordance with the ordinances of Islam. . . . The Messenger of God . . . was indeed a true shadow of God. (225–26)

This is a remarkable claim. The phrase "shadow of God" was originally used during the sixteenth century to describe the relationship between God and the rulers of the Safavid dynasty (1501–1722). Established by a messianic Sufi order, the Safavids were first ruled by Shah Ismail, a charismatic *sheykh* who encouraged his disciples to believe that he was the reincarnation of the Twelfth Imam. Eventually this messianic claim ran its course, so that the most a Safavid ruler could assert was that his respect of God's laws gave him the right to be the "representative" of the Twelfth Imam and thus rule as God's "Shadow on Earth"; it was never claimed, however, that God's "shadow" was divinely inspired. Yet in his speech Khomeini recasts the term in a manner that recalls his activist view of *'esmat*: he implies that a man becomes the "shadow of God" when his "practice" brings him "close to God and the Messenger." This double formulation suggests a ruler who is God's instrument or "shadow," but who rationally embraces a Qur'anic model of Prophetic activism to effect change in this world. As Khomeini puts it in the final moments of his sermon: "We constantly read in the Koran that the Pharaoh acted in a certain way and Moses in another . . . but we don't think about *why* the Koran tells us this. It tells us this so that we may *act* like Moses toward the Pharaoh of our age" (226–27).

Summary: Blinded by the Light?

Khomeini was luckier than Moses, who saw but never touched his Promised Land. Unlike the liberator of the Hebrews, Khomeini not only returned to the country from which he had been expelled fifteen years earlier; but, on January 31, 1979 also was delivered from the heavens on the wings of an Air France Boeing 747. To his fervent followers looking for their modern-day Moses, no matter how much this event was made possible by Western technology, it seemed like a miracle. And why not? Along the highway that took him to Behesht-e Zahra cemetery—the final resting place of many revolutionary martyrs—and finally to Tehran, Khomeini was greeted by thousands of Iranians, eagerly proclaiming him their Imam. Clearly, the return of the Twelfth Imam, the Mahdi was closer than it had ever been. In the ensuing "Ten Days of Awe," as the period came to be known, Khomeini's followers took to the streets in ever-greater numbers, ignoring the bullets that rained down on them. Then suddenly the Shah's troops stopped shooting. On 11 February 1979, the Shah fled Iran, thus seeming to confirm the miracle that Khomeini had predicted.

Hannah Arendt has written that "mass leaders in power have one concern which overrules all utilitarian considerations: to make their predictions come true." The "propaganda effect of infallibility," she adds, "the striking success of posing as a mere interpreting agent of predictable forces, has encouraged in totalitarian dictators the habit of announcing their political intentions in the form of prophecy."[48] Khomeini grasped this instrumental logic: he was certainly willing to declare—as he had done in reference to the 1978 Qom protests—that the defiant actions of his followers were fulfilling a divine prophecy. Moreover, he surely knew that by toppling the Shah, these valiant deeds had enabled an act of messianic return that exemplified the "extrinsic *'esmat*" of which he had written in 1972. Yet there was much more to it than that. Khomeini was not the manufacturer of his own charisma. His lifelong immersion in mysticism, combined with an enduring fervor to defend his fellow Shi'ites against unjust rulers, endowed him with a genuine sense of his own divinity. That he thought such transcendence could be a product of human action in no way diminishes the earnestness of these feelings. Still, this charismatic sensibility by itself could have no *social* consequences. It was the fusion of a profound crisis of social dislocation with this magical sensibility that transformed it into the twentieth century's final example of pure charisma. Beyond the structural conditions that melted the institutional and symbolic walls between elites and masses, Khomeini's charisma intensified the longings of his followers because it articulated a messianic sensibility deeply rooted in Shi'ite, and possibly Persian, culture. Thus, as Dabashi writes, when the crowds welcomed Khomeini as their Imam, they expressed

> the terms most sacred of . . . [their] shared imagination. There is scarcely any term more sacred than "Imam" in the cherished remembrance of a Shi'i mind. . . . Khomeini earns the thankful recognition of "Imam" from an ecstatic crowd which . . . invests every ounce of its collectivity . . . in the man who would deliver the earthly experience of the sublime. "Imam Khomeini" demands, indeed exacts, obedience. . . . You utter it . . . and you are in. "In" is that fantastic realm of mystical operations where time stands still and place is irrelevant.[49]

Were the leaders of the Islamic Left, as well as their colleagues in the nationalist and communist camps, as smitten with Khomeini as the *mostaz'afin*? Had they embraced this "fantasy" as completely as the masses? Were they as "in" as the rest of the crowd? Two years after the revolution, one Iranian offered the following stinging judgment: "There was," she wrote, "a powerful element of self-delusion. Given the overwhelming ideological, political, and organizational hegemony of Khomeini . . . many political currents . . . read their own political beliefs . . . into Khomeini's views."[50] Yet this phenomenon involved more than an act of calculated self-delusion. The desire to experience transcendence was not limited to the *mostaz'afin*: whatever their rational expectations, some leaders of the intelligentsia—and certainly many of their followers in the universities—were momentarily "blinded by the light" of messianic fervor. Moreover, if intellectuals such as Bazargan could "read their own political beliefs" into Khomeini, this was because before the revolution, the Imam had absorbed the Islamic Left's populist instrumentalism into his own worldview—and, as we have noted, even into the ideology of *velayat-e faqih*. Thus perhaps we should not be so quick to blame Bazargan, who like many of his colleagues was soon to learn that multiple notions of authority could be embedded in a myriad of institutions, doctrines, and even founding constitutions.

5 Dissonant Institutionalization: The Imam in Power

> Before the revolution, I believed that once the revolution succeeded then there would be honest people to carry out the task. . . . . Therefore I . . . stated that the clergy would leave and attend to their own profession. But I later realized that . . . most of . . . [the honest people] were dishonest. . . . I later stated . . . that I had made a mistake. This is because we intend to implement Islam. Accordingly . . . I may have said something yesterday, changed it today, and will again change it tomorrow. This does not mean that simply because I made a statement yesterday, I should adhere to it. Today I am saying that . . . the *ulema* should continue with their jobs.[1]
>
> —Imam Khomeini

> The chief qualification of a mass leader [is] . . . infallibility; he can never admit an error.[2]
>
> —Hannah Arendt

Implementing Islam

Khomeini's extraordinary statement cited above was made in December 1983. Having secured nearly absolute power in the name of *velayat-e faqih* ("Rule of the Jurist"), he now confessed that he had first wanted to restrict the *ulama* (Islamic scholars) to their "own profession." Moreover, the Imam admitted that having "said something yesterday," he might "[change] it today . . . and will again change it tomorrow." Such vacillating hardly fit the image of the "True Believer" that Khomeini's disciples associated with the Imam, leader of the Muslim community. How could the "Shadow of God" admit that he had "made a mistake"? Moreover, if charismatic authority derives from the belief of its bearer *and* his followers that the leader exudes the divine, what explains the admission by this seeker of "complete perfection" that he not only knew of no clear path to messianic redemption, but that from the outset he also was undecided as to whether the clerics should form the vanguard of the Islamic Revolution? Didn't this principle serve as the very foundation of *velayat-e faqih*?

The previous chapter has anticipated these questions: Khomeini's vision of Islamic government had no single foundation, no one core logic. The notion of a divinely inspired activist-prophet who implements God's laws was important to him, as was the utilitarian idea of a political ruler who strives to defend the Muslim community's interests. Khomeini's desire to lead a revolution conflicted with his aspiration to "implement Islam"—a pragmatic goal in whose name a contradictory array of political institutions, ideologies, and decisions could be invoked.

Students of Iran's revolution are well aware of the competing ideologies preceding it. That Khomeini had courted the Islamic Left prior to his return to Iran is not news. But because this fact has been fitted into conventional theories of charisma, its *enduring* significance for the ideological dynamics of the revolution has not been fully appreciated. Most scholars hold that the fate of the Islamic Left confirms the teleological view of revolutions outlined by Crane Brinton. He maintained that every revolutionary elite contains moderates and true believers. The former use "grand words and phrases as a consolation and a joy to their listeners and to themselves. But . . . they . . . do not really believe a heavenly perfection is suddenly coming to man on earth."[3] In contrast, the radicals *believe* in the idea of messianic redemption but cannot attain it without the moderates. Once the latter have served their purpose, they are promptly removed.

This dialectic certainly *seemed* to have occurred in Iran. During the first two years of the revolution, Khomeini appointed many leading Islamic Leftists to positions in the Provisional Government. The Council of the Revolution's decision in February 1979 to appoint Mehdi Bazargan prime minister, and the creation of a cabinet *dominated* by people affiliated with the Iran Freedom Movement (IFM),[4] suggested that the Islamic Left would play a prominent role in the political process. This trend culminated in the election of Abolhasan Bani-Sadr as president in January 1980. Yet within two years, every member of the cabinet who had ties with the IFM was either forced out of power, executed, or dead under "mysterious" circumstances.[5] Bazargan's resignation, following the 4 November 1979 occupation of the American Embassy by militant students, was crucial. His departure signaled the beginning of the end of the *entente* between the old generation of Islamic Leftists and the radical clerics. Discussing these developments, Cheryl Benard and Zalmay Khalilzad echo Brinton by concluding that the "appointment of the modernists" was a "tactical move, intended to avoid antagonizing the modernist political groups" and to "buy time" for Khomeini.[6]

This view of the revolution certainly captures one reality, but it downplays another. Because the Islamic Left had helped to define the ideological terrain of the revolution, and because the radical clergy had absorbed some of its ideas, Khomeini and his allies could not completely eradicate—nor dispense with—the political logic of the Islamic Left. Moreover, as we shall see in the last section of this chapter, while the 1979 hostage crisis may have discredited the more liberal wing of the IFM, it empowered a new generation of quasi-Marxist clerics and lay intellectuals whose social and political projects echoed 'Ali Shari'ati's unique blend of utopianism and rationalist instrumentalism.

This chapter explores this process of ideological accommodation through the lens of dissonant institutionalization, a process by which contending visions of authority are embedded *within* a diverse array of official and semiofficial arenas (as outlined in chapter 1). These domains include, but are not limited to, competing ideological factions within the state, formal constitutions or other written documents, and the everyday political rhetoric of leaders. Although I address the issue of ideological factionalization in the final section of this chapter, my focus will be on analyzing the accommodation of contending visions of authority in two arenas: the Islamic Republic's 1979 Constitution, and Khomeini's daily political discourse. As we shall see, the framers of the Constitution tried to adjust Khomeini's charismatic theory of *velayat-e faqih* to the traditional logic of clerical guidance and to the modern notion of popular sovereignty.

Similarly, an analysis of Khomeini's speeches and edicts will show how the Imam zigzagged between a messianic notion of politics and a more utilitarian view, which called for creating political institutions and stable laws for defending the interests of the people. In analyzing these speeches, my purpose is not to give a comprehensive account of the revolution; instead, my more modest goal is to illustrate how a genuinely charismatic leader can evince competing ideological commitments in a remarkably open fashion. While this dynamic anticipates the phenomenon of complex routinization analyzed in the next chapter, dissonant institutionalization revolves around the effort to *accommodate* different notions of authority, whereas complex routinization centers on attempts by a leader and his disciples to forge a more stable and coherent form of government and authority. This chapter explores the dynamic of dissonant institutionalization during the 1979–82 period. These were the years of Iran's *grande terreur,* a time of revolutionary upheaval during which the regime and its clerical vanguard gave full vent to their charismatic aspirations. Their campaign revealed itself in the regime's quest to mobilize the people through Revolutionary

Committees against domestic and foreign enemies, and in its efforts to compel all social groups to demonstrate absolute obedience to the Imam. While incarnating this quest for charismatic action and total loyalty, the Imam also evinced profound ambiguity about the practical and philosophical consequences of revolutionary action. Pressed by contending allegiances, Khomeini demonstrated that the road to heaven can be paved with multiple intentions.

Revolution versus Order: The Paradoxes of Clerical Power, 1979–80

The prevailing assumption that Khomeini hid his real agenda in order to secure the support of the "modernists" is correct.[7] He wanted to derive legitimacy from the quasi-socialist–quasi-democratic agenda of Islamic Leftists such as Bazargan and Bani-Sadr without subordinating his revolutionary agenda to theirs. But this explanation simplifies reality in two ways: first, by confounding the results of a complex historical process with Khomeini's intentions; second, by assuming that Khomeini was motivated by a coherent set of strategic goals. There is, however, evidence to suggest that he initially took a flexible approach to power that not only reflected tactical considerations, but also revealed a more fundamental desire to accommodate competing visions of Islamic government. Khomeini may not have been completely forthright in declaring to a reporter three months before returning to Iran that "[t]he ulema themselves will not hold power in the government . . . [but instead] exercise supervision over those who govern and give them guidance";[8] but he did not abandon his previous promise to "fulfill no governmental function. I will be content, as in the past, to be my nation's guide."[9] Indeed, during the winter of 1979 he seemed open to the idea that the clerics should retain their traditional role as moral guides. For example, in a statement linking this traditional view of clerical power to a utilitarian concern with creating order, he argued that to prevent "anarchy and chaos," the *"ulema* and the preachers [must] . . . go to mosques and call on the people to observe peace and friendship."[10] Then, to the surprise of many, he "retired to Qom in late February and closed his office, referring all matters to the [provisional] government."[11]

In the ensuing weeks, the proliferation of independent Revolutionary Committees invited the very chaos he feared. Khomeini responded by reiterating a functionalist view of government, according to which revolutionary zealotry would be tamed by the compartmentalization of governmental tasks. "Islamic revolutionary committees," he warned in a fourteen-point decree, "are duty-bound . . . to refrain from *interfering* in government." To ensure that they acquitted themselves in a "humanitarian fashion," the *ulama*, as "guardians of the Koran and Islam," were "not to . . . deprive anyone else of his freedom." Given their role as ethical guides, Khomeini cautioned, the "learned *ulema* . . . should be looked after," and nothing should be done to harm "the status of this group."[12]

This statement articulates a dilemma with which Khomeini would constantly wrestle in the coming years. By assigning the *ulama* a specific and delimited set of responsibilities, advocates of Shi'ite traditionalism had tried to distance the clerics from the corrupting influence of politics. In this sense, the *ulama*'s "status" derived from their autonomy from the state and power politics. Khomeini's dilemma—as revealed above and in other speeches—lay in his desire to retain this advantage and yet at the same time inject clerics into the heart of politics. At times this dilemma became very personal. For example, Khomeini issued the above-cited decree prior to the 30 March 1979 referendum on declaring an Islamic Republic. In the days before the referendum, he hesitated about the proper bounds of his *own* authority: "I demand of you, my sisters and brothers, to go and drop that ballot card . . . which says 'yes.' "[13] The next day he shifted ground, insisting that "you are free to vote for whatever you like. . . . But I recommend that . . . to obey the orders of God . . . you should try and vote for the Islamic Republic."[14] At this point Khomeini seems unsure as to how far the scope of his authority—as well as that of his clerical allies—should reach.

Khomeini's readiness to bring leaders of the Islamic Left into government reflected such indecision. He may have reasoned that if he could count on Bazargan and company to focus on everyday matters, the clerics could distance themselves from the political fray and thus retain their status as defenders of the moral order. This reasoning seemed to have partly figured in Khomeini's insistence that high-ranking clerics *not* occupy formal positions in the Provisional Government. Yet taking this position did not mean that Khomeini and the clerics had relinquished power to Bazargan and his allies. The former continued to influence the regime through their involvement in the Council of the Revolution, a secret body that included clerics and Islamic Leftists. Moreover, Khomeini did not hesitate to impose limits, as he did in late February 1979, when he rejected Bazargan's proposal to call the new state a "Democratic Islamic Republic." While he endorsed the idea of a republic, a term he had not used in his book *Islamic Government*, Khomeini rejected the concept of democracy, since he associated it with his secular opponents and the West.[15] With this stipulation he backed

Bazargan's government. But as spring approached, the Imam began to see in Bazargan's actions the makings of a counterrevolution.

Khomeini's suspicions were heightened by the 1 May assassination of his disciple (and Revolutionary Council chairman) Ayatollah Morteza Motahari, and by an unsuccessful attempt to kill his close ally, Hashemi Rafsanjani. These attacks came at a bad time for Bazargan. He had been pushing for a national election to send delegates to a constituent assembly, a body that would review a draft Constitution previously prepared by lay intellectuals in Paris. Inspired by the constitution of the French Fifth Republic, the draft did not mention *velayat-e faqih*, proposing instead an elected assembly whose laws could be reviewed for Islamic propriety by a Council of Guardians in which clerics would be a *minority*. Khomeini smelled a rat.

Trying to Act as a "Revolutionary"

What was to be done? Despite Khomeini's abiding dedication to the principle of clerical rule, he already had evinced concerns about the potential risks of charismatic revolutionary action—particularly when it was led by those who supposedly were closest to the divine. But reconciling these concerns proved difficult. The publication of a preliminary draft of the Constitution on 26 April provoked his suspicion that opponents of clerical rule were imposing their agenda on the document. In what may have been an allusion to Bazargan himself, Khomeini warned of "those who want to speak behind a veil . . . [of a] democratic Islamic Republic." They "want freedom but without Islam," he insisted. "We hate freedom without the Koran. . . . We hate their saying: Islam without the clergy." This talk was unacceptable. "The slightest deviation from the Islamic Republic," Khomeini warned, "is against the course of Islam."[16] One month later, after the final version of the draft Constitution was announced, Khomeini lashed out at the remaining advocates of a constituent assembly: "This presents a danger for Islam and for the Prophet of God," the Imam intoned. "The ratification of the constitution by the constituent assembly . . . poses a danger for the Hidden Imam." In what may have been another elliptical message to Bazargan, he cautioned intellectuals backing this assembly that they should "know that I like them and do not want them to be suspected of ill-intentions."[17]

Yet having exhibited such hostility to opponents of clerical rule, Khomeini wavered. In theory, he knew that clerical rule was legitimate and necessary. But in practice, he found it could backfire when the clergy competed in a manner that blemished their reputation as moral guides. Nonetheless, Khomeini the mystic had always known that far from giving man the means to transcend his earthly desires, politics could corrupt him. Alluding to this dilemma, he warned that "we are facing a . . . danger greater than that posed by the former regime. This is the danger of unbridled freedom *(afsar gosikhteh)*, which means that [when] . . . the walls of dictatorship are crumbling . . . [man] commits any deed his heart desires." Worse yet, this dangerous condition had infected the clergy. For, he seemed to imply, by competing for the right to execute the *functions* of the Prophets, the clerics were acquiring the opposite of extrinsic *'esmat* (infallibility): those "who are man's teachers," he declared, "[those who have] succeeded the Prophet," whose "profession is that of the prophets," had given the impression that "we are ensnared by the tyranny of the clergy, [that] the clergy is a dictator." If this situation persisted, the very survival of the Islamic Republic would be in jeopardy. "Even Imam Ali was defeated by Muawiyah," Khomeini reminded his audience.[18]

In these warnings Khomeini evinced concerns about two potential arenas of conflict. One was the Revolutionary Committees, whose "street justice" was turning the revolution into chaos. "If the committees, . . . God forbid, should act against the rules of Islam," Khomeini cautioned, "they have failed our school." While the task of spreading the revolution "is a great undertaking for the clergy," by overstepping its bounds, the clergy is "losing the key to the nation's victory." That key was political order, the foundation of which was "unity of expression." Concluding with a popular citation from the Qur'an, he warned his followers, "Hold fast all together by the rope of God."[19] The second arena from which Khomeini demanded "unity of expression" was the media, where a fierce debate over the proposed constituent assembly was unfolding. Seemingly unaware that his own rhetoric had inflamed such divisiveness, Khomeini insisted that the clerics resolve their differences peacefully. Thus his efforts to mitigate the negative effects of clerical activism had a schizophrenic quality. On the one hand, they were marked by calls for harmony and fairness. "Set aside other objectives in the interests of Islam and . . . join hands," he told the clerics. On the other hand, they were characterized by a sectarian demand for revolutionary action against all forces that hindered the quest to realize Islam's intrinsic harmony. "Don't sit back while foreignized intellectuals . . . give their views [on the draft constitution]," he told the clerics.[20] Mincing no words, Khomeini stated, "I issue the same emphatic warning to the press. . . . If I should sense a serious danger, I will bring up the problem with my dear nation."[21] Two months later he went even further. Using the example of a rebellion in Kurdestan to make a broader point, he warned that "we will give these corrupt strata a little longer. . . . If they do not put their affairs in order . . . God knows that I will act as a revolutionary."[22]

By the time he had issued this caution in late August 1979, Khomeini seemed to have chosen the path of revolutionary-charismatic action. Following his wishes, the idea of a constituent assembly was dropped in favor of a seventy-three-seat Assembly of Experts. The election of the assembly on 3 August was then manipulated by Khomeini's clerical allies to ensure that clerics received at least two-thirds of the seats. Two months later the Assembly of Experts approved a constitutional clause that made Khomeini the Supreme Jurisprudent. Thus the deed was done. In words that his opponents would surely grasp, the Imam proclaimed that the era of *velayat-e faqih* had arrived:

> Theocracy is something that God, the exalted, . . . has ordained. . . . Wake up, you gentlemen, . . . because the deviationists are . . . trying to . . . smash our movement. . . . [They] . . . speak out [against] the concept of theocracy. . . . I shall strike you in the mouth. Stop this talk. . . . Enough is enough: what ought to be done must be done.[23]

Prelude to Contradiction: Debating the New Constitution

By November 1979 Khomeini had achieved "what ought to be done." On the fifteenth of that month the Assembly of Experts approved a new Constitution. Yet the results were far from the theocracy that Khomeini had zealously proclaimed. Instead of producing a coherent constitutional map, the clerics blended several different ones, thus institutionalizing a new political order based on contending visions of authority. Surveying the various opinions expressed by the Assembly of Experts, we can distinguish three schools of thought: orthodox, populist revolutionary, and democratic. Advocates of the first position objected to the very notion of constitutionalism and popular sovereignty, which they claimed were Western imports. "We all know," explained one cleric, "that parliament was forcibly imposed on the *Shari'ah* [sacred law of Islam]." For those who advocated this position, Islamic government meant the Rule of the Jurist, pure and simple.[24] In contrast, although the revolutionaries championed the idea of one Supreme Ruler, they argued that some form of popular sovereignty was essential to selecting or "recognizing" the *faqih* (Supreme Leader). Led by Ayatollah Mohammad Hoseyn Beheshti, a loyal disciple of Khomeini's, this group echoed 'Ali Shari'ati's

Leninist notion of an intellectual vanguard that realizes the collective consciousness of the masses through the propagation of an ideology, or *maktab*. Thus while asserting that "the leadership and legislation cannot be left to the majority at any given moment . . . [because] this would contradict the ideological character of the Islamic Republic,"[25] Beheshti argued in the same breath that having joined together to overthrow the Shah, "with their first selection, they [the people] will limit their future selections of the *maktab*."[26] This implicit call for Iranians to subordinate their personal freedoms to *la volonté générale* was supported by Hassan Ayat, Mohammad Fawzi, and Ayatollah Mohammad Yazdi. Yazdi suggested that having freely chosen Islam and its sacred laws *(Shari'ah)*, the people had given their blessing to the principle of *velayat-e faqih* and thus would henceforth exercise their freedoms strictly within these limits. Ayat agreed. Citing Jean-Jacques Rousseau's social contract, he ventured the claim that "[i]f the social contract were once in reality realized, it was in relation to Islam."[27] Pushing this circular logic as far as it would stretch, Ayatollah Dastgheyb concluded that the *faqih*'s authority became a divine commandment *only when the people demonstrated a readiness to embrace it*.[28]

Lay intellectuals and clerics associated with the Islamic Left articulated a more democratic vision of Islamic government. This group advanced three arguments. First, they asserted that the term *velayat-e faqih* should be understood in its symbolic sense. Thus Bazargan, Ezzatollah Sahabi, and Rahmatollah Maraghe'i distinguished between "true vice-regency, [which] belongs to the *ma'sum* [i.e., the Imams],"[29] and a philosophical *velayat* (vice-regency), by which they meant the sovereignty of Islam and the *Shari'ah* over humanity. Understood in this light, Maraghe'i argued, *velayat-e faqih* could not be equated with the idea that "a special social class should make a monopoly of Islam for itself."[30] Second, they held that by delegating executive, judicial, and legislative powers to the jurists, the supporters of clerical rule were sowing the seeds of their own de-legitimation. For, the democrats warned, the people would eventually reject such an autocracy, and with it, the very idea of an Islamic political order. Some of the most vociferous defenders of this position were moderate clerics. Highlighting the global and domestic ramifications of establishing a new dictatorship, Ayatollah Makaram Shirazi cautioned that "our domestic and foreign enemies will accuse us of dictatorship and hostility to the people. . . . They will say that a small handful of religious scholars have . . . framed a constitution which establishes their own dominion." Recapitulating this argument in words that would sound prophetic fifteen years later, Hojjat al-Eslam Hojjati Kermani warned that "[r]umors concerning . . . the despotism of the clergy have been spread throughout the country. . . . Tomorrow the mass of the homeless, the unemployed, the hungry and the discontent will join with the disgruntled intellectuals."[31] Finally, seeking to justify their support for Khomeini and thus avoid their total political (if not physical) elimination, several Islamic Leftists argued that the Imam's role in the political system was justified by his "superior qualities"[32] and by the exigencies of the times, which demanded someone who could "guarantee achieving the goals . . . of the revolution, and . . . assure the stability of the Islamic Republic."[33] This familiar excuse for authoritarianism was advanced by Bazargan himself, as well as other IFM leaders. They held that despite the contradiction between popular sovereignty and *velayat-e faqih*, Khomeini's charisma was needed to "stabilize" a revolution that was vulnerable to domestic and foreign enemies. Yet, in what was not a completely unreasonable rationalization of this awkward position, they reasoned that because the idea of clerical rule was not mandated by divine revelation, this contradiction might eventually be resolved in favor of popular sovereignty![34]

The tension between this democratic position and the orthodox and populist revolutionary visions must have been obvious to all participants in the Assembly of Experts' debates. The Islamic Left had contributed much to the language and authority of the clerics, but like the socialist "moderates" of whom Brinton has written, many of these leftists would eventually pay a high price for championing utopian symbols. Lacking sufficient allies outside the assembly (leading clerical traditionalists such as Ayatollah Mohammad-Kazem Shari'atmadari asserted that Khomeini's theory of clerical rule had no basis in Islam, but he was completely isolated), and weakened by the ongoing hostage crisis (discussed later in this chapter), Bazargan, Bani-Sadr, and others had to acquiesce to the assembly's final draft of the Constitution. On 2–3 December 1979 the document was ratified—as would be expected—by more than 99 percent of the population.

A Multiple Constitution

Despite their confused objections, the remonstrations of the moderates had some impact on the debates of the Assembly of Experts. Rather than jettison their arguments, Beheshti and company attempted to reconcile the Islamic Left's blend of rational constitutionalism and charismatic instrumentalism to the charismatic utopianism of Khomeini and his disciples. The result was an ideological mishmash that is probably unmatched in the history of constitutionalism. Nowhere does this effort to accommodate competing notions of authority come through more clearly than in the Preamble to the 1979 Constitution.[35] The millenarian aspirations of Khomeini's followers are enshrined in this declaration: "Government from the Islamic perspective does not stem from class position or the domination of an individual or a group, but is rather the realization of the political idea of a nation which shares the same customs and way of thinking, and which organizes itself so that . . . it makes its way toward the ultimate goal (movement toward God)." Echoing Khomeini's efforts to place the quest for transcendence in the context of an all-encompassing government, the Preamble states that "the constitution provides the groundwork . . . for participation at all phases of significant political decision-making for all members of the community, so that in the process of attaining perfection, every individual takes part. . . . This will be the realization of the government of the oppressed of the earth." But this effort cannot be left up to the individual: "Based upon the concept of the Mandate of the Imamate, the constitution lays the groundwork for the realization of the leadership of a member of the eminent clergy who is recognized by the people as their leader in order to guarantee that various organizations do not deviate from their real Islamic duties." Ultimate authority is thus vested solely in Khomeini, not merely because the doctrine of *velayat-e faqih* demands it, but because the Imam's authority has crystallized in a mass uprising of a "people" that has *"recognized"* him as their leader. As the Preamble puts it, the "alert conscience *(vojdan)* of the nation" was ultimately "led by His Eminence and Supreme Holiness the Ayatollah Imam Khomeini."[36]

Yet Khomeini's holy authority does not merely flow from his ability to incarnate this crisis of conscience. The Preamble repeats several times that the Imam has taught Iranians the importance of "adhering to the true ideological and Islamic path of struggle." This distinction between ideological *(maktabi)* and Islamic *(eslami)* is revealing. We have seen that Shari'ati had argued for the creation of a mobilizing Islamic ideology. The term *maktabi* is used in this instrumentalist sense throughout the Preamble and the rest of the Constitution. Advancing a corollary distinction between "faith and ideology," the Preamble asserts that a "Revolutionary Corps" will also be an "ideological army," and that "just, ascetic and dedicated people (the just clergy)" are responsible for creating the political institutions from which an "ideologically oriented" society will emerge.

This revolutionary vision also has utopian and universalistic elements. The purpose of ideology is to "construct a model society," whose shining moral example will produce a "movement towards the victory of all oppressed people . . . [thus creating] a basis favorable to the endurance of this revolution at home and abroad." Following the lead of other millenarian movements, Iran's revolutionaries expect that their utopia will, to use Karl Mannheim's telling phrase, "burst the bounds of reality" and thus open "the way for the establishment of a unified worldwide community." Yet this quest for universal liberation is not lauded in purely transrational terms. Instead, the Preamble links this aspiration to a process of *political representation* whose institutional parameters—we are told—are laid out in the Constitution. Offering the latter as a "guarantee against any kind of ideological and social despotism," the Preamble promises that the quest for an "ideological society" will not only prevent "ideological despotism," but also make the slogan "Independence, Freedom and Islamic Government" a constitutional reality! After all, "the constitution is an attempt, also made by other Islamic and democratic movements, to open the way for the establishment of a unified world community."

In retrospect, this reference to democracy appears to be an ideological slip of the tongue. In the Constitution itself, the word *democracy* is never mentioned. Yet it retains the idea of blending some form of popular sovereignty with clerical rule: in its hundred-plus Articles, the document specifies a variety of competing political institutions and authorities—but without indicating how each one was to coexist with the other. Imam Khomeini's charismatic authority is enshrined in Articles 5 and 107. The former states the following:

> During the Occultation of the Glorious Lord of the Age. . . . The Mandate to Rule *(velayat-e amr)* and The Imamate of the People *(Emamat-e omat)* devolve upon a just and pious *faqih*, well-informed with his times, courageous, resourceful; . . . recognized and accepted by the majority of the people as a leader *(rahbari)*. Should there be no jurist endowed with such qualifications . . . his role will be undertaken by a . . . Leadership Council consisting of religious jurists meeting the above mentioned requirements in accordance with Article 107.

Article 107 reiterates the main points of the above, but relates them directly to Khomeini as Imam:

> When one of the *foqaha* [scholars of the law] who fulfills the conditions mentioned in Principle 5 . . . is recognized . . . by a decisive majority of the people for the position of *marja'* [religious guide] and leader *(rahbari)*—as is the case with the Exalted and Source of Imitation *(marja'-e taqlid)* and leader *(rahbar)* of the Revolution Ayatollah Al-Uzma Imam Khomeini—then this leader will have charge of governing and all the responsibilities arising from it.

Not only did these two articles echo the functionalist view of the *faqih*'s authority set out in *Islamic Government*; but, by suggesting that Khomeini's right to rule was a direct product of both his character and his actions, they also resolved his earlier failure to define how such a leader would be selected. It will be recalled that in Khomeini's *Islamic Government* he had argued that the leader had to be just, knowledgeable of the law, and morally qualified to be a leader of the people; but he had not defined how such qualifications would be ascertained. Now, by stipulating that a "just *faqih*" could earn the "recognition" of his people through a display of uncommon piety, courage, and resourcefulness, the Constitution made it very clear that Khomeini's authority was based on a charismatic bond between him and the people. It was on this basis that the roles of divinely inspired religious guide *(marja'-e taqlid)* and political leader were fused into one office designed expressly for Khomeini: that of *rahbar*, or leader.[37]

Article 110 gives the *rahbar* extraordinary powers: he appoints the six *foqaha* who sit on the twelve-member Council of Guardians; he appoints all the highest judicial authorities; he is commander of the armed forces and thus empowered to appoint the chief of staff and commander-in-chief of the Islamic Revolutionary Guard Corps *(Sepah-e Pasdaran)*; and he has the right to dismiss the president if the Supreme Court or the *Majles* (Parliament) can demonstrate that the president has harmed the national interest through incompetent or illegal acts. Yet while these legislative and judicial powers are considerable, the Constitution does not place Islamic government on a par with the power of the leader. Instead, it attempts to accommodate the Imam's charismatic powers to both the traditional and legal-rational demands of Islamic government. The result: 12 chapters and 175 articles of constitutional syncretism. For example, Articles 2 and 56 echo the elitist principles proclaimed in Articles 5 and 107 by stating that sovereignty belonged to God, while the duty of "continuous leadership" fell on the *foqaha*. But Articles 6, 71, and 113 contravene these elitist provisions, the first by stating that the "affairs of the country shall be administered . . . in accordance with public opinion, expressed through elections"; the second by providing for a popularly elected "consultative assembly," or *Majles*, that was empowered to "establish laws on all matters, within the limit of its competence as laid down in the Constitution"; and the third by providing for a popularly elected "president" who, "after the leadership . . . is the highest official position the country." Similarly, Article 57 holds that the legislative, executive, and judicial branches were "independent of each other," but then undermines this provision by placing these branches under the "jurisdiction . . . of the Imamat." Finally, Article 96 affirms the continued centrality of traditional Islamic authority by providing for a clerically dominated Council of Guardians that was empowered to veto all laws deemed un-Islamic. Article 99 further circumscribes the legal-rational authority of the *Majles* by giving the council the nebulous right to "supervise" the election of the president and *Majles*.

However, the Constitution makes no clear provision for settling disputes between the *Majles* and the council, or between the president and the prime minister—a flaw that would bedevil the regime for years to come. Paradoxically, the chaotic division of powers delineated in the document favor the *rahbar*'s charismatic authority by inviting conflicts between the *Majles* and the Council of Guardians that can only be settled by the *rahbar* himself. Thus the most striking feature of the 1979 Constitution is its effort to accommodate charismatic rule to the long-term exigencies of routinizing a revolution through enduring laws and institutions. Ayatollah Montazeri—at the time president of the Assembly of Experts—put it best. The final document, he observed, "is not ideal. . . . It is a compilation of different views put together with the central objective of producing a Constitution that is in accordance with Islam."[38]

Bani-Sadr, Khomeini, and the Clerics: Harmony versus Zealotry

With the adoption of the Constitution in December 1979, Khomeini could now focus on translating its articles into political practice. Although he had previously welcomed the adoption of the Constitution as a victory for theocracy, in 1980 he began to back away from such revolutionary statements in favor of a pragmatic approach emphasizing the authority of the *Majles* over that of the Council of Guardians— and even the *rahbar* himself. These efforts mirrored those articles in the Constitution favoring popular sovereignty. However, the combined effect of the hostage crisis and the challenge posed by President Bani-Sadr to Khomeini's authoritarian rendering of *velayat-e faqih* soon encouraged the Imam to change course; once again he would subordinate his utilitarian and traditionalist commitments to the pursuit of an ideological war against the "enemies" of the Islamic Revolution. Yet the Imam's speeches and actions suggested that he was not as zealously committed to this revolutionary course as his own followers might have assumed.

Khomeini demonstrated his utilitarian proclivities in January 1980. With presidential elections about to be held, he vetoed Ayatollah

Beheshti's quest for the presidency. A longtime ally of the clergy and leader of the clerically dominated Islamic Republican Party (IRP), Beheshti zealously advocated Khomeini's version of *velayat-e faqih*. But despite Khomeini's aspirations, he continued to argue that the *ulama* should not occupy high government positions.[39] He not only opposed clerics running for high office, but also refused to exercise his constitutional authority as *rahbar* to affirm the eligibility of the candidates. "I do not intend to recommend anyone," he explained, "[and thus] . . . ask the parties, groups and individuals not to attribute their candidacies to me."[40] The only stipulation he made was that those who had voted against the Constitution were barred from running. This opened the race to Dr. Bani-Sadr. A French-trained Islamic Leftist who had advised Khomeini from his headquarters outside Paris, Bani-Sadr proceeded to win the presidential election.

To some observers, Bani-Sadr's election was a fluke. With Beheshti barred from running, the IRP was forced to find a suitable lay candidate just weeks before the 25 January election. This fortuitous timing—combined with Bani-Sadr's considerable popularity in comparison with the IRP's Hasan Habibi—assured Bani-Sadr's victory. Yet if serendipity played a role in his election, this was not the only logic at play. Khomeini's own desire to keep the torch of utilitarian Islam burning thwarted the effort of his clerical allies to undermine the new president. After all, Bani-Sadr had contributed to the fueling of this torch. The son of a well-respected cleric, he attended Ayatollah Seyyed Mahmud Taleqani's Qur'an interpretation sessions during the early sixties, and then moved to France, where he studied economics. His exposure to a world of multiple imaginations yielded a body of literature that assailed Iran's dependence on the West while celebrating the notion of a symbolic or "generalized" Imamate. This concept called for an Imam whose considerable authority would eventually be diffused to the people, thus turning each individual into an Imam or leader.[41] How this Lutheranized vision of the Imamate was to be achieved remained a mystery, but Bani-Sadr's devotion to it was so strong that it led him to Khomeini in 1972. Eventually, Bani-Sadr came to view himself as Khomeini's "devoted son." While it is not easy to assess the effect of Bani-Sadr on Khomeini's thinking, by the time they joined forces outside Paris, the Imam had developed a certain respect for the French-trained intellectual. Once in Iran, Bani-Sadr's attempts to push the revolution in a populist direction met with some success. For example, his defense of individual rights during the Assembly of Experts' debates apparently influenced the final version of the Constitution, especially its Preamble. Subsequently, the widely held perception that Bani-Sadr "was the personal choice of Khomeini" helped to secure his election.[42] When Khomeini then declared that the people should support the president-elect, it seemed that the ideas of the Islamic Left would still have some role to play in the revolution.[43]

In the ensuing months Khomeini gave unprecedented attention to the task of institution building. While it was true that Bani-Sadr played a central part in encouraging this pragmatic emphasis, it is unlikely that Khomeini would have defended this position so forcefully had he not shared his "spiritual son's" belief in the principle of creating an enduring political order. Toward this end Khomeini rallied support for the first elections of the *Majles*, which were held in March 1980. Marking this event, he insisted that all candidates put aside their differences to create a "central power on which all other powers will depend." Remarkably, he added that the "Majlis is higher than all the positions which exist in the country."[44] While this claim blatantly *contradicted* Khomeini's constitutional powers as *rahbar*, it attested to his enduring desire to create a rational basis for the assembly's authority. Yet it was not easy to adjust this desire for an institutionalized revolution to the demands of sustaining revolutionary fervor. In the ensuing weeks and months, Khomeini once again tried to have it both ways—to rationalize institutional authority on the one hand, and to encourage spontaneous revolutionary action on the other. For example, in March 1980 he issued a series of guidelines to revolutionary organizations. While supporting the Revolutionary Guard Corps—a paramilitary organization that played a leading role in arresting enemies of the revolution—he warned that the "slightest violation [of someone's rights] would lead to prosecution." The corps, he insisted, must "deal with all people with kindness and with Islamic manners." Khomeini then turned to the Revolutionary Courts, which had been established to try and duly dispatch with anyone deemed an enemy of the revolution. He declared that they "have no right to have armed forces of their own. They should act according to the Constitution and, gradually, the Islamic judicial system should take over." Yet after repeating this judicious message, he called in the very same speech for a "revolution . . . in all the universities" and a "purging" of all "deviant groups . . . engaged in mixing Islamic ideas with Marxist ideas"![45] One month later, Khomeini declared a "cultural revolution." In the ensuing year thousands of alleged counterrevolutionaries were purged from the universities as well as the military and government bureaucracy.[46]

Khomeini's increasing stridency can be partly attributed to the hostage crisis. The seizing of the American Embassy on 4 November 1979 by a group of students and young revolutionaries mentored by Ayatollah Kho'eyniha had given student radicals and their clerical mentors an ideal cause with which to humiliate the United States and isolate Iranians favoring reconciliation with Washington. The failure of President Jimmy Carter's administration to rescue the hostages in April 1980 only strengthened the students' hand at the expense of Bani-Sadr and others who sought restored relations with the United States. Moreover, just one month after the botched rescue attempt, the Iranian government revealed that it had thwarted no less than four planned coups d'état by elements linked to the Iranian army.

These events had a predictable effect. Speaking to a large crowd in Qom, Khomeini contradicted his previous warnings against revolutionary justice by insisting that "you should make sure that these people who indulge in corruption . . . are crushed with full force. Such people, wherever they are, should be sentenced to death."[47] But, having issued this violent summons, and in the midst of his "cultural revolution," Khomeini marked the opening of the *Majles* six days later by warning the deputies to "act with calm and mutual respect and . . . shun . . . the unprincipled taking of sides in order to crush the opposite." Moreover, in an implicit reference to the emerging conflicts between the president and the *Majles*, Khomeini insisted that the "Majlis and the government act harmoniously . . . to overcome the difficulties of the country."[48]

This was not the first time that Khomeini had tried to promote cooperation between the *Majles* and the president. From March through July 1980, the convening of the *Majles* had been stalled due to a conflict between Bani-Sadr and deputies affiliated with the Islamic Republican Party (an umbrella organization of radical clerics and lay political activists, many of whom had roots in the Islamic Left) over the selection of the prime minister. Although his position as *faqih* gave him ample authority to do so, Khomeini did not intervene in this conflict. Finally, in August 1980 the president was forced to accept the nomination by the *Majles* of Mohammad 'Ali Raja'i, a hard-liner who was deeply suspicious of Bani-Sadr.

The Emergence of Khomeini as Imam?

Although this development suggests that Khomeini had begun to support Bani-Sadr's opponents, it is remarkable how long it took Khomeini to take decisive action against the president. While the hostage crisis was certainly one of the factors promoting this dynamic, growing support for Bani-Sadr from both nationalist and religious leaders was the decisive factor. Opposition to the principle of clerical rule by venerable clerics such as Ayatollah Mohammad-Kazem Shari'atmadari was a particular concern for the Khomeini regime. These clerics, Khomeini held, had mistakenly believed they could "deceive me" with "words . . . from the Koran and the *Nahj al-Balagha*" (a collection of sermons attributed to Imam 'Ali). Furiously spurning those who dared speak another Islamic language, Khomeini dismissed the "turbaned" impostors, who were "infiltrating the clergy and engaging in sabotage." What is more, he added indignantly, they had formed "imam committees. Who is this imam? . . . Anybody who wishes to do something puts it under the name of the imam." This was unacceptable: "I warn . . . the clergy. . . . I tell them all and discharge myself of my final responsibility, to repulse all these mullahs."[49]

By July, in a veiled attack on Bani-Sadr and his allies, Khomeini seemed to hint that he had reached a decision. In the beginning of the revolution, he explained, "we were two groups; one . . . from the seminary and the other . . . from abroad [i.e., Islamic Leftists such as Bani-Sadr]. They [the latter] had revolutionary experience, but these people from the seminary made the revolution." Counting on those from "abroad" was wrong, Khomeini implied. "Right from the beginning we made mistakes . . . we were not experienced . . . and a person [i.e., Bani-Sadr] was elected." But such errors would not be repeated. Henceforth, Khomeini insisted, the "Majlis must be 100% religious . . . 100% revolutionary and ideologically motivated."[50] To assure revolutionary spirit, Khomeini finally did what he had avoided doing since March 1980: he intervened in the conflict between Bani-Sadr and the *Majles*. Bani-Sadr, he complained, had permitted people "whose thoughts are not revolutionary" to "be heads of the ministries. . . . Mr. Bani-Sadr should not introduce such people into the Majlis." From now on, Khomeini insisted that all those opposed to Islam

> should be purged. I cannot tolerate seeing anyone changing his mind about what he wants to be. Now I want to be a Democrat, now I want to be Nationalist, or I want to be an Islamic Republican. We have received blows from that. They are our enemies, we do not want them.[51]

Khomeini's intolerance for "anyone changing his mind about what he wants to be" was ironic, given his own ambivalence regarding the penalties exacted by revolutionary action. Indeed, only two weeks after making the above speech, he again vacillated. In a speech to army officers that mirrored his fear of the negative effects of revolutionary zeal, he warned, "you are all brothers. . . . All forces should unite. This is a religious duty . . . for the Majlis deputies, to cooperate with the government and the president." Such cooperation, Khomeini asserted, began with the principle that all governmental or official institutions should stop "interfering" in the affairs of the other. "If everybody were to interfere in everybody else's affairs this would not be a proper country," he insisted. "The law has determined everyone's responsibilities. . . . If one were to forsake the law . . . he would act contrary to religion."[52] Yet despite this call for cooperation, Khomeini maintained his veiled if erratic attacks on Bani-Sadr throughout the summer. Iraq's invasion of Iran in September 1980 temporarily saved Bani-Sadr from Khomeini's wrath. With Iraqi forces on the offensive, Khomeini asked him to take charge of the military. Thus, for a time, the Iranian president could protect himself from his domestic enemies.

However, by late winter 1981 several events increased the tensions between Bani-Sadr and Prime Minister Raja'i to the breaking point. First, a group of prominent intellectuals led by Bazargan sent a letter to the government attacking it for violating human rights. This was followed by violent clashes between Bani-Sadr's supporters and those of Khomeini's. As these events unfolded, Khomeini came under pressure to act against his "spiritual son," but he still hesitated to use his powers to remove Bani-Sadr. Such action would not only signal the regime's rupture with the modernist forces which Bani-Sadr represented, but also would have highlighted the political system's dependence on Khomeini's charisma. Khomeini's words suggested that he wanted to avoid this day of reckoning. "God forbid," he warned in early February, "there should come a time when I feel obliged to do my duty [*ehsas-e vazifeh konam*]. I advise them to keep calm. . . . If this obligation to do my duty arises, I will take back whatever I have given to other individuals."[53] Four months later, he kept his promise. Following a march by the National Front against recently proposed Islamic legislation, Khomeini condemned the demonstration as an "invitation to rebellion . . . against the explicit direction of the Koran." He then went even further issuing a remarkable statement that in effect equated his authority with Imam 'Ali's! In this statement Khomeini exclaimed, "What makes me feel sorry is . . . to face those who did not let Imam 'Ali finish his duties." Such behavior left him little choice but to invoke his powers. "What can I do. You did not listen to my advice. . . . The National Front is condemned as of today."[54]

Several days later, Khomeini's disciple Chief Justice Ayatollah Beheshti suggested that Bani-Sadr be tried for treason. The besieged president went into hiding, and on 16 June the *Majles* began impeachment proceedings. These events were followed by the 28 June bombing of the headquarters of the IRP, in which some seventy of Khomeini's supporters, including Beheshti, were killed. Two months later, two more allies of Khomeini's, Raja'i (elected president in July 1981) and Ayatollah Mohammad-Javad Bahonar (named prime minister by the *Majles* in August 1981), died in another bomb blast. Enraged by the death of his allies, Khomeini decided to stop excluding the clergy from top governmental posts. In August 1981 he appointed a Presidential Council consisting of Ayatollah Abdolkarim Musavi-Ardabili, 'Ali Akbar Hashemi Rafsanjani, and Ayatollah Mohammad Reza Mahdavi-Kani. Two months later, Ayatollah Khamane'i's election as president signaled that the generation of Islamic Leftists who had served in the first government of the Islamic Republic would henceforth be marginalized. Having isolated Bazargan and his allies, Khomeini then launched a campaign against his clerical foes. This crusade would eventually culminate in the April 1982 "defrocking" of Ayatollah Shari'atmadari and the purging of Khomeini's clerical opponents in the seminaries of Qom.

Dissonant Institutionalization in the *Majles*

Khomeini's victory was bittersweet. In the ensuing years, the political involvement of leading clerics ensured that differences among them would become a matter of public record. Khomeini, as we have seen, had long understood the dangers inherent in such a development. Indeed, in February 1981 he had already given what he called an "emphatic reminder to the clergy" that "they should in no way interfere in matters for which they are not qualified." Their interference, he cautioned, "will be an unforgivable sin, because it will lead to the nation's mistrust of the clergy."[55] Khomeini repeated this theme two months later, insisting that "the clergy . . . keep to their assignment and . . . not exceed their limits."[56]

Why then did Khomeini eventually turn on Bani-Sadr? Was this development preordained by a logic intrinsic to all charismatic leadership and revolutions? Viewed through the lens of contending authorities, Khomeini's actions clearly were not part of some grand scheme; instead, they stemmed from his enduring concerns about the paradoxical consequences of clerical rule. As Khomeini's speeches reveal, he understood that the clerics' authority could be quickly compromised by the perception that these servants of God were doing the devil's work. Thus he did not subscribe to Beheshti's view that the "president counts for nothing."[57] On the contrary, he shared Bani-Sadr's belief that an elected president had a popularly important role to play. As Shaul Bakhash notes, Khomeini "disapproved of IRP attempts to undermine the discipline of the armed force . . . [and] had no desire to alienate the type of . . . left-of-center 'Islamic' political groups and intelligentsia that Bani-Sadr represented."[58] It was this concern that had impelled Khomeini in March 1981 to convene a summit during which he tried to get Bani-Sadr and IRP leaders to resolve their differences. But the two sides were determined to fight it out, thus giving Khomeini little choice but to exercise his "revolutionary duties" by siding with clerics whose actions deeply worried him.

Nonetheless, the purging of Bani-Sadr and his allies from the highest reaches of government did not bring an end to the ideological influence of the Islamic Left. Its ideas were not only reflected in the Constitution and in Khomeini's own political rhetoric, but also found their way into the *Majles* itself. Paradoxically, some of the highly Islamic radicals who had vigorously opposed Bazargan, Bani-Sadr, and other Islamic Leftists now became the principal inheritors of the Left's populist instrumentalism. The hostage crisis set the stage for this development. Radical activists such as Behzad Nabavi, who led the Iranian delegation negotiating an end to the hostage affair, and Ayatollah Musavi Kho'eyniha, spiritual leader of the "Students Following the Imam's Line," the militant group that seized the American Embassy, used the crisis to discredit Bani-Sadr and other "tools of the West." Their efforts facilitated the election of a radical bloc of clerics and lay intellectuals to the First *Majles*.[59] Although a diverse group, the radicals agreed on three points: they viewed the state as the principal vehicle for establishing social justice and economic independence; they opposed any reconciliation with the United States; and they viewed politics and ideology in highly rationalist if instrumentalist terms. These Islamic Republicans held that to be a genuine "Follower of the Imam's Line" required a firm commitment to promoting the people's participation in national politics through the agency of the *Majles*.

In the wake of the April 1980 elections, Khomeini signaled his sympathy with this populist perspective. Thus he not only handed primary responsibility for resolving the hostage crisis to the *Majles*, but in May 1979 proclaimed that "[t]he center of all law and power is the Majlis. It guides all and it should do so"[60]—a phrase he would often repeat in the coming years. Yet if Khomeini endorsed the idea that the *Majles* should be a principal—if not the leading—seat of authority, he did not favor any one *Majles* faction. The Imam wanted the benefit of balancing different factions without the costs of factionalism: the radicals, he argued, had to learn to live with other factions, since "all the powers of the nation are concentrated in this group" (i.e., the *Majles*).[61] This position allowed him to retain his authority as paramount arbiter of the political system; what is more, it facilitated the dissonant institutionalization of contending authorities. Henceforth, the *Majles* became *the* arena through which competing social forces sought to accommodate conflicting interests and ideologies.

Summary: The Dilemmas of Power

Although the function of the *Majles* was to address and thus circumscribe social conflict, we shall see that the resumption of clerical disputes—particularly between the *Majles* and the Council of Guardians—soon presented Khomeini with a vexing dilemma. If, on the one hand, he intervened in these conflicts, such unilateralist actions would invariably highlight the political system's dependence on his own charisma. Although this charisma gave Khomeini the personal authority to intervene in political disputes, it suggested no concrete solutions to Iran's mounting social difficulties. If, on the other hand, Khomeini remained on the sidelines, clerical disputes could easily spin out of control, once again exposing the inherent costs of clerical involvement in politics. The choice thus seemed to be between exercising personal authority at the expense of institutionalizing power and solving pressing social problems, or permitting clerical disputes to undermine public confidence in the very notion of an Islamic Republic. As chapter 6 will show, by vacillating between these two poles, the Imam inadvertently accentuated the dilemmas of power. In time this vicious cycle would compel him to give greater—if not decisive—weight to Iran's interests—over and even against the demands for a continuous revolution against foreign and domestic enemies. But before this could happen, Khomeini would have to overcome his profound desire to sustain the antieconomic charismatic ethos of his Islamic Revolution.

6 The Trials and Tribulations of Complex Routinization

> It would seem to be an observable fact of human behavior that large numbers of men can stand only so much interference with the routines and ritual of their daily existence. . . . Social systems composed of human beings can endure but for a limited time the concerted attempt to bring heaven to earth. . . . Thermidor comes as naturally to societies in revolution as an ebbing tide, as calm after a storm, as convalescence after fever.[1]
>
> —Crane Brinton

> It is not acceptable . . . that in the name of revolution . . . somebody should be oppressed. From now on, this is the time for stability and construction. . . .[2] The main thing is that we serve. . . . Serving the government is the same as serving Islam. . . . We should no longer say we are in a revolutionary situation.[3]
>
> —Imam Khomeini, December 1982

The Storm before the Calm?

When the storm of charisma emanates from the very soul of a charismatic leader, it is no easy task to transform this revolutionary aura into doctrines and institutions that legitimize social order. Messianic redeemers, according to Edward Shils, "see themselves moving towards a culmination of history." Because they view constant movement as an end rather than a means, "to live from year to year . . . to solve the problems of the year . . . are not enough."[4] As the Russian anarchist Mikhail Bakunin declared, "I do not believe in constitutions or in laws . . . We need something different. Storm and vitality and a new lawless and consequently free world."[5] Nonetheless, it has been a cardinal principle of Western social science that the tempest of revolution must eventually dissipate. Crane Brinton ascribed this "observable fact of human behavior" to a collective exhaustion born of one too many efforts at building "heaven on earth." Anticipating this argument, Max Weber identified three forces that impel routinization: first, the resolution of the crisis that first sparked the quest for cathartic experience or "re-enchantment"; second, the development of *economic* interests on the part of disciples as patrons of the leader's ruling institutions. Since these interests "become conspicuously evident with the disappearance of the personal charismatic leader,"[6] they are inextricably linked to the third force that prompts routinization: the issue of succession. Faced by the need to choose a new ruler, the "charismatic staff" repackages the original leader's magical aura so that it legitimates both the authority of the successor, and the authority of the institutions through which the new leader and his allies rule.

As suggested in chapter 1, this process is fraught with contradictions. While Weber notes that such leaders may "desire to transform charisma . . . into a permanent possession of everyday life" (1121), their rationality has limits: consumed by a desire for revolutionary action, the leaders are not only "free of the ordinary worldly attachments and duties of occupational and family life." More fundamentally, they "[reject] as undignified . . . all rational economic conduct" (1112). In short, they cannot fully routinize their charisma without denying their very identity. Yet because "the great majority of [their] disciples . . . 'make their living' out of their 'calling'" (249), these followers must somehow find way to address material realities without impinging on their leader's charisma. This is why the struggle to "capture" charisma only reaches a crescendo *after* the leader's death (1122). Although some charismatic leaders designate their successors, the *full elaboration* of a new authority structure occurs only when their disciples are free to establish "norms for recruitment" that a "genuine charismatic leader" might otherwise oppose (249). At this point charisma is routinized by one of three mechanisms: hereditary rule, modern law, or the transfer of the leader's powers to a traditional "office" or ruling institution.

As noted in chapter 1, instrumentalist accounts of ideology and authority provide a useful window onto this process of routinization. By highlighting human agency and the calculated manipulation of symbols by political elites, instrumentalist theory illuminates the two dynamics that are central to routinization: the political struggle among disciples to encourage their leaders to address social, economic, and political problems; and the contest by competing factions within ruling establishments to redefine the leader's ideological legacy so that the authority of a new leader and the social interests of his allies are legitimized. This second contest pivots around *ideas*: no serious contender can afford the perception—or worse, the accusation—that he has betrayed the leader's ideals. Instead, all contestants must show that their political or social vision is an authentic expression of the founding leader's values. In short, routinization entails a dual dynamic: a struggle to enlist the leader behind a given sociopolitical project, and a contest to redefine the leader's ideological legacy.

While my analysis of this twin dynamic draws on instrumentalist approaches to routinization, it departs from the linear view envisioned by symbolic and instrumentalist accounts of charisma. I argue that where dissonant institutionalization has defined the political and social terrain, a linear transition from "pure" to "manufactured" charisma is unlikely. Instead, "complex routinization" consists of a prolonged and even chaotic struggle to overcome or mitigate the destabilizing effects of dissonant institutionalization. Two facets of this process complicate the struggle. First, because the original charismatic leader imbibed contending visions of authority, he is as apt to support as he is to oppose routinization. Under these conditions, his disciples' efforts to secure his blessing for a given sociopolitical project may advance one day and reverse the next. Second, because the charismatic leader bequeaths a multifaceted ideological legacy, when he dies and the routinization battle swings into full gear, every faction can plausibly argue that its rendering of that legacy defends the leader's ideals. As a result, the attempt by any one group to legitimate its hegemony by selectively appropriating the leader's ideals can be challenged with relative ease. Under these conditions, routinization is as likely to move forward and back, or left and right, as it is to proceed along a straight path.

Chapters 6 through 8 illustrate the *particular* features of this chaotic process. I emphasize *particular* because by its very nature, complex routinization is indeterminate. Its fate depends on the content of a leader's ideological legacy, and on the organizational and rhetorical strategies that contending social forces bring to their twin struggle to enlist his support and reinterpret this legacy. This chapter focuses on the first facet of this struggle: the efforts of competing *Majles* (Parliament) factions to push the Imam toward endorsing their respective social and political agendas. The latter section of this chapter, and the bulk of chapters 7 and 8, highlight the second facet: the contest to appropriate Khomeini's legacy.

The endeavor of Khomeini's disciples to enlist his support for their respective agendas pitted radical advocates of statist development against conservative and pragmatic proponents of private enterprise. At times the two sides compromised, only to see the Council of Guardians, which supervised all legislation for Islamic propriety, veto their reforms. This quintessential standoff between traditional and rational-legal authority could not be broken without amending the Constitution to give a clearer line of authority to one or more ruling bodies. Yet the *Majles–* council conflict also obscured a more fundamental tension: that between the personal-charismatic authority of Khomeini, and the *institutional* authority of the legislative and judicial branches. As long as Khomeini's place in the regime was secure, this conflict was not fatal to his rule. After all, Khomeini could always invoke his authority as *rahbar* (Supreme Leader) to break the stalemate between the *Majles* and the Council of Guardians. But in doing so he would invariably accentuate the political system's dependence on a charismatic, yet mortal leader. Assuming that no successor could match Khomeini's exceptional stature, the constitutional procedures for selecting the next *faqih* would have to be changed so that his authority derived from his position or *office*, rather than his personal qualities. As a result, political and socioeconomic routinization were inextricably linked. Without tackling the first, little progress could be made on the second.

Khomeini's response to this double challenge illustrates the contradictory dynamics of complex routinization. On the one hand, his mystical-charismatic vision of social justice hindered his ability to articulate a clear social project and also frustrated his disciples' efforts to gain his endorsement of their respective economic agendas. On the other hand, Khomeini's long-held desire to strengthen the ruling institutions of the state encouraged him to seek concrete solutions to the problems of social and political authority. As a result, a beguiling cycle emerged. Instead of intervening, Khomeini would encourage the *Majles*, government, and Council of Guardians to resolve their differences. When such cooperation failed to emerge, he would support one faction. But such intervention simply revealed the dependence of the political system on Khomeini's personal charisma, thus hindering Khomeini's own efforts to institutionalize power. The frustrated Imam would then seek refuge in a mystical vision that was as alluring as it was ineffective. This pattern of failed conflict resolution emerged in full bloom during the Iran–Iraq War. Since Khomeini believed the war provided a vital outlet through which Iran's young martyrs experienced mystical transcendence, he was loath to give it up. Finally, prompted by *Majles* Speaker 'Ali Akbar Hashemi Rafsanjani, and facing economic crisis, Khomeini issued his 1 January 1988 edict on the interests of the state. Eight months later he accepted a cease-fire and then backed Rafsanjani's campaign for constitutional reform. The new Constitution, promulgated within days of Khomeini's death in June 1989, not only diminished the charismatic authority of the *faqih* by separating the positions of *marja'* (or "highest religious source of imitation") and *faqih;* but, by still providing for the direct, popular election of the president, and the indirect selection of the *faqih* by a clerical assembly, it also created the *potential* for serious rivalry between the president and Supreme Leader.

The implications of this failure to coherently routinize authority were at first unclear. The principal concern of Khomeini's disciples was to show that supporting—or opposing—these constitutional reforms was consistent with Khomeini's wishes. Thus the second facet of routinization, the struggle to appropriate a leader's ideological legacy, began within days of Khomeini's death. Rafsanjani and his allies realized the above reforms by manipulating the utilitarian aspects of Khomeini's speeches and edicts. Yet Rafsanjani's actions, as those of his rivals, signaled only the opening skirmish in a prolonged ideological war. Chapters 7 and 8 highlight the conflicting twists and turns that this contest took during the nineties.

Utilitarianism and Charismatic Mysticism: "Islam Is Everything"

No single domain of "this-worldly" activity displayed the contradictory impact of Khomeini's charismatic-mystical commitments better than Iran's socioeconomic policy.[7] Although he had absorbed the Islamic Left's dedication to social justice and political mobilization, this perspective was tempered by his enduring devotion to Islamic mysticism. Given the impact of Khomeini's eclectic vision on the efforts within the regime to enlist his support for institutionalizing the Islamic Revolution, I will summarize the mix of mysticism and utilitarianism that made this vision deeply alluring, yet profoundly unrealistic. To do so, I will cite from several speeches that the Imam gave in 1979, a tumultuous year during which he repeatedly outlined his understanding of social justice.

Echoing Jalal Al-e Ahmad's book *Weststruckness*, Khomeini begins a "Speech to Craftsmen" by blaming the West and its Muslim allies for the Iranians' failure to understand the comprehensive nature of their "ideology." Foreigners, he asserted, "imprisoned" Islam in two false realms. The first consisted of the "schools and mosques" over which the clergy presided. These clerics behaved as if Islam "allowed only spiritual aspects," failing to notice that in the Qur'an "there also are chapters on government . . . laws and all that is related to . . . government." People who "sacrificed spiritual values for material considerations" filled the second false realm. These "materialists"—in other words, Islamic Leftists—turned "every chapter of the Koran" into "a worldly issue," as if "nothing existed in the invisible world." They mistakenly believed that the revolution was either about "democracy, when most of [the Iranian people] never heard of the word 'democracy' "; or that it was about "an improvement in their material life"! This claim was patently refuted by the other-worldly concerns that had impelled Iranians to sacrifice their lives in the struggle against the Shah, Mohammad Reza Pahlavi:

> Does it seem reasonable for a person to shout for his stomach and then give up his life, is this reasonable? Could anyone wish his child to be martyred to obtain a good house? This is not the issue. The issue is another world. Martyrdom is meant for another world. This is a martyrdom sought by all of God's saints and prophets. . . . The people want this meaning.

Having asserted that Islam was neither exclusively about reason nor transcendence, Khomeini identified what he held to be the essence of Islam: "Islam is everything," he asserted. It came to "transform man" by uniting his spiritual and physical existence. Thus he explained, using a famous *hadith* (saying) attributed to Imam 'Ali, "man is a miniature universe. . . . Man embodies all the things that exist in all things . . . good and evil."[8] But by himself man cannot unite body and spirit. This was the task of the "prophets . . . to take man by the hand . . . and guide him to the light . . . through teaching." This evocation of Khomeini's devotion to the idea of "wholeness" struck a chord in his audience because it addressed the spiritual and social alienation that had gripped many of them. Khomeini understood that in their readiness to die, the youth were paradoxically expressing a desperate desire to regain a vital sense of life. As he put it on another occasion, "Dying does not mean nothingness: it is life."[9]

Yet Khomeini never let his audience forget who supposedly bore the guilt for taking their humanity away. Echoing the populism of the Islamic Left, he warned that the "superpowers are stripping us naked. . . . One of their big plans is to . . . replace [our brains] . . . with European ones: to . . . rob us of our intellectual independence." This reference to dependency found a particularly receptive audience among *bazaaris*, the traditional merchant middle class that had paid a high economic and spiritual price for the Shah's modernizing policies. Linking both forms of alienation, Khomeini again echoed Al-e Ahmad: "We have forgotten our industries: tile work, inlaid work, carpet-weaving. . . . We forgot these things because they *made* us fall in love with the West" (italics mine). Things had gotten so bad that when one of the Shah's relatives developed tonsillitis, "a doctor was fetched from abroad. . . . This was such a slap to our doctors. . . . What shame and degradation it is for a country that it has to stretch its hands toward America." Having tapped into this vein of humiliation that many Iranians felt at being "made to fall in love with the West," Khomeini warned his audience that they should not be "satisfied with saying 'God Willing' . . . or just praying." Instead, he asserted, "you should act."

Khomeini invariably prescribed three courses of action. First, he insisted that Iranians cut all "economic and cultural links with foreign countries." This was not merely a political matter. Khomeini held that Iranians could not effect this divorce without *humiliating* the American government. That government, he insisted, should be "slapped in the face," and "punched in the mouth."[10] Second, Khomeini asserted that the time had come to "replace . . . our colonialists' brains" with "an independent brain." Doing so required replacing "this Western pattern . . . with an eastern pattern . . . an Islamic pattern." This was the third element in Khomeini's prescription. By "eastern pattern," he meant unifying people's physical and spiritual sides in a way that checked their propensity for evil self-indulgence. This was the way of the "prophets . . . [who] would never fight among themselves because fighting comes from selfishness and flaws in the human being." The prophets "destroyed the flaws, and crusaded," because "He who wants God has no quarrel with anyone."[11] In sum, Khomeini argued that social antagonisms bequeathed by socioeconomic and intellectual dependency had robbed Muslims of their *innate* ability for spiritual and social unity. By breaking the spell of dependency through rational intellectual and political endeavors, as well as through cathartic acts that "slapped" the United States and its Iranian supporters, and by following the guidance of the clergy, Iranians would not only regain control of their economy, but also rediscover the "miniature" reflection of God's mystical universe that was inside their very being.

1981–83: Social Justice versus the Mystical Catharsis of War

Because Khomeini's vision offered no concrete solutions to the marked conflicts over social and economic policy that paralyzed Iran during the eighties, it was ultimately unsustainable. The achievement of social justice would remain a utopian dream lacking a means for addressing mundane economic issues. The transition from vision to reality required two corollary initiatives: a change in the Constitution that gave the president and/or the *Majles*—rather than the Council of Guardians or even the *rahbar* (leader)—full or at least increased authority over political and social policy, and a readiness by Khomeini to consistently back one *Majles* faction or the other.

These requirements created a dilemma for Khomeini's disciples. How could any one faction enlist his support in mundane economic tasks without seeming to diminish his charismatic aura? One possible solution was to emphasize Khomeini's populist-utilitarian commitments, but without giving undue credence to the mystical ethos that made his vision of social justice so emotionally compelling but ultimately impractical. The leaders of the radical *maktabi* (ideological) *Majles* faction were well suited for this delicate balancing act. As noted in chapter 5, most were clerics or lay activists who had imbibed the ideals of the Islamic Left, particularly the utopian instrumentalism of 'Ali Shari'ati. The multiple biography of Mir Hoseyn Musavi, who became prime minister in October 1981, was typical of this generation. An Iranian-trained architect who spent a year in the United States before the revolution, Musavi saw the state as the primary vehicle of social change. Joining him in this were, among others, then Deputy Speaker Ayatollah Musavi Kho'eyniha; Asadollah Bayat; Morteza Alviri; Hojjat al-Eslam Hadi Ghaffari, leader of the radical *Hezbollah*, or Party of God; and Hojjat al-Eslam Hadi Khamane'i, the younger brother of President 'Ali Khamane'i. Champions of the "masses," they welcomed the Imam's call for the First *Majles* to issue "serious proposals . . . for the welfare of the oppressed classes."[12]

It was soon clear that Musavi's economic program could not succeed without facing the task of political routinization. His regime's efforts at land and foreign trade reform illustrated this point. Musavi's bid in 1981 and 1982 to enact land tenancy laws and trade reform provoked the wrath of the conservative *hojjatiyeh* faction in the *Majles,* and of the Council of Guardians. The *hojjatiyeh* faction was led by clerics who had close ties to the *bazaar.* Although its existence was not publicly mentioned until 1983 (in part because many of its members opposed the doctrine of *velayat-e faqih,* "Rule of the Jurist"), the *hojjatiyeh's* opposition to statist policies helped dilute the reform laws proposed by Musavi's government.[13] At the same time, whatever reform legislation that did get passed was vetoed by the Council of Guardians, which claimed that such legislation violated the Qur'an's defense of private property.[14] While this situation could only be resolved by convincing Khomeini to overcome his charismatic preference for unity, few deputies had the authority—or the courage—to approach the Imam.

One would think that the socioeconomic and human costs of the Iran–Iraq War might have encouraged Khomeini to acquiesce to routinization. Precipitated by Iraq's September 1980 invasion, the war underscored the state's desperate need to get its economic and institutional house in order. Yet the bloody fighting did not compel the

Imam to be more pragmatic: on the contrary, the martyrdom of thousands of young men filled his head anew with mystical visions. But this sad development was not completely irrational. Technologically ill equipped for a blitzkrieg, the regime sought to stop the attack by throwing waves of young "volunteers" at the Iraqis. Thus Khomeini openly defended the calculated and political use of Shi'ism's symbols to mobilize the youth. Two months after the invasion and on the eve of the holy month of Muharram, he told a group of clerics:

> Do not imagine that in the mourning ceremonies you are weeping for the sake of the Lord of Martyrs. No, the Lord of Martyrs has no need for this weeping. By themselves, these ceremonies achieve [nothing]. However . . . [they] unify the people. . . . The prophets with their divine mission wished to mobilize . . . the nations through various *means*. Islamic issues are political issues and the political aspects *predominate* over its other aspects.[15]

Yet if Khomeini's speeches had clear political intent, something more profound than mere opportunism was going on. As the war dragged on, the content of his speeches suggested his growing conviction that martyrdom was the supreme form of mystical experience. Khomeini had hinted at this idea earlier. In an October 1980 speech that echoed his mystical belief in man's "incompleteness," Khomeini had argued that "the natural world is the lowest part of creation. . . . The true arena is the divine world which is inexhaustible." But, he continued, "even in animal ambitions man is different from the rest of the animals." Man achieves the divine by ceasing to be a "slave of nature" and instead pursue the "path of God." "Our youngsters," who "welcome martyrdom," demonstrated that point. By *not* being "a material being," they were helping Iran become " a divine country."[16] Gripped anew by this mystical idea, in a March 1981 speech Khomeini told the clerics that the solution to their power struggles lay in reaching "the stage where you . . . overlook yourself." "When there is no self to contend with," he claimed, "there is no dispute, no quarrel."[17]

These appeals did not quell the disputes within the clergy. Clearly upset, Khomeini again shifted toward a utilitarian approach to resolve the Council of Guardians–*Majles* deadlock. His endeavors were encouraged by *Majles* Speaker Hashemi Rafsanjani. A loyal ally who had avoided linking himself to any one *Majles* faction, Rafsanjani was well positioned to seek the Imam's intervention without appearing to disdain Khomeini's charismatic belief in unity. Thus after the council vetoed a bill providing for landownership in the cities, Rafsanjani asked the Imam to openly support the new law. Such intervention, Rafsanjani implied, was justified by the principle of public necessity, which holds that when the interests of the Islamic community are at stake, clerics can legislate "secondary ordinances" regarding issues not directly legislated in the Qur'an or the Sunna (example of the Prophet and Imams as revealed in *hadith* literature).[18]

Khomeini had endorsed the utilitarian principles of public necessity and secondary ordinances in his book *Islamic Government*. Eleven years later, he appeared ready to respond positively to Rafsanjani's assertion that "as the guardian of the community, [the Imam] can exercise authority in situations of extreme importance."[19] Yet to the apparent dismay of Rafsanjani, Khomeini delegated this authority to the *Majles*! "Whatever concerns the safeguarding of the Islamic Republic order," he wrote, "and whichever is necessary . . . once the majority of deputies . . . recognize the topic in question, they are authorized to . . . implement it, while stressing its temporary nature."[20] This effort to routinize his charisma by delegating authority to the *Majles* failed because it did not resolve the conflict between the *Majles* and the Guardians' Council. It was somewhat bizarre, therefore, that only two months after his half-baked attempt to shift his authority to the *Majles*, Khomeini issued a decree that heralded the institutionalization of his revolution. In a kind of Islamic Bill of Rights, he held that "it is not acceptable . . . that in the name of revolution . . . somebody should be oppressed. From now on, [this] is the time for stability and construction."[21] The following week he added a utilitarian twist to the above decree, declaring that: "The main thing is that we serve Islam. . . . Serving the government is the same as serving Islam. . . . We should no longer say we are in a revolutionary situation."[22]

However, the revolution could not be institutionalized merely by issuing proclamations. Thus barely a week later, the *Majles* and the Council of Guardians were again locked in a fierce battle. Frustrated, Khomeini once again tried to break the deadlock by invoking the concept of secondary ordinances—but now with a novel interpretation. Clerics had traditionally argued that the governments could issue secondary ordinances when addressing a narrow range of contractual issues not directly addressed in the Qur'an. But now Khomeini told the *Majles* that "we cannot imagine that God would not have looked at every aspect of any problem." This dictum even applied to "secondary provisions [which] . . . have been ordained for the very reason that problems may arise in a particular society. . . . These are also ordinances from God."[23] By thus implying that secondary rulings were also mandated by God, Khomeini virtually equated the clerical power to issue such rulings with the authority of God himself! Yet in retrospect this grandiose claim was only a dress rehearsal for a more dramatic transformation that took another five years to unfold. A few days later, the Imam again assigned the task of determining secondary principles to the *Majles*, thus failing to address the root problem, which was the Constitution's confusing division of powers. Confounded by his own failure to resolve this crisis, Khomeini again sought solace in mysticism. In a speech that celebrated the successes of the revolution, he exclaimed, "Your youths have crossed the border in one night. . . . They have suddenly achieved what the mystics and mystical poets have been dreaming of."[24] Three months later, he declared that the "trenches . . . are centers for worship of God"; there, he asserted, the martyrs had attained "mystical and divine stages."[25] Khomeini then extended this argument by virtually recasting the concept of martyrdom. Instead of defining it as an unforeseen act by which Muslims *inadvertently* die in the defense of Islam, he now held that the very survival of the Islamic Republic required the *deliberate pursuit* of martyrdom:

> If the great martyr . . . confined himself to praying . . . the great tragedy of Karbala [where Imam Hoseyn was martyred] would *not* have come about. . . . Among the contemporary ulema, if the great Ayatollah . . . Shirazi . . . thought like these people [who do not fight for Islam] a war would *not* have taken place in Iraq . . . all those Muslims would *not* have been martyred.[26]

These shocking statements proved no more effective in 1983 than they had in years past. By the end of 1983, the Imam admitted his failure to institutionalize the revolution. As he put it, "my only fear is that we may fail to hand over things to the next generation in a consolidated manner."[27]

1984: Economics Is Hell

Although the economic and social crises plaguing Iran had failed to move Khomeini in any one clear direction, by the mideighties the country's dire economic situation was finally getting his disciples to focus on effecting appropriate policy. After all, the revolution had promised the *mostaz'afin* (disinherited) social justice, whereas the government's own Planning and Budget Organization reported that from 1979 through 1985, absolute poverty rose by nearly 45 percent![28] Compelled by such news to make difficult decisions about the national economic policy, the clerics became even more divided. Joining the radical *Majles* faction was Ayatollah Mehdi Karrubi. A longtime disciple of Khomeini's, by late 1983 Karrubi's control over the powerful Martyr's Foundation had earned him the leadership of the radical deputies in the *Majles*. Backed by Ghaffari, whose control of the *hezbollahi* shock troops gave him a strong base for mobilization outside the *Majles*, these two men pressed Musavi's government—in Karrubi's words—to concentrate on "acting rather than . . . making excuses."[29]

These demands had the unintended effect of coalescing an alliance of clerics and lay deputies around Rafsanjani's "pragmatic-conservative camp." With each side controlling about 120 seats, power was divided between Prime Minister Musavi and his radical allies, and Speaker Rafsanjani and his supporters. Thus "executive-legislative relations were virtually at a stand-still."[30]

This standoff set the stage for the fierce political battle during the spring 1984 *Majles* elections. The introduction of a new election law restricted the political playing field by requiring all candidates to demonstrate "spiritual, as well as revolutionary commitment to Islam" and "total loyalty to the 'Great Leader' Imam Khomeini, and the institution of *faqih*."[31] On this basis, the Council of Guardians disqualified leaders of the Iran Freedom Movement (IFM) from participating in elections, thus leaving two main *Majles* factions to fight it out.[32] While Khomeini backed this measure, he openly—if inconsistently—fretted that it might be seen to favor the imposition of clerical control over the popular will: "In the previous regimes [i.e., that of the Shah], efforts were made . . . so that [the government] could have a free hand in electing certain people." This mistake, Khomeini implied, should not be repeated. "Today," he insisted, "no power in Iran can impose anything on the people and the elections are in the hands of the people." Thus, "the Majlis needs people who are committed to Islam and . . . the Islamic Republic, and, at the same time, those who are statesmen, economists and knowledgeable about the world situation."[33]

Khomeini's statements bolstered the radicals. With their presence in the *Majles* increased, Musavi proclaimed that the Second *Majles* would be the "true representative of the toiling . . . oppressed people, . . . a revolutionary Majlis."[34] Yet as he had done before, Khomeini tried to avoid decisively backing any one faction. Implicitly rebuking the leaders of the new *Majles*, he warned that "[o]ne should not be concerned with being elected to the Majlis or being elected President or appointed minister. . . . You are Shi'ites, like me. I place as much value on these positions as I do on these old shoes. . . . You should take care not to bring about the same problems of the past."[35] But such problems were unavoidable. Although the radicals had made gains in the elections, Rafsanjani had scored a victory by winning 1.9 million of the 2.3 million votes cast in Tehran.[36] Buoyed by this success, he was reelected *Majles*

Speaker. Rafsanjani then began a concerted, if quiet, effort to secure Khomeini's support for a series of moderate economic reforms. This campaign met with some success. Meeting in August 1984 with the prime minister and his cabinet, Khomeini contradicted his previous warnings against causing dissension by asserting that Musavi's radical economic approach, in Bahman Baktiari's words, "contradicts Islam, the constitution and the nation's interests."[37]

The Momentary Triumph of Messianic Universalism: 1985–86

This appeal to interests was no more successful in breaking the logjam than were Khomeini's previous ones. Tension within the *Majles* continued, as did the stalemate between it and the Council of Guardians. Although in January 1985 Musavi assailed the council's veto of laws dealing with taxation, land distribution, foreign trade, and limitations on the scope of the private sector—and although the Iran–Iraq War was exacting an ever-higher human and economic cost[38]—Khomeini could not, or would not, resume his previous attempts to encourage progress on economic issues. On the contrary, he again took refuge in mysticism. In a speech marking the anniversary of the Islamic Revolution, he warned the clerics that "all corruption and problems of the world stem from an illness called self-conceit *(khod-bini)*."[39] One month later, he again maintained that the complete spiritual awakening of humanity would be achieved only through death. Thus, he insisted, Iran's recent setbacks on the battlefront represented a *gain:*

> At times a calamity becomes a blessing. . . . It is under pressure that the spirits soar to the higher world. . . . If we Muslims . . . were like other nations, and had been running after wealth, status . . . or were running for bread and sex, many would have been disappointed. But the nation that goes to war for martyrdom . . . such a nation can hardly think of anything else. As for its economy, it does not matter. These matters are for those who are tied to economies.[40]

For Khomeini, the Iran–Iraq War not only represented the primary arena through which Iranians experienced spiritual transcendence; by 1985 he appeared convinced that this battlefield also had become *the* testing ground upon which Iran's revolution would succeed or fail at realizing its global aspirations. Khomeini had often declared that the "Islamic Revolution . . . is being exported . . . [so that] . . . with the dispensations of the Supreme Lord, the banner of Islam is likely to be hoisted throughout the globe in the not-too-distant future."[41] Because this messianic vision suggested that the revolution's success at home depended on its expansion abroad, Khomeini argued that the defeat of the "satanic" alliance had to be achieved *at all costs*. "It is our belief," he explained in April 1985, "that Saddam [Hussein, leader of Iraq] wishes to return Islam to blasphemy and polytheism." Thus "if America becomes victorious . . . and grants victory to Saddam, Islam will receive such a blow that it will not be able to raise its head for a long time. . . . The issue is one of Islam versus blasphemy, and not of Iran versus Iraq."[42] This sentiment was reinforced by Khomeini's messianic conviction that in defeating Iraq and the West, the Islamic Republic of Iran was fulfilling a goal that all the Prophets—*including* Mohammad—had *failed* to achieve. "I should say," he declared in November 1985, "that so far the purpose of the Prophets has seldom been realized. Very little." Knowing that some clerics would find this claim blasphemous, he warned that "tomorrow court mullahs . . . [should] not say that Khomeini said that the Prophet is incapable of achieving his aims." But the reality was that those aims had *not* been achieved. If they had, "we would have the American Government and others." Since the prophets would never have intended for this unfortunate situation to endure, it was incumbent upon the IRI to finish the mission the prophets had started. "The aim of the prophets," Khomeini added for good measure, was "to guide mankind toward knowledge of God. *All other issues* are subsidiary to it."[43] Repeating this mystical theme some weeks later, Khomeini insisted that the aim of the prophets "was *not* to bring about social justice . . . not for the sake of people . . . but for God."[44] Iran's mission was about universal redemption—not the hell of economics or politics.

1987–90: Absolute *Faqih* or Absolute Government?

Because such messianism failed to provide any concrete solutions to the many conflicts that had immobilized the *Majles*, by late 1985 that body was gripped by a new dispute. The discord was sparked by the efforts of recently reelected President Khamane'i—a conservative—to block the reappointment of Musavi as prime minister.[45] Seeking to deflect this initiative, 134 out of the 270 *Majles* deputies sent a letter to Khomeini in which they defended Musavi. At the same time, Musavi's supporters from the Islamic Left repeatedly insisted that they had the support of the Imam. Concerned that this development heralded a new round of clerical disputes, Khomeini angrily warned that those who were opposing

Musavi should "not create obstacles" that would eventually defeat the government.[46] One month later, when the Council of Guardians met with Khomeini to complain about Prosecutor General Kho'eyniha's attacks on private property laws, the Imam gave a response that could not have satisfied either faction. Citing a *hadith* from the Prophet, he replied obliquely that "the poor share in the wealth of the rich." He then refused a request from *Majles* Deputy Ayatollah Ahmad Azari Qomi—owner of the conservative daily newspaper *Resalat*—to replace Prime Minister Musavi with Ayatollah Mohammad Reza Mahdavi-Kani.[47]

In the ensuing two years, the attempts by competing *Majles* factions to obtain Khomeini's support for their agenda repeatedly failed. The core of the problem was the Imam's contending commitments. If in October 1985 he could call upon the cabinet to give the private sector more power, only to claim one month later that "the aim of the prophets was *not* to rule,"[48] how could his disciples chart a coherent political and social project? However, in 1987 things began to change. Indeed, Khomeini not only began to address fundamental political and social matters; but, in time, also emerged as one of the principal routinizers of his charisma. This dramatic shift was precipitated by the 1986 Iran-Contra affair. By implicating *Majles* Speaker Rafsanjani in the efforts of U.S. president Ronald Reagan's administration to sell weapons to Iran and thus momentarily threatening Rafsanjani's political survival,[49] the scandal emboldened the radicals. Despite the efforts of Azari Qomi and other advocates of a market economy, by the close of 1986 the conservatives had failed to block several reform bills championed by the radicals. Rafsanjani tried to prevent further polarization by again appealing to Khomeini. Karrubi's radical faction, he warned, was about to prevail, a development that would permanently divide the *Majles* while threatening the interests of the *bazaar*. In May 1987 Khomeini responded by advocating the dissolution of the Islamic Republican Party, which had served as a stronghold of radical activism.

It appears, however, that by the summer of 1987, Khomeini's heart ailment had weakened him. Sensing that time was running out, Rafsanjani asked Khomeini to back a labor law that the Council of Guardians had vetoed. But Khomeini refused to intervene. Instead, all he would do was allude to "Islam's mysticism, Islam's gnosticism, at the head of which are the spiritualities of Islam."[50] "This is a transitional world," he told *Majles* deputies, "everyone's time will come. I will part first, and you will follow later."[51] However, only two months later, Khomeini put aside such morose thoughts to give unprecedented attention to mundane political and social matters. Angered by the Council of Guardians' refusal to accept the labor law, he took the one step that he had long avoided:

in a blunt speech, he not only commanded the Council of Guardians to accept this legislation, but did so in words that unambiguously upheld the utilitarian prerogatives of government. "The state can," Khomeini insisted,

> by using this power, replace those fundamental . . . Islamic systems, by any kind of social, economic, labor . . . commercial, urban affairs, agricultural, or other system, and can make the services . . . that are the monopoly of the state . . . into an instrument for the implementation of general and comprehensive policies.[52]

This unprecedented intervention provoked a sharp rebuff from the conservatives. In a letter to Khomeini, Council of Guardians member Ayatollah Safi warned that the "people believe that this *fatwa* has opened the door to those who want to use it to bring about any kind of social or economic order."[53] This bold remark surely provoked Khomeini's wrath. Never before had one of his allies so openly challenged his judgment. But far from getting him to back down, such defiance seems to have prompted the Imam to extend the notion that the state could "replace those fundamental Islamic systems, by any kind of . . . other system" to its most logical extreme.

The occasion for this development arose as a result of a speech given by President Khamane'i. In an effort to deflate the radicals' aspirations by defending what he called "freedom in economic matters," Khamane'i asserted that "the executive branch . . . should have a permanent presence in society . . . *within the limits of Islamic laws and Islamic principles.*"[54] By implying that the government's actions were constrained by Islamic law, this speech angered Khomeini. Rebuking the president for failing to clarify that the *faqih* was not merely the interpreter of the law, but in some sense the *vehicle* of law itself, on 1 January 1988 Khomeini declared the following to a Tehran University audience:

> Government is among the most important divine injunctions and has priority over all peripheral divine orders. Your interpretation of what I said, that is, the government [or state] has jurisdiction within the framework of divine injunctions, is . . . contradictory to what I said. . . . The government, which is part of the total [or absolute] vice-regency of the Prophet . . . is one of the foremost injunctions of Islam and has priority over all other secondary injunctions, even prayers, fasting and the hajj. . . . The government is empowered to unilaterally revoke any lawful agreement . . . if the agreement contravenes the *interests* of . . . the country. It can prevent any matter, whether religious or secular, if it is against the *interests* of Islam.[55]

By equating the "divine injunction" of government with the "total vice-regency of God," and by asserting that the *faqih* could take any action to defend the "interests of Islam and the country"—interests that were ultimately defined by the *faqih* himself—Khomeini implied that the vice-regent of God had the authority to *create* both divine and secondary injunctions.

We have already seen that this formulation did not come out of the blue. Khomeini had long believed in the utilitarian tasks of government, and had used the term *interests* in that context as far back as 1941. And, as noted in chapter 3, after he invoked the term in a spring 1963 attack on the Shah, many of Khomeini's clerical allies began to use the concept of *maslahat* (expedient interests). Later, in the wake of the revolution, the ruling clerics frequently cited national/ideological interests to justify new legislation.[56] Even so, Khomeini's January 1988 edict took the term to unprecedented heights. He now appeared to have embraced an absolute utilitarianism that defied the most sacred principles of Islam—a utilitarianism implying that sovereignty belonged not to God, but to the *faqih* himself! How could this approach provide an enduring solution to the constitutional crisis that paralyzed his country? After all, despite its utilitarian aspects, the idea of an "absolute" or "total" *faqih* seemed to define the very essence of charismatic authority. The answer is that Khomeini's formulation was hardly definitive. For example, although he had spoken of the "total vice-regency from God," he had *not* linked this vice-regency exclusively to himself. Instead, he had tied it to a nebulous entity he called the "government"—an entity that was not only a "divine injunction," but also somehow "part of the total vice-regency of the Prophet." But Khomeini was unclear about what constituted "government," how it was "part" of the vice-regency, or who was to define state "interests." This ambiguity opened the door to the possibility that he was not speaking merely about the personal power of the *faqih*, but also about the institutional power of government itself. By design or default, then, Khomeini's vagueness set the stage for a struggle among competing *Majles* factions over his legacy.

For our purposes, we can divide this contest into three phases. The first phase, which we shall cover in the remaining pages of this chapter, unfolded during the last few months of Khomeini's life and the first few days after his death in June 1989. During this period the debate over his legacy was not about "big versus small state," but rather about *the very nature and role of the state*. While "institutionalists"—a loose alliance of radical, pragmatic, and conservative deputies—sought to routinize Khomeini's charisma in the *Majles* and government, the "charismatists" tried to rescue the idea of charismatic rule by defending the investment of all authority in the *person of the* faqih. Once this issue was apparently resolved through a wholesale amendment of the Constitution (discussed later in this chapter), the debate over Khomeini's legacy shifted to economic issues, and finally to more distinctly political matters. We will now turn to the first phase of this debate and see how it lay the groundwork for the dramatic constitutional reform of July 1989.

Khomeini's Legacy: The First Debate

While the contest to appropriate a charismatic leader's ideological legacy is a key feature of routinization, it usually begins in earnest only after the leader has died. This makes sense: to misrepresent that legacy during the leader's lifetime means courting his wrath. In the case of the Islamic Republic, however, that struggle began while Khomeini was still alive and in command. Indeed, the ink was barely dry on his 1 January 1988 edict when Rafsanjani and his allies in the institutionalist camp realized that it offered a potential solution to the crisis that had paralyzed the country. They saw that by tying the vague concept of the "total vice-regency from God" to a nebulous entity called the "government," Khomeini had left open the intriguing possibility that the "Rule of the Jurist" had as much to do with institutions as it did with the ruler's personal authority. As a result, Rafsanjani could plausibly argue that a reform of the Constitution that strengthened governmental institutions (even at the expense of the clerics) fulfilled the Imam's wishes!

The institutionalists wasted no time in exploiting this possibility. As Rafsanjani put it six days after Khomeini issued his edict, "The views expressed by . . . the Imam . . . illustrate the depth of his . . . leadership." The true "meaning of proper leadership," Rafsanjani claimed in an elliptical reference to Khomeini's populist utilitarianism, "is that leadership should respond to the call of the people." In answering this call, "the Imam's line has become clear": Islam must "demonstrate its power on essential issues of the state." In fact, Rafsanjani implied, this pragmatic principle had always been clear. "The day that the Imam graciously said: 'If the majority of the Majlis approves something' . . . the day that the Imam granted this permission, the issue should have become clear to everyone." By thus implying that Khomeini's words had affirmed the delegation of his authority to the *Majles* or the government, Rafsanjani tried to diminish the Ruling Jurist's power while appearing to defend Khomeini and the nation. "Today the views of the Leader are our final authority," he asserted. "If everyone accepts the Imam's line, there should no longer be any division among us."[57] Prime Minister Musavi then took a cue from Rafsanjani. In an interview with Tehran Radio, he expressed his delight with "the recent message of his excellency the Imam." The cabinet "treated this message seriously" because it "clarifies a great number of ambiguities" and enables "the holy system of the Islamic Republic to deal with the . . . problems it is facing." Thus it was time to "implement" Khomeini's "message" by forming "the required Majlis committees," and by appointing "revolutionary specialists who follow the Imam's line." Such a policy, Musavi added for good measure, was the foundation of the "Imam's *Islamic Government,*" which outlined a "concept of an Islamic government" capable of solving "various problems."[58]

Rafsanjani's opponents in the charismatist camp quickly grasped the transformation that was occurring under their very feet. "O Imam," they warned two days after Musavi's interview,

> The enemies of Islam and the opportunists made diverse interpretations regarding the response of the Master [Khomeini] and the query of the student [Khamane'i] which cast doubt in the minds of the divine nation. . . . In the name of defending . . . jurisconsult and Imamate, they had engaged in insinuation. . . . Their main aim was to . . . destroy the man who raised the call of the Islamic Revolution. . . . rather than to explain the absolute divine jurisconsult.[59]

But Rafsanjani's allies were unrelenting. On the very day that the above statement was issued, students at Tehran University proclaimed their absolute support for Khomeini: "With the statement of . . . the Imam . . . in which he described government as one of the primary principles of Islam, there is no longer any ambiguity in the Islamic government's plans for solving the country's economic and social problems."[60] Emboldened by this popular celebration of Khomeini's utilitarianism, Rafsanjani then gave an extraordinary sermon in which he pushed the Imam's 1 January declaration in a direction that Khomeini himself probably found dubious.

At the outset of his sermon Rafsanjani tried to outflank his opponents by implying that the dispute over Khomeini's words was merely a misunderstanding. There was no power struggle in Tehran as the foreign press had reported. Instead, the Imam was simply defining "the reality of *velayat-i faqih* and Islamic government . . . for it is something which is not yet clear to the people." But "if in the Imam's interpretation it transpires that some persons were correct and others were mistaken" (i.e., if it turned out by some fluke that Rafsanjani was correct and his foes were wrong), "then it was not what the Imam intended." After this clever suggestion that Rafsanjani's view of Khomeini was untainted by politics, the Speaker emphasized that the Imam's edict concerned the institutions and prerogatives of government. Government, Rafsanjani explained, "is responsible for implementing affairs and regulations." Thus, "the Majlis, as his holiness has repeatedly said, is above all affairs, it is the axis of things." Indeed, the Majlis was responsible not only for implementing laws, but also for passing "laws within the framework of Islam."

Although this notion was contestable, Rafsanjani directly addressed the controversy by making the very utilitarian argument that Khomeini had used. "Not all the laws which were implemented during the time of the Prophet were divine rules communicated in the Quran," he explained. Instead, "there were certain matters in governmental affairs which were left to the Prophet . . . as a ruler and vice-regent . . . that was his governmental authority."[61] The Imam's delegation of this authority allowed the *Majles* to pass such legislation. Mincing no words, Rafsanjani added:

> Our legitimate right to interfere comes from the Imam, since you know that this is the issue of *velayat-i faqih*. . . . I am Hashemi Rafsanjani. . . . I have no right to enact laws for people. I am their representative, yet I . . . do not have this right. The Imam can give me this right. *Velayat-i faqih* gives me this right. . . . The entire system's legitimacy stems from the position of the Imam.

Did the delegation of the Imam's absolute authority signal a new despotism? No, Rafsanjani insisted, "all those analysts who . . . reason dictatorship out of this are very wrong." *Velayat-e faqih*, he continued, had in fact created a "democratic system. . . . There are councils, the Majlis, and the right to vote. Decisions start with the people. They all have the soul of *velayat*. . . . So, as you see, democracy is present in a form *better* than in the West" (italics mine). Indeed, Rafsanjani concluded in words momentarily placing him closer to Gettysburg than Tehran, "the system is not moving towards . . . absolutism. . . . This healthy style of government of the people by the people, with the permission of *velayat-i faqih*, will continue."[62]

Although Khomeini had repeatedly declared the *Majles* to be "the head of the nation's affairs," it is difficult to imagine that Rafsanjani's bold assertion pleased him. While the term *democracy* had been used in the Preamble of the 1979 Constitution, and while the Islamic Left had bequeathed a Rousseauian notion of direct representation that many radicals favored, the Islamic Revolution's anti-Western credo had obscured the influence of such Western ideas on the *Majles*. As far back as 1984, however, Rafsanjani had reminded his fellow deputies of this tradition. Responding to the conservatives' assertion that a proposed tax bill was "un-Islamic," he observed, "You are sitting in Parliament. Where is the precedent for parliament in Islamic history . . . [or for] a president, cabinet or ministers, prime minister and the like."[63] But despite this prudent reminder, Rafsanjani had not spoken of democracy, a form of government that most clerics still equated with the "Great Satan." Yet by 1989 the times were changing. Although few of his allies were ready to speak of democracy openly, many echoed Rafsanjani's pragmatic focus on government. President Khamane'i, for one, declared that "the legitimacy of all bodies—legislative, executive or judicial—is a product of their affiliation with the rule of jurisconsult." Yet, the president added almost as an aside, "if the supreme jurisconsult gives some of these powers to a person or body, that person or body will possess [these] powers."[64]

Khomeini Supports the Institutionalists

By seizing the initiative, the institutionalists had created a political climate receptive to the notion that Khomeini's words required a reinvigoration of the *Majles* and a diminishing of the power of the high-ranking clergy. Although Khomeini's opinion of this development is difficult to determine, his actions and his words suggest that he did support Rafsanjani. In this way, Khomeini emerged as a primary routinizer of his own charisma.

One such act of routinization occurred in February 1988, following another demand by *Majles* deputies that Khomeini intervene against the Council of Guardians. Once again, Khomeini's initial response was to hesitate. Although he had done much to strengthen the *Majles*, he was still reluctant to oppose a body that mirrored his enduring belief in the moral leadership of the clergy. But a choice had to be made, lest the Imam sacrifice the very efficacy of the Islamic Republic. Thus he agreed to form a Consultative Council to Ascertain the Interest of the State (*Majma'-e Tashkhis-e Maslahat-e Nezam*).[65] More than any other ruling body, it enshrined Khomeini's vision of utilitarianism. Known as the "Expediency Discernment Council," it was empowered to override a veto by the Council of Guardians. What is more, in its original form it consisted of six members of the Council of Guardians, six deputies (including Rafsanjani and two of his allies, Khamane'i and Kho'eyniha), and the minister involved with the legislation being assessed. With the addition of this thirteenth member, the balance of power in the Expediency Discernment Council could potentially favor politicians over theologians. This power shift was demonstrated in the ensuing year, when the council repeatedly overruled the Council of Guardians' rejection of several social reform laws.

Khomeini also advanced the institutionalists' fortunes by backing the candidacy of technical "specialists" during the April and May elections for the Third *Majles*. Several weeks before the voting, Khomeini insisted that "the people act freely in these elections, they do not need guardians." The total absence in this speech of *any* reference to the clerical role in the elections suggests that Khomeini was issuing a subtle reproach to the clergy. The only advice from this "old father" (as Khomeini called himself) was that the people should vote "for those representatives who are committed to Islam, who are faithful to the people." The *Majles*, he again asserted, "is the house of all the people and the source of hope for the deprived."[66]

The election results seemed to follow Khomeini's wishes. The "professional clerics" (*mo'ammamin*, "those who wear the turban") lost nearly one-fourth of their seats in the 270-member assembly. Instead of the near majority of 122 seats they had in the Second *Majles*, the clerics won a paltry 71. Meanwhile, the laymen took an overwhelming 189-seat majority, 42 more than in the previous *Majles*. What is more, of the entire assembly, only 68 members had a traditional or religious education, as compared with 153 in the Second *Majles*![67] Khomeini appeared pleased with this outcome. In a message to the *Majles* read by his son Ahmad, he expressed his thanks to God that "the elections . . . were carried out in a sound manner." It was the "people's only desire," Khomeini insisted, "for the Majlis to resolve problems . . . and alter the country's extremely complicated administrative system." Toward this end, he instructed the *Majles* to "propound laws and bills in the committees on the basis of dear Islam" and give "priority to implementing the country's infrastructural policies."[68]

Toward Constitutional Reform:
The Limits of Complex Routinization

Over the ensuing six months the institutionalists obeyed the Imam's call to "alter the country's . . . complicated administrative system." Although the new Constitution did not provide for the level of coherent institutionalization that Rafsanjani may have wanted, this stunted form of routinization laid the foundation for the subsequent efforts of clerics and lay activists to push for more dramatic political reforms. Two factors encouraged Khomeini and the institutionalists to promote the revision of the 1979 Constitution: the increasingly desperate situation on the Iran-Iraq battlefront and the complex issue of succession to the Imamate.

We have seen that Khomeini's burning desire for revenge against Iraq, as well as his belief that the revolution's messianic fervor would either prevail or die on the battlefield, impelled him to pursue the Iran–Iraq War despite its terrible costs. However, by mid-1988, the Iraqis had scored several victories in this eight-year battle. The July 3 downing of a civilian jetliner by an American naval vessel—an act that Khomeini apparently believed was perpetrated deliberately by the United States to aid the Iraqis—finally convinced the Imam that the very survival of his Islamic state required ending the war. Some three weeks later, in a bitter speech, he accepted the United Nations cease-fire resolution:

> Accepting resolution [598] was truly a very bitter and tragic issue for everyone, particularly me. . . . At this juncture I regard it to be in the interest of the revolution and of the system. God knows that had it not been for the motive whereby all of us, our honor and credibility, should be sacrificed in the interests of Islam and the Muslims, I would never have agreed to this. Death and martyrdom would have been more bearable to me. . . . How unhappy I am because I have survived and have drunk the poisonous chalice of accepting the resolution.[69]

Having drunk this "poison," Khomeini turned to the political issue that he had not resolved in January 1988: the failure of the Constitution to provide the *Majles* with a clear basis of authority. Before he could do so, however, he had to deal with the task of endorsing his successor. Khomeini had already addressed this question in 1985 by signaling support for his loyal student, Ayatollah Hoseyn 'Ali Montazeri . However, by the late eighties, Montazeri's succession presented two problems, one political and the other constitutional. The political complication derived from the fact that by 1988, Khomeini's disciple had become a vocal critic of the government's human-rights violations and lack of democracy. In February 1989 Khomeini lashed out by sending Montazeri a letter warning him that "I shall not allow the government to fall into the hands of the *liberalha*."[70] One month later Montazeri resigned, thus leaving the problem of succession unresolved. This development also raised a basic constitutional issue. The two articles of the Constitution that specify the qualifications for being *faqih* had been tailored to Khomeini's charismatic specifications. They stipulate, among other things, that in addition to being a man of justice and superior political judgment, the *faqih* has to be *the* leading *marja'*, or religious "source of emulation." With Khomeini's death it was unlikely that any Iranian cleric—including Montazeri—would have the charismatic and traditional qualities necessary to be *marja'* and *faqih*. The Constitution had anticipated this problem by stipulating that in this event a "Leadership Council" of three to five Grand Ayatollahs was to be created. Nonetheless, not one high-ranking cleric (with the possible exception of Montazeri) accepted Khomeini's concept of the Ruling Jurist! Moreover, even if such a council could be formed, it was unlikely that it could replicate the authority of a single leader. As Ayatollah Azari Qomi put it, it was ridiculous to expect the masses to replace their acclamation for the Imam with "slogans like: 'We are your soldiers, Oh Council of Leadership.' "[71] Given that neither a qualified *marja'* nor an effective Leadership Council could assume the mantle of the Ruling Jurist, the only solution was to amend the Constitution so that it diminished the charismatic basis of the *faqih's* authority.

From Reconstruction to Constitutional Reform

In the winter of 1988 the institutionalists launched a campaign to gain the Imam's blessing for a revision of the Constitution that would provide the *Majles* with a clear basis of authority. To marshal public opinion, they linked this project to the fundamental issue of economic reconstruction. In a letter signed by President Khamane'i, *Majles* Speaker Hashemi Rafsanjani, Chief Justice Ayatollah Abdolkarim Musavi Ardabili, and Prime Minister Musavi, the reformers invited the Imam to issue a "ruling regarding the extent of their authority in the matters of reconstruction." Khomeini responded with a letter that gave the institutionalists the opportunity they sought. He began his message by insisting that the principle of "neither East nor West" guide reconstruction. But after reaffirming this familiar call for independence, the Imam added that the "strategy of reconstruction" was to be led by "experts, in particular cabinet ministers, the appropriate Majlis committees . . . scientific and research centers . . . inventors, discoverers, and committed specialists."[72] Encouraged, the institutionalists turned to the challenge of constitutional reform. President Khamane'i raised the issue in a Friday sermon in which he argued that "[t]he constitution is the embodiment and manifestation of the revolution." But there were "cases when a certain difficulty not foreseen by the constitution" would arise, as was demonstrated by the deadlock between the *Majles* and the Council of Guardians. In such cases, the president explained, the "chief jurisconsult creates an assembly . . . and says that the difficulty will be resolved through this body"—an implicit reference to Khomeini's creation of the Expediency Discernment Council. But, the president added (choosing his words carefully so as not to appear to be defying Khomeini), while this assembly was "not contrary to the constitution," and even "augmented" it, it did not resolve the Constitution's ambiguities. To drive home this point, Khamane'i *negatively* contrasted the practice of government in Iran with its Eastern and Western counterparts:

> In socialist countries . . . the party defines policy. In . . . Western democracies, the person who wishes to lead announces his policies. . . . The people [then] . . . vote for them. [But] in our society this is not the case. . . . The Constitution does not specify such an authority. . . . *We need a source of authority as well as a center*, an assembly, an organization to define the country's policies.[73]

Khamane'i's candor suggests the extent to which the need to rationalize authority had overtaken the familiar rhetoric of "neither East nor West." This bold critique was soon echoed by other *Majles* deputies. In a gathering at Tehran University's Department of Law and Political Science on 5 December, one hundred deputies addressed a letter to Khomeini in which they called for forming a committee to amend the Constitution. Three months later, the Imam responded by issuing a decree that created a "Council for the Reappraisal of the Constitution" chaired by Ayatollah Meshkini.

The participants in the May 1989 debate on constitutional amendments had at their disposal a decade of statements, speeches, and *fatvas* (religious edicts) by the Imam himself. Having articulated contending visions of authority, each side could draw on this rhetorical reservoir to make a case for or against a particular amendment. The institutionalists skillfully mined Khomeini's utilitarian legacy to justify the controversial proposal to separate the position of *marja'* from that of *faqih*. Consider, for example, the clever response of Prosecutor General Kho'eyniha to a reporter from *Keyhan*, a daily newspaper. Asked if the division of these two posts entailed "separating religion from politics," this longtime radical asserted that "[t]he question should be turned around." There is, Kho'eyniha stated, "no question of religious leadership being separated from a political one. [Rather], the issue is to see if the condition for being a leader is also to be a source of emulation." This, he asserted, was not the case, since selecting the *marja'* "is a personal matter, quite separate from affairs of the country or running the nation." This argument echoed Khomeini's utilitarian thesis that the qualities needed to perform the *function* of leadership were *extrinsic* to the leader himself. But Kho'eyniha did not stop here. Having suggested that the moral authority of the *faqih* flows from his actions rather than from any intrinsic attributes, he deduced that the separation of religion and politics would be prevented by the leadership's defense of religious values, not its reliance on the personal qualities of the *faqih*. "It depends on how much the *regime* pays attention to religion," he explained. "If the Islamic Republic . . . stresses Islamic principles, the Muslim people will support it." But if, on the other hand, "officials . . . deviate from religion," the "danger of religion separating from politics" would become real. Thus, Kho'eyniha implied, the paradox: those who held that the *faqih* should be the *marja'* were unwittingly promoting the separation of politics from religion! Mincing no words, Kho'eyniha warned that "[i]f, God forbid, there is a leader who is also a source of emulation, but who puts away religious principles, the people will start to have problems with him. At that point religion *will* separate from politics."[74]

Khomeini had never pushed this utilitarian argument to such a radical, if plausible conclusion. Instead, he had two contradictory wishes: keep the clerics out of politics, thus protecting the idea of an Islamic state from being soiled by the propensity of humanity for evil; and strengthen the clerics' moral authority as guides of the people. During the spring of 1989 the advocates of routinization not only cleverly exploited this and other loopholes in Khomeini's thinking, but did so during the very year that the Berlin Wall came tumbling down. In a sign of the times, the Council for the Reappraisal of the Constitution assessed several constitutions, including that of the United States, to aid them in rationalizing Iran's multiple document.[75] A decade after a revolution had spurned the "Great Satan," the leaders of the Islamic Republic again looked to the West![76]

Note that all of this occurred while Khomeini was still the *faqih*. Although it is possible that the institutionalists manipulated Khomeini's vision in a manner that defied his will—particularly given that his death occurred two months after the constitutional commission began its deliberations—there is little evidence to support this interpretation of events. On the contrary, Khomeini played a direct role in the overall process of revising the Constitution. He not only issued instructions for amending critical articles such as Article 109 (see below), but justified these and other changes by invoking the concept of *maslahat*, or expedient interests.[77] Thus it should come as no surprise that institutionalists such as Hadi Khamane'i (the president's brother) and Amid-Zanjani emphasized the close adherence of their positions to the guidelines laid out by the Imam himself.[78]

Such maneuvering clearly annoyed the charismatists. On the issue of the *faqih*'s powers, they insisted—in the words of an editorial in the newspaper *Jomhuri-ye Eslami*—that the "Imam's guidelines are extremely clear." But they expressed concern that the Council for the Reappraisal of the Constitution would "make a mistake" by stretching "the limits of responsibility . . . of key posts to take into account specific individuals who have performed at a high level."[79] By "specific individuals," the editorial was alluding to Rafsanjani, who had declared his support for strengthening the authority of the president by abolishing the position of prime minister.[80] Indeed, Rafsanjani's determination to create an independent executive was such that he had initially proposed *permanently* replacing the position of *faqih* with a "Leadership Council"! While this proposal was quickly dismissed, charismatists continued to worry that the more modest proposal to separate the positions of *marja'* and *faqih* would weaken the latter's authority. "Let us assume," stated an editorial in the daily newspaper *Ettela'at*, "that a future leader will not personally be a religious leader. . . . Then, if in his era there happen to be many distinguished, influential religious leaders . . . excelling . . . in scholarship, and popularity . . . how can we prevent the . . . evitable clashes . . . between them and the Leader?"[81] The institutionalists responded by affirming that the Leader' s authority derived purely from *rational* criteria. Thus, argued an editorial in *Keyhan*, since knowledge of the law was an important qualification for being Leader, "presence in political and social sciences" as well as "reputation for prudence and good management" should be emphasized in the revised Constitution.[82] Although this answer hardly resolved the very real problem of competing authorities within the executive branch as raised by Rafsanjani's opponents, the announcement of Khomeini's death on 3 June 1989 robbed the charismatists of their final court of appeal.

The Imam's passing was a painful event for the entire country. Attesting to this fact, the authorities kept Khomeini's corpse frozen for three days to permit millions of people to pay their respects in a field in northern Tehran before the body was moved to Behesht-e Zahra Cemetery in the southern part of the city. In the resulting frenzy Khomeini's shrouded corpse fell out of its open coffin and momentarily disappeared in the crowd—as if signaling that the people would not release their cherished hero. Yet the institutionalists acted swiftly. Although they mourned the Imam, they solidified their gains one day after his death by having the Council of Experts elect 'Ali Khamane'i Leader. They then enacted an array of amendments to the new Constitution, which was ratified by national referendum on 9 July 1989.

The 1989 Constitution

Mehdi Mozaffari has described the transmutation of Khomeini's authority as a transition "from paternalism to presidentialism."[83] This summary gives only part of the story, however. It is true that the new Constitution partly reinforced the president's authority; it did so by abolishing the position of prime minister, diminishing the independent authority of the Council of Guardians, and, most of all, separating the position of *marja'* from that of *faqih*. But in several ways the new Constitution also enhanced the *faqih*'s powers. For example, it transferred one of the president's key tasks, coordinating the three branches of government, to the office of the *faqih* (see below).[84] Moreover, the separation of *marja'* and *faqih* was a double-edged sword. Although this change undermined the *faqih*'s charismatic-religious authority, it created the real possibility that either the democratically elected president, and/or a *marja'* within or outside the clerical establishment, might develop their own charismatic following. Thus the traditionalization of Khomeini's authority in the *office* of the *faqih* perpetuated rather than transcended the phenomena of "dissonant institutionalization."

The attempt to create a presidential system is enshrined in Article 60, which abolishes the post of prime minister. This measure was designed to prevent the bifurcation of executive and legislative power that had paralyzed previous governments, and *did not* make the president more powerful than the Leader. Article 113 stipulates that the presidency was the "next highest official position . . . after [that] . . . of Leader." However, the Leader's position was weakened by changes in Articles 5, 107, and 109 that stripped him of his charismatic-popular base.[85] The original version of Article 5, it will be recalled, stipulated that the "leadership" was to "devolve upon the just and pious *faqih*," who was "recognized and accepted as leader by the majority of the people." The latter provision celebrated Khomeini's charismatic link to the people. However, the new version of Article 5 dropped all references to any popular acclamation of the Leader. Indeed, because the 1989 Constitution stipulates that the Leader is to be selected by indirect election (see below), the president emerged as the sole *elected* representative of the entire nation.

Article 109 picks up where Article 5 leaves off by redefining the qualities of the Leader in strictly rational terms. In its original form Article 109 stated that the Leader was to be a man of "learning and piety, as required for the functions of . . . *marja'*." In its new version the article demotes the Leader by dropping the criteria that he be

a *marja'*. Instead, it holds that the Leader should have the qualifications of "scholarship, as required for performing the function of *mufti*
in . . . fields of *fiqh*." To reinforce this point, Article 109 requires that
"in case of a multiplicity of persons fulfilling the above qualifications,
the person possessing the better jurisprudential and *political* perspi-
cacity will be given preference"(italics mine). It is worth reiterating
that Khomeini himself had directly promoted this change. Indeed, he
had written the chair of the Council for the Reappraisal of the Constitution, not only insisting that "we cannot let our Islamic regime go
on without a supervisor," but adding that "I . . . from the very beginning . . . insisted that the condition of the *marja'iyyat* was not necessary . . . a just *mujtahed* who is confirmed by the honorable experts . . .
will be sufficient."[86]

Article 107 reaffirms this critical shift from charismatic to traditional
authority. The original version of this article stated that a *marja'* was
to be recognized by a "decisive majority of the people." Where such
popular acclamation was not in the offing, the article stipulates that an
elected "Assembly of Experts" would either select a *marja'* or appoint
a "Leadership Council" consisting of three to five qualified *marja's*.
But in the new Constitution, Article 107 was completely rewritten.
Its opening paragraph implicitly affirms that the era of Khomeini has
passed; henceforth, the Leader would be chosen in a manner that broke
the bond between the people and the *faqih*:

> After the demise of the eminent *marja'-i taqlid* and great Leader of the uni-
> versal Islamic Revolution . . . Imam Khomeini—who was recognized . . . as
> *marja'* and Leader by a decisive majority of the people, the task of appointing
> the Leader shall be vested with the experts elected by the people.

These experts, the article continues, were to select a new Leader
from among the *fuqaha* (religious jurists), "possessing the qualifications
mentioned in Article 109"—in other words, the Leader was *not* to be
chosen from among the *marja's*, but rather from among religious scholars
having the requisite legal and political skills. As if the rational source
of the Leader's new authority required more emphasis, Article 107
concludes with the stipulation that "[t]he Leader is equal with the rest
of the people . . . in the eyes of the law."

The other crucial change in the Constitution concerned the Council
of Guardians. While the council's veto power was retained, Article 112
turns the "Expediency Discernment Council" into a *permanent* body.
Empowered to "discern the interest in matters arising between Parliament and the Council of Guardians," its membership was stacked.
By requiring the council to include two "temporary members"—the

cabinet minister most relevant to the issue in question and the chair of the relevant parliamentary committee—Article 112 all but ensures that the six clerics sitting on the council would be in a minority.[87]

While the new Constitution represented a step forward on the path to routinization, it also perpetuated the phenomenon of dissonant institutionalization. On one level the document provides one of modern history's most succinct examples of the institutional traditionalization of charisma. Under the new Constitution, the *faqih* inherits Khomeini's authority as the Supreme Leader. What is more, Article 110 includes an expanded list of the *institutional* powers of the *faqih*, including the following: (1) delineation of the general policies of the Islamic Republic; (2) supervision of the proper execution of the general policies of the system; (3) issuance of decrees for national referenda; (4) assumption of supreme command of the armed forces; (5) declaration of war and peace; (6) appointment, dismissal, and acceptance of the resignation of the *foqaha* on the Guardian Council, the supreme judicial authority, the head of radio and television, the chief commander of the Islamic Revolution Guard, and the supreme commander of the armed forces. In contrast, Article 113 specifies that the president is responsible for "implementing the constitution and acting as the head of the executive, except in matters directly concerned with [the office of] the Leadership." Yet if these provisions reinforced the traditional authority of *faqih*, by entrusting a president (who was no longer facing competition from a prime minister) with the task of "implementing the constitution," the president became the guardian of the constitutional order. Given that he is the only directly elected leader who represents the entire nation, it was possible that the President would acquire a measure of charismatic authority that was unavailable to the indirectly elected *faqih*.

No one could predict where this peculiar arrangement would lead. Rafsanjani's initial opposition to reintroducing the single-leader concept suggests that he feared that the president would face a *faqih* who was jealous of his popular authority.[88] It would be better to work with a Leadership Council than one wounded *faqih*—particularly since the latter was still the "supreme" authority. Yet this was not to be. In the end, all of Iran's presidents would have to live with a political system that left them with two uncomfortable options: exercise authority as the democratically elected guardian of the Constitution, thus risk alienating the *faqih*; or subordinate themselves to the Supreme Leader, and in so doing defer to traditional authority at the expense of the modern office of president and the constitutional authority of the *Majles*.

Summary: The Opening Skirmish

Despite the aforementioned shortcoming, the reform of the Constitution set Iran on a path from which there was no turning back. Henceforth, authority no longer rested in the hands of a manifestly charismatic man. Yet the routinization process that had begun in late 1988 was far from complete. The 1989 Constitution divided authority between a *faqih*, who derived legitimacy from a traditional office, and the president, whose authority derived from a modern, legal-rational institution. Standing between them were the Expediency Discernment Council and the Council of Guardians. Although the latter might be counted on to back the *faqih*, the ideologically heterogenous makeup of the former made it unpredictable. By thus perpetuating dissonant institutionalization in a new form, Rafsanjani and his allies ensured that the travails of complex routinization would continue for years to come.

Although an economic crisis aggravated by war set the stage for the constitutional reforms of 1989, it is difficult to ascribe Khomeini's decision to promote these changes to any one set of material interests. Sometimes he fought routinization with every mystical fiber in his body, while at other moments he abetted it. Such wavering stemmed from his multiple moral, social, and political commitments. Khomeini's 1 January 1988 edict on the "interests of the state" is a case in point. Why did he issue it? Some scholars argue that he wanted to strengthen the radicals, while others argue the opposite.[89] Ervand Abrahamian holds that Khomeini was a creature of the traditional bourgeoisie, but then writes that "Khomeini had issued his controversial 1988 decree . . . to strengthen the *étatists* against the *laissez-faireists*."[90] Further on in the same book he asserts that "Khomeini's intentions" were "not so much to undermine the middle class as to strengthen the Islamic Republic, which, in his eyes, was the main defender of the long-term interests of Islam, the sacred law, and thereby private property."[91] For what, then, did Khomeini make his charismatic strivings, and toward what end?

Among these various possibilities, Abrahamian's emphasis on interests seems the most persuasive. When finally pressed to choose between contending visions of authority, Khomeini chose in favor of the state—or, shall we say, the *system*. Facing failure on the battlefront and economic chaos, he drew on a conviction that he had articulated twenty years earlier, namely that "Islam came in order to establish order. . . . It is our duty to preserve Islam. This duty . . . is more necessary even than prayer."[92] The Imam may have not anticipated the paradoxical consequences that would ensue from his reiteration of this pragmatic principle in January 1988. But neither was he completely "defeated"—as one scholar puts it—"by the cunning of history."[93] Instead, his efforts to routinize his own charisma suggest that in the end, Khomeini selected the one interest that trumped all others: state or governmental authority.

Although Rafsanjani and his allies cleverly invoked Khomeini's January 1988 *fatva* to legitimate their agenda, his political victory owes as much to their rhetorical skills as it does to the fact that their focus on "interests" echoed the utilitarian aspects of the Imam's legacy. But Rafsanjani's success was also a product of material realities: after eight years of war, Iran desperately needed an executive having the authority to reconstruct the economy. Rafsanjani hoped that the private sector—of which he was a part[94]—would advance this change. Thus after his election on 28 July 1989, he appointed a cabinet that reflected his government's hopes for economic reform. The new cabinet was dominated by technocrats, no less than one-third of whom had studied in the West.[95] To the dismay of the radical members, these individuals sought to revive the private sector and enlarge the role of Western investment in the nation's overall economic development (with the exception of funds from the United States).

These events were paralleled by the selection of 'Ali Khamane'i as the new *faqih*. From Rafsanjani's perspective, this was an auspicious event. After all, Khamane'i had proclaimed his support for liberating the post of president from the constraints of a prime minister. "A single person must be in charge," he insisted in May 1989. "People must make demands of him, protest to him, hold him responsible. . . . This view relies on the popular vote, popular emotions, and demands."[96] Such enthusiasm from an unelected *faqih* who was not only "one among equals" but not even a qualified *mojtahed* (legal scholar) to boot, must have warmed Rafsanjani's heart!

However, as we shall now see, things would not go as smoothly for the new president as the reconstructionists (those within the ruling elite who backed Rafsanjani's plans for economic reform and reconstruction) had envisioned. Rafsanjani's efforts in 1991 and 1992 to recast the Imam's legacy in a manner that legitimated a further rationalization of the economic system did meet with some success. Even so, he had to contend with a multifaceted legacy that was preserved in the Constitution and the very workings of the *Majles* itself. Thus spring 1989 turned out to be merely the opening skirmish in a protracted battle to reshape the Imam's legacy. Neither Rafsanjani nor the new *faqih* could foresee the paradoxical paths that this struggle would take during the first few years of the Iranian Second Republic.[97] It is to this subject that we now turn.

7 Children (and One Father) of the Revolution

> After the triumph of the Islamic Revolution and the fateful events of the eight-year sacred defense . . . the death of the founder of the Islamic Republic, and the leadership of Ayatollah Khamanei, the most fateful historic event is establishing the uniform foreign exchange rate.[1]
>
> —*Majles* Deputy 'Ali Zadsar, January 1993

> I was the first casualty in a suspicious and mysterious attack aimed at the children of the Islamic revolution. Today the time has come for more casualties, and I am certain that sooner or later the other friends of the Islamic Revolution and the Imam [leader of the Muslim community] will have their turn.[2]
>
> —*Majles* Deputy Behzad Nabavi's letter to President 'Ali Akbar Hashemi Rafsanjani, April 1992

Traditionalization versus Radical Islamism

And so it came to pass that twelve years after the Islamic Revolution, after the many sacrifices and hardships suffered by Iran's youth, *Majles* Deputy Zadsar reached the staggering conclusion that the "most fateful historic event is establishing the uniform foreign exchange rate." Zadsar made this claim some months after President Rafsanjani and Supreme Leader 'Ali Khamane'i had purged the *Majles* of many radicals. Determined to silence the critics of a controversial economic reform program, Rafsanjani stood by as conservative clerics accused former Minister of Heavy Industries Behzad Nabavi and other radicals of undermining the revolution's Islamic principles. Stunned, Nabavi sent Rafsanjani an open letter in which he recounted his stalwart efforts to defend these values and warned that the "children of the . . . revolution" were being purged by the very state that they helped to create.

To students of revolution, this story has a familiar ring. Most regimes that have aspired to utopia have inevitably produced their own Robespierres. Yet the persecution of the persecutor *can* have a salutary effect.

Confronted by a growing chasm between reality and dogma, the occasional true believer might be induced to reconsider the ideals that
animated the revolution in the first place. In the wake of the 1989 revision
of Iran's Constitution, some observers expected that Rafsanjani would
play this role. His references to a democracy "of and by the people"—
with, of course, "the permission of the *faqih*"—had raised such hopes.
Theoretically speaking, such a development would have made sense.
Max Weber argued that under some conditions, routinized charisma can
become the handmaiden of democratic ideology. As he puts it, "when
the charismatic organization undergoes . . . rationalization, it is readily
possible that, instead of recognition being treated as a consequence of
legitimacy, it is treated as the basis of . . . *democratic legitimacy*."[3] Yet even
if this process has a certain intrinsic logic, it is hardly inevitable. As
Juan Linz and Alfred Stepan remind us, in post-totalitarian societies,
reformers face an imposing legacy: an ideology that retains a "social
presence" in the institutions and founding documents of the revolution.[4]
Overcoming such legacies not only requires new political alliances, but
also demands "soft-liners" who have the skills to legitimate and advance
reform *without* antagonizing the "hard-liners," those for whom even the
hint of change constitutes a slippery descent into chaos.[5]

Although the first skirmish over Khomeini's legacy suggested that
Rafsanjani had the talent to push that legacy in a more democratic direction, it soon became clear that he had neither the allies nor the personal
desire to do so. On the contrary, with Supreme Leader Khamane'i's
support, the new president manipulated Khomeini's ideas to legitimate
a project that was economically liberal, politically authoritarian, and
philosophically traditional. This "traditionalization" strategy—echoes
of which could be found throughout the Middle East—provoked a
hostile response from *Majles* radicals.[6] They used Khomeini's letters,
edicts, and speeches to discredit the economic, social, and ideological underpinnings of Rafsanjani's "reconstruction" program. With this
counterattack, the battle over Khomeini's legacy shifted into high gear.
In the ensuing decade, every effort to routinize the revolution occurred
under the imposing if ambiguous shadow of the late Imam.

This chapter traces this second stage in the battle over Khomeini's
legacy and evaluates how it helped reshape the ideological contours of
post-Khomeini Iran. While highlighting what Ahmad Ashraf has called
the "disintegrative" potential of Khomeini's charisma,[7] I will endeavor
to demonstrate that the process by which the Imam's legacy fragmented
into its constituent parts was *not* wholly random. Indeed, if the 1991–
92 purges encouraged some children of the revolution, and one of its
fathers, to advance a more democratic—even liberal—interpretation

of Khomeini's legacy, this development owed much to a utilitarian and populist logic that was central to the Imam's dissonant ideological vision.

I begin by analyzing the rhetorical contours of Rafsanjani's traditionalization strategy. Two factors—both of which stemmed from the enduring effects of dissonant institutionalization—pushed the president to adopt this plan. First, as we have seen, the new Constitution did not coherently routinize authority. While it weakened the *faqih*'s (Supreme Leader's) charismatic authority by separating his post from that of *marja'* (religious guide), it strengthened his powers. This situation caused a dilemma: although Rafsanjani's direct election gave him a popular base far wider than the *faqih*'s, any attempt to enhance his democratic credentials might be seen as an effort to diminish Khamane'i's authority. As a result, this constitutionally blessed arrangement created an institutional incentive for cooperation between the president and the *faqih*.

Second, the dissonant institutionalization of conservative and radical factions in the *Majles* pushed Rafsanjani to back the conservatives. Because the new *faqih* was merely "one among equals" and lacked the personal charisma to contain this conflict, the radicals felt free to assail Rafsanjani's economic reforms with abandon. These attacks antagonized conservative deputies, many of whom favored the president's reforms, while at the same time depriving Rafsanjani of the political allies he needed to enact a political reform program. Thus the president responded not by promoting greater openness, but by insisting that Khomeini's legacy required *absolute* loyalty to the *faqih*. In this way he played a leading part in "manufacturing" Khamane'i's charisma. The radicals answered this retraditionalization strategy in two ways: first, they engaged in what might be called "recharismatization." Casting the Imam as a quasi-divine figure, they held that the government's social, political, and economic policies should be based solely on Khomeini's edicts, speeches, and *Last Will and Testament*. Second, they invoked the *Majles'* constitutionally decreed authority to evaluate and criticize the actions of the executive. They held that neither Rafsanjani nor the *faqih* could make policy without considering the view of the *Majles*. These two strategies backfired by encouraging the *faqih* and the president to cooperate with each other all the more. The subsequent purge of radical *Majles* deputies by the conservative clerics in the months leading up the May 1992 elections provoked a storm of protest. Suddenly, a language that had rarely been used on the *Majles* floor now made itself heard: the language of individual rights, personal freedoms, and ideological pluralism. Although riddled with ambiguities and inconsistencies that mirrored its self-serving function—as well as the enduring effects of dissonant institutionalization—the fact that this hobbled vision of political and ideological pluralism was legitimated by invoking the Imam's legacy suggests that by 1992 the Islamic Republic was already moving in new directions.

Capturing the Imam's Legacy: Rafsanjani Anticipates the Radicals

In the fall of 1989 newly elected President Rafsanjani announced that his cabinet would push for a revised Five Year Plan that called for an expansion of the private sector through the privatization of public-sector assets, the repatriation of capital, and the promotion of foreign investment.[8] This break with the populist policies of former Prime Minister Mir Hoseyn Musavi's government was bound to provoke protests. Although Rafsanjani no longer had to contend with a prime minister, his allies in the pragmatic-conservative camp numbered some 90 deputies, while the radicals held 160 seats.[9] Moreover, the prevailing socioeconomic conditions made market reform dangerous. Although Iranians generally supported reconstruction, reform was bound to harm the many groups that benefited from state subsidies, and who had vested interests in a highly protected economy, the major assets of which had been 85-percent nationalized.[10] Armed with this knowledge, the *Majles* radicals began to stir up trouble months before Rafsanjani announced his reconstruction policy. The 19 August 1989 dismissal of Interior Minister 'Ali Akbar Mohtashami foreshadowed this turn of events. A former ambassador to Syria and proponent of exporting Iran's revolution, he greeted his dismissal with this caution: "Our enemies, the U.S. and the West, will only be satisfied when Islam and the Islamic Revolution are annihilated." Implicitly linking Rafsanjani to this agenda, Mohtashami warned that "offering any new plan and principle contrary to [the Imam's] principles is a blatant violation of the Imam's clear path."[11] To head off this challenge, Rafsanjani had to demonstrate that his conception of economic and political reconstruction would honor the Imam's vision of social justice and economic independence—no simple task. His "reconstructionist cabinet" was hardly revolutionary: 12 of the 22 nominees were new, 7 of them had doctorates, 9 were engineers, and only 4 were clerics. Worse still, 6 had been educated abroad, 4 of them in the United States![12] Although radicals complained that these nominees lacked "a good revolutionary record," Rafsanjani nevertheless mustered a vote of confidence for his cabinet by emphasizing that the new *faqih* supported his policies—a claim that foreshadowed his dependence on the conservative clerics.[13] But this momentary victory hardly resolved Rafsanjani's key ideological challenge, namely to align his policies with the Imam's populist legacy.

Rafsanjani had long anticipated this problem. Indeed, he began a campaign to capture the Imam's legacy only four days after Khomeini's death. Addressing a people still in shock, he explained that "while the Imam belonged to all of us . . . we have the right to judge . . . because we were witnesses to the . . . Imam's mental imaginings and his wishes."[14] Having asserted his interpretive credentials, he then gave an account of the Imam's biography, the object of which was twofold: first, to suggest that Khomeini's legacy was far more complex than might otherwise be assumed—and thus imply that only his closest disciples had a right to interpret it; second, to suggest why Ayatollah Khamane'i was Khomeini's rightful heir. In enumerating the Imam's many dimensions, Rafsanjani began by describing his "talent, which differed very much from ordinary people." Clearly this gift had a charismatic quality: "It was that which forced one to be persuaded. . . . Whoever asked him a question would become certain." Yet Rafsanjani was careful to add that this talent was *not* divine. "I do not want to suggest that His Graciousness should have the position of the Prophets or the Imams," he declared. "But how should I put it? It is that among ordinary people, such a person stands out. He really had faith." Rafsanjani described this faith in ways that echoed Khomeini's notion of "extrinsic" infallibility. The late Imam's ability to "persuade" his followers rested on *actions* that prepared the "groundwork" *(zamineh)* for his message. "Miracles are exceptions," Rafsanjani asserted. "God does not rule the world through exceptions. He rules . . . in accordance with laws and regulations, and with unchanging *traditions*." Khomeini's life exemplified this rationalist logic. During each stage, from his early education, his years of "seclusion" and contemplation, his struggle against the Shah, and finally his emergence as the conscience of the people, the Imam prepared the groundwork for what was to come. Thus it followed that the Imam had carefully prepared the political field for his death by "directing the issues of leadership towards a specific path": a successor who would emulate the Khomeini's activism by demonstrating an equal capacity for *political* leadership.

To bolster this argument in favor of a rational conception of the *faqih*'s power, Rafsanjani read his audience the letter that Khomeini had written Ayatollah Meshkini, who was then chair of the Committee for Reappraising the Constitution. The letter began by stating the principle that Khomeini had indicated should guide the revision of Iran's Constitution, namely that "whatever the gentlemen deem to be in the *interests* [of the regime], then they may act accordingly." Yet the Imam was not content to leave the utilitarian function in the hands of clerics whose training was strictly religious. Instead, Rafsanjani argued, Khomeini had specified that "you must elect an individual who can defend our Islamic honor in the world of *politics and deceit*." To emphasize the political nature of the *faqih*'s authority, Rafsanjani resumed reading from the Imam's letter: "Since the very beginning . . . I insisted that the condition of *marja'iyat* was not necessary. The just *mujtahid* [legal scholar] who is confirmed by the honorable experts . . . will be sufficient." By thus emphasizing that Khomeini himself had initially opposed the idea that the *faqih* should be *marja'* (religious guide), Rafsanjani gave this separation of religion and politics the seal of Khomeini's charismatic authority. This done, he then delivered the coup de grace. The Imam, Rafsanjani asserted, wrote that "[i]f the people vote for the experts . . . and they appoint an individual to take over the leadership . . . that [entails] a pledge of allegiance [*bey'at*]. . . . In such a case he becomes the elected *vali* [guardian] of the people."

This was a daring statement. The notion that the indirect election of the new *faqih* would replicate the charismatic pledge of allegiance that the masses had once sworn to Khomeini was a stretch. Indeed, the Assembly of Experts had been empowered to select the new *faqih* precisely because the clerics wanted to monopolize this decision. Yet however implausible, because Khomeini had argued in his letter to Meshkini that the Assembly of Experts' selection of the *faqih* constituted the people's choice, Rafsanjani could give this assertion the Imam's blessing. Having done so, the president then made an even bolder claim. The so-called election of the *faqih*, Rafsanjani argued, made it "incumbent upon the *marja'* to obey" the *faqih*! Thus, although the new Constitution separated the positions of *faqih* and *marja'*, and although the authority of a *marja'* derived in part from the strength of his popular following, Rafsanjani clearly implied that the political authority of the *faqih always* took precedence over the religious authority of any *marja'*.

This crucial point established, Rafsanjani then got to his main concern, the issue of succession. Again invoking his privileged access to Khomeini, Rafsanjani asserted that during a meeting with the Imam, "the head of three branches, Ayatollah Ardebili, myself, the Prime Minister, Hajj Ahmad Aqa [Khomeini's son] and our present leader" asked Khomeini who would fill the "leadership vacuum." At this point, the Imam "pointed to Mr. Khamanei." This inclusion of Khomeini's son Ahmad in Rafsanjani's story was important. Knowing that Ahmad's testimony would bolster his account of Khomeini's actions, Rafsan-jani emphasized that Ahmad told him of his father's belief that 'Ali Khamane'i "is truly worthy of the leadership." Thus the *isnad*, or chain of testimony, was clear: Khomeini had chosen Khamane'i to succeed him.

Rafsanjani concluded by warning his listeners against questioning the new *faqih*'s qualifications. Unwittingly giving credence to those who did, he held that "[w]e do not have even a grain of doubt that the leader . . . we have selected is a *mujtahid*." Moreover, the "Imam's words" clearly showed that this *mojtahid* had to have a wide array of practical talents. "The *mujtahid* in the seminary . . . cannot as easily issue an edict about shortcomings in banking . . . as one who is responsible in administration." Indeed, Khamane'i's "familiarity with national is-sues . . . is far more important than all the other conditions such as the struggle, knowledge, justness and others."

Traditionalizing Khomeini's Legacy: The Quest for "Revolutionary Reconstructors"

Rafsanjani had certainly gone a little overboard. Khomeini may have declared in January 1988 that the interests of the state were superior to religious obligations; and while he had often said that knowledge of religion was a necessary but *insufficient* condition for leadership, he had never argued that having a "familiarity with national issues" *took precedence* over being a just *faqih*. Yet while cleverly using Khomeini's legacy, Rafsanjani had not betrayed it. If in the ensuing two years he and Khamane'i effectively invoked the Imam's words, this success stemmed from Khomeini's rich legacy, of which an emphasis on national issues and political expediency was merely one part. This said, Rafsanjani and Khamane'i went out of their way to argue that only certain priv-ileged people had the requisite grasp of Khomeini's life to elucidate this complex legacy. For example, in November 1989 Rafsanjani stated that Khomeini was an "exceptional person" because he had combined the study of "jurisprudence, philosophy, mysticism and morals." Al-though his love of mysticism had "remained hidden," Rafsanjani held that since the Imam's "life was the source of scrutiny and study for me," he (Rafsanjani) could fathom these mysteries.[15] Six months later Supreme Leader Khamane'i made a similar case. "It would be wrong," he warned,

> to say that one can only detect what the Imam really had at heart by looking at his political vision. What the Imam truly believed can be grasped by

looking at all aspects and dimensions of his being and thought . . . such as his political cries, mystical poetry, his smile, or even when he shed a tear.[16]

Khamane'i's warning to look beyond the Imam's "political vision" notwithstanding, the key dimension of Khomeini's legacy that the reformers emphasized was anything but mystical. As Rafsanjani put it in a speech to the nation, "the only solace is the fact that I heard the report and the content of the decree from the voice of . . . [Ahmad Khomeini] . . . my comrade in arms." The essence of Ahmad Khomeini's message was that the Imam "used to solve problems." Although "God's prophet had departed," there was no reason Iran could not "keep the same principles, lines, and rules. . . . I believe that the new, competent, efficient and revolutionary management will . . . unravel all the knots which now exist."[17] The *chief* manager, Rafsanjani maintained, was Khamane'i, and he thanked God that "we now have a leader who is familiar with the country's pain."[18] Khamane'i repaid the compliment. Noting that "you witnessed how our great Imam used to praise the government again and again," the *faqih* invoked Khomeini's utilitarian legacy to issue this warning: "We expect the Majlis, while maintaining its freedom . . . to observe the *interests* of the country and the expression of its views."[19]

This reference to freedom not withstanding, the key question was, which institution had the *ultimate* right to define and defend these interests: the executive or the legislature? In the coming months Rafsanjani and Khamane'i seemed to have this response: the "freedom" of the *Majles* was subordinate to the *faqih's* right to define "interests." Sometimes this answer was expressed rather circuitously. For example, during his 17 August 1989 speech marking the convening of the new *Majles*, the new president declared, "I personally have always hated dictatorial despotism." Acknowledging that "we have not been able to give" constitutionally guaranteed rights such as "freedoms and respect [for] individuals" to "the people," Rafsanjani quickly added that this situation had prevailed because the "people themselves have . . . opted *not* to ask" for these rights! Such self-sacrificing behavior was necessitated by the eight year-war with Iraq, he explained. Thus, while "job opportunities have been foreseen by the people," it was only now—with the end of the war—that the conditions had finally allowed Iran to achieve these "rights" and thus to "achieve economic independence."[20]

This quest for "economic independence" had long been central to the Islamic Revolution, particularly the ideology of the radicals. Rafsanjani's use of this phrase signaled the intent of his government to appropriate it for its own agenda. Henceforth, "social rights" and "economic independence" would be equated with market reforms, and with a distinctly nondemocratic approach to securing such reconstruction. Thus Rafsanjani made the following argument: "The Prophet used to say: 'Poverty is the source of shame in this world' . . . especially deliberate poverty, not imposed poverty." By "deliberate," Rafsanjani implied that bad economic policies created self-inflicted poverty. Such policies precluded independence, since "anybody who is in need will not be independent." Enumerating a familiar list of inefficiencies associated with state-led development, he observed that the government was buying sugar "from our own . . . mills" for forty tumans and selling it for twenty-seven. As a result, the state had created a "dependent industry" that had to be bailed out by running a budget deficit. The only solution to this bitter paradox was to "go through a stage" of production-driven growth that was backed up by a plan to reduce the inefficiencies of government bureaucracy. What then remained of his call to give the people their constitutional rights? Having equated these rights with jobs rather than with political rights, Rafsanjani implied that the struggle for social rights would *not* be accomplished democratically. Economic reform, he asserted, could only be achieved with "serious cooperation and fellowship . . . between executive officials, Majlis deputies . . . the judiciary, and the people themselves."[21] Echoing this patrimonialist vision in religious and utilitarian terms, Khamane'i insisted some days later that in the "*interests* of the people . . . support for . . . the top officials in the country is absolutely essential. Weakening it is a religious taboo *[haram]*."[22] Of course, there was no question that this call for solidarity was in line with Khomeini's wishes. "You saw during the time of the dear Imam," Khamane'i asserted, "how he placed emphasis on the support of the people for the officials. . . . It is the same today."[23]

Still, even the *faqih* could not deny that after ten years, the revolutionary flame that had burned in the hearts of the youth was now flickering. "Do not let the spirit of revolutionary zeal . . . die," he instructed.[24] But what would keep this flame from dying out? In his quest to inspire the kind of charismatic love that Khomeini had enjoyed, Khamane'i faced a dilemma that confronts all postrevolutionary regimes: how to sustain zeal while ensuring that it doesn't subvert social order. The solution was to associate the very concept of revolution with the regime's reformist economic agenda. For example, while Khamane'i insisted that "the younger generation . . . does not have the right to forget" the "bloody days" precipitating the revolution, he added that "the best reconstructors are *revolutionary* reconstructors."[25] To give this revisionist line as much revolutionary authenticity as possible, Khamane'i aimed it at those groups most associated with Khomeini's charismatic legacy. Thus in a speech to the Grand Assembly of the *Basij*, or Mobilization Corps (a wing of the Islamic Revolutionary Corps), Khamane'i maintained that "if during the reconstruction period, the government can . . . enable the Islamic system to provide answers for the material and spiritual needs of the nation . . . the greatest blow will be delivered to world arrogance." In other words, the superpowers would henceforth be humiliated by the triumph of economic progress. As a result, "the mobilizers of the faithful . . . should regard reconstruction . . . as their goal, in addition to . . . the revolution." That this message was delivered in the vast mausoleum that housed the "immaculate tomb of His Holiness Imam Khomeini" (in the words of the press report) was not lost on those attending the meeting. Stepping up to the lectern, the president reiterated the link between Khomeini and the regime's economic policies. "At the outset of the Revolution the founder of the IRI [Islamic Republic of Iran] . . . paved the way for the entry of the best members of society into the arena of *jihad* [holy war or effort], selflessness, and reconstruction [*sazandagei*]." Having equated *jihad* with reconstruction, Rafsanjani noted that with twenty thousand of its members entering the universities in 1989, the *Basij* could spread the "spirit of resistance and selflessness in education" as it had "in all fronts."[26]

The "front" that mattered most was the economy. In a Friday prayer sermon on "principles of production and work," Rafsanjani seemed to echo Weber's *Protestant Ethic and the Spirit of Capitalism*. Those who believe "that religion does not give serious consideration to production and proliferation of society's wealth" were propagating an "un-Islamic viewpoint." Islam, the president maintained, fully attended to "such rationalities." Had the Prophet not "kissed the coarse hands of a worker . . . to stabilize the cult of labor?" Commenting on the Arabic word *'amal* (which, he claimed, means both "work" and "worship"), Rafsanjani then asserted that the Prophet believed that work constituted a form of worship. Thus the failure to spread the "cult of labor" had nothing to do with Islam. "The problem lies with our society, our culture," Rafsanjani insisted. "We must remove this obstacle," not merely by "eliminating those psychological problems," but by applying a reformed "attitude" to the "unhealthy economy." In this way Iran would create "an independent society" and realize the "guidelines of our great demised Imam."[27]

The Radicals Respond: Recharismatization I

Farzin Sarabi has noted that the radicals were united more by their opposition to Rafsanjani's policies than by a clear set of common priorities.
Some, such as *Majles* Speaker Ayatollah Mehdi Karrubi and Ayatollah
Musavi Kho'eyniha, sought to promote mass political participation and
maintain state control of the economy. Others, such as Mohtashami and
Hojjat al-Eslam Sadeq Khalkhali, focused on opposing the West.[28] Yet
it would be a mistake to minimize their shared values. Most radicals
saw themselves as the defenders of 'Ali Shari'ati's revolutionary Islamic vision—a vision that, they claimed, *fully accorded* with Khomeini's socioeconomic and political legacy. Seeking to revive this equation
in June 1990, Hadi Khamane'i (the *faqih*'s brother), Abolhasan Ha'eri-
Zadeh, Asadollah Bayat, and Mohammed Ebrahim Asghar-Zadeh held
a seminar, "Shari'ati and the Renaissance of Islamic Thought," at Tehran
University. Getting to the heart of the issue, Bayat said, "Had our great
Imam not distinguished between the Pure Mohammaden Islam and the
American Islam, some of Shariati's writings would not have been prop-
erly understood." In other words, Khomeini had recognized Shari'ati's
quest to transform Islam into a revolutionary *maktab* (ideology), thus
taking it out of the hands of those who had viewed it merely as a spiritual
religion (i.e., "American Islam").[29] The radicals' mission was to protect
this legacy. This meant championing the *mostaz'afin*'s (disinherited's)
socioeconomic rights (or opposing market reforms); defending national-
cultural independence (or opposing any reconciliation with the West);
and articulating the collective will of the people (or opposing those who
sought to skirt their will).

The radicals possessed many institutional assets, such as *Majles*
deputies, control of powerful organizations such as the *Bonyad-e Shahid*
(Martyr's Foundation), and a dominant role in the Students Following
the Line of the Imam, the militant group responsible for taking American
hostages and occupying the American Embassy in 1979. Seeking to
coordinate their actions, in fall 1989 several radical clerics founded the
Association of Combatant Clerics of Tehran. This organization (whose
main opponent was the conservative Combatant Clergy Association)
was headed by Speaker Karrubi, who also chaired the Martyr's Foundation. Yet while these organizations offered an effective vehicle for mass
mobilization, they did not provide a solution to the central *ideological*
challenge facing the radicals: how to oppose the regime's economic
policies without appearing to question the *faqih*'s authority as "Supreme
Leader." The radicals' first solution to this bind was to sanctify Khomeini's legacy. The Imam's words and statements, they argued, constituted

a kind of divine revelation, the timeless authority of which could not be contradicted by any mortal—*including* a living *faqih*. Although this position invited ridicule from Rafsanjani's allies—who, as we shall see, *correctly* observed that Khomeini's theory of *velayat-e faqih* ("Rule of the Jurist") was meaningless without the people's readiness to obey the commands of a *living faqih*—the radicals pursued this deification strategy to its logical end.

Interior Minister Mohtashami had the audacity to pursue this plan of action. In a speech marking the martyrdom of Imam Hoseyn at the hands of Sunni Caliph Yazid, he began his remarks by placing Khomeini in the line of the infallible Imams. "One of the achievements of . . . the *maktab* of Husain," Mohtashami asserted in Shari'atist language, "is the negation of the hegemony of arrogance and the evil of Yazid and other Yazids of history." The latter reference was to contemporary "Yazids" such as the United States, the primary representative of world "arrogance." Courageous defiance of this enemy was the key to following in Hoseyn's footsteps:

> A person who utters the word "God" with faith . . . is freed from the clutches of every kind of slavery. . . . Such a person becomes the manifestation of divine power . . . the Imam . . . that great spirit of God, who negated the United States. . . . Thanks to . . . the prophetic leadership of our late Imam . . . the front of justice is known in the world arena today with an ever-increasing power.

This remark carried with it an implicit rebuke: any leader who defied this legacy of opposition to contemporary Yazids lacked "divine power."[30] Encouraged by Mohtashami's defiant words, other radicals soon emulated him. Thus, only a few days after the minister's speech, Kho'eyniha declared, "The ultimate and greatest goal for a human being . . . is to ascend the pinnacle of servitude to God. . . . The secret of the amazing and miraculous victory of the Imam was in this fact. . . . This is the rare characteristic of divine leaders, not the characteristic of any leader in any revolution." Having issued this oblique critique of "any leader of any revolution," Kho'eyniha focused on the charismatic quality of Khomeini's legacy. "There is no doubt," he said, "that one of the valuable legacies of this revolution has been the . . . world-wide confrontation with global arrogance." Yet the ultimate purpose behind confronting the United States was not to create any particular order. "The Imam's objective . . . was the implementation of religious obligation, not the establishment of the Islamic Republic of Iran." He did this by defying the Shah and the United States, thus creating a "divine movement so emotional, so heroic, so deep and vast that today the Imam . . . is the Imam all across the world."[31]

The Radicals Respond II:
Asserting the "Constitutional" Rights of the *Majles*

These remarks did not intimidate Rafsanjani. By fall 1989 his government had not only unveiled a new Five Year Plan, but also was exploring the possibility of renewing ties with a host of lesser "Satans," including Saudi Arabia and France. There was even talk in Tehran of a thaw in diplomatic relations between the United States and Iran.[32] As these developments unfolded, the radicals intensified their assault on the president. One of the first signs of this came during a debate over the case of Roger Cooper, a British citizen who had been jailed for spying. In a letter signed by 110 deputies, radicals assailed Judiciary Chief Ayatollah Mohammad Yazdi for discussing the possibility of clemency during a meeting with Cooper's sister-in-law. Although Supreme Leader Khamane'i had endorsed the meeting, Khalkhali asserted, "If the release of Cooper had been in the interest of the revolution, the Imam would have personally taken a decision." Insisting that "we cannot release a person whom the Imam had not released," Khalkhali implied that the late Imam's authority took precedence over that of the living *faqih*.[33]

While this de facto deification of Khomeini may have stirred some souls, it presented a number of practical problems. It not only implied defiance of the *faqih* and perhaps even of Khomeini's wishes (see below), but also suggested that the very group proclaiming its desire to solve the social issues of the day was obsessed with a memory. To effectively challenge Rafsanjani's government, the radicals had to show that Khomeini's legacy also gave them a *constitutional and timely right* to assert their authority over the government (and, by implication, the *faqih*). The Roger Cooper controversy offered an occasion upon which to make this case. Responding to Judiciary Chief Yazdi's claim that the judiciary had sole discretion over this case, Deputy Asadollah Bayat insisted, "The Majlis has every right to interfere in each and every affair relating to the government." Indeed, Bayat even asserted, "No other branch of government but the legislature has the right to determine the policy [of the government] and strategy of the entire ruling system." Thus, he warned, "we will resist any violation of the constitution."[34] At the same time, Deputy Khalkhali reassured his colleagues that this defense of *Majles* "freedoms" did not flout the *faqih*'s authority: "I have not seen . . . any deputy who has intended to disobey the orders of the leadership, [which are] a duty for us." That said, Khalkhali added—almost casually—that such loyalty "does not mean that advice shall not be given." In this spirit he recalled that "there was a time that the Imam sent Mr. Ahmad [Khomeini] . . . to the Majlis three times to get a vote of confidence for Mr. Mir Hussain Musavi." In other words, the Imam had repeatedly backed the radicals. Insisting that "the Majlis cannot be emptied of revolutionary people," Khalkhali implied that those who backed this goal were tools of the United States. "The hand that is trying to eradicate the revolutionary people is the hand of America. . . . That hand must be cut off. . . . We learned the way of struggle from our Imam."[35]

This truculent statement suggests that despite the risks, by mid-1989 the radicals had set upon an irreversible course. Thus on the tenth anniversary of the November 4 storming of the American Embassy, the Association of Combatant Clerics of Tehran declared that "the preservation of our revolutionary rage against America . . . will show that the path of the 'Great Khomeini' did not end with his death."[36] Yet it turned out that young people were more interested in soccer than in expressing their "revolutionary rage." Instead of joining anti-Western rallies, many stayed home to watch the live broadcasts of the Peace and Friendship Cup! The radicals were certain that such apathy resulted from the efforts of nefarious characters in state-controlled media to divert attention from Khomeini's revolutionary legacy. Declaring November 4 "National Anti-Imperialism Day," they reminded the public of the central role that the student-occupiers of the American Embassy had played in defeating the "group [which] insisted that the . . . youth return to their homes and leave the management of the revolution's affairs to them." Having vanquished "both America and the moderate lines . . . [with] the decisive support of his holiness the Imam," Deputy Hasan Habibi insisted that the "children of the revolution, who have . . . the legacy of that great divine man in their hearts . . . keep the spirit of struggle with America alive." This required that the "nation's executive organizations . . . not permit imposters, people who believe in the West . . . to . . . persuade the people to silence and isolation."[37]

These statements were aimed at Mohammad Hashemi Rafsanjani, director of the Voice and Vision Broadcasting Company (henceforth VV) and the president's brother. Mincing no words, one deputy asked whether "our cultural propaganda tools were being used to keep alive the Imam's sacred principles?"[38] Echoing this sentiment, another deputy chastised media officials for ignoring the *Majles*. While that body had "designated November 4 as the 'National Day for the Struggle against

Imperialism,' " the VV had reserved Sports Day for that very date! "I wish to remind Majlis deputies," he added, "that after the leadership, the Majlis is the highest authority and it is *other* people who must obey [it]." Speaker Karrubi agreed: "Our enemies should know that November 4 is the day of struggle against aggressors. . . . The policies of the IRI are the same as those that the Imam defined for our officials."[39]

The Imam's Will versus the Constitution: The Limits of Sanctification

As the above account suggests, an inherent contradiction ran throughout the radicals' position. On the one hand, they wanted to exalt the Imam by insisting that the government's policies should follow his edicts and commands to the letter. On the other hand, they claimed that as the representative of the people, the *Majles* had the constitutional right to make policy in the present—over, and perhaps against, the wishes of the *faqih*. Left unexplained was how the radicals' evocation of Khomeini's charisma was to be reconciled with the right of any other state institution to exercise *its* constitutional powers—not least of which were those accorded the *faqih*.

This contradiction became glaring during the fall of 1989 and into winter 1990, a period during which the radicals pressed their constitutional-rights argument while redoubling their efforts to deify Khomeini's legacy. The first occasion for this effort was the debate over Rafsanjani's Five Year Plan. Responding to the incessant lampooning by Rafsanjani's allies in the *Majles* of former Prime Minister Musavi's economic policies, radical deputies proudly defended his reputation by linking his name with that of another Musavi. "Our father and leader," one deputy cried, "when you, the great Ruhollah Musavi [Khomeini], departed, the Musavis of your line [i.e., Prime Minister Musavi] were also dismissed." After that, "some divided your legacy . . . and told us: 'This broken pot for making soup is mine, this ladle of sweets is yours.' " Worse yet, this same capitalist group "encourages us to eat . . . the forbidden wheat" of foreign debt. They want us "to be driven out of the paradise of your Islamic revolution. . . . O Imam, O Leader! . . . In the Third World . . . the oppressors infiltrate through gold, power or trickery and then devour . . . the pure blood of the revolutionaries. Let us be . . . careful about borrowing!"[40]

In the ensuing months, radical deputies continued to press their case. However, their attacks failed to discredit Rafsanjani. Lacking any credible alternative, and most likely aware that the people would blame them if the *Majles* failed to make headway on the president's reconstruction program, some of these deputies endorsed the government's Five Year Plan. Still, the radicals did not concede defeat; instead, they pursued their assault on Rafsanjani's policies by reasserting the constitutional rights of the *Majles*. The December 1989 visit of the Romanian dictator Nicolae Ceauşescu to Tehran offered an ideal opportunity to do so. Ceausescu was scheduled to meet with Supreme Leader Khamane'i during the very week that Romanian police were shooting protestors. Several days before the planned meeting, the radicals assailed the Foreign Ministry—and by implication Khamane'i—for inviting the despot. Leading the attack, Khalkhali declared that "the Iranian Republic, as a protector of the oppressed . . . should not have received a bloody dictator on its soil."[41] These remarks were echoed in a slew of editorials, all of which emphasized a point that the *faqih* surely grasped: as the newspaper *Jomhuri-ye Eslami (Islamic Republic)* put it, "any effort" that contradicted the "revolutionary, Islamic and popular nature of the Islamic Republic" was "unacceptable."[42] Several days later forty-five deputies summoned Foreign Minister 'Ali Akbar Velayati to answer questions about the affair. Capturing the mood in the *Majles*, Seyyed Hadi Khamane'i insisted that "the Majlis and the deputies, based on the Constitution, have equal rights before the nation."[43]

The radicals' actions clearly worried the *faqih*. In the wake of their criticisms, he not only canceled his meeting with Ceauşescu, but also gave a speech that echoed the radicals' populism. Thus Khamane'i noted that "in our revolution, we understood . . . from the outset . . . that . . . any system that is not based on the people's will . . . will meet the same fate [as Romania's system]." Yet practically in the same breath, the *faqih* added that "the nation must pay attention to . . . the unanimity of words . . . and the effort to build the country." This required a strong state, along the lines suggested by Khomeini. "To follow our great Imam," Khamane'i declared, "I strongly oppose the weakening of institutions which shoulder sensitive duties, including . . . our foreign affairs. . . . Today, the banner of Islam . . . cannot be preserved if you engage in rows among yourself. . . . You must preserve unity."[44]

No one misunderstood the *faqih*'s point. Indeed, Rafsanjani seized upon Khamane'i's speech to strengthen the authority of his government and make clear his total loyalty to the *faqih*. "We hope the fatherly reprimand which was heard today will be the last of such affairs," Rafsanjani declared. "Henceforth, everybody must . . . move within the limits of the views of the leadership."[45] Similarly, the Association of Qom Seminary Clerics issued a statement applauding Khamane'i's remarks, while the Combatant Clergy Association declared that his speech had a "deep impact, like the wise guidance of the great Imam . . . on the hearts of the followers of the school of Imamate and Velayat." Not to be outdone, Judiciary Chief Yazdi declared that "God has ranked obedience to the vice-regent in an equal position as obedience to God and the Prophet."[46] Some 130 deputies subsequently echoed this sycophantic loyalty in a letter pledging absolute loyalty to Khamane'i. But suddenly a problem surfaced. To the dismay of the regime, a majority of deputies failed to sign the letter to Khamane'i! This embarrassing development emboldened the radicals. Led by Speaker Karrubi, they launched a campaign that successfully prevented the letter from being read on the *Majles* floor.[47] Karrubi then convinced 217 deputies to sign a second letter that displayed a more independent spirit. "It is clear to everyone," the deputies affirmed in this communication, "that the vice regency of the jurisconsult is *one of* the indestructible pillars of the sacred system . . . and that it is *among* the religious and revolutionary duties of . . . this nation to support it." After giving this equivocal pledge, the deputies then asserted that the Imam himself accorded supreme authority to the *Majles*:

> after the vice regency of the jurisconsult . . . comes the Majlis, which is granted some 40 specific rights . . . under the Constitution. His eminence Imam Khomeini . . . described the Majlis as "the supreme power," "the head of all affairs," the "essence of the nation's virtues" and "the center of all powers and laws. . . . Naturally, all these powers are within the framework of preserving the system's general interests and contributing to the implementation of popular sovereignty.

Such defiance left many deputies uncomfortable. Fearing Khamane'i's wrath, thirty-three legislators who had signed the second letter then tried to give it a pro-*faqih* spin by attaching a separate note to it. "I have read the text of the letter," wrote 'Ali Akbar Nateq-Nuri, "which appears to be more a discussion of supporting the leader than of supporting and defending the Majlis." While "the Majlis seems to have been put on the same level as the Leader," Nateq-Nuri added that "the Leader is one thing and the Majlis is another. . . . Anyway, the part concerning support for the Leader is approved."[48]

The central lesson of the Ceauşescu affair was that the radicals could not wrap themselves in the reassuring warmth of their constitutional rights without provoking a legitimate counterattack from the *faqih* and his allies. Perhaps it was this sobering lesson—combined with the continuing successes of the Rafsanjani-Khamane'i alliance—that led the radicals to once again employ their deification strategy during the early months of 1990. Now, however, this plan reached unprecedented heights. Instead of arguing that all of the Imam's words and edicts should dictate the parameters of socioeconomic policies (a position that offered a wide berth for reinterpreting Khomeini's ideas), the radicals specified that his *Last Will and Testament* furnished the *sole* guidelines for determining economic, social, and political policy.

This effort to imbue Khomeini's *Will* with supreme revelatory authority was not totally far-fetched. Khomeini had described his thirty-five-page, handwritten testament in grandiose terms, insisting that it was intended as a "recommendation to all Muslim nations."[49] When the *Will* was issued in June 1989, its publishers echoed this grandiosity by concluding a short biography of Khomeini with these words: "Imam Khomeini is no longer with us . . . but his spirit is very much alive, and his . . . commands continue to guide millions of Muslims around the world for ever."[50] But this was not all. The language of Khomeini's document accorded with the radicals' revolutionary, anti-Western agenda. Downplaying the Imam's many dimensions, the *Will* repeated Khomeini's familiar call to combat "deviant elements" at home, including the "capitalists, land-grabbers, and the upper class," and the "Shaytanic powers" abroad.[51] The imperative of fighting these domestic and foreign enemies dominates the *Will*, even eclipsing its passing reference to *velayat-e faqih*. Stripped of all nuances, this document could be offered as an authentic expression of the Imam the masses knew best: a charismatic revolutionary who struggled to topple all expressions of modern and traditional authority.[52] Thus only one month after pledging his support to the *faqih*, Speaker Karrubi stated that the "political, economic and cultural bases that the Imam propounded . . . in his *Will* are important. . . . The provisions of the will are for the post-imam period . . . the Imam's principles . . . are to guide the people after him."[53]

This new deification strategy soon ran headlong into the central theoretical contradiction to which it had always been vulnerable: one could not argue that the Imam's *Will* superseded Khamane'i's authority without denying the core premise of *velayat-e faqih*, namely that authority should rest in the hands of a *living faqih*. Rafsanjani's allies seized on this contradiction to mock the radicals' sanctification of Khomeini. Thus Ayatollah Ahmad Azari Qomi, publisher of the conservative daily newspaper *Resalat*, held that Karrubi's remarks "indicate his inadequate information about our dear departed Imam's culture regarding the absoluteness of the vice-regency." Is it "in the Imam's *Will*," he asked, "that all his orders regarding anyone or anything continue to be implemented until judgment day?" That this position negated the essence of the Imam's wishes—and even the very will of God—was not surprising. After all, Azari Qomi implied, the radicals' deification of Khomeini was little more than a rationalization of their selfish interests:

> The people recognize . . . the group obstructing Mr. Hashemi-Rafsan-jani's . . . programs. What answer will they give God? What answer will they give the Imam? Do they think they are dealing with . . . a stupid nation? Have the people forgotten the Imam's exhortations. . . . The Imam said: "On my behalf, tell my revolutionary offspring that extremism will yield bad results."

Having reminded his opponents of Khomeini's supposedly natural proclivity for moderation, Azari Qomi got to his main point: "Ayatollah Khamanei," he explained, "and his auspicious leadership have the dear Imam's endorsement . . . they have absolute *velayat*," and thus the "power of the Majlis, the Cabinet, the judiciary, the Armed Forces, and everyone else." Given this authority, Azari Qomi asserted in another dig at his opponents, can it be claimed that the "absolute *velayat* pertains basically to two people? Is it possible that during the Imam's life, he was the absolute *velayat* as well as Ayatollah Khamanei?" Such a notion was ludicrous. "Had this same logic prevailed after the Prophet's death, it would have implied that 'Ali's leadership constituted a "sacrilege regarding the holy Prophet." In other words, it would have obviated the need for leadership, a need which was at the very heart of Khomeini's revolutionary Shi'ism! "By the same logic," Azari Qomi intoned, "where is the need for the Imam? This is Americanized Islam . . . according to which some people ignore the Leader's . . . rulings on the pretext of using 'the Imam's traditions.' . . . By using his eminence the Imam . . . they are ignoring his most important precept—the rule of Islam." In branding his foes advocates of "Americanized Islam," Azari Qomi was not merely turning the tables on his rivals. Instead, he *correctly* implied that the radicals had stripped Islam of its most vital element—its ability to rule through the authority of the Leader. This had to be a *living* authority, not one relegated to the heavens. By placing the Leader beyond man's reach, by in effect rendering unto Khomeini what was his and unto Caesar what was Caesar's, the radicals had Christianized Islam, in defiance of Khomeini's legacy. Those who *truly* wanted to "love the Imam," Azari Qomi added, "should implement his most important bequest . . . the rule of the supreme jurisconsult, which to-day is on his Eminence Ayatollah Khamenei's shoulders with all its absoluteness."[54]

Embracing a Father of the Revolution: From Political Offense to Political Purge

In mid-April 1990 Grand Ayatollah 'Ali Araki issued a *fatva* (religious edict) in which he declared that "in regard to morning prayers, there is no difference between moonlit and other nights."[55] Seemingly innocuous, this ruling was in fact potentially momentous: its issuance constituted the first time that a "source of emulation," or *marja'*, had directly contradicted one of Khomeini's decrees since the Imam's death in June 1989. The Constitution's separation of *marja'* and *faqih* had made this circumstance possible. Lacking the qualifications of a *marja'*, Khamane'i did not issue a single religious ruling during his first four years as *faqih*! Although this did not prevent some of his closest allies, such as Judiciary Chief Yazdi, from advocating his selection as *marja'*, Khamane'i's lack of religious stature was such that the regime had little choice but to endorse Araki for that position. From the regime's perspective, this decision made sense. Given that Araki was one hundred years old, in frail health and thus unlikely to challenge Khamane'i, the *faqih* could endorse Araki *providing* that he limited his edicts to strictly religious matters—such as whether worshipers should wait for the light of dawn before starting morning prayers. Moreover, since leading clerics such as President Rafsanjani and Judiciary Chief Yazdi had pledged their absolute loyalty to Khamane'i, the *faqih*'s position as supreme guide was completely secure. This said, the relationship between the *marja'iyyat* and *faqih* was hardly settled by late 1990. Given that the authority of a *marja'* rested as much on his scholarship as on the scope of his popular following, it was possible that a charismatic *marja'* might earn a following eclipsing that of the *faqih*. While few clerics had the qualifications—or the guts—to cultivate this kind of authority, there was one who was capable of acquiring it: Ayatollah Hoseyn 'Ali Montazeri.

Although Montazeri was one of the fathers of the Islamic Revolution, Khomeini had effectively silenced him in March 1989. Several events prompted this action, not least of which was Montazeri's support for Mehdi Hashemi, a relative who had embarrassed the government two years earlier during the Iran-Contra affair. However, it was Montazeri's repeated public criticisms of the government's human rights record that led to his political demise. While these criticisms were partly motivated by a desire to protect his family, Montazeri's words were not prompted by pure opportunism. Indeed, from the early days of the revolution, he had displayed a certain ambivalence with regard to Khomeini's theory of *velayat-e faqih*. Thus in 1979 he proclaimed, "The people's right of self-determination . . . means that they choose whom they wish." Though he admitted that this principle could not be applied comprehensively to the selection of the *faqih*, Montazeri insisted that the people "choose the ruling jurist, directly or through the experts."[56] In the ensuing years he tried to maintain some distance from the regime's repressive policies. Thus it is reported that in 1984 he initially rejected Khomeini's request that he succeed him as *faqih*, insisting instead that the choice of successor be left to the Assembly of Experts.[57] Two years later, and several months *before* the arrest of Mehdi Hashemi for his role in the Iran-Contra affair, Montazeri told intelligence officials that "we must be moderate towards the people" and not undertake "extremist actions."[58] One month later he not only again warned the regime that it should "not monitor the people so much," but also defended the notion of cultural pluralism. "One woman is without a veil," he noted, "another wears it badly. Do not expect everyone to be the same. . . . We must make allowances and look the other way."[59] Two years later, in a move that antagonized Khomeini and his clerical allies, Montazeri gave a series of lectures in Qom—published in the pages of the daily newspaper *Keyhan*—that offered a pluralistic view of Islamic government. These lectures presaged a bolder critique of the regime. Following the execution of several thousand political prisoners during the autumn of 1988, Montazeri sent Khomeini two letters in which he faulted the Imam for having failed to "take note of how your orders, that concern the lives of thousands of people, are carried out."[60] Then, in an interview published in *Keyhan* in early 1989, he challenged Khomeini in language that helped seal his political fate:

> The denial of people's rights, injustice and disregard for the revolution's true values have delivered the most severe blows against the revolution. Before any reconstruction [takes place], there must first be a political and ideological reconstruction. . . . This is something that the people expect of a leader.[61]

While this audacious letter left no room for a reconciliation between Montazeri and the Imam, in the summer of 1989 Khamene'i, the new *faqih*, invited Montazeri to resume teaching in Qom. Apparently, the regime hoped that the senior cleric would now keep quiet. But this was not to be.[62] By December 1989 Montazeri's supporters were distributing "night letters" that questioned Khamene'i's qualifications to be *faqih*.[63] Islamic Revolution Guards responded by detaining and humiliating Montazeri, forcing him to wear his nightcap rather than his white turban.[64] Prosecutor General Hojjat al-Eslam Mohammad Mohammadi Reyshahri added fuel to the fire by threatening Montazeri's followers for making remarks that Reyshahri claimed were designed to "weaken the system."[65] Given that Reyshahri had recently been appointed the head of the Special Clerical Tribunal—a body created in 1987 following the Iran-Contra scandal—his attacks suggested that the regime was determined to prevent Montazeri and other senior clerics from allying with *Majles* radicals against the *faqih*.

In the ensuing weeks several developments induced the regime to escalate its attacks on the radicals. As a result, the very alliance that Rafsanjani wanted to prevent now became more likely. The first of these developments occurred during the December 1989 midterm elections, when the regime suffered a major symbolic defeat: several of its outspoken critics, including Mohtashami and former Minister of Heavy Industries Behzad Nabavi, won seats in the Tehran electoral district. Prior to that, the regime had tried to isolate these radicals by dismissing Mohtashami from the cabinet (as we have seen) and by trying to disqualify Nabavi from running for the *Majles*. Having failed on both fronts (Nabavi's disqualification was overturned by the Council of Guardians), the regime braced itself for the inevitable counterattack. Iraq's August 1990 invasion of Kuwait and the West's ensuing bombing campaign provided the occasion: although Rafsanjani and his foreign ministry remained neutral, Mohtashami and Khalkhali embarrassed the president by calling upon the *faqih* to declare a *jihad* against the United States and its allies. This was followed by further attacks on Rafsanjani's economic policies and overtures to Western financial institutions. These assaults compelled the president to reinforce his alliance with the conservative clerics. Ominously, the Council of Guardians disqualified nearly all radicals candidates from the fall 1990 Assembly of Experts elections because they had failed to pass written and oral tests in Islamic jurisprudence![66]

This action turned out to be merely the regime's first strike against the radicals. In July 1991 the *Majles* passed an amendment to the election law that made absolute loyalty to the *faqih* a condition for running in *Majles* elections. Since Article 99 of the Constitution gave the Council of Guardians the power to supervise these elections, the radicals concluded that the regime planned to make them pay a heavy price for having challenged Khamane'i's authority. Four months later their suspicions were confirmed. Rafsanjani's supporters pushed for an "expanded" interpretation of Article 99, according to which the Council of Guardians could actively judge a candidate's eligibility, rather than merely supervise the elections. With elections for the Fourth *Majles* scheduled for April 1992, the handwriting was on the wall.

Rather than retreat, the radicals sought the very alliance that the regime wanted to prevent. In a not-so-secret trip to Qom, one hundred deputies visited Montazeri. Upon their return, Deputy Morteza Alviri gave a defiant speech. After lambasting the regime's Five Year Plan, he told the *Majles* the following:

> The matter of following a source of emulation is not something that can be spelled out in orders. . . . A point of pride in Shi'ism is the "freedom of emulation." . . . Thus no one can ask me—or some 80 to 100 . . . deputies, who independently of any political line follow the esteemed source of emulation His Holiness Grand Ayatollah Montazeri—"why do you follow him?"

Indeed, Alviri insisted, such support for "His Holiness Grand Ayatollah Montazeri" was consistent with the Imam's wishes! After all, in his letter of dismissal to Montazeri, hadn't the Imam reassured him, "God Willing, with your teaching and discussions, you will give warmth to the seminary and the government." If then "we are committed to the Imam's advice . . . how can a meeting with someone who was mentioned in this way . . . be taken as a 'plot against the commands of His Holiness the Imam?' " Such a position, Alviri added, not only defied the Imam's will, but also contradicted the Constitution, which stipulated that "the rank of 'source of emulation' has become separate from the Leader."[67] The regime's sharp response was encapsulated the next day in a *Jomhuri-ye Eslami* editorial. "The status of *faqih* and source of emulation," the paper warned, "cannot resolve . . . [those] incidences . . . [when] people who are pursuing their own private political goals can make the best use of such titles." In short, religion was one thing and politics another! The deputies' visit to Montazeri was a "political maneuver . . . carried out by self-interested . . . parties" who could not possibly claim fidelity to Khomeini's legacy. "The Imam," the editorial continued, "is that figure who when placed alongside zero, zero becomes more than nothing. . . . Deputies . . . without commitment . . . to the Imam's line, even when there are 100 of them, are 100 zeros." Worse still, these "zeros" had misrepresented the Imam by citing his words out of context. After all (the editorial *correctly* observed), Alviri had failed to read that part of the letter in which Khomeini had told Montazeri to "purge your house of unsound people." Excluding these words, the paper sarcastically observed, made as much sense as repeating the hallowed phrase "There is no God but God" *without* the last two words! Such sophistry could not hide the truth. Insisting that "[y]ou understand the Imam's intent very well," the paper warned Alviri and his allies that they could not have it both ways: pledge "obedience to the Leader" and still try to prevent "the successful implementation of the Five Year Plan."[68]

The visit to Montazeri was the last straw. As vice-president for parliamentary affairs Attaollah Mohajerani put it, "The Islamic Republic cannot afford a tug of war between the *Majles* . . . and the administration."[69] Citing that portion of the electoral law that required candidates to show "practical commitment to Islam and to the Islamic government," and invoking the government's enhanced interpretation of Article 99 of the Constitution, the regime purged many of its most determined critics. In the winter and spring of 1992 nearly one-third of the 3,150 candidates were rejected. These included 39 incumbents from the Third *Majles*, most of whom were attached to the radical faction Association of Combatant Clerics of Tehran. To the radicals' dismay, Khalkhali, Nabavi, Bayat, and Hojjat al-Eslam Hadi Ghaffari were sent packing because they lacked the proper "Islamic" credentials![70]

From Islamic Republicanism to Islamic Liberalism?

This purge was hardly as violent or as decisive as the one that many radicals had meted out to their "liberal" enemies a decade earlier. Indeed, despite the regime's meddling, Karrubi, Kho'eyniha, and Mohtashami ran in the April 1992 poll. This said, the government's efforts to discredit the radicals did discourage voters from supporting them. Prevented from joining the only institution from which they could formally represent the people, many children of the revolution were condemned to a kind of internal political exile that for a few would be permanent.[71] Subsequently, some *Majles* radicals began to protest. For example, in a speech he gave in February 1991, Speaker Karrubi asked how the government could insist that candidates demonstrate "practical commitment to Islam and the government" without "specifying" the "limits" for such conditions. He said this demand was "problematic," since "anyone can say that others . . . have or do not have this qualification according to his views, his likes and dislikes."[72] Karrubi, it seems, had learned the hard way that arbitrary rule respects no ideological boundaries. Having made this discovery, he and his allies sought to defend themselves by invoking several political ideals against which they had long fought. Because this implicitly liberal defense signaled the beginnings of an ideological shift within a core constituency of the revolutionary state—and because this shift was legitimated by invoking Khomeini's dissonant ideological legacy—it merits our critical attention.

This change unfolded on the *Majles* floor both before and after the May 1992 elections.[73] Deputies expressed their concern about a range of issues, including the rule of the law, the separation of powers, individual (as opposed to collective) rights, and cultural or ideological pluralism. Making a case for the rule of law was relatively easy. After all, regardless of their ideological affiliation, all deputies agreed that their duty was to follow the sacred commands of the *Shari'ah* (sacred law of Islam). As for the radical deputies, they had always given this traditional notion a populist-utilitarian twist by insisting that the people expressed divine law through the agency of the *Majles*. Pushing this idea one step further, several of these individuals expressed a view that seemed suspiciously akin to the Western notion of "natural law." Thus one deputy insisted in November 1991 that "the law . . . is something that has sprung from within the people. . . . This also means that instead of people supervising the law, the law supervises everything." This being the case, "we must close the doors to all types of individual manifestations when writing new laws. . . . We all recall that in the last few months of his life the Imam announced clearly that we must all move in the direction of implementing the constitution."[74] Echoing these thoughts, another deputy held that there was also a practical reason for respecting "lawful criteria in political, economic and social affairs." If, he noted, "appointments, dismissals, and praise do not follow a specific law, the result will be that every time a group or faction gets into power . . . they will decide to eradicate their political opponents." This situation would plunge "the nation's affairs in disarray." Under such conditions, the people would "become disappointed and turn away from officials—and everyone will lose."[75]

Among the most vociferous advocates of this argument were those deputies whose political fortunes suffered as a result of the state's abuse of the law and the judicial institutions charged with upholding it. Speaker Karrubi, who had recently been investigated by the Special Clerical Tribunal for "financial corruption," boldly challenged the government one month before the elections. He insisted, "We must always remember the guidelines of the Imam" by assuring that "during elections, executive officials, supervisors sent by the Council of Guardians, and their representatives . . . regard all candidates in the same manner." Zeroing in on his target, he added that "as an old soldier of the revolution," it was "necessary to issue a warning." The "respected Council of Guardians," he declared, "has the duty not to come under pressure. It must keep its neutrality." If, instead, it acts "in favor of one faction . . . then we, too, will carry out our duty. . . . We will speak with the Leader."[76]

These warnings had little effect on the government. As a result, the radicals focused on two themes, the defense of which proved a bit more tricky: individual freedom and personal and/or civil rights. We have seen that the idea of freedom had long played a central role in the lexicon of the revolution in general, and the Islamic Left in particular. But the radicals had conceived of freedom in Rousseauian terms, insisting that these rights should be subordinated to the will of the majority. But now there was a subtle shift away from this collectivist tradition. For example, having been informed of his disqualification by the Council of Guardians, Deputy Yadollah Eslami explained, "I speak for the sake of the threat to social liberties and for the sake of justice." Eslami's choice of the phrase "social liberties" was probably a defensive maneuver employed to deflect the charge that he was defending individual liberties and thus emulating a Western or "liberal" agenda. But his meaning was clear. "In which court," Eslami intoned, "and where in the world is a person . . . deprived of his social rights without being informed of the crime or being tried? Does this conform to justice?" Deputy Ghaffari concurred. "What has happened to a number of people," he noted, "including myself," was a violation of rights. "What religious or rational justification," he asked, "is required for the violation of the rights of these individuals?"[77]

The theoretical problem with this position was obvious: having played a part in legitimating the notion that the clerics had the right to define such "rights" for the *umma* (Islamic community), Ghaffari and his colleagues were not well positioned to suddenly assail the abuse of this practice. Acknowledging this point, Ghaffari admitted, "I happened to defend the clerical tribunal and recognized it as legitimate, which is how I feel today." Yet, he added, "I accept it as a religious organization, and I have no complaints. I only object to the verdict that was issued."[78] By contrast, Sadeq Khalkhali—who had earned the nickname the "hanging judge" by presiding over dozens of "revolutionary tribunals" during the early years of the revolution—objected to the very idea that the Council of Guardians or Special Clerical Tribunal had a right to question his actions. After complaining that one of his critics had threatened to "DDT whoever does not agree with . . . [my] tastes,"[79] Khalkhali reproached another deputy for asserting that "because you [i.e., Khalkhali] killed many people in the revolution courts . . . you do not have the right qualifications to be in the *Majles*." If this reasoning were correct, Khalkhali pointed out, "then the Imam 'Ali . . . would also not have enough credentials, because he also did such things to many people." Proudly recalling his bloody role in the revolution, Khalkhali implied that it was sheer hypocrisy for his opponents to suddenly assert that his previous actions had violated human rights. The real difference was that his critics were now in the driver's seat, whereas Khalkhali and his allies were the *true* defenders of Khomeini's legacy. "As God is my witness," he declared, "the Imam put in writing that, 'I will not forget your actions favoring the movement and the revolution.' "[80]

As we have seen, this evocation of Khomeini's charismatic legacy hardly provided deputies with a sound basis upon which to defend their individual or civil rights. To make a compelling argument, the radicals had to show that the Constitution protected these rights. In theory, making this case seemed simple; the Constitution contained many articles that protected the rights of freedom of speech, assembly, and even due process. However, as noted in chapter 5, these rights were qualified by the caveat that they could not conflict with the interests of the community or of Islam. Since the *faqih* and his allies in the judiciary ultimately defined these interests, the radicals could not defend their position by resting their case solely on such qualified rights. Instead, they had to prove their argument by embracing political norms that were *universal*. Anticipating this ideological shift, Deputy Morovatollah Partow made the following remarkable statement:

> Since Montesquieu and other political and social thinkers raised the issue of the separation of powers, the evolutionary course has evolved and become more complete, to the point that as far as possible, these three branches do not interfere in one another's affairs, while each control and accompany the other. . . . They should especially not violate the Constitution.

Indeed, Partow added for good measure, hadn't the Imam himself drawn this same conclusion when he declared that the *Majles* "must be at the head of all affairs and powers?"[81] Deputy Masha'allah Heydari-Moqaddam agreed, citing eight articles in the Constitution that the executive had violated in its effort to disqualify him. But then he went one step further. Linking the constitutional powers of the *Majles* to a document that had been endorsed by the United Nations (a body maligned by the Imam and the radicals as a tool of Western colonialism), Heydari-Moqaddam explained that "according to Paragraph 3 of Article 14 of the Covenant of Civil and Political Rights . . . signed on December 16, 1966 by the U.N. General Assembly and by the Iranian legislature on September 8, 1974, anyone accused of committing a crime must have at least five guarantees."[82] That a deputy would defend this position by reminding his colleagues that the Shah's discredited Parliament had endorsed a U.N. document not only suggests the extent to which some deputies were ready to go to defend their rights; it also suggests that some clerics were now prepared to distance themselves from the radicals' claim that such rights were merely a tool of Western ideological hegemony.

Beyond focusing attention on this array of principles, *Majles* radicals articulated a more general theme: ideological pluralism. Admittedly, their primary goal was to prevent their exclusion from the *Majles*. Responding to the repeated efforts of conservative clerics to belittle their role in this institution, radicals such as Nabavi and Ghaffari reminded their colleagues that Khomeini had always accorded their comrades pride of place in the Islamic Revolution. Yet in defending this viewpoint from a narrowly instrumentalist angle, some radicals began articulating a much more general philosophical principle—albeit in a language that was riddled with confusion and inconsistencies. Take, for example, Behzad Nabavi's open letter to Rafsanjani, in which he protested the Council of Guardians' decision to disqualify him from running in the 1992 elections. Most of this letter consists of a long narrative of Nabavi's contributions to the revolution. Nabavi proudly recounts the role that he played discrediting President Abolhasan Bani-Sadr; the contributions he made, as head of Iran's negotiating team, to ending the 1979–80 hostage crisis; and the personal support that the Imam gave him after "counterrevolutionary" elements tried to rid the regime of radicals. Today, Nabavi claims, these same forces "want to gradually push aside those who believe in the Islamic revolution . . . and let those who are in opposition . . . take over." While this group has taken many forms—"liberals, hypocrites [i.e., *Sazman-e Mojahedin-e Khalq-e Iran*, Organization of the Iranian People's Holy Warriors], leftists, and finally the right"—its efforts to remove the "children of the revolution" can only lead "to the acceptance of the will . . . of the enemies of the Islamic Revolution." This will happen, Nabavi argues, because the revolution's greatest asset—its tolerance of "rivals inside the family of the Islamic revolution"—will be destroyed. Once this occurs, the remaining wing of the revolutionary family will be isolated and thus vulnerable to the West and its "domestic agents." For this reason, Nabavi states, he always opposed "the unacceptable methods of seeking monopoly and eliminating people." Indeed, "I have believed in political freedom and the necessity of having a . . . rivalry of ideas." This said, Nabavi admits that there *were* moments during which both he and his comrades didn't practice what they preached. "We protested the freedom of opponents of the government," he concedes. Yet, he goes on to say, these actions were undertaken with the best of intentions: "because we believed that they [the regime's opponents] should clarify their duty to the government." Once clarified "within the framework of the law," even the regime's critics could contribute to "sound political competition and respect for the votes of the nation," all of which will "guarantee the perpetuation . . . of the Islamic revolution."[83]

Nowhere in this ten-page letter does Nabavi address the theoretical fault lines that run throughout his letter. By what philosophical, religious, or practical measure can one determine who has the right to belong to a revolutionary "family"? And who does the determining? While Nabavi seems aware of these questions (his admission that he protested the "freedom of opponents" suggests as much), he is either unable or unwilling to address these tricky issues, perhaps because in doing so he can only open an ideological can of worms. Yet seen in terms of a broader learning process, Nabavi's letter constituted a lively defense of an albeit hobbled vision of ideological pluralism.

By its very nature, such arguments eventually encompassed cultural questions as well. Assailed by the Special Clerical Tribunal for cultural and financial "corruption," some radicals defended a vision of the revolutionary family that was both ideologically and culturally pluralistic. For example, one unlucky deputy named Ahmad Robati had been disqualified from running in the 1992 *Majles* elections after the tribunal had discovered several incriminating photographs of him. One, from 1975, depicted a blue-jeans-clad Robati standing next to a suspicious-looking woman! Addressing the *Majles* while Speaker Karrubi passed this photo around to his colleagues, Robati explained that the woman in the photo was his fiancee. "You know what society's conditions were in those days," he stated, hoping to remind his audience that during the seventies most students wore jeans, so there was nothing untoward about the photo. On the contrary, it was taken on the day that he, his parents, and his brother went to ask for the hand in marriage of the woman in question. "If that is a crime," Robati exclaimed, "if that is against religious law, then so be it."[84] A few minutes later another deputy, Ebrahim Asghar-Zadeh, came to Robati's rescue. He too had worn Western clothing, but this had not stopped him from playing a leading role in the 1979 takeover of the American Embassy. Addressing his beleaguered comrade, Asghar-Zadeh affirmed the following:

> To the gentleman who came and said that he had worn Lee Jeans, I say, brother, I am among the forces you know. At the beginning of the revolution, I was a spokesman for the students following the Imam's line. In that same American Nest of Spies [i.e., the occupied Embassy], I appeared time and time again wearing an American jacket. But I was not aware of this issue until the Imam asked if what I was wearing was made in our homeland. When the Imam pointed this out, I knew the mistake I had made. But this was only advice.

Asghar-Zadeh's colleagues surely grasped his point: while it may have been a "mistake" to wear an American jacket, even the Imam had not *forced* the militant student group Followers of the Imam's Line to correct this error. Instead, all he did was offer "advice." Such remarkable tolerance was now being extinguished by the *Majles*—the very same body that in 1989 had written to the Imam and declared, "We have to return to the constitution." Reminding his audience that the Imam had responded to the *Majles* with a letter in which he stated, "I believe we have to go back to the constitution," Asghar-Zadeh asserted that the rights accorded by this document were indivisible. "In the constitution there is a whole chapter about the rule of the people, which is something that cannot be split apart." Thus "we cannot destroy the people's rights" by banishing "all those people" who had made such "sacrifices for the revolution."[85]

Ultimately, one of the most compelling defenses of cultural/political pluralism came from deputies who believed that the clergy's assault on intellectual freedom might discredit the very idea of an Islamic state. For example, Deputy Ayatollah Morteza Panahandeh warned that their attempts to monopolize "power in the hands of a particular faction . . . will bring dictatorship." God forbid, he explained, "that we should lose these people. God forbid that we should chop off our own roots."[86] Following the May 1992 elections, Hadi Khamane'i echoed these warnings. The government's supporters, he noted, had shamelessly used whatever arguments they felt would effectively discredit their enemies. "The accusation varied with the psychology and beliefs of the audience," Khamane'i claimed. The "capitalists" were told that the "radicals are the enemies of your capital"; the "cultural liberals" learned that "the radicals are fanatics and oppose social liberties"; and the "trades people" were told that "these heavy taxes . . . are the work of these extremists." Last but not least, "the . . . believers" were warned that "this faction is against religious guardianship." Such methods, Khamane'i promised, had sown "a bad seed . . . which will threaten the values of the revolution. . . . It is a flood that will take everything along with it."[87]

"Without Love for Khamanei, One Cannot Love . . . Khomeini"

Hadi Khamane'i's warning was prophetic. During the 1991–92 parliamentary debates, many speakers argued that the most effective way to ward off the threat of "Western culture" was to strengthen the rule of law, the protection of individual liberties, and the separation of powers among the three branches of government. While some radicals may have failed to notice the irony in taking this position (i.e., their use of Western ideas to ward off Western culture), it did not go unnoticed by conservative clerics, for whom the paradoxes of Iran's "Islamic" revolution were culturally and ideologically intolerable. Throughout 1992 and even more so during the next two years, the clerical establishment increased the state's repression of all those forces that it had believed had facilitated the West's "onslaught" against Islamic-Shi'ite culture.

As with most cases of ideologically driven repression, that which swept Iran during the early nineties was glorified by an intellectual vanguard that saw itself as the last defender of a divinely ordained revolutionary ethos. Emboldened by the radicals' defeat, conservative deputies made it clear that henceforth, supreme authority would rest in the hands of the *faqih*. As always, they did this by invoking Khomeini's legacy, especially its utilitarian strands. "Have we not learned," asked one deputy, "that . . . the interests of the regime take precedence over *all else*?" After all, he observed, "the Imam himself had said, 'It was to determine the interests . . . that I would give up all.' " Thus, it is "obligatory . . . to use the directives of the Imam and the Grand Leader in our writing and speaking."[88] Note the equation between the directives of the Imam and those of the "Grand Leader," an obvious rebuke to the radicals, who had tried to subordinate the commands of the second to those of the first. All that seemed finished. "I ask the exalted leader," Deputy Heshmat Musavi fawned, "to every so often favor the dear people of Iran with his Imam-like commentaries." This request was followed by the affirmation that "without love for Khamanei, one cannot love . . . Khomeini."[89] Gone was any mention of the constitutional prerogatives of the *Majles*. As another deputy succinctly put it, "It would be appropriate for us *Majles* deputies to accept the commands of the exalted leader unconditionally."[90]

Although the conservative clerics succeeded, from the perspective of Rafsanjani, the 1991–92 purges produced contradictory consequences. Having isolated the radicals, he now had to rely on a conservative clerical establishment that opposed any Western encroachment in the economy. The president could talk all he liked about the value that Islam supposedly ascribed to work; but when it came to implementing his "reconstruction" program, he had to move very cautiously lest he alienate his right-wing supporters.[91] However, on another level, the purges of 1992 proved an unintended boon to the fortunes of Rafsanjani and his band of reformists. By putting the radicals in the dock, they forced some "children of the revolution" to expose the contradictions animating their dissonant ideology. That radicals such as Karrubi had repeatedly invoked the populist and utilitarian dimensions of Khomeini's legacy to both embarrass the conservative clerical establishment and defend the constitutional rights of the *Majles* suggested possibilities for a political and ideological realignment of forces that might eventually free Rafsanjani of his dependence on conservative clerics.

Paradoxically, these clerics inadvertently encouraged this revisionist dynamic. Keenly aware of the contending ideas that inspired the radicals, the conservatives made hay out of these contradictions. Consider the stinging critique leveled by Seyyed Akbar Parvaresh against the radicals in April 1992: "They memorize the Koran and drink wine," he claimed, thus pointing out the admiration many radicals had for the very civilization they supposedly despised. Continuing his assault, Parvaresh asserted that the radicals "make an amulet of the Koran and kill the eloquent Imam." In other words, while proclaiming their support for Islam, the radicals embraced doctrines that defied the Imam's authority. Finally, Parvaresh argued, the radicals' populism was a smoke screen behind which lurked an arrogant elitism. "If the people follow them [the radicals], and do what they want them to do, then the people are great, dear and esteemed." If, on the other hand, "the people turn away from them or elect someone else, then the same people are called hesitant, confused . . . and discouraged."[92]

Summary: Contending Visions

All three of the above critiques had more than a grain of truth. The products of multiple and shared imaginations, the radicals wanted the freedom to wear jeans, yet demanded a culturally authentic and unified Islamic government. They wanted democracy, political participation, and individual freedoms, but saw themselves as an intellectual vanguard that spoke for the supreme interests of a transcendent, collective, people. Last, but not least, they proclaimed support for *velayat-e faqih* while asserting that the *Majles* had the constitutional right to interfere in the decisions of the executive. The radicals' initial efforts to square these circles were often unconvincing. As we have seen, men like Nabavi were caught in an ideological web of their own making. Yet if their subjective responses to the 1991–92 purges were inconsistent and their motivations self-serving, objectively speaking, their answers performed a vital function: they suggested that in the continuing struggle over Khomeini's legacy, Iran's leaders would have to make more clear-cut *choices.* Could one embrace Montesquieu's concept of separation of powers and continuously vilify the West? Could one pursue a struggle against the domestic accomplices of Western culture and still demand the rule of law? And could one accept clerical rule and yet argue, as Karrubi had, that the *faqih* was just *"one of* the indestructible pillars of the sacred system"?

These questions can also be phrased in more theoretical terms. The struggle over Khomeini's legacy during the early nineties represented a second phase in a prolonged process of complex routinization. Para-doxically, because this dynamic never fully transcended the effects of dissonant institutionalization, it tended to reproduce it. For every step forward, Iran's leaders devised new ways to accommodate contending visions of political community. Whether the 1991–92 purge of the radical members of the *Majles* was enough of a blow to break this cycle is a question we shall address in the next and final chapter, and also in the conclusion of this book. We shall see that in their efforts to make hard philosophical or ideological choices, prominent radicals such as Mohammad Khatami and Abdolkarim Soroush soon found themselves both echoing and moving well beyond Khomeini's legacy. In doing so, they did not simply set the stage for a dramatic realignment of Iranian politics. On a more personal level, many disillusioned Islamic Leftists soon discovered that wearing jeans and American jackets did not necessarily constitute a counterrevolutionary act.

8 Disenchantment, Charisma, and . . . Reform?

> From the first days that the Imam took center stage, he began his religiously inspired struggle against tyranny, dependency, corruption. . . . He was aware that if religious leaders, thinkers and intellectuals are not confronted with practical problems, they will not think of solutions. . . . The Imam's greatest legacy is indeed the establishment of Islamic government.[1]
>
> —Mohammad Khatami

> All religious governments . . . [must] . . . determine whether human rights have a foundation that is independent from that of religious law or not. . . . If we view the government as the public's guardian, then we are speaking from the premise of responsibilities, and if we consider it the public's trustee, then we are speaking on the basis of the rights of the people. All of the problems come from the effort to combine these two things.[2]
>
> —Abdolkarim Soroush

What Is Islamic "Government"?

In the struggle within the regime over Khomeini's legacy, every competing faction claimed the Imam for itself. If conservative *Majles* Deputy Seyyed Akbar Parvaresh could justifiably accuse the radicals of "trying to portray the Imam as solely your own," his allies on the Right also strove to monopolize Khomeini's memory.[3] Few obeyed the Imam's final instruction, namely that "whatever statement is, or will be, attributed to me is not acceptable unless I have said it in my own voice . . . or it has my signature."[4] But while the battle over Khomeini's legacy continued into the midnineties, its political significance changed. Henceforth, that contest served as a surrogate for a fundamental debate over the very nature of authority. Following the 1991–92 purges by the regime of the radical faction of the *Majles* and its campaign against "cultural onslaught," several lay thinkers and clerics began asking whether a political system based on contending notions of authority could long endure. Convinced, as Abdolkarim Soroush put it, that "all of the problems come from the effort to combine" conflicting principles, these thinkers implied that the very survival of the Islamic Republic of Iran required pruning Khomeini's legacy of its more glaring ideological contradictions.

Yet what did this mean? Which values were in conflict and which were in sync? Which could be accommodated and which deserved discarding? And could a system based on the dissonant institutionalization of contending visions of authority be prodded in a more coherent direction without undermining its very ideological foundations? The answer to this last question was not merely theoretical: the effort to routinize Khomeini's authority could easily provoke a counterattack from conservative clerics. As with all hard-liners, they saw any reform as an invitation to their demise. The challenge facing the reformers, then, was to show that the opposite was true, namely that without reform, the entire system might collapse under the weight of popular discontent.

By the midnineties the growing spiritual and symbolic disenchantment of the postrevolution generation seemed to be pushing Iran in this very direction. Alienated as much by the state's dogma as by its intolerance of just plain fun, many youths either became apathetic or committed an even more shocking act: they turned to Western culture for inspiration. The clerics responded by intensifying their campaign against cultural onslaught. But such efforts only led to greater disaffection. At this point the reformists stepped in. Seizing the initiative, they tried to lift the young out of their existential doldrums by recasting Khomeini's charismatic legacy in a more democratic and pluralistic light. For a second time Iran's history, disenchantment gave way to charisma, although this time the quest for what Durkheim called collective "effervescence" was designed to promote reform and joy, rather than revolution and collective rage.

Conservative clerics inadvertently triggered this cycle. Having prevailed in the *Majles*, they launched a campaign to purge other state institutions of potential reformists. In late 1992 Minister of Islamic Guidance Seyyed Mohammad Khatami was forced to resign for failing to correctly "guide" the youth. Next to go was Mohammad Hashemi Rafsanjani, the director of the Voice and Vision Broadcasting Company. By 1994 hundreds of intellectuals and supposed dissidents were in prison, and some had been executed. Yet this campaign only encouraged a new wave of reformist thinking. Among these intellectuals was Mohammad Khatami. A member of the clerical Left, after his forced resignation from the Islamic Guidance Ministry he answered his critics by arguing that the only way to address the challenge of Western culture was to create a tolerant vision of Islamic civilization. Abdolkarim Soroush, a lay intellectual, endorsed this thesis but went further: he argued that the creation of a rational and open Islam *required* distancing clerics from political power. Although this was clearly a more harmonious vision of Islamic community in comparison with that of Khatami, the structural and ideological forces that drove the two men were similar. The products of multiple shared imaginations, both reformists had once occupied important positions in Khomeini's revolutionary state, only to become disillusioned when that state turned on some of its own children. As victims of the very state they had helped to create, Khatami and Soroush tried to push the populist and rational aspects of Khomeini's legacy in a new direction without appearing to betray it.

The hard-liners held that this bid to sort out Khomeini's legacy was in fact an exhibition of disloyalty to it. Citing Khomeini's own words, Ayatollah Mohammad Reza Mahdavi-Kani and his allies reduced this legacy to one simple formula: fanatical opposition to Western "civilization" and the repression of all "liberals" who dared question the ultimate authority of the *faqih* (Supreme Leader). Thus the conservatives scorned the reformists' argument that the *faqih*'s role as guide of the overall political system should be accommodated to the rule of law and the authority of the *Majles*. While Khatami and his allies argued that this definition of the *faqih*'s authority in such transpolitical terms would enhance his stature, the conservatives feared that this was a recipe for the Islamic state's self-destruction.

Why, given the conservatives' fierce opposition to the reformists, did Khatami prevail in the May 1997 elections? His success was partly due to his rhetorical skills: by trying to show that his revisionist agenda was consonant with Khomeini's "greatest legacy . . . the establishment of Islamic government," Khatami diluted—although by no means prevented —opposition from Supreme Leader 'Ali Khamane'i. But Khatami's victory also stemmed from the overwhelming popularity of his message. By addressing the burning desire of Iran's youth for a pluralistic, democratic, and spiritually uplifting vision of the future, he galvanized the country. In doing so, Khatami demonstrated the validity of Max Weber's argument that in modern societies, charisma can serve as a handmaiden of democratic legitimacy and change. In what was no small paradox of history, Khatami's rise to stardom echoed Khomeini's own success in transforming alienation into a political movement. This said, it would be premature to conclude that Khatami's electoral victory made the transition from charisma to pluralist democracy inevitable. Given the enduring institutional authority of the *faqih*, as well as the conservatives' capacity to mobilize supporters of the "old system," Khatami may well conclude that his political fate rests in accommodating rather than opposing the system of contending authorities. This is an issue that I will take up in the conclusion.

Disenchantment, Part Two

Khatami's 1997 electoral victory gave voice to the youth's profound need for spiritual re-enchantment. Disillusioned by a system that had failed to give the new generation a morally uplifting vision of the future, they looked beyond Iran's borders for hope. Statistics tell part of this story. During the eighties, the population grew by a staggering average of 2.8 percent per year, jumping from 39 million in 1980 to 56 million in 1990. By 1995, about half of the country's 60.5 million people had been born after the Islamic Revolution.[5] While these young people had not directly experienced Khomeini's charisma, they were subject to the state's efforts to transform the Imam's ideas into a ruling ideology. From the vantage point of the state, this endeavor occurred in concert with three potentially troubling trends. The first of these was increasing urbanization. By the mideighties nearly 60 percent of the total population lived in cities. Tehran's population alone grew from four million to seven million between 1980 and 1990, and was expanding by one hundred thousand a year by the end of that period. Therefore, the potential for collective action—or opposition—in the capital increased. The second potentially destabilizing trend was growing literacy.[6] From 1980 to 1991 the percentage of literate men rose from 54 percent to 66 percent, while the percentage of literate women leaped from 30 percent to 59 percent. As a result, the regime faced an increasingly mobilized and politically conscious population. Finally, Iran experienced a dramatic expansion of secondary and higher education, as the following table indicates.[7] The implications of this trend merit particular attention.

The Expansion of Higher Education in Iran, 1977–97

					Enrollment						
1977	1982	1984	1986	1988	1990	1992	1993	1994	1995	1996	1997
155.8	135.7	171.5	204.3	292.6	312	374.7	436.6	909	1,048	579	625

					Teaching Staff						
1977	1982	1984	1986	1988	1990	1992	1993	1994	1995	1996	1997
15.5	11.5	13.7	14.9	17	23.3	30.2	32.9	36.4	52.8	40.5	44.1

SOURCE: UNESCO, Division of Statistics: <http://unescostat.unesco.org/database>.

NOTE: The UNESCO reports as provided on the Internet do not account for the sudden rise in higher education enrollments in 1994, nor the equally sudden drop in enrollments in 1996.

The expansion of higher education had a paradoxical impact. It will be recalled that Iran also had experienced a steep increase in students pursuing secondary and higher educations during the sixties and seventies. The growing support for a radical Islamic ideology during the seventies was brought about in part by the thinning of the intellectual and institutional walls between the seminaries and the universities. With the universities reopening in 1982 and the Islamization of higher education, the clerics intended to complete this process. But they were far from successful. Indeed, given the absence of qualified instructors, the state had little choice but to retain Western-educated faculty members, many of whom emulated Western curricula. Thus, complained the traditionalist publication *Sobh*, "We should not be surprised to see that our universities are entirely impervious to Islamic values."[8] Such alienation might have been expected among a new generation that had not lived through the revolution; a good number of whom had pursued higher education for largely utilitarian reasons.[9] But even those students who were supposedly philosophically committed to the regime became increasingly disaffected. Thus while 60 percent of the admissions each year were reserved for students who came from families of martyrs—an ideological mainstay of the regime—the wall between universities and *traditional* seminary life reemerged in the nineties.[10] This familiar process of social mobilization and growing alienation was particularly marked in the female population. We have already noted the dramatic increase in literacy among women, which doubled during the Khomeini decade. Because education and literacy rates far outstripped opportunities to participate in political and economic activities,[11] many women became even more determined to remedy their political, economic, and cultural disenfranchisement, one of the factors for their playing an increasingly important role during the reform movement of the nineties.[12]

Iran's intellectual elite began to openly debate the aforementioned developments during the early and midnineties. Of particular concern were studies indicating that an increasingly disenchanted population was looking West for symbolic inspiration. For example, in April 1995 the biweekly publication *'Asr-e Ma* (Our Era) reported the results of an opinion poll of three hundred students in Tehran. Twenty-seven percent of these youths, the journal reported, "indicated . . . pessimism towards politics, while 41 percent expressed indifference." More alarmingly, 51 percent reported that they "experienced a feeling of nihilism and lack of identity," while a whopping 81 percent had "a lower inclination toward religion." But apathy was not the sole or dominant response to this crisis. Eighty-eight percent of the subjects "said they favored wearing fashionable clothes and having unbridled relations."[13] Moreover, when asked "a question on the behavioral model of the youths and students, 61 percent . . . referred to Western artists, while only 17 percent cited the country's officials as their behavioral model." Indeed, "50 percent of the subjects declared that they favored Western music, while only 15 percent said they liked revolutionary songs and music." Noting that these respondents distinguished between Western jazz, classical, pop, and even electronic music, the journal concluded that "the subjects are so interested in the products of Western culture that they are even meticulous and choosy about them."[14]

Such striking conclusions were echoed by other studies. For example, the spring 1998 issue of the reformist journal *Goft-o-gu* (Dialogue) offered an illuminating picture of the "cultural and social development" of the youth of southern and northern Tehran. The comparative focus was revealing, since at the outset of the revolution the citizens of southern Tehran had been poorer, less well educated and more traditional in comparison with those in the northern part of the city. One of the aims of the Islamic Revolution was to close this cultural and economic gap with programs designed to create a new "Islamic man." However, the *Goft-o-gu* study showed that while this north–south gap had narrowed, this process had not produced the ideological transformation that the regime had hoped for. Exposed to the domestic forces of education and the international forces of globalization, the youths of the north and south alike were suffering a profound identity crisis. "Today's youth," the journal reported, "are, on the one hand, constrained by customs . . . and on the other, are *seized and enchanted by the modern world and the future*. They are aware that the speed of global developments make it quite difficult to predict the future." The journal's survey indicated that instead of responding to these changes by becoming apathetic, most youths turned to the "educational and personal development aspects of recreation," particularly sports, television, and video. Overall, the journal reported, "the need of the youth for independence and freedom was natural and all young people expressed this need."[15]

From Mini-Glasnost to "Cultural Onslaught"

Although the Iranian media was filled with stories about cultural onslaught and the growing disenchantment of the youth, there was little consensus as to the remedy. Such differences were not simply a matter of conservatives versus radicals. The transcripts of the 1991–92 *Majles* debates show that the radicals were more divided than the conservatives when it came to devising an effective *means* for addressing this problem. While some radical diehards demanded that the state use repressive measures to combat foreign culture, reform-minded radicals called for a more pluralistic approach. What then was to be done? Absent an effective safety valve, the youth's discontent might turn into collective rage. But 'Ali Akbar Hashemi Rafsanjani's government could not countenance making sweeping changes without associating his regime with "liberal" forces. Such fears were provoked by a flurry of angry articles that appeared in the press following Rafsanjani's presidential election in July 1989. Inspired by his inaugural speech, the writer 'Ali Akbar Sa'idi-Sirjani published an essay that summed up both the frustrations and the renewed hopes of Iran's liberals: "Why," he asked,

> has anger drawn such a blood-drenched curtain before the eyes of the tyrannized that we are unaware . . . of the meaningful smile that is curving the corners of their lips when they [Westerners] observe that while we shout our slogans "Death to America," columns of smoke from Winston cigarettes dance in the air?

This biting critique of a "tyrannized" people who mouthed revolutionary slogans while smoking American cigarettes might have sufficed. But Sirjani went further. Affirming that "we cannot return the people of our contemporary, closely linked world to the life of 100 years ago," he declared that "when a country hears from its president's tongue that despotic tactics are not lasting, the light of hope appears on the horizon." Thus Sirjani implied that Rafsanjani's program was consonant with a liberal agenda that sought to reconnect Iran to a "closely linked world"![16] Over the next two months, conservative papers attacked the hapless writer in an attempt to disassociate Rafsanjani's government from Sirjani's attack.[17] Given that Rafsanjani had his hands full contending with radical *Majles* deputies, he could hardly tolerate attacks from liberals who linked his government to a domestic and foreign policy agenda despised by his clerical allies. Yet if the Sirjani affair made political reform that much more risky for Rafsanjani, his administration still had an interest in promoting a degree of cultural glasnost. By easing restrictions on film directors, television producers, and novelists, the administration might placate a state-dependent intelligentsia that had tired of state repression, while at the same time giving young people a medium through which their frustrations could be articulated by fictional characters. The trick was to promote this cultural venting *without* sanctioning a full-blown critique of the state and its ruling institutions.

Two of Rafsanjani's allies played an important role in trying to strike this delicate balance. Minister of Islamic Guidance Seyyed Mohammad

Khatami did so by promoting a rebirth of Iran's film industry. Khatami had declared his intention to do so back in December 1987. Taking a cue from Khomeini, who had recently issued an edict calling for relaxing the application of film codes, Khatami asserted that "cinema is not the mosque. . . . If one feels that leisure time has . . . become homework . . . we have deformed society."[18] Yet while films such as Dariush Mehrju'i's *Ejareh Neshinha* (Tenants, 1986) or Rakhshan Bani Etemad's *Kharej az Mahdudeh* (Beyond the City Limit, 1986) addressed sensitive social issues, it was not until the late eighties and early nineties that films by directors such as Mohsen Makhmalbaf and 'Abbas Kiarostami began to explicitly tackle controversial political, social, and sexual issues.[19] By encouraging this trend, Khatami attracted the wrath of conservative clerics. Meanwhile, Mohammad Hashemi Rafsanjani pursued a similar glasnost policy as director of the Voice and Vision Broadcasting Company (VV). Hashemi allowed for the production and broadcasting of serials and films that were not fully in keeping with the cultural and religious standards of the conservative clerics. Moreover, his ministry broadcast foreign films which, while censored for "inappropriate" sexual, religious, or political content, sometimes provided a relatively positive view of the West. Because he was President Rafsanjani's brother, and because television and radio reached a wider audience than books, Hashemi's activities drew considerable attention.

This mini-glasnost did not achieve its intended results. Instead, by feeding the youth's desire for Western products and ideas, it provoked a backlash. We have noted the attacks that had been directed against the VV's coverage of sports in 1989. In the ensuing year such assaults were often accompanied by attacks on Khatami. As one *Majles* deputy put it, "it is mandatory for all officials . . . to be mobilized against the cultural invasion of global oppression." Rather than sit idly by, he called upon the "Ministry of Guidance . . . the great clerics, the seminaries, the VV, and all the newspapers . . . [to] join hands, and utilizing the talents of the youth . . . neutralize all the plans of the enemy.[20] Soon, the *faqih* himself repeated such attacks. His unrelenting critique of the cultural onslaught played a part in forcing Khatami to resign in July 1992. Celebrating this event, Deputy Mohammad Reza Rahimi illustrated the cultural contamination Khatami had supposedly let loose. Thus, he claimed, the film *Two Halves of an Apple* had "crossed the line by implying that a veiled woman in the southern part of the city [i.e., Tehran] is stupid but the unveiled woman in the northern part of the city is intelligent. This film does not conform to the goals of the revolution." Worse yet, "the Minister of Islamic Guidance did not react to the instructions of the Grand Leader. . . . After another warning to the officials, the resources of the ministry should have come to this battlefield."[21]

This situation was to change quickly after Dr. 'Ali Larijani became the new Minister of Culture and Islamic Guidance. Declaring that "it is very simplistic for Islamic cinema and art to . . . prove itself by trying to seek help from rank sexual romance," he promised that his ministry would design "a proper system for the young people," the hallmark of which would be the "true and lofty freedom that is a divine tradition." After all, Larijani asked, how "can we soon forget the call of the divine guardian, our late Imam, who emphasized our own cultural richness?" With this legacy in mind, he promised cultural policies that showed "the deceptive face of the West that infiltrates the societies in the guise of human rights and democracy in order to achieve its filthy purpose of domination."[22]

Larijani kept his promise. In November 1993, following the issuing of a scathing report by the Legislative and Parliamentary Affairs Division of the *Majles*, Mohammad Hashemi Rafsanjani and many of his colleagues at the VV were forced to resign. The *Majles* committee's detailed and scathing fifty-plus-page report, and Hashemi's biting response to it, suggests how polarized the debate over the "cultural invasion" had become. Reviewing VV programming from 1988 through 1991, the report asserted that out of nine hundred films broadcast on television, seven hundred were foreign! "A Muslim Iranian youth," it warned, "during the most sensitive period of the formation of his personality, has been influenced by such serials which . . . bring divine spiritual values into question." The report voiced particular concern that "pre-college male and female students who have been prohibited from having relations . . . begin to contemplate." Worse yet, even *Iranian* films failed to tow an Islamic line. "In the serial *Hazardastan*," the "deviation of the [1906] Constitutional movement is shown," but there was "no sign of the spiritual leaders of the nation." As for children's programming, it consisted of cartoons in which "wine drinking, unveiling, and relations between boys and girls exist . . . to the extent that children accept them as normal." Even the "attractive animation *Around the World in 80 Days*" posed grave dangers. While "the main hero . . . is a . . . powerful, brave . . . and ever-victorious character [who] . . . enchants children," he was "explicitly introduced as an Englishman." This was too much: "If . . . our youth who were born *after* the victory of the revolution are inclined towards Western culture, it is because . . . one hour per day, they have been shown the very attractive material and spiritual qualities in . . . the Western world." These shocking lapses were ascribed to pro-Western or even pro-Shah elements. The "outside space, the hallways and workshops," the report complained, were "empty of any Islamic and revolutionary signs." More ominously, the report asserted that "[t]he . . . VV has artists who are artistic and cultural dependents of the Tyrant" (i.e., Shah Mohammad Reza Pahlavi). Their presence explains "the inability of the system to . . . purge the ideas of undesirable producers."[23]

The aggressive nature of Mohammad Hashemi Rafsanjani's 31-page-plus response the *Majles'* report suggests that he assumed—incorrectly, as things turned out—that his more powerful brother would protect him. The response began by maligning one of the report's authors, Deputy 'Ali Akbar Parvaresh, who, the report claimed, had been a member of the *Hojjatiyeh* Society[24] (a group that had been purged from the *Majles* for opposing *velayat-e faqih*, "Rule of the Jurist"). Hashemi then argued that because Khomeini was a "jurist and proven source of emulation," it was incumbent upon the investigating committee to base its judgments solely on the "religious decrees and . . . opinions of the late Imam." Displaying a *handwritten* copy of one of Khomeini's letters, Hashemi's response readily admitted that the VV had broadcast music. But, it added, the VV had done so precisely *because* such programming was "in accordance with the jurisprudential opinion of the Imam." Alluding to *fatva*s (religious edicts) in which Khomeini had declared the broadcasting of music acceptable,[25] Hashemi deduced that it was the actions of the *Majles* investigating committee, rather than those of the VV, that constituted "an actual example of cultural invasion." Indeed, he continued, "the enemy [spoke] against the . . . Imam through the mouths of the members of the Inquiry and Investigation Group." Finally, in a bid to defend the VV's staff, which had been accused of pro-Shah sympathies, he concluded by invoking a contradictory mix of principles. Thus having asserted that foreign serials such as *The Inspector* conformed to revolutionary guidelines by questioning "the British judicial system beautifully," Hashemi then advanced an implicitly liberal argument to defend its programming! "Does the Inquiry and Investigation group," he asked, "believe that in the Islamic society artists are not free and are forced to make programs under the pressure of government?"[26]

Yet it was not this defense of free speech that did Hashemi in. Rather, by asserting that the Imam's opinions should serve as the foundation for cultural policies, he had implicitly questioned Khamane'i's authority.[27] When Hashemi then took the risky step of printing the first part of his report without the *faqih's* permission, Khamane'i issued an order that forbade publicizing the remainder of the response. Hashemi's resignation was followed by a crackdown on independent and state-supported intellectuals. By October 1994 the situation had gotten so bad that 134 of Iran's leading intellectuals took the unprecedented step of issuing an open declaration denouncing "certain individuals, institutions and groups related to the government" for using "arbitrary interpretations" of art "to vilify, humiliate and threaten writers." Affirming that "our collective presence is the guarantee of our individual independence," the signatories asserted that "defending the human and civil rights of every writer is . . . the professional duty of all writers."[28] One month later the writer Sa'idi-Sirjani—who was not one of the signatories of this letter—died under mysterious circumstances while in administrative detention. His death was followed by further arrests of intellectuals, and by a partial purge of pro-Western faculty members in the universities in 1995–96.

Multiple Imaginations:
Khatami Rethinks the "West"

The October 1994 letter demonstrated that the intelligentsia had become thoroughly alienated. By reminding intellectuals of the paradoxical fate of those radical deputies who had been purged from the *Majles* in 1992, the regime's actions brought together a heterogenous universe of thinkers and activists who might otherwise have gone their separate ways. Moreover, because these children of the revolution articulated an estrangement that the new generation shared, disillusioned radicals such as Khatami could make a persuasive case that their solution to the cultural onslaught addressed the authentic needs of a mass constituency whose very loyalty to the revolution was now in peril.

Before we examine Khatami's initial response to this crisis, we need to review the ideological and cultural legacy of the Islamic Left. It will be recalled that the political consciousness of 'Ali Shari'ati and his followers was shaped by their encounter with the West and by their Marxist and existentialist thought in particular. Shari'ati had accommodated these two influences to a millenarian sensibility that reflected his earlier immersion in Shi'ite thought and mystical Islam. The result was a peculiar mix of instrumentalist rationalism and transrational utopianism. Shari'ati sought to create a totalistic Islamic ideology that would mobilize the masses behind a messianic vision designed to realize political and social ends.

One of the peculiar aspects of such instrumentalist ideologies and their many variants—including existentialism—is that they can invite diametrically opposed prescriptions for political action. A Pareto or a Sorel might argue that in the absence of any one objective truth, the duty of the elite is to create and impose one grand myth that can command the disciplined loyalty of the masses. By contrast, a Mosca or a Shils might arrive at a more pluralist perspective, namely that the very absence of one objective political "truth" requires both a tolerance of competing ideas, and a readiness to encourage the masses to sort out these ideas democratically.[29] During the nineties, a number of Iran's radical Islamic thinkers and political activists began to make this second case.[30] Although their earlier encounter with Third-Worldist ideologies had inclined many of them toward a totalistic mind-set, their shared multiple imaginations created among some Islamic Leftists an affinity for a more liberal approach to *creating* political order. Moreover, for many of these children of the revolution, their suffering at the hands of an "Islamic" autocracy crystallized this pluralistic inclination. That this shift began during a period of increasing cultural, economic, and social globalization that saw the Western powers triumphing over the Soviet Union only deepened the readiness of some Islamic Leftists to address the West's cultural onslaught with a new and more pluralistic political project.

Khatami's "multiple biography" prepared him for just such a transformation. Born in 1943, he was the first son of the popular prayer leader of Yazd, Ayatollah Ruhollah Khatami. An open-minded cleric, the father encouraged his children to listen to radio news broadcasts, read poetry, novels, newspapers, and, as Elaine Sciolino has noted, delve into "books banned by other clerics."[31] In 1961 Khatami pursued religious studies at Qom Theology School, where he became a disciple of Ayatollah Khomeini. Inspired by Khomeini, Khatami then pursued the study of philosophy at Esfahan University, where he obtained a bachelor's degree. It was during this period that he began to read Western political thought, a topic to which he returned over the next two decades. Khatami also became a political activist at this time. Joining the Association of Muslim Students of Esfahan University, he was exposed to the ideologies of the Islamic Left.[32] After completing his degree, Khatami returned to Qom and resumed studies in religious interpretation *(ejtehad)*. He subsequently completed a master's degree in philosophy at Tehran University, and returned again to Qom, where he resumed studies in philosophy. In 1978 he moved to Hamburg, where he replaced Ayatollah Mohammad Hoseyn Beheshti as director of the Hamburg Islamic Center. This first direct encounter with the West also put him in contact with *the* largest community of Iranian students in Europe. During the first year of the Islamic Revolution, Khatami remained in Germany, where he learned German as well as some English. In 1980 he returned to Iran and was elected to the First *Majles*. After a brief stint as director of the *Keyhan* Publishing House, to which he had been appointed by Khomeini, he became Minister of Islamic Guidance in 1982. Over the next few years he defended the state's autocratic policies through the ministry and by assuming additional responsibilities, not least of which was his position as chairman of the War Propaganda Headquarters. The intrinsic demands of these tasks obscured Khatami's growing misgivings with the state's repressive policies. By 1987 he was already calling for a more open cultural regime. With the death of Khomeini in 1989, Khatami's policies provoked the wrath of the conservative clerics. Yet his dismissal in July 1992 did not leave him totally isolated. Appointed head of Iran's National Library and cultural advisor to President Rafsanjani, he pursued his studies of Islamic and Western political thought away from—but still within a comfortable distance of—the political limelight. He did so with gusto, producing a series of books that sought to bridge the "civilizational" gap between the East and the West.

The 1991–92 *Majles* purges set the stage for this development. After all, Khatami's fate had become entangled in the heated debate about the cultural onslaught that had accompanied the campaign against the radicals. When deputies such as Elyas Hazrati sarcastically observed that "creating a climate of opposition to the Minister of Islamic Guidance is announced as strengthening Islam and . . . the government, whereas questioning [another] minister . . . is regarded as weakening the government,"[33] they drew attention to the arbitrary logic that the conservative clerics were using against Khatami. Similarly, when other deputies warned that slogans such as "videos are agents of corruption and fornication" would make "curious young people . . . even more suspicious of our conceptual horizons,"[34] they provided a compelling rationale for forging a more pluralistic answer to the youth's growing malaise. Emboldened by the pluralist rationale informing these and other remarks, Khatami took on his critics during his last months as minister. Blanket censorship, he warned, was counter-productive. "If there is a dispute against a piece of film or music," he explained, "we cannot declare films or music as inadmissible and thereby spoil the whole issue."[35] Such arguments failed to assuage his critics. After resigning, Khatami sent Rafsanjani a letter of resignation that anticipated his comprehensive rethinking of political authority.

Predictably, Khatami began the letter by aligning his cultural policies with the populist-utilitarian legacy of Khomeini. "The Imam," he declared, "had the truth of religion *and* the rights and greatness of the people on his side." With these two great assets, he was able to promote "change in society in areas such as culture" by "creating an atmosphere that befits the basic needs of the human being of our time." This effort to break "down the walls of ignorance" was precisely what "drew fair-minded companions . . . into the domain of . . . cultural crusading." That legacy was now in danger of being trampled by policies that "suspend thought" and "deny lawful freedoms." Warming to his thesis, Khatami cautioned that by using methods that are "completely outside the bounds of logic and law," the state was creating a "disturbed atmosphere . . . the most immediate effect of which is disappointment and lack of confidence on the part of sound thinkers and artists, reputable people, *even those who believe in and love the Islamic revolution and Islam.*" Khatami would not be an accomplice to the state's self-administered demise. In an oblique reference to the purge of the *Majles* radicals, he noted that the events of "recent years" had taught him that "rigidity, inflexibility and backwardness" were the "the greatest plague on the government." Thus, Khatami concluded, he had no choice but to seek another position from which he could "defend legitimate rights and freedom of society and individuals."[36]

The initial impression one gets from *Fear of the Wave*, the first book that he published after becoming director of the National Library, is that the Khatami of 1993 still adhered to the nativist construction of Western civilization that had inspired the Islamic Revolution. After all, he not only insisted on describing the "West" in monolithic terms, but followed Shari'ati's lead by holding that this entity sought to "replace its old colonialism . . . with neocolonialism," a project that requires propagating a "world-view that lures its prey into subjugation."[37] It is here, as Mohsen 'Alina has argued, that Shari'ati's existentialist notion of a collective "return to the self" seems to have influenced Khatami.[38] Yet while he may genuinely subscribe to such nativist thinking, Khatami's use of Shari'atist language is also highly instrumentalist: it not only attests to Khatami's revolutionary credentials, but also appears designed to make ideologically palatable a new and very different understanding of cultural "onslaught" and Islamic civilization.

Khatami elaborates this thesis in the first pages of his study. While he cannot decide whether the West is "worn out and senile" or, on the contrary, "maintains tremendous political, economic, military, social and technological power," he is no longer convinced that civilizations can be understood as monolithic or self-contained. Rather, "the give-and-take among civilizations is the norm of history" (2, 13, 1). Indeed, " 'new' civilizations are never new in the true sense, for they always feed on the work of previous civilizations, appropriating and digesting all that fits their needs, dispensing with all that does not" (1–2). While this observation hardly breaks new ground, it anticipates a distinction fundamental to Khatami's thinking: namely, that between what he calls the "idea of religion itself" and "the many different interpretations" of religion that give rise to "civilizations." The latter, he implies, are subjective; they address "the specific needs and dilemmas of a community in a particular time and place." In contrast, religion is objective; it has an "eternal life" that "transcends civilization" (11). Khatami implies that the very future of the Islamic Republic depends on grasping this distinction between religion and civilization *and acting upon it.* This is *not* the task of the masses. Rather, it is the duty of "religious intellectuals," three of whom made seminal contributions to the revolution: Shari'ati, Jalal Al-e Ahmad, and Khomeini! By giving the Islamic Republic "its dynamism, relevance and ability to provide answers to the people's problems," these men helped create a new Islamic civilization (26).

The fact that Shari'ati and Al-e Ahmad were not clerics poses no problem for Khatami. On the contrary, because he views each civilization as the distinctive product of *independent religious thinkers*—people who use culture to achieve a wide range of cultural, economic, *and* political ends—Khatami *opposes* the very notion of clerical hegemony. This said, he is careful to reach this conclusion *through* Khomeini. Thus while citing the Imam's oft-repeated warning that "until the clergy are active in every sphere, they will not realize that religious authority and knowledge are not enough," Khatami adds that because clerics lack adequate knowledge of issues extrinsic to Islam, the times require "a new vision" for which "relying on current religious leadership is necessary but not sufficient" (40, 42). In an apparent echo of Shari'ati, he again argues that "religious intellectuals" must forge this vision. Their task is to "understand *real* Islam"—which Khatami naturally insists is "the same Islam that the late Imam epitomized . . . particularly in the last years of his life" (50, 55–56; italics mine).[39]

If "religious intellectuals" *create* civilization out of the timeless verities of religion, does it follow that they should do so on behalf of the state or ruling party? While both Shari'ati and Khomeini answered this question in the affirmative, Khatami argues that in today's world, autocratic methods no longer provide a useful means of creating Islamic civilization. With the emergence of a new era of global communications, the only way to capture the youth's imagination is for the state to promote a climate in which the young freely develop an "Islamic utopian ideology" or "vision" that gives "their lives . . . direction, [and] in whose shadow they feel pride, greatness and tranquility."[40] In short, Khatami implies that genuine spiritual re-enchantment can only occur when it is unencumbered by compulsion or what he calls "dogma" (48).

Has Islamic republicanism metamorphosed into Islamic liberalism? Khatami disagrees. Once again embracing a nativist approach, he insists that when it comes to the West, "we are confronted with our philosophical and moral opposite" (15). Yet having made this assertion, he admits that the East has gained much from the West! "Western civilization," he asserts, "rests on the idea of 'liberty' or 'freedom.' " Indeed, Khatami affirms, [these are] "the most cherished values for humans of *all* ages." But that is not all. Khatami then asserts that when it comes to religion, the West has made a *positive* contribution by casting "aside the deification of regressive thinking that had been imposed on the masses in the name of religion." Thus the Reformation was clearly a positive development. Yet if Islamic civilization has much to gain from the West, Khatami holds that "the view of the West about humans and freedom has been . . . one dimensional." Alluding to the familiar Islamist charge that Western notions of freedom subordinate the moral imperatives of community to the greedy needs of the individual, Khatami challenges Iranians to create a new civilization that can "absorb the positive aspects of Western civilization and [possess] the wisdom to recognize the negative aspects" (17, 19). By definition, this balance cannot be struck by thoughtlessly negating the West. On the contrary, to forge a new synthesis, "we have no choice but to correctly and comprehensively understand the West." This requires abandoning—or at least revising—the nativist ideology of the revolution:

> This approach is different from a rigidly political appraisal of the West. Those who cannot separate *the political West from the nonpolitical West* are acting against the interests of the nation and the Islamic Revolution, even though they may be doing so inadvertently. Here, introspection, rationality, and objectivity will be effective, not harsh words and violence. (19)[41]

The catch-22 for Khatami is that it is difficult for Islamic civilization to absorb this pluralistic ethos in the absence of freedom itself. Under these conditions—which Khatami implies actually exist in Iran—any "closed-minded and dogmatic person can use the excuse of conspiracy" (i.e., the excuse of being a bogeyman of the West) "to oust his opponents from the political stage. . . . Anyone can mount an attack on thoughts different from his . . . with the excuse of defending the interests of the system, the revolution and religion."[42] Nor does government-imposed "restriction" provide an answer, "since . . . in today's world . . . the global broadcast of mass-communicated electronic images . . . is under no government control. How can we prevent dynamic and curious minds from accessing what they desire?" (46) In short, repression only aggravates the problem, either by fomenting endless struggles between "dogmatic" persons, or by whetting the youth's appetite for the very Western ideas that the government wishes to deny them. Thus, Khatami argues, "when confronting the opponent in the name of rejecting the West and defending religion, if we step on freedom we will have caused a great catastrophe" (17). To avoid this catastrophe, Khatami offers a twofold approach. First, in a clear echo of the argument that some of his allies made on the floor of the *Majles* in 1991, he asserts that "our system needs accountability and discipline." At the same time, the Islamic Republic requires a "cultural strategy" that will make "our people immune . . . to . . . the cultural onslaught of the West." By definition, this strategy cannot be based on "isolation." Quite the reverse: "An active, evolving society must be in contact and communications with different, sometimes opposing views, to be able to equip itself with a more powerful, attractive, and effective thought than that of the opponent" (47–48).

While advancing these proposals took courage, they were peppered with contradictions and tautologies that reflected the dissonant roots of Khatami's thinking. Rather than resolve the aforementioned catch-22, Khatami suggests that to foster freedom, one must create the preconditions for it. He does not explain how a state that was created to further a revolutionary ideology can be compelled to give up this mission without undermining its very *raison d'être*. Nor does he explain how Iran can absorb the West's love of freedom and liberty without being contaminated by the "virus" of Western civilization (47). Stated otherwise, he cannot have his Shari'atist cake and eat it too, by both affirming and negating the notion of two coherent and (presumably) mutually opposite "civilizations."

I would guess that Khatami was aware of the tensions in this thinking. A product of multiple imaginations and a system that thrived on dissonance, Khatami was not about to renounce what he himself called the "utopian visions" that "came to define our ideology." For this reason he readily praised *'erfan,* or Shi'ite mysticism, for its ability to "address supernatural phenomenon," while resolutely calling for a more rational and democratic approach to politics.[43] Thus for its time and place, Khatami's book made a valuable contribution by pushing the rationalization of Khomeini's legacy forward. It did so by calling upon the state to make society *the locus* of charismatic or spiritual inspiration; proposing that a broad category of independent "religious intellectuals" transform religion into a foundation for rational civilization; and suggesting—however inconsistently—that because civilizations are the porous *creations* of humanity, their survival requires a sober and open dialogue rather than an incessant struggle over the truth.

Multiple Imaginations:
Soroush's Existentialist Mystical Liberalism

The work of Abdolkarim Soroush is important for three reasons. First, while it did not directly engage the arguments of Khatami, in a general way the ideas of the latter provided a point of departure. Like Khatami, Soroush argued that the very survival of an Islamic system hinges on rethinking both the West and the nature of religious authority in the Islamic Republic. But unlike Khatami, Soroush was ready to push this rethinking in directions that a cleric could not endorse without placing himself outside that clerical establishment. Second, Soroush disseminated his ideas through his university lectures, and through journals such as *Kiyan*, a publication that offered clerics and lay intellectuals a regular forum for open discussion. Thus, until Khatami was elected president in May 1997, Soroush's circle of influence was wider and more diverse. Finally, Soroush represented the very "religious intellectual" who Khatami argued should play a leading role in renewing Islamic civilization. He was not only an independent lay-thinker, however: as with Khatami, Soroush's ideas represented the revisionist thinking of one of the revolution's disillusioned ideologists.

Soroush's multiple biography is typical of the Islamic Leftists who helped influence the revolution. Born in 1945 to lower-middle-class parents who lived in southern Tehran, he spent seven years at a Islamic primary school before entering the recently established Alavi High School. Established by merchants, the school's mission was to "educate individuals who were both well-equipped with the modern science and also possessed of religious conviction."[44] The latter sensibility was reinforced by none other than Khomeini, whom Soroush met after his release from prison in 1963, and who made a profound impression on the young Soroush.[45] He then pursued the study of Islamic law and exegesis, or *tafsir*, while at the same time studying mathematics. After graduating, Soroush obtained master's degree in pharmacy at Tehran University. Later he briefly studied at the *Hoseyniyeh Ershad*, where he was deeply influenced by Shari'ati.[46]

In 1973 he left for London to pursue advanced studies in analytical chemistry at the University of London. But scientific training was not his first or only love. In the early seventies he began doctoral studies in the history and philosophy of science at Chelsea College, London. During the ensuing five years, Soroush wed a love of neo-Marxist political theory, the hard sciences, mysticism, and philosophy to produce an eclectic view of authority. This perspective not only echoed his own training, but also reflected the ideas of some of the leading ideologues of the revolution, including Ayatollahs Beheshti and Morteza Motahari as well as 'Ali Shari'ati. Soroush returned to Iran after the revolution began, and was appointed by Khomeini to the seven-member Cultural Revolution Institute. The mission of this body was to Islamicize the higher education curriculum prior to re-opening the universities in 1982. Yet Soroush was never fully at ease with this task. As he put it, during the revolution, "I was under the control of my passions, and you know, revolution is not rational."[47] Like other Islamic Leftists, his encounter with the irrationalities of revolution induced Soroush to rethink his Shari'atist-Khomeinist views. In 1984 he resigned from the institute (now renamed the Cultural Revolution Council) and took up a position in the Institute for Cultural Research and Studies in Tehran. He also began teaching philosophy and mysticism at Tehran University, and even hosted a series of televised lectures on the *Masnavi*, the famous work by the mystic Rumi. Thus although he no longer assisted the state's Islamicization efforts, he retained ties with the new generation of young intellectuals. It is this organic link between Soroush and university students—not merely his ideas—that explains the state's expulsion of him from the universities in 1996.

Rejecting Weststruckness

It is no coincidence that one of the first articles that Soroush published in *Kiyan* (August 1994) addressed the relationship between Muslim identity and modernization. While Khatami had poked a few hesitant holes in the monolith called the "West," Soroush's goal was to refute the idea that "Western civilization, the printing industry, photography, democracy, computers, aircraft . . . have all come about together." The West, he argues, is not a "strong factory . . . whose products are produced side-by-side and with full interdependence." The very idea that the West constitutes an integrated entity "has never been empirically demonstrated." Moreover, those Iranian intellectuals who view the West in these holistic terms are caught in a double paradox. First, their ideas are derived from the writings of Friedrich Hegel and Oswald Spengler as well as more recent postmodernists, "who have portrayed everything, including knowledge, to be the result of power." Thus Iranian thinkers have chosen an antimodernist, anti-Western methodology that is distinctly Western. "In their zeal for opposing the West," Soroush astutely notes, "they want to denounce modernism . . . with reasoning taken from foreigners themselves!" Second, from a practical point of view, this very attack on modernism transforms Iranians into passive victims of the West. "Those who invented the term 'plagued by the

West,' " Soroush declares in a reference to Al-e Ahmad and his followers, are "fatalistically worshiping history, philosophizing, waiting passively, submitting to the Western storm, and waiting for the arrival of its age."

The challenge, Soroush argues, is to devise a way to meet this "storm" that does not limit Iranians to the usual choices: submitting blindly to the West, embracing a supposedly "authentic" Muslim alternative, or selecting those aspects of the West that are useful, and dispensing with the rest. Instead, the key is to distinguish between the universal attributes of knowledge and the societal, civilizational, and cultural forces that give knowledge its "existence . . . but not its essence." The existential world may shape the *questions* that each culture asks, but, Soroush argues, the *answers and procedures* used to get to these answers "are not relative." Instead, they constitute the foundation for a new "realism," which, while it may be the "child of modernity and Western civilization . . . is a child who leaves its mother immediately after birth and casts the shadow of its thesis over all peoples, local and foreign." By breaking down "the walls of civilization," this universal ethos will allow Iranians to place their "politics, government, the economy, and morality . . . into a new order."

This prescription was infused with the tautological logic that often colors such Socratic arguments: by making the distinction between the universal "essence" of knowledge and its cultural or historical forms, Soroush can then arrive at the logical deduction that Iran can engage the West while avoiding the usual suspects: cultural surrender, cultural superiority, or mechanistic "borrowing." What is important, however, is not so much the coherence of Soroush's argument as its very articulation. In August 1994, Soroush challenged his readers to think beyond the hesitant revisionism to which Khatami and other reformist clerics felt compelled to adhere.[48]

Redefining the Clergy

The aforementioned article was something of an esoteric trial balloon. In the spring 1995 edition of *Kiyan,* Soroush addressed one of the hottest issues of the day: the future of the clergy. He minces no words in setting out his thesis. "To be a member of the clergy," he writes, "must not constitute a job or profession, or else it harms the religion to the benefit of the professional clergy and results in the destruction of the very thing that the clergy claim to protect, namely the religion itself." To defend this controversial proposal, Soroush begins by discussing the views of two scholars who influenced his own thinking: Ayatollah Motahari and Dr. Shari'ati. The latter, he notes, was a "withouter": a lay intellectual, he believed that the only way to strengthen religious ideas was to deprive the clerics of their control over interpreting religion. Yet, he observes, Shari'ati resembled those he attacked. His desire to "create an ideology of Islam . . . would have led to the formation of a class of ideological interpreters plagued with the same faults and calamities he was attempting to eradicate." This astute remark introduces an idea that was to become central to Soroush's writing: being complex, grand, and ultimately mysterious, religion cannot and should not be transformed into a man-made ideology. To defend this bold argument Soroush turned to the late Ayatollah Motahari, a student of Khomeini's whose writings played a significant role in the Islamic Revolution. Motahari, Soroush argues, defined the clergy as a group that makes "a living through religion, that is through religious knowledge or religious functions." Thus the critical thing was the *method* by which clerics gained their "livelihood." Motahari, Soroush implies, believed that the clergy was a "professional group" that, like any other similar group, has a "collective identity and shared interest."

Whether Motahari defined the clergy in these sociological terms is debatable. But Soroush is certainly correct when he argues that Motahari feared that the clerics' corporate identity might be undermined by their financial dependence on the wider populace. For while they had not been coopted by the state (as was the case with their Sunni counterparts), their dependence on the masses made them vulnerable to the irrational passions of society. Motahari argued that the solution was to create a central financial fund that would be controlled neither by the government, nor by the followers of a *marja'* (religious guide). But, Soroush maintains, this is no solution at all. The root of the problem lies in the clerics' lack of "detachment" from *all* mundane interests. Creating a central fund would turn the clerics into just another corporate group, whereas, he argues, the "defense of religious truth" should *never* be mixed with the "defense of legitimate professional and personal interests."

To make the case for a total detachment of the clergy from corporate or mundane interests, Soroush invokes the authority of several other thinkers, among them the eleventh-century Muslim philosopher Abu Hamid Mohammad Ghazali and the decidedly more contemporary Imam Khomeini! Ghazali's notion of "reliance of God," Soroush argues, holds that for the clerics to truly know God, they must "teach, pray, give advice, and fulfill other religious duties without worrying about their livelihood." Khomeini, he continues, adopted the same position when he admonished the clergy to, in Khomeini's words, "practice piety so that your honor among the masses can be protected." Yet, Soroush recognizes, Khomeini's phrase is opaque. Indeed, it can be interpreted in at least two ways: "piety" can be understood as a means of gaining the support of the masses, and thus constitutes a "worldly thing rather than a spiritual characteristic." Or, the statement can be understood to mean that "practicing piety becomes desirable . . . not because it gains worldly respect for the clergy but because it shows that the clergy can live in a way that is free from gaining material benefits from religion." This second view, Soroush claims, is consonant with Shi'ite mystical tradition, the essence of which is that the "work of religion is for those who are in love with religion. . . . Only such lovers are capable of abandoning everything else." Having cleverly reminded his audience of Khomeini's ambivalent feelings toward clerical activism, and having linked his own mystical incitations to those of the Imam, Soroush is well positioned to argue against placing a cleric "in a position [by which] he may be tempted to betray the religion." Citing the Sufi saying "I have been placed in the midst of water, yet I am expected to remain dry," Soroush concludes that the link between religion and *all* forms of worldly *power* must be totally severed if religion is to retain its moral and spiritual authority.

It is interesting to note that in the last pages of his essay Soroush insists that his thesis hinges neither on Marxist theory nor on Islamic mysticism. Instead, this scientist turned Islamist invokes the insights of a post-Marxist sociology of knowledge that is closer to Karl Mannheim and Thomas Kuhn than Karl Marx or Molla Sadra. Yet upon closer inspection we find that his analysis is neither as radical, nor as post-modern, as it seems. In fact, Soroush affirms that the modern professions are "controlled" by *objective* scientific codes, whose ultimate authority rests *not* on the short-term interests of the professional community, but rather on concrete empirical results. "Physicians," he notes, "cannot act in any way they want. . . . If patients are not treated, the society of physicians will lose its legitimacy." The same rule, however, does *not* apply to clerics. "Religious opinions," Soroush asserts, "do not have experiential impact on this world. Their full impact is revealed in the next world."[49] This remark suggests that despite his protests, Soroush's point of departure was philosophical and mystical. By tapping into these traditions, he not only speaks to a cultural sensibility that still resonated fifteen years after the revolution; equally important, he reminds his audience that Khomeini himself had been deeply influenced by mystical Islam. That Soroush's Sufism is shorn of the messianism that was central to Khomeini's mysticism is precisely the point. Viewing the carnage of ideological revolution to which he had briefly contributed, Soroush seems keen to introduce a type of charismatic experience that might appeal to the young, but would be denuded of the destructive chiliasm that animated the ideas of Khomeini and Shari'ati.

Deconstructing Secularism

In his subsequent *Kiyan* essays, Soroush never fully consummated this marriage of neo-Marxist sociology and mystical individualism. Instead, his writings constituted a work in progress whose importance lay in the provocative way it challenged Iranians to rethink religion and politics. Consider his essay on secularism that appeared in the summer 1995 edition of *Kiyan*. While the essay is extremely complex, its esoteric style hides its political message.

Soroush propounds a double thesis. On the one hand, he argues that pious Muslims have *totally misunderstood* "secularism." On the other hand, he wants to show that once Muslims grasp the intricacies and paradoxes of secularism, they will see that separating religion from politics *protects* rather than undermines religion. Soroush admits that this case is a hard one to make. "In the modern age," he notes, "secularism has been presented as a conscious discarding of religion from the affairs of life and politics." But this view misrepresents a more complex reality. "A secular government," he says, "is . . . not opposed to religion, but neither does it make religion the *foundation* of its legitimacy or the basis of its actions." Religion cannot legitimize politics because modern governments base their actions on scientific knowledge, which is intrinsically distinct from religion. Thus he defines *secularism* as "nothing other than rational and scientific social management." Muslims, Soroush adds, are not unfamiliar with this idea. Indeed, the Arabic term *'alamaniyat* means "knowledge practice." However, they have failed to grasp that this type of practice is "indifferent" rather than opposed to religion. Because scientific management addresses issues that do not "raise the subject of religion," it exists on a separate plane from religious knowledge.

Some Westerners obscured this notion of different kinds of knowledge. Because they assumed "religion to be false," they deduced that the "entry of a false idea into . . . politics [is] . . . damaging." Others, however, took a more sober view. They "considered religion to be true, but did not accept the idea that religion should have the right to mix with the impurities and the thinking about interests in politics, or for something sacred to be in the service of something worldly and non-sacred." It is this notion of secularism—as a system that ensures the moral and practical integrity of different types of knowledge—that Soroush wants to rescue from the misunderstandings and abuses to which it has fallen victim in the Islamic world, and in some parts of the West as well.

To make this case for multiple and distinct bodies of knowledge, Soroush insists on distinguishing between the ontological nature of secular thought on the one side, and its sociopolitical roots on the other. In what at first seems to be a familiar account of its historical determinants, he argues that secularism was the paradoxical product of the uniting of church and state. "The conversion of the church to a great bureaucracy," he notes, transformed the church into the "ideological child of the government." By thus sacrificing "its best and most vigorous internal forces to the enormous idol of the absolutist state . . . the political and cultural removal of the church was . . . done by the church itself." However, while this argument has momentous implications for the future of the Islamic Republic's clergy—if not the Islamic Republic itself—Soroush doesn't highlight the destructive effects of the church-state alliance merely as a prelude to an uncritical lauding of the "liberating" effects of the Reformation. On the contrary, echoing Mannheim's work on ideology and utopia, he argues that "both the confirmation and negation of secularization took the form of ideology." For in the religious wars that ensued from the Reformation, each side tried to annihilate the other's version of truth. The philosophers of the French Enlightenment were especially guilty of this sin. Instead of recognizing that their view of knowledge was merely a "tradition among traditions," they insisted on sitting "on the seat of 'precise science and knowledge' "—thus "cutting off . . . dialogue with other traditions" in a manner that transformed their ideas into "pure ideology." Such totalistic thinking, Soroush argues, was worse than religious absolutism. "One must . . . avoid," he warns, "the secular religions, meaning the human 'ideologies' which function more dogmatically than the celestial religions. They also call upon the people to be their servants, but slaves to themselves, not slaves to a kindly God."

But, Soroush insists, this ideologization of knowledge was by no means inevitable or intrinsic to secular thinking. On the contrary, the ontological roots of secular thinking have always resisted such totalistic logic. Tracing these roots, Soroush argues that secular thinking is rooted in Greek civilization, particularly in the philosophical distinction that Aristotle drew between "essences" or "nature" (and the metaphysical concepts that name these essences) on the one side, and the ultimate truths that God has bestowed on the other. Once "essences . . . became intrinsically independent from God. . . . God's only task became to give being to essence." Quoting Avicenna's assertion that "God did not make an apricot an apricot; rather he created it," Soroush deduces that the various types of knowledge created by God also have their intrinsic natures. Thus, anything that has its own prior essence . . . can no longer be considered intrinsically religious, because one thing cannot have two intrinsic natures. . . . For example, 'water' has its own structure. . . . For this reason, we do not have religious water and non-religious water . . . or religious and non-religious wine. The same applies to justice . . . knowledge . . . and the like. Similarly, we cannot have an intrinsically religious government. Do the secularists say anything other than this?

Having reasserted this Socratic-essentialist view of secular thought, Soroush then describes its two most important features, both of which he believes can contribute to "the well-being of humanity and . . . prepar[e] conditions for better understanding of the *true contents of revelation* [italics mine]." First, secularism has created a rational foundation for assessing the policies of government. As Soroush puts its, this perspective "does not just have the negative definition of 'non-religious,' but also the positive attribute of criticism and supervision." In a not-so-subtle reference to the position of the *faqih,* Soroush then asserts that in a system guided by secularism, "we have no . . . position, office or rule that is above general supervision, from the ruler himself to the manner of exercising. . . . [Thus] when a policy is not sacred (meaning it is scientific), and religion remains sacred, those two become separated, and this is the reason and meaning of the separation of religion and politics in secularism." But, he adds, this arrangement does not mean that faith-based knowledge loses its importance with the growth of science. On the contrary, "a human being can know God and be a religious practitioner and at the same time make use of scientific management." Nonreligion may be "getting a foothold" in politics at the same time that "a kind of scholarly and studied religious practice is forming at a higher level and is being realized." Thus, he reasons, it is precisely the *separation* of sacred and nonsacred knowledge that allows for this flowering of *society-based* piety: it encourages "intelligent people" to take "delight in God and religion in the domains of politics, society and nature," while at the same time using their scientific faculties to assess—and supervise—the policies of government. This, he adds almost as an aside, has certainly been the pattern "abroad" (i.e., in the West), where "the government follows society, and one of its characteristics is that if society is religious, the government also takes on a religious hue."

After implying that Western, society-based secularism may be doing a better job of protecting religious piety than state-enforced Islamic orthodoxy, Soroush proceeds to spell out an even more controversial thesis. The second advantage of secular thinking, he argues, is that it has been accompanied by, and in some ways helped to create, a profound change in society's understanding of its relationship to political authority. To explicate this point—which, as it turns out, is his central *political thesis*—Soroush relies on a familiar Weberian distinction. Religious thinking, he asserts, conceives of the individual as an "obligated being" who has a "duty" to obey. By contrast, the modernization of knowledge has produced the "entitled human being," a person who believes that he has "rights," and that it is the *duty* of government to protect them. These rights, Soroush adds, include the right *not* to practice religion. Where secular thinking prevails, religion is a *choice* rather than an obligation; it is on this basis that religion rises or falls in a modern society. Thus when modernization reaches a point where people see themselves "as master of the house, and indeed as the creator of the world," a society will *inevitably* make the transition from a conception of duty to one of rights. This is why, *in the long run,* mixing these two types of knowledge is pointless. "Islamic rights," Soroush asserts, makes as much sense as the phrase "Islamic water." The former not only substitutes one essential thing for another, "it is one philosophy taking the place of another."

Yet while inevitable, Soroush admits that this transition to a system of rights can be blocked or delayed, particularly when one of two conditions prevail: when government and the people have conflicting views of authority, or "where the boundaries between" competing notions of authority "become blurred and dark" such that "both ruler and subject speak and act on the basis of rights part of the time, and part of the time on the basis of responsibilities." Here, of course, Soroush implicitly assails the system of contending authorities that exists in the Islamic Republic—and to which he once contributed. "The discussion about the vice-regency and the idea of government as trustee," he then states, "and the opposition between these two things has to do with this very subject." Navigating in perilous waters, he adds that "if we view the government as the public's guardian, then we are speaking from the premise of responsibilities, and if we consider it the public's trustee . . . we are speaking on the basis of . . . rights. . . . All of the problems come from the effort to *combine* these two things" (italics mine).[50] Thus in one fell swoop, Soroush had not only impugned one of the guiding principles of the Islamic Left (and Khomeini)—namely, that populist-democratic and traditional-authoritarian notions of authority can be fruitfully accommodated; but also used a spirited defense of secularism to launch a barely disguised attack on the authority of the *faqih*!

Minus this attack, Soroush's argument might have attracted less probation from the regime (discussed later in this chapter). After all, one of his goals was to highlight secularism's propensity to transform into amoral instrumentalism or what he called "pure ideology." Writing in the same article, he asserts, "It is the duty of religious reformers and thinkers to make the human beings who have arrived at the rights of the devotee . . . aware of their responsibilities of being devotees." Indeed, this "is the work of religion," a task which Soroush has evidently defined for himself and other "religious reformers." But how was this noble task to be achieved? What kind of religious knowledge would support it, and how could this knowledge be relocated from the state to society without impugning the new Shi'ite institution and its effective "pope"? Regarding the first question, Soroush had little to say. Instead, he clung to a mystical notion of religion, even while acknowledging that mystics "fought the philosophers" because the former believed in a form of human existence that "would transcend causality." Soroush defends the notion of essences because he believes that it has served as a bulwark against all totalitarian efforts to "create a new man" or "pure ideology." Yet he implies in the same breath that religious knowledge existed in a sacred sphere that was beyond the rational perception of humans. This coexistence formed Soroush's own version of contending authorities. In his view, the coexistence of religious and scientific knowledge required separating the quest for the divine from the state; but, like Khatami, he was unsure how to create a new class of free "religious intellectuals" when an Islamic state hindered the freedom to pursue this very mission.

The Capitalist (and Democratic) Roots of Mysticism?

That key role of mystical thought in Soroush's work was revealed in a talk he gave at Tehran University that was subsequently published in *Kiyan*. Entitled "Livelihood and Virtue," the lecture assailed two of the principal ideological foundations of the Islamic Revolution: the notion of revolutionary, mass asceticism; and the collectivist, anticapitalist vision that flowed from it. In a clear echo of his previous writing on essences, Soroush begins the article by distinguishing between "dominant" and "subordinate" values. The first, he asserts, are "beyond nationality, beyond history, fixed and eternal. They include goodness, justice, sacrifice and courage." The second "are in the service of life." These values are clearly utilitarian; their "function . . . is to make life calmer, more desirable, more possible, and more complete." Soroush makes a point of tracing these "subordinate" values to the West. They evolved, he suggests, in a society in which the constant interaction of virtues and sins had the unintended consequence of serving the public good. Soroush doesn't hesitate to declare that "Bentham, Hume, Adam Smith" and most of all Bernard Mandeville were the "inventors of the modern age." Nor does he deny that most Islamic mystics opposed the worldly, individualistic ethos that these men praised. But neither is Soroush willing to cede the territory of Islamic mysticism to the ascetics. Instead, he suggests that certain mystical practices lend themselves to the guiding hand of unhindered political and social intercourse. "The great ones such as Ghazali, Mowlavi [Rumi], and Thomas Aquinas," he writes, "understood that sinners and impure people carry half the weight of society's livelihood on their shoulders. Through their . . . undeclared cooperation with the devout and noble, they help balance and perpetuate social life." Thus, Soroush asserts in a mystical celebration of functionalist theory, "in the workshop of existence, unbelief is inevitable."

Soroush then takes this provocative argument one step further. Rejecting the "Sufi-like morality [that is] based on asceticism, elevating poverty, and fleeing from the world," he notes that many of the Islamic world's greatest mystics—such as Mohammad Shamsoddin Hafez— did *not* "regard being a man of paradise as being in contradiction with seeking pleasure and living like a human being." Turning the logic of mystical asceticism upside down, Soroush argues that financial and personal contentment *opens the door* to experiencing "primary values," not least of which is spiritual knowledge:

> Values such as justice, freedom . . . remain fixed, but people are who busily struggling will have no opportunity to address those things. . . . For those caught in a struggle to make a living, even God is a god of oppressed people, not a god of mystics. . . . As soon as the veil of preliminary needs is ripped away, the beautiful sunshine of Truth will appear in the mirror of the higher and more refined mystical needs, and religion . . . in the true sense will return.

Beyond religious revelation, the satisfaction of worldly needs also makes pluralist democracy and freedom of expression possible. Soroush argues that pluralism is both a consequence of modernization and a prerequisite for it. Its value stems not merely from the fact that it allows "for crying out against injustice and oppressors. . . . More importantly, freedom of expression is for understanding the knowledge of others and presenting one's understanding to others. . . . Democracy is a method for managing a society that has the new values and information." In short, democracy is not so much an end as a means to the pursuit of "primary values." The latter requires certain preconditions, beginning with the creation of a "culture of wealth" and followed by the establishment of democracy itself. Nor do wealth and democracy contradict the essence of Islamic-Iranian culture and religion; on the contrary, Soroush implies that they establish the conditions for the flowering of a society's culture. Thus, he concludes, the challenge that Western culture poses to Islamic identity cannot be met by "following Spengler's lead in issuing unsubstantiated decrees every moment about the decline of Western civilization." Rather than embrace Jalal Al-e Ahmad's "Weststruckness," Iran's youth should "take refuge with . . . and also seek liberation from . . . tradition" by recognizing that the "morality of science" (which includes democratic governance) and "the morality of wealth are two forms of constructive tradition of which we are now more in need than ever."[51]

Widening the Debate:
Mysticism, Neotraditionalism, and Populism

Guillermo O'Donnell and Philippe Schmitter argue that the transition from authoritarianism has often been hastened "by exemplary individuals, who begin testing the boundaries . . . imposed by the . . . regime." This process "leads to mutual discoveries of common ideals, which acquire enormous political significance just because they are articulated publicly."[52] Soroush's eclectic blend of traditional liberalism, Shi'ite mysticism, Socratic essentialism, and neo-Marxist postmodernism opened the door to this very dynamic. It did so by impugning the revolution's central premise, namely that piety can be best protected by making the state its chief guarantor. Religion, Soroush implied, is *not* "everything." Rather, it constitutes its own distinct domain—a mysterious essence whose contemplation must be encouraged by free intellectuals, but never imposed from above, lest it transform into "pure ideology" and lose its spiritual force. However, if these bold ideas sparked a veritable rethinking of the revolution's ideology, they did not always produce the "common ideals" of which O'Donnell and Schmitter have written. Instead, Soroush's critique, as well as that of Khatami, set the stage for at least three distinct, if occasionally overlapping, intellectual trends. While it is beyond this scope of this inquiry to undertake a comprehensive review of these three trends, it is useful to identify and briefly evaluate their main lines of contention.

The first trend was inspired by the reformationist logic implicit in Soroush's ideas. The reformationists addressed the central challenge posited by Soroush: how to rescue religion by locating it in a realm that was autonomous of all power politics.[53] This topic was implicitly tackled in a four-part roundtable on secularism and pluralism published by *Kiyan* in the winter of 1995. Joining this discussion were four intellectuals, Hojjat al-Eslam Mohammad Mojtahed-Shabestari, Mahmud Sadri, Ahmad Sadri, and Morad Farhadpur. Despite their differences—some spoke from a postmodernist perspective, others from a more liberal or modernist vantage point, and still others from a religious one—all discussants debated one of Soroush's basic propositions, namely that Islamic mysticism *might* provide a lens through which young people could rediscover a personally liberating form of piety. The presence of Mojtahed-Shabestari lent credibility to this idea. A cleric and scholar of mystical philosophy whose ideas Soroush occasionally quotes in his own writings, Shabestari did not share his colleagues' postmodernist sensibility. However, while he rejected all forms of relativism, insisting that there indeed is an "ultimate truth," he added that "this is an absolute that is manifest in my human limitations, and engulfs me." Indeed, he affirmed, it is an "existential" absolute. Echoing the logic of mysticism, he asserts that "I only face the ultimate truth in my own religious experience. . . . Religious truth must be faced through a path of 'change and transformation,' not through a logical path. . . . *It is personal and dialectic* [italics mine]."

While some of his fellow discussants indicated difficulty with the notion of an absolute truth, they found in the existentialist quality of Mojtahed-Shabestari's mysticism (and by association, that of Soroush) a culturally inspiring foundation for religious and political pluralism. Yet several participants also suggested that mysticism might be lacking in two basic respects: first, it does not address the issue of religious law; second—and in the words of *Kiyan*'s chair of the discussion—"most mystical experiences occur for the elite rather than the common people." Mojtahed-Shabestari's answers to both points were not only tautological; more important for our purposes, they inadvertently highlighted the intrinsic limitations of a mystical approach. Addressing the link between mysticism and *Shari'ah* (sacred law of Islam), Mojtahed-Shabestari tried to define away the problem. "A religious law," he asserted, "is acceptable that is created compatible with the fluidity of religious experience." This sweeping mystical statement is not merely circular. If law issued from the constant flow of "religious experience," the clerical establishment would have to surrender its control over the interpretation of texts, an act tantamount to dismantling the Islamic state. As for the elitist nature of mysticism itself, Mojtahed-Shabestari's answer suggested that he was in fact comfortable with the need for religious leadership. Indeed, he explained that he *agreed* with those "mystics [who] say that the human problem is the problem of correct interpretation of religious experience and not the religious experience itself. . . . Prophets were leaders who taught man the correct interpretation of religious experience." While this point echoes Soroush's argument for "religious intellectuals," it also implies a degree of "guidance" (a term Mojtahed-Shabestari himself uses) that would dampen the supposedly liberating nature of mystical practices. This, perhaps, is why Farhadpur indicated that he prefers post-modernist solutions (which, he believes, do not imply guidance), while other roundtable participants endorsed mysticism over postmodernism solely for *pragmatic* reasons; in other words because, as Sadri puts it, the "post-modernist situation is . . . built on foundations that we lack."

While intriguing, the esoteric nature of these ideas diluted their political significance. As far as the regime was concerned, two other ideological trends presented a more serious and immediate challenge. The first came from dissident clerics who addressed the problem of clerical authority by advancing a neotraditionalist interpretation of *velayat-e faqih*. The death of Ayatollah 'Ali Araki in late 1994 set the stage for this development. By raising the hopes of Ayatollah Mohammad Yazdi and *Majles* Speaker 'Ali Akbar Nateq-Nuri that Khamane'i might be declared the *marja'*, Araki's death rekindled the long-simmering debate about the *faqih*'s authority vis à vis society in general, and the clerical establishment in particular. Leading this debate was none other than Ayatollah Hoseyn 'Ali Montazeri. Infuriated by the treatment accorded to him, his family, and other senior clerics who were critical of the regime, in October 1994 Montazeri warned in a twelve-page letter that "the political, economic, and cultural damage inflicted upon the Islamic system . . . because of mistakes and excesses by the selfish and incompetent individuals" would "weaken the religious beliefs of the faithful." Assailing the Special Clerical Tribunal, Montazeri insisted that its existence contravened the Constitution! Finally, in an ideological coup de grace, he assailed the very principle of *velayat-e faqih* by asserting that the Leader's particular "interpretation" of this principle "contradicts religious principles." "*Velayat-i faqih*," he is reported to have written, "does not mean that the Leader is free to do whatever he wants without accountability."[54]

Within a year, similarly bold ideas were being repeated in journals such as *Iran-e Farda* (Iran tomorrow). Reviewing the history of the concepts of *vali*, or guardian, and *marja'*, Hasan Yusefi Ashkevari asserted that "if the religious source of imitation and political leadership are to be concentrated in one person . . . what will become of the separation of powers, peoples' rights and the presence of political parties?" By reminding his audience that "Imam Khomeini is a prominent example of the ability to initiate a great movement against the ruling regime," the writer laid bare the central paradox of the Islamic Republic: namely, that in taking away the clerics' freedom, it had deprived the *maraje'* of their very moral authority.[55]

This neotraditionalist defense of religious pluralism was meant to save religion by taking it out of the hands of a ruling clerical elite.

However, uncoupling faith and political authority suggested its own problems, not least of which was the absence of a mechanism by which one or another interpretation of religion was to influence the social and political realms. The separation of the positions of *marja'* and *faqih* set out in the 1989 Constitution was supposed to have remedied this problem. But as Montazeri's own critique suggested, and as the efforts by Khamane'i's allies to declare him the *marja'* also showed, this distancing of religion from politics only encouraged renewed attacks on the idea of an absolute "political" *faqih, without* producing an alternative or coherent vision of the source and boundaries of the *faqih*'s authority.

The third trend sparked by Soroush's writing sought to remedy this problem by subjecting the *faqih*'s authority to democratic institutions and procedures. This populist approach was advocated by prominent Islamic Leftists, several of whom had survived the 1992 purge of the *Majles* by establishing powerful footholds in the publishing world. Among them, perhaps the most important was Ayatollah Musavi Kho'eyniha, who had become managing editor of the newspaper *Salam* (Hello). We have already seen that in 1988 Kho'eyniha argued that separating the positions of *marja'* and *faqih* would *strengthen* religious faith by making it less likely that the people would blame all of Islam for the particular actions of an evil or incompetent *faqih*.[56] But experience showed that this solution could not stop the *faqih* from abusing his "political" powers. Reacting to the regime's assaults on lay Islamists and the clergy, Kho'eyniha shifted ground: he now advocated a democratic interpretation of *velayat-e faqih* that was clearly designed to limit these political powers. "God," he argued, "has given the people the right to form a government, for their society to choose a ruler." Thus,

> the extent of the vice regency . . . are subject to the views and decisions of the people. If the people delegate all of this right . . . to one individual . . . then [he] . . . has absolute vice regency. [But] if the people have stipulated a structure for the nation's political and executive system, have distributed power based on this structure, have provided bodies and responsibilities for managing the country's affairs, then . . . the vice regency . . . does not belong to an individual but rather to the entire Islamic government.[57]

This argument raised many more questions than it answered. If the *faqih*'s authority were a product of popular sovereignty, the defense of Islam would henceforth be subject to the changing political and social tastes of the masses. Such a solution was far removed both from Soroush's reformationist orientation, and from Montazeri's neotraditionalist stance. Moreover, the direct election of a *faqih* could invite the real possibility that the people would choose a Supreme Leader who favored separating the clerics from political life! This was certainly not acceptable to the ruling clerics. Alternatively, if Kho'eyniha's position were interpreted *not* as a sweeping demand for the direct election of the *faqih*, but rather as a more modest call for subjecting the Leader's authority to that of other constitutional bodies such as the *Majles*, how could such a reconciliation of patrimonialist and rational authority be achieved in practice? As far as the ruling clerics were concerned, any such reconciliation was impossible: once it began, it could only lead to the destruction of the very position that it was ostensibly meant to protect.

The Regime Responds to the New "Martin Luthers"

From the vantage point of the regime, the theoretical problems raised by the aforementioned three trends were of less import than the growing popularity of revisionist thinking itself. Given the widening debate about the relationship between religion and politics in general, and the authority of the *faqih* in particular, the challenge facing the regime was whether it could still put the cat back in the proverbial bag. That it hoped it could was amply demonstrated by two things: by its verbal attacks on Soroush, and its efforts to associate all its critics—regardless of their differences—with Soroush's reformationist agenda. Thus in a direct response to Kho'eyniha's statements in *Salam*, a writer in the conservative newspaper *Resalat* began by noting that "these days, the doors to debate have been opened on government, the political philosophy of Islam, the political system, and other things." This has resulted not only in debates in the universities (God forbid!). More ominously, the "enemies of Islam" were now referring to these debates "as a 'Renaissance,'" while "pointing out various 'Martin Luthers' to the people." Citing Khomeini's writings, the writer then made the wholly plausible argument that Kho'eyniha's ideas were a slippery slope to democratic pluralism. Lambasting the notion that "the right of vice regency is . . . delegated from the people," he argued that "this theory" was not only "exactly the opposite of the Imam's . . . view," but also "the same theory of liberal democracy with a dash of 'materialistic Islam'. . . . Did the people . . . stand up to the Shah's fascist regime . . . only to get a 'liberal democratic' regime?" Taunting Kho'eyniha, the writer then asked, "in whose name" should this "new discovery" be recorded, "in your name, [or] Mr. Soroush . . . ?"[58] This attempt to associate Kho'eyniha with one of the regime's chief critics was not to be taken lightly. In late 1993 the editor-in-chief of *Salam*, 'Abbas 'Abdi, had been arrested and imprisoned, in part as a result of the attention that his paper had paid to the case of Montazeri.[59]

The regime and its allies supplemented this and other attacks with verbal—and eventually physical—assaults on Soroush himself. Leading this campaign was none other than the *faqih*. In November 1995, during a speech before university students that conveyed his concerns about Soroush's influence on young people, Khamane'i warned that "students at universities, seminaries and high schools" must "identify the enemy"; in other words, those "waging an onslaught against the clerical system." While not referring to Soroush by name, the *faqih* implicitly addressed Soroush's controversial analysis of the clergy. "As long as the clergy exists," Khamane'i promised, "there is a central organization which is recognized by the people as speaking in the name of religion." But, he immediately added, this organization was "not dependent on any of the organs of power." In other words, the *faqih* implied, Soroush was wrong to argue that the clergy was a bogeyman of the state. On the contrary, precisely because the "Shi'ite clergy . . . does *not* rely on the ruling machinery for money, for a living . . . they are free to speak." This said, Khamane'i then added that the clergy had earned this "freedom" by virtue of their skills and knowledge. "It is not as if anyone can come from anywhere and start interpreting the Koran and the Sunnah [example of the Prophet Mohammad and Imams as revealed in *hadith* literature]." In an unwitting affirmation of Soroush's central thesis, he then asserted unambiguously that "if religion . . . does not have an official custodian and guardian," it can easily be "brought in line" with any kind of thinking! "Understanding truths in such a distorted way," the *faqih* declared, "this is sedition."[60]

Khamane'i's words brought swift, if limited, results. Official discussions of Soroush's ideas in the universities were soon stopped, and after several physical attacks carried out by the regime's supporters, Soroush ended his public lectures and left the country for some months. But the regime's campaign not only failed to extinguish the fires of dissension. In addition, Khamane'i's attacks suggested that his regime was now on the defensive. To make matters worse, the outbreak of riots in 1995 further demonstrated the regime's isolation. Provoked by a sharp decline in oil prices and deteriorating economic and social conditions, in April the protests reached the outskirts of Tehran, where rioters, "armed with clubs and stones," shouted "Down with the Islamic Republic, Down With Khamanei."[61] These events set the stage for a realignment of forces in the *Majles*. During the spring 1996 parliamentary elections, a new coalition of Islamic Leftist reformers, businesspeople, and technocrats scored a major victory.[62] While these groups did *not* share a common economic agenda, they all wanted political liberalization. Henceforth, *Majles* Speaker 'Ali Akbar Nateq-Nuri could no longer rely on an automatic majority to align the *Majles* behind the conservatives' agenda. On the contrary, because new groups such as the Servants of Construction—a moderate faction drawn from the business and professional community—were close to Rafsanjani, the president could now push for reforms without having to rely exclusively on the authority of the *faqih* and his allies.[63] Thus in the ensuing months, Rafsanjani worked behind the scenes to promote Prime Minister Mir Hoseyn Musavi's candidacy for president. After Musavi declined to run, Rafsanjani shifted his support to Khatami, who after his 1992 dismissal had remained as an advisor to the president.

The 1997 Presidential Elections: Rights versus Duties

It is not clear why Khatami's initial decision to enter the political field did not provoke an immediate reaction from the ruling clerical establishment. One reason may be that the clerics were overconfident and thus could not imagine a scenario in which their candidate would lose. Another reason may be that Khatami's opponents failed to recognize the potentially subversive message embedded in his writing on Islamic civilization and the West. As a member of the clergy who, as we have seen, used a nativist discourse while subtly undermining it, since his resignation in 1992 Khatami had not provoked the kinds of concerns within the clerical establishment that the likes of Soroush, Montazeri, and Kho'eyniha had repeatedly sparked. Still, this did not mean that Khatami would have an easy time of it. The dual challenge facing him in the presidential campaign of 1997 was to seize the initiative without dashing the hopes of university students, intellectuals, women, and businesspeople for dramatic change, while reassuring the conservative clerics in general—and the *faqih* in particular—that his election would not strengthen the very forces the regime had been trying to silence.

As always, the most effective way for Khatami to walk this fine line was to align his political agenda with the legacy of the Imam. This he did with great rhetorical skill. Before and throughout the April 1997 campaign, he held that the Imam's legacy not only countenanced reform, but in fact *demanded* a reinvigoration of the constitutional authority of the *Majles* (and by implication that of the president) as well as a reinvigoration of civil and human rights as set out in the Constitution. In response, his opponents embraced the Imam's legacy in an effort to discredit the reformers.

Khatami first outlined his case for reform during a February 1997 interview published in *Jomhuri-ye Eslami*. The transcript suggests that the representative of this hard-line paper wanted to trap Khatami by pegging him into the ideological hole of liberalism. Khatami's response was to spurn all ideological badges while implicitly embracing the spirit of political liberalism. The interviewer begins by noting that Khatami is a member of the Association of Combatant Clerics of Tehran, some of whose members—it will be recalled—began to articulate a more liberal agenda during and after their 1992 purge from the *Majles*. "Do you think," the interviewer then asks in an implicit reference to the Islamic Left's democratic orientation, "that populism is merely a temporary slogan or a permanent strategy?" Khatami responds by explaining that while he is indeed a member of the Association of Combatant Clerics of Tehran, "I formulate . . . my program" on the basis of the "priority and needs of the society." Having distanced himself from the radicals, he then makes it clear that for him, populism means "people will be able to vote for ideas" or "programs" and "not for individuals." In other words, patrimonialist values should not be the basis for choosing a leader. "People," Khatami insists, have "the *natural* right . . . to vote for the best [italics mine]." But what does such a criterion mean in terms of "programs," the interviewer asks? It is at this juncture that Khatami makes the link to the Imam. Implicitly invoking Khomeini's utilitarianism, he states that "the most important . . . [problem] is the preservation of the system and of our Islamic values. . . . The Imam . . . exerted great efforts for the revolution to flourish. . . . What is a priority is that this system should be preserved, improved and strengthened. . . . It should be made strong and stable."

This was hardly the first time that an Iranian leader connected a reformist agenda to Khomeini's utilitarian focus on preserving the Islamic state or "system." As we saw in chapter 6, Rafsanjani did precisely this after Khomeini issued his 1988 edict on the "interests of the state." Khatami's goal is more ambitious: he wants to enlist Khomeini's rationalism to support the principal thesis that Khatami had been repeating since 1992, namely that the very survival of the system hinges on aligning each and every one of its parts—including the *faqih*—with the rights, duties, and roles established by the Constitution.

In an effort to advance this argument, Khatami reminds his interviewer that "The revolution . . . arose from the people's hearts and established . . . this bond between the people and the ruler." Evidently, this bond had begun to weaken. In strikingly nationalistic terms, Khatami affirms that while every "Iranian with nationalist sentiments *should* know . . . that today he has grandeur and 'the upper hand' and is not 'subjugated' " [italics mine], many Iranians have not grasped such momentous changes. This is because the old revolutionary instincts are still around. "We should free our society from the old mentality of law-evasion," Khatami declares, "and replace it with the mentality of respect for the constitution. . . . Security, justice, freedom, participation, and development too should be interpreted and implemented *within* this [constitutional] framework" [italics mine]. For, he insists, the time has finally come: "our society has the necessary stability to take the constitution seriously."

What then is the role of the clerics within such a framework? Reminding Khatami that he "recently . . . told a gathering that society should rely on all the people and not only on the elite because this elite may deviate from the correct path," the interviewer then asks whether Khatami considers "elitism to be an accepted theory." Khatami at first treads very lightly through this ideological minefield. "While in an ideal society everyone is a leader," he acknowledges, this view "is not inconsistent with the need for the presence of the immaculate Imam as the pivot of society." This said, Khatami then implies that clerical leadership is a matter of talents and skills, not divine inspiration: "All talents are not equal in society, and important duties are handed to people who have a higher degree of knowledge." But such duties do not justify patrimonialism. Echoing his populist roots, Khatami insists that "experts should serve the people. . . . Ruling should serve the people and not vice versa."

Such declarations did not satisfy Khatami's interviewer. Two questions remained: first, can a constitutional system be squared with the authority of the *faqih*? And second, will political reform invite the West's "cultural and mental onslaught"? Regarding the first question, Khatami attempts to square the *faqih*'s authority with the principle of popular sovereignty by again invoking the concept of the system. Khatami's intent is not only to distinguish between this system and the daily grind of politics, but to imply that the *faqih*'s ability to protect this system derives from remaining *above* the political fray. Thus while affirming, à la Kho'eyniha, that the "pivot of the system which was created by the people is the supreme jurisconsult," Khatami adds that "the Leader is everyone's leader and the leader of all those who have accepted the system." This is why, he insists—in a clear reference to conservative clerics—that those who "portray themselves" as the *faqih*'s "only" supporter are "actually demoting and discrediting" the *faqih* "from his position at the head of society." These people are "inflicting a blow on the revolution," whereas "those who . . . love the system of the Islamic Republic" have shown a refusal to "exploit such an important issue."[64]

Having used this distinction between politics and the system to argue for a transpolitical vision of the *faqih*'s authority, Khatami then employs it to tackle the issue of cultural invasion. Insisting that "whoever accepts the system can enter the system," Khatami implies that loyalty to the system does not require adherence to any particular ideology or politics other than the system itself. Moreover, while affirming that "anyone intending to harm Islam will be confronted with the Islamic system," he then adds the crucial observation that since this system is "founded [on] the tradition of criticizing the rival in society . . . plotting ideas aimed at your youth . . . should be . . . answered with counterthoughts. Thoughts cannot always be answered with prevention and negation." In short, the most effective response to cultural invasion is dialogue and openness rather than repression.

Apart from criticizing the intrinsic problems associated with a repressive response to the cultural invasion, Khatami also agues that the need for a pluralistic response to the West is dedicated by global realities. Noting that even the Europeans worry about their national identity, he adds, "I do not believe that America has initiated a cultural onslaught against Europe because of political determination." In short, Iran is *not* facing an organized plot. Instead, Khatami implies, the challenge facing Iran is systemic. It is a product of "information networks" and "superior technology" whose force is inexorable. "What will we do if tomorrow television sets can receive satellite programs? Can we say that television sets should be gathered? Today the Internet is much more important than the satellite. . . . All the elements are not in our hands to close down the doors for ever." Thus the solution is not coercion but "prevention." Naturally, this policy was Khomeini's approach. The Imam, Khatami asserts, "brought new ideas on the basis of principles," the most important of which was "elevating society's power of thought . . . an Islam which was to solve the problems of man. . . . Getting to know the world and the various schools of thought . . . strengthening Islamic and native culture are all solutions to confront the West's cultural onslaught."

Khatami directed the above defense of pluralism and constitutionalism to his most important constituency—university students. Noting that one of the revolution's greatest achievements was that "university intellectuals started speaking the same language as the people," Khatami implicitly acknowledged that this space between the university life and popular faith was once again widening. "Preserving Islamic values," he notes, "is a difficult job. . . . We still have a long way to go in the universities to achieve spiritual and mental changes." This can only be done by observing "the principle of rivalry" and "diversity," since ultimately, "human creativity is based on diversity . . . within the system, which means the acceptance of the rules of competition and respect for rivals."[65]

In his subsequent talks, interviews, and speeches, Khatami linked this very Western notion of institutionalizing the "rules of the game" to the role and authority of the *Majles.* Citing Khomeini's oft-repeated statement that "the Majlis is the essence of the nation's virtues," Khatami deduced that "government is, in a sense, determined by the Majlis. It is true that the president is directly elected by the people's votes. But . . . the Majlis has the upper hand. . . . The executive branch has to answer to the legislative branch." What is remarkable about this statement is not merely that it diminishes the authority of the president, but that it suggests that the *faqih* is also subject to the authority of the *Majles.* Indeed, Khatami goes on to remind the interviewer that the very origin of the word *parliament* is *parler,* meaning "to discuss." The original function of parliaments in France, he correctly observes, *was not to rule.* Instead (and jumping to the present), Khatami states that "the Majlis plays the role of a court which is defending authorities, limits, and rights." Having made this reference to the notion of natural rights, he then asserts that the *Majles* "reforms the structure of government to the benefit of the people." As for the Supreme Leader, in this interview he barely got a mention. Nevertheless, Khatami cannot resist again reminding his audience that as far as he is concerned, because the Leader is the chief protector of the system, he does not champion any particular ideology. Pushing this logic one step further, Khatami then argues that the *faqih* "is the leader of all those who do *not* believe in religion but who have accepted the system" [italics mine].[66] This remarkable claim may have been consistent with Khatami's modern view of authority, but it was hardly compatible with the conservative clerics' understanding of *velayat-e faqih!*

Embracing and Extending Khatami's Charismatic-Utilitarian Message

In a strange sort of way, Khatami's idea of the *faqih's* authority seemed to be more in line with the eclectic blend of charismatic and utilitarian thinking that characterized Khomeini's view of that office than with the traditional vision of the *faqih* advanced by the ruling clerics. Khomeini struggled to remain above the political fray; his charisma derived in part from the perception that while he personified the *umma*, or Islamic community, the "interests" of that community required enduring institutions that transcended the authority of the Leader himself. While Khatami seemed to invite Khamane'i to recapture this dissonant legacy and link it to a more constitutional form of government, it is hard to avoid the conclusion that during the course of the campaign itself, Khatami—or at least his followers—began to conceive of the president as the primary vehicle for linking charisma and democracy. As Khatami traveled around the country, his natural charm, enthusiasm, and good looks became as important as the ideas he was advocating. Indeed, Khatami's statements reflect his awareness that the election was as much about addressing the existential problems of the youth as it was about solving concrete social problems. The critical issue, he noted, was the "physical, mental, and spiritual needs" of young people, not least of which was their need to "enjoy the present."[67] Iran's intelligentsia and students eagerly embraced this message. Not only were his rallies well attended, particularly in the universities, but a wide range of student, professional, women's, musical, and artistic associations endorsed Khatami's candidacy. Moreover, leftist or reformist newspapers such as *Salam* and *Hamshahri* gave their implicit, but influential, support to his campaign. In a country where the minimum voting age was sixteen, this explosion of enthusiasm among the young had profound, if not revolutionary, implications.

This point was not lost on Khatami's closest supporters and advisors, many of whom came from, or identified with, the radical *Majles* deputies who had been purged by the regime in 1992. Buoyed by the manifestations of popular support for Khatami, as well as by his vigorous defense of constitutionalism and the people, these children of the revolution were soon hard at work trying to push his ideas as far as they would go. To what may have been Khatami's distress, many of these zealous reformers published articles that aggressively addressed the one issue that Khatami had tried hard to finesse: the authority of the *faqih*. Some radicals, such as Mehdi Karrubi, who at the time was Secretary of the Tehran Militant Clerics Society, did so carefully. "All of us," he affirmed, "accept the absoluteness of *velayat-i faqih*. . . . All of us accept this and obey him." Indeed, having received permission from the *faqih* to resume its activities, the leaders of the association "entered gingerly and gradually."[68] Others, however, were less diplomatic. Behzad Nabavi, who, as we noted earlier, had launched a vigorous protest after his disqualification from running in the 1992 *Majles* elections, insisted that "80 percent of the Imam's opinions were on the same track as our own viewpoints." Having thus aligned the radicals with the "true" legacy of the Imam, Nabavi asserted, "Only in one place did the Imam speak about the absolute guardianship, and there were no other discussions." In other words, Khomeini's January 1988 edict on the "absolute *faqih*" was not the be-all and end-all of the Imam; on the contrary, Nabavi implies, it was something of an exception. And even if it were not, the edict had to be understood in the broader context of the Imam's overall vision—which, of course, the radicals grasped more clearly than anyone: "Our understanding of the absolute guardianship which the Imam spoke of is the authority of the Islamic government, not the authority of a single person." Thus, Nabavi insisted in language that seemed to reflect Khatami's, "The guardianship of the religious jurist are rules of the regime in the same way that the place of the people in the regime is a rule."[69]

The Counterattack: Too Much, Too Late

That by design or default Nabavi's statements echoed Khatami's was logical. As we have noted, the position of the political reformers had always been that Khomeini's January 1988 edict was as much if not more about government than about any one individual. What Nabavi did was express this idea in terms that seemed to question the very legitimacy of the *faqih*, or at least to subordinate his authority to the will of the people. Such ideas went much further than had Khatami's rhetoric. Indeed, they had more in common with Kho'eyniha's populist-democratic concept of the *faqih*'s authority. That such ideas were now being commonly expressed in papers such as *Salam* confirmed the clerical establishment's fears that Khatami's reformism was opening the door to a counterrevolution along the lines of the 1906 Constitutional Revolution. However, unless the *faqih* himself both shared such fears and *acted on them*, it was unlikely that the clerics' counterattack—however stinging—would reverse the gathering momentum in favor of Khatami.

The clerics' response took three forms: one was articulated by Khatami's chief rival, Speaker 'Ali Akbar Nateq-Nuri; another was voiced by Khamane'i himself; and a third was expressed by a leader of the conservative clerics, Ayatollah Mahdavi-Kani. We can dispense with Nateq-Nuri's response quickly, for he minced no words: "By raising the question of scientific management and jurisprudential management . . . the enemies come to the conclusion that the former is the best. . . . [Their] aim is to undermine the root of *velayat-i faqih* in the long run." Declaring himself a loyal supporter of Khamane'i, Nateq-Nuri lashed out at all those who claimed that economic issues should take precedence over culture and identity, and particularly over the struggle against Western "arrogance."[70] Such attacks left most young Iranians uninspired, to say the least. Although Nateq-Nuri was the same age as Khatami, he was perceived as much older and far less wise. With a good part of the Islamic Left having abandoned such rhetoric, and with students looking for a new vision, the *Majles* Speaker seemed to be speaking into the wind.

Yet if Nateq-Nuri's attacks left many Iranians cold, Ayatollah Mahdavi-Kani's verbal assault surely sent shivers through the opposition. As secretary of the conservative Combatant Clergy Association, which was closely aligned with the influential Qom Theological Lecturers' Association, he was well placed to mobilize the clerical establishment against Khatami and his supporters. Wasting no time, in February 1997 Mahdavi-Kani launched a series of blistering attacks, the purpose of which was twofold: first, to link Khatami's candidacy with the 1906 Constitutional Revolution, which, as we have noted, ended with the creation of a largely secular Parliament; and second, to argue that the reformists had completely distorted, if not betrayed, Khomeini's legacy. "Beware," Mahdavi-Kani warned,

> that the events of the constitutional revolution are being repeated with this talk. When they dare to speak in the Islamic Republic and at the center of Shi'ism and to say that the legitimacy . . . of the guardianship of the commander of the faithful [Ali] was based on popular demand, then nothing will be left of your guardianship. . . . It is foolish not to prevent these deviations in the name of freedom!

What was worse, those who had championed a democratic guardianship had not only done so in the name of Khomeini, but had done so by proffering a mystical vision of the Imam that Mahdavi-Kani claimed was completely false. "We have role models and we don't need Sufi games and gurus," he declared—an oblique reference to attempts by thinkers such as Soroush or Mojtahed-Shabestari to link Khomeini to their mystical-reformist agenda. Insisting that "I never remember the Imam . . . saying a single word about having [transcendental] contacts or being in [transcendental] states," Mahdavi-Kani tried to deflate the notion that mystical experiences might offer the masses a less privileged access to the divine.[71]

Such attempts to recapture Khomeini's legacy for the conservative camp were replayed in the pages of the conservative paper *Resalat*. Warning that "even countries that regard themselves as cradles of democracy and liberalism consider freedom permissible only within the framework of the red lines of their own regime," Mohsen Azhini lambasted radicals for calculatedly misrepresenting Khomeini's words so that they equated the guardianship of the jurisconsult with "dictatorship, theocracy, and the monopolism of the clergy." Examining in excruciating detail several essays about *velayat-e faqih* that had been authored by Islamic Leftists such as Nabavi and Asadollah Bayat, Azhini used his impressive knowledge of Khomeini's writings to argue that while "the regime of the religious jurist" cannot be established "without being elected by the people," it "also has divine and religious support, which is a divine appointment." In other words, the *faqih*'s authority came from God, not the people. Moreover, Azhini added, Khomeini's January 1988 edict clearly stated that the *faqih* had "absolute authority" to defend the "interests of the Islamic country." Contradicting his initial reference to the "people's will," Azhini held that the *faqih*'s authority was practically unlimited, a position which he tried to support by citing from Articles 4, 57, and 110 of the Constitution. "Those who may be pursuing certain intentions by using the 'constitution' as an excuse," he warned, "must be told that this is not a suitable excuse, because the religious guardian . . . is a person who . . . believes in the constitution more than anyone else."[72]

In the beginning Khamane'i did not match these verbal assaults. Indeed, he stated in February 1997 that "it is fitting for the experts to carry out academic debates on the details of the issue of *velayat-i faqih*." This said, he added that the "exalted leader of the Islamic revolution [i.e., Khomeini] said that . . . safeguarding the system was the most important responsibility." In contrast to the reformers, who had embraced this utilitarian principle in order to advance their more pluralistic vision, the *faqih* insisted that this principle must be given "priority with . . . all power."[73] This shift to a more defiant position suggests that Khamane'i had initially assumed that the state's propaganda resources—which were made available to Nateq-Nuri—would assure Khatami's defeat, or that an open verbal assault on Khatami might backfire. However, by late May he had begun to change his tune. With Khatami's popularity on the rise, Khamane'i now gave an implicit endorsement to Nateq-Nuri, the authoritarian terms of which contrasted sharply with Khatami's vision of political authority:

> Every day there is talk of . . . separating religion from politics. . . . Inside
> the country, too, some people repeat these utterances. . . . You should make
> the people understand that just as participating in an election is duty,
> making a good choice is also a duty. . . . The people accept the principle
> of receiving help for the clergy. . . . No member of the clergy should think
> that he has no . . . duty in this respect. They should not say that the people

228 / Chapter Eight

should go and do whatever they like. . . . You should issue . . . guidelines to the people.[74]

Expanding on this theme several days later, Khamane'i insisted that "if anyone, out of those people who enter into the arena of the presidency shows the slightest sign of being soft toward the United States . . . toward the cultural and political attacks of foreigners . . . the nation will definitely not vote for such a person."[75] But by then, this crude attack came as too much, too late. To have stopped the election would have meant courting open civil conflict. On 23 May 1997, Khatami scored a stunning victory by winning 70 percent of the thirty million votes cast.

Summary: The "L-Word"

If Khomeini's revolution was about anger, Khatami's was about happiness. While it would be an exaggeration to say that Khatami's election constituted a charismatic revolution, it certainly demonstrated the ability of an alluring personality to harness the existential angst of young people behind a vision for a better world. In this sense, it echoed Mannheim's notion of utopian movements, which, he argued, attempt to "burst the bounds" of reality in the quest for a different world. That said, most Iranians viewed this "second *khordad*" in sober terms. By 1998 the vast majority of the population was sick of revolutionary slogans and promises. Although inspired by Khatami's pluralist vision of Islam, the majority of Iranians agreed that reform—rather than revolution—was the order of the day.

But what kind of reform? What central idea inspired Khatami's victory? Most Iranians knew the answer but refused to utter it: liberalism. Through a process of ideological metamorphosis whose broad outlines we have already traced, the collectivist vision of democracy and popular sovereignty that had inspired the revolution in 1979, and which was institutionalized along with other contending political principles, slowly reemerged in pluralist form. Thus a revolution that began by speaking in a nativist, anti-Western language was transformed into a reform movement whose chief spokesman could barely hide the principal philosophical foundation of his political vision. Asked in early 1997 for his opinion on liberals and liberalism, Khatami explained, "I believe that a true human being who believes and has accepted Islam cannot be a liberal." This was because "liberalism is based on man's wants, wishes, and his materialistic needs," whereas Islam concentrates on the "spiritual and ethical improvement of man." Having defined liberalism and Islam in these broad, ultimately meaningless terms, Khatami then proclaimed that there was not one person among the groups that supported the revolution who could be a called liberal![76] Such sophistry demonstrated the continuing and debilitating influence of dissonant institutionalization. As I shall discuss in greater detail in the conclusion, despite the considerable progress represented by Khatami's election and his subsequent efforts to push for an "Islamic Civil Society," many groups and institutions still sought to maintain what Khatami called the "old mentality."

Conclusion:
Fear and Joy

A carnival celebrating the Iranian revolution for the first time featured
U.S. cartoon characters, dancing and music. . . . Actors dressed as Mickey
Mouse, Bugs Bunny and a variety of animals sang and danced in a
procession of more than a dozen floats that circled *Enqelab* (Revolution)
Square, entertaining a crowd of 5,000 people. Called "Carnival of Joy,"
the carnival was organized by the Ministry of Culture as part of the
celebration leading up to the twentieth anniversary of the 1979 overthrow
of the U.S.-backed Shah on February 11.[1]

—*Iran Weekly Press Digest*, 5 February 1999

The Supreme Leader vowed on Wednesday that "Iran would stay on its
20-year-old Islamic Revolutionary path. . . . The Islamic Revolution has
destroyed any fear of bullying foreign powers and exposed their false
shows of friendship. . . . The young people of today can review this short
but eventful 20-year period, and never be fooled by the tricks and the
smiles of America and Zionism."[2]

—Supreme Leader Ayatollah 'Ali Khamane'i, 10 February 1999

The Inevitable Victory of Mickey Mouse?

On the twentieth anniversary of Iran's Islamic Revolution, Tehran's
Revolutionary Square played host to Mickey Mouse and Bugs Bunny.
Apparently, the young people who flocked to this event were not both-
ered by the spectacle of American cartoon characters celebrating the
fall of the Shah. But the same could not be said of Supreme Leader 'Ali
Khamane'i. As far as he was concerned, the five thousand participants in
this Carnival of Joy were suffering from a bad case of false consciousness.
After all, he insisted some days later, "The young people of today can . . .
never be fooled by the tricks and smiles of America and Zionism."
Yet while it is easy to lampoon Khamane'i's fear of joy, we would be
mistaken to assume that the austere asceticism and anti-Americanism
that he articulated has lost its foothold in the ideologies and institutions
of the ruling elite. Mohammad Khatami's experiences during the three
years following his presidential election demonstrated that he faced
a tricky dilemma. On the one hand, his overwhelming victory at the
polls encouraged his followers to push for an immediate opening of the

political and cultural field. On the other hand, his conservative detractors seized every occasion to undermine Khatami's allies in government, the media, and the universities. Khatami's dilemma was to respect such forces without alienating the millions of young people who embraced his message of hope, joy, and political reform.

Khatami skillfully negotiated these countervailing pressures. In so doing, he secured an unprecedented measure of *glasnost* in the cultural and intellectual fields. Moreover, he raised the hopes of his young followers for a new kind of Islamic Republic without provoking a politically fatal backlash from the *faqih* or his allies. However, the assumption held by many "transitologists"—namely, that such experiments in political liberalization are inherently unstable, and thus either set the stage for a breakthrough to competitive democracy, or provoke a counterreform from "hard-liners"—may be wrong.[3] Rather than move forward or back along a linear path, the system of contending authorities forged by Khomeini and retooled by 'Ali Akbar Hashemi Rafsanjani and Khamane'i may endure in new institutional and ideological forms. This appears to be Khatami's objective. As we shall see, during the first two years of his presidency, Khatami strove to sustain *and* transform Khomeini's dissonant legacy. Moreover, in a tribute to its enduring symbolic power, Khatami and his opponents again invoked that legacy in furthering their aims. While the February 2000 parliamentary elections, during which reformists crushed their conservative rivals, suggest that the reformists had stretched the Imam's words about as far as they would go, I will argue in the "theoretical reprise" that concludes this chapter that domestic and global realities may very well *facilitate* Khatami's efforts to reform, rather than eclipse, the system of contending authorities that he inherited in May 1997.

Khatami's "Dialogue of Civilizations"

During his first months in office, Khatami spelled out an eclectic worldview that expanded upon many of the ideas he had raised in his earlier writings. Of course, this vision was fully consistent with the Imam's legacy. Thus in his 4 August 1997 inaugural address before representatives of the *Majles*, Judiciary, Council of Guardians, Assembly of Experts, and Expediency Council, Khatami explained that the revolution had been "led . . . by a Mujahid jurisprudent, a revolutionary mystic and yet, a statesman immersed in moral virtues." Celebrating Khomeini's "far-reaching dimensions," Khatami declared that the "mandate and mission of the President" was to "institutionalize the rule of law, and the Constitution, first and foremost." This, he held, was "the only way through which the continuity of the Revolution, the dynamism of the system and the power and dignity of the noble people of Iran can be ensured." While such aims would be achieved by a government that "felt duty-bound to base its programs and policies on the *essence* of Islam" [italics mine], Khatami swore to fulfill the duties that the *law* imposed on him by protecting the "freedom of individuals and the rights of the nation . . . [through] . . . constitutionally guaranteed liberties, strengthening . . . the institutions of civil society . . . and preventing any violation of constitutional rights." After noting—almost in passing—that "the Leadership . . . will . . . guide and assist us in performing these duties," he asserted that "the legitimacy of the government stems from the people's vote. . . . The Islamic government is the servant of the people and not their master."[4]

What was *essentially* "Islamic" about this inspiring formulation? In a speech before the Eighth Session of the Islamic Summit Conference, held in Tehran on 9 December 1997, Khatami elaborated a vision of "Islamic" politics that revealed the considerable impact of globalization and Western political thought on his thinking. "In our view," he declared, "a new order based on pluralism is taking shape in the world." The challenge for Islamic societies was to join this world while rediscovering "the essence of our identity." Yet, he then implied, "such a return to . . . [our] common identity" was really not a return at all. Echoing the instrumentalist thesis he had laid out in his book *Fear of the Wave,* Khatami invited Muslims to *create* a "new Islamic civilization," the heart of which would be the "realization of the 'Islamic civil society' in our respective countries." While he insisted that this society was based on a "unique and distinct view of existence" that was "fundamentally different from the 'civil society' rooted in Greek philosophical thinking and Roman political tradition," Khatami's notion of an "Islamic civil society" was clearly inspired by the West.

Khatami hinted at this point during his 7 December speech. The "accomplishments . . . of Western civilization are not few," he noted, even if its "negative consequences . . . for non-Westerners are plentiful." The challenge was to "utilize" its "positive scientific, technological and social accomplishments" without being seduced by its negatives. This goal could only be realized through a "dialogue among civilizations and cultures, with people of intellect taking a pivotal role."[5] Though hardly an original prescription, Khatami made a case for adapting a particular Western concept that most clerics had long scorned: the distancing of religion from politics. Thus in a Friday sermon Khatami began by asserting that an "Islamic civil society . . . is not . . . uniform." The "real achievement," he argued, is to . . . compromise," while "the danger is when we label one tendency as Islamic and the other as against Islam." To avoid these dangers the clergy had to remain "aloof from the unwanted negative consequences of being too close to power and government, which could prevent them from their essential mission of providing spiritual and religious guidance to society."[6] Although this demand was partly motivated by Khatami's desire to discourage maverick clerics such as Ayatollah Hoseyn 'Ali Montazeri from criticizing the government and thus putting Khatami and his reformist allies in an awkward position (discussed later in this chapter), his call for distancing clerics from political power also reflected a sincere conviction. As Khatami put it in a January 1998 interview with CNN, the roots of American civilization went back to the Puritans, a people whose vision was "in harmony with republicanism, democracy and freedom." Recalling Alexis de Tocqueville's *Democracy in America*, Khatami noted that the French statesman had attributed the admirable nature of American democracy to the "fact that liberty found religion as a cradle for its growth, and religion found protection of liberty as its divine calling." This unique relationship, he argued, was precisely what made America so appealing to Iranians. "We feel that what we seek is what the founders of American civilization were also pursuing four centuries ago."[7]

The Return of the Islamic Left: From Louis XVI to François Mitterand?

This remarkable statement was fully in keeping with Khatami's previous writings. His message, that religious freedom encourages rather than discourages piety, found a receptive audience in a society exhausted by dogma. That Khatami believed that such an arrangement could exist in a system over which the *faqih* presided did not diminish the potency of his message. That said, the political significance of Khatami's ideas, and even more so those of Abdolkarim Soroush and his young followers, extended far beyond their ideological or emotional appeal. By 1998 their eclectic vision had inspired a mass reform *movement* linking three generations: prominent "fathers of the revolution," most critically Ayatollah Montazeri; "children of the revolution," many of whom came from the Islamic Left as well as from liberal-nationalist circles; and finally "grandchildren of the revolution," the new generation of high school and university students who constituted the movement's mass base. In some ways, the fate of the reform movement itself hung on Khatami's ability to inspire *and* control this third generation. The new president accomplished both goals by promoting an array of institutions through which his politically experienced allies in the Islamic Left addressed an increasingly impatient and frustrated youth.

Khatami's cabinet provided an official—though hardly inviolate— arena within which reformists advanced their case. While composed of religious conservatives, moderates, and more radical reformers, Khatami's thirty-two-member cabinet gave pride of place to "children of the revolution." Khatami's official senior advisor was none other than Mir Hoseyn Musavi, the former prime minister whose office was abolished in 1989. The executive vice president was Mohammad Hashemi (brother of former President Rafsanjani), who in 1993 had been forced from his post as director of the Voice and Vision Broadcasting Company. Musavi and Hashemi were joined by several other prominent "children of the revolution," all of whom shared one or both of the following characteristics: they belonged to the generation of the sixties and seventies whose "multiple imaginations" had been formed by direct or indirect exposure to Western ideas; or, they were part of, or had close ties to, the cadre of radical *Majles* deputies who were purged in 1992. The cabinet included First Vice President Hasan Ibrahim Habibi (educated in France and a friend of 'Ali Shari'ati's), Minister of Foreign Affairs Kamal Kharazi (educated at the University of Texas, Houston), Vice President and Head of Planning and Budget Organization Mohammad 'Ali Najafi (educated at M.I.T.), and Vice-President for Environmental Protection Ma'soumeh Ebtekar.[8] Raised in the suburbs of Philadelphia but educated in Iran, during the 1979–80 hostage crisis Ebtekar served as an interpreter for the Students of the Imam's Line, the militant organization that occupied the American Embassy during the crisis. Her position in the cabinet encouraged those who wanted Khatami's government to expand opportunities for women in public life. Finally, mention must be made of Abdollah Nuri, Khatami's first Minister of the Interior. A prominent member of the clerical Left, he brought solid revolutionary credentials to the reform struggle. This explains, in part, why in 1998 hard-line clerics forced him to resign, and later put him on trial for espousing "un-Islamic" ideas.

Control over the ministries of Interior and Culture proved crucial; these two ministries gave licenses to a host of civil society organizations, the most important of which were located in the media. This development had a profound impact on the ideological disposition of the reform movement. Excluded from Parliament since 1992, Islamic Leftists flocked to the opposition press—the backbone of a reemerging civil society. The role that Ayatollah Musavi Kho'eyniha and 'Abbas 'Abdi played in the daily newspaper *Salam* (Hello) has already been mentioned in chapter 8. By 1998 their daring criticisms were already being echoed in papers such as *Khordad*, edited by former Interior Minister Nuri; *'Asr-e Ma* (Our era), a biweekly edited by Behzad Nabavi (former minister and chief negotiator during the 1979–80 hostage crisis whose letter to former President Rafsanjani was also discussed in chapter 8); *Rah-e No* (New way), edited by Akbar Ganji, a former contributor to *Kiyan* who was close to Soroush; and *Jame'eh* (Society). Many of these reformers also played a major part in forming new organizations such as the Islamic Iran Participation Front (IIPF). Established in December 1998, IIPF counted among its one hundred founders most members of the Association of Combatant Clerics of Tehran, as well as leading lay Islamists such as Mohammad-Reza Khatami (President Khatami's brother), 'Abbas 'Abdi, Ma'sumeh Ebtekar, and Sa'id Hajjarian.[9]

Not only were these reformists prominent members of the Islamic Left, but no less than five of them—'Abdi, Kho'eyniha, Nabavi, Ebtekar, and Hajjarian—had been leaders of, or otherwise linked to, the Students of the Imam's Line. While many Western observers suggested, in the words of one *New York Times* correspondent, that it was "paradoxical" that some of the "most prominent advocates for opening the country . . . and institutionalizing democratic values were either hostage-takers or supporters of the seizure" of the American Embassy in 1979, the reader will appreciate why this development was eminently logical.[10] As we have seen, Islamic Leftists were originally inspired by a discordant blend of utopianism, instrumentalist existentialism, and radical republicanism. Their suffering at the hands of a state they had helped to legitimate cured most of them of their utopianism. As Ganji noted, "I was an Islamic leftist, a Revolutionary Guard, and I worked at the Ministry of Islamic Guidance. . . . We wanted to change everything. We wanted to create new kinds of human beings. I can tell you I don't have any desire like that any more."[11] It is particularly significant that this transformation began in the post–Cold War era and *in tandem* with a global process of democratization. The latter captured the imagination of many in the Islamic Left. If in the seventies the radicals were following Shari'ati by using Western ideas to defy "Western decadence," by the late nineties many had concluded, along with Khatami, that the Islamic Republic of Iran was poised to reconcile with a "civilization" whose pluralistic traditions Islamic Leftists had often denounced but grudgingly admired.

Such a conclusion also reflects a rationalist view of politics that still animates the Islamic Left. As 'Abdi put it, his generation had long believed that "whatever works is good." Echoing this utilitarian ethos in terms that many of his middle-class counterparts in Eastern Europe and Latin America would surely grasp, he explained that while the "chaos [and] anarchy" during the "first days of the revolution" demanded centralized rule, the revolution's successes had now made a new form of "freedom" possible. Disabused, as he explained in an interview with me, of the notion that "freedom and equality were the same, that when the second would be achieved, the first would naturally follow," 'Abdi and his colleagues now sought to link the aspirations of Iran's new generation to what they believed was a global struggle for democratic reform, human rights, and pluralism. "What you did in two centuries in Europe," he asserted, "we have done in 20 years in Iran. We have traveled the distance between Louis XVI and François Mitterand in two decades."[12]

Assailing and Defending *Velayat-e Faqih*

The opposition media also gave dissident senior clerics effective channels through which to address both the regime and the reform movement. One of the first to add his voice to the debate was Ayatollah Ahmad Azari Qomi (d. 1999). Although he had enthusiastically defended the prerogatives of the *faqih* during the early nineties, in the ensuing years the persecution of Montazeri—as well as several other Grand Ayatollahs such as Seyyed Mohammad Ruhani, Ya'sub al-Din Rastgari, and Seyyed Mohammad al-Shirazi—infuriated him. Forced in 1995 by 'Ali Akbar Nateq-Nuri and Mohammad Reza Mahdavi-Kani to resign as editor of *Resalat* and secretary of the Qom Theological Lecturers' Association (QTLA), Azari Qomi could not risk openly confronting the government. Khatami's election, however, emboldened him. In November 1997 Azari Qomi sent a thirty-four-page "Letter of Pain" to the QTLA in which he assailed the method by which the *faqih* had been elected and decried the regime's persecution of senior clerics such as Montazeri and al-Shirazi. Demanding to know "whether it is the same inquisition of the Middle Ages," he warned that if such "crimes" continued, "the people will consign us to the dustbin of history." Turning his attention to Khatami, he admonished him "not to become the last of the presidents of the IRI [Islamic Republic of Iran], for this is what may well be your fate if you do not act now to stop . . . present injustices committed in the name of Islam."[13] These bold words sparked violent protests by pro- and antireform student groups alike. When *Hezbollahis* (paramilitary thugs closely linked to Khamane'i and the conservative clerics) ransacked the homes of Azari Qomi and Montazeri, the latter retaliated by giving a rousing speech in which he maintained that a "republic means the government of the people." Acknowledging that "in our constitution, we have a *vali e- faqih*," he added that this did not mean that "one man concentrates all the power in his hands. No . . . the *vali* [guardian] . . . we envisaged in the constitution has his duties and responsibilities clearly defined. His main responsibility is to supervise . . . not to create for himself a royal guard . . . bigger than the world's kings." Therefore, Montazeri warned the *faqih* to stop trying to "imitate the Imam because you are not him. . . . Stop dealing with religious matters and content yourself to supervise."[14]

By assailing the regime in such vitriolic language, this "father of the revolution" encouraged still more dissent within the clergy. Indeed, one of the first younger clerics to echo Montazeri's critique was his former student, Mohsen Kadivar. A scholar of mysticism and Islamic philosophy who had earlier pursued studies in the hard sciences, Kadivar advocated an Islam of joy and love whose mystical core had much in common with Soroush's reformist vision. As early as 1995 Kadivar stated that the "central question that the clergy faces today is whether it can preserve its independence . . . in the face of an Islamic state, since it does not want to fall victim to the fate of the Marxist parties of the former communist states."[15] Now, in the wake of Khatami's election, Kadivar's critical reassessment of the doctrine of *velayat-e faqih* ("Rule of the Jurist") inspired reformists and university students. Moreover, Kadivar's critiques were echoed by other clerics such as Hojjat al-Eslam Mohammad Mojtahed-Shabestari, who, as we have seen, had contributed to the *Kiyan* debates during the midnineties. In a statement that could have been written by his colleague Soroush, Mojtahed-Shabestari insisted that the "institution of *velayat-e faqih* is a purely political rather than religious one. Our constitution . . . juxtaposes divine rights and the rights of the citizen. This mix . . . is the source of many of our problems. We must escape from this contradiction by adapting to the exigencies of modernity."[16]

To the regime's dismay, by late 1997 student leaders were repeating the above positions. This turn of events represented a particularly sharp blow to the conservatives. Afer all, during the early nineties some of these very same leaders, such as Heshmatollah Tabarzadi and Manuchehr Mohammadi, had defected from the dominant *Daftar-e Tahkim-e Vahdat* (Office for Consolidation and Unity) to create new student unions that *backed* the efforts of Rafsanjani and Khamane'i to purge Islamic Leftists! However, Khatami's election, combined with the subsequent efforts by the security establishment to rein in the university student movement, apparently encouraged Mohammadi and Tabarzadi to abandon the conservatives and seek an alliance with liberals and Islamic Leftists. Thus in the fall of 1997 Tabarzadi—the leader of the Union of Students' Islamic Association—raised a storm of controversy by arguing that the "best way to stop" the misuse of the *faqih*'s powers was for the people to elect him to a limited term in office.[17] That such demands echoed *Salam*'s provocative editorials is no coincidence; both Kho'eyniha and 'Abdi had maintained close links with the student movement since the early eighties.[18]

Khatami and Khamane'i:
The Tricky Dynamics of Cohabitation

Conservative clerics reacted to the increasingly bold reform movement in two ways. First, as one might predict, they launched vitriolic attacks on the critics of *velayat-e faqih*. Second, through the semiofficial media, they tried to undermine Khatami's authority by insisting—in the words of the newspaper *Jomhuri-ye Eslami (Islamic Republic)*—that Khatami "break" his silence regarding the conflict between Khamane'i and Montazeri, or "face the same fate as that manipulated naive [man]." *Resalat* was even more emphatic: it suggested that if Khatami believed that he could no longer work under the prevailing conditions, he should "go to the Leader, offer his resignation, and explain his reasons to the public."[19]

Such attacks put *both* leaders in awkward positions. Khatami's dilemma was that while he wanted to promote greater freedom, this was difficult to do without appearing to assail the *faqih*'s authority or provoking his hard-line allies. During the last months of 1997 and throughout 1998, Khatami tried to reconcile these competing goals by repeating an argument he had made during the presidential campaign. "Our law," he stated, "has turned *velayat-i faqih* into *one* of the principles of the system. It is also mentioned in the constitution, and any opposition to it would be tantamount to opposition to the system" (italics mine).[20] By again placing the *faqih*'s powers within the constraints of law and the Constitution, Khatami could appear to be taking a hard line against those Iranians who were "opposed to the system," but without giving credence to the notion that the *faqih*'s authority was absolute or above the law. This clever solution also helped Khatami to deflect the politically explosive demands being made by Montazeri and Azari Qomi. By attacking Khamane'i and in the same breath calling upon Khatami to make good on his spirited defense of "the rule of law," both clerics had the new president in a bind. Khatami navigated through this ideological minefield by arguing that because the position of the *faqih* was both sacred and constitutionally mandated, any attempt to politicize it by claiming that "whoever is with this camp is a proponent of *velayat-i faqih* and whoever does not share this tendency is anti-*velayat-i faqih*" would harm the system itself. Assailing those who used "our sacred values for justifying their own viewpoints," Khatami seemed to defend the office of the *faqih* while implicitly criticizing reformists and hard-liners alike for politicizing that sacred office.[21]

In some ways, Khamane'i faced an even more complex dilemma. On the one hand, his authority as *faqih* derived—as Khatami himself argued—from his ability to remain above the political fray. From an ideological perspective, Khamane'i was not ill-suited for this task. No simple product of the conservative clerical establishment, he had absorbed some of the populist notions of the Islamic Left years before he turned against it. Thus he appeared inclined to try to push for ideological consensus. On the other hand, because Khamane'i occupied an office whose supreme mission was to defend Khomeini's principle of *velayat-e faqih,* and because that principle was undergoing attack by Khatami's supporters, he had to rely on the conservative clerical establishment *without* encouraging it to launch a wholesale assault on the new president and his allies. Such an assault would only undermine Khamane'i's authority as Supreme Leader and unifier of Iranian society by further polarizing the political arena.

At first Khamane'i seemed to have found the magic formula. Rather than directly criticize Khatami, whose character he sometimes praised, the *faqih* tried to curry favor with conservative clerics by implicitly assailing Khatami's call for a "dialogue of civilizations." Thus during the December 1997 Organization of Islamic Conference Summit Khamane'i spurned Khatami's public praise of Western civilization by warning Muslim leaders that "[t]he West, with its comprehensive invasion, has . . . targeted our Islamic faith . . . [and] exported the . . . disregard for religion and ethics [that will] indubitably . . . engulf the present Western civilization and wipe it out."[22] In the ensuing year, a pattern emerged. With few exceptions, each time Khatami called for civilizational dialogue or "Islamic civil society," the *faqih* retaliated with a hail of nativist ideological barbs. When this was insufficient, he tried to intimidate Khatami's supporters by menacingly associating them with liberal or Western influences. That Khamane'i feared such influences, and that he shared the conservative clerics' zealous opposition to opening Iran to the West, reinforced his readiness to level such verbal attacks. But in so doing Khamane'i inadvertently invited the efforts of hard-liners to repress the reformists.[23] Led by hard-line deputies in the *Majles* and by Chief of the Judiciary Ayatollah Mohammad Yazdi—who brought the full weight of his ministry to bear—in 1998 the hard-liners vented their wrath upon every political official, newspaper, or institution that supported Khatami's reform agenda.

The first to feel their ire was Minister of Culture Atta'ollah Mohajerani. Having promised in August 1997 that there would be "no more illegalities in Iran's cultural sphere, such as burning down book shops . . . or beating up university lecturers" (a possible reference to the experience of Soroush), Mohajerani became the target of stinging criticism on the floor of the *Majles*, as well as of an unsuccessful attempt to impeach him in early 1999.[24] Hard-liners then turned on Interior Minister Abdollah Nuri, whose close ties with the reformist media and whose many appointments of Khatami loyalists to official posts in the provinces and municipalities led to his impeachment in July 1998.[25] That same summer, the mayor of Tehran, Gholamhoseyn Karbaschi, was put on trial for "corruption." His arrest the previous spring had provoked a public confrontation between Khatami and his cabinet on the one side, and Yazdi and his ministry on the other. In an effort to prevent further polarization at upper echelons of government, Khamane'i met with the heads of the judicial, executive, and legislative branches. But the *faqih*'s effort to place himself above the factional dispute mollified no one. While it may have dissuaded the judiciary from imposing a harsher penalty (Karbaschi was sentenced to five years of imprisonment), the hard-liners continued their assaults.

Opposition newspapers were regularly banned but then reopened under new names. For example, *Jame'eh* was closed down in June 1998, then reopened in its new incarnation as *Tus*, was shut down in October 1998 and then reopened as *Neshat* (Joy), only to be shut down in October 1999. Prominent writers such as Faraj Sarkuhi (editor of the monthly *Adineh* [Friday]), Morteza Firuzi (editor of the English-language daily *Iran News*), and Akbar Ganji were summarily arrested, tried, and convicted on a range of charges, including "sedition" or "opposition" to the *faqih*. Finally, when such measures failed to quell the reform movement, elements within the state's security apparatus resorted to extrajudicial measures. In the fall and winter of 1998 Iran was shaken by the murders of six leading intellectuals, including nationalist opposition leader Dariush Forhuhar and his wife, Parvaneh, and two prominent writers, Mohammad Ja'far Puyandeh and Mohammad Mokhtari, who had attempted to reestablish the banned Iranian Writers' Center.

The murders of dissident intellectuals by agents linked to the Ministry of Information (i.e., intelligence) amply demonstrated that

Khamane'i's efforts to pacify conservative clerics without encouraging regime hard-liners were unsuccessful. Indeed, the assassinations not only showed that the *faqih* had failed to control a key part of the state's coercive apparatus, but also suggested that Khatami could not shield his allies from the worst forms of state violence. Faced by these twin pressures, during the first months of 1999 both men made attempts to work more closely together. A certain "cohabitation" at the top was reflected in Khamane'i's language, which began to echo that of his president. While this trend was partly a response to the Islamic Republic's first local council elections (which reformists swept in late February 1999), the *faqih*'s assertion that the "demands, resolutions, and faith of the people . . . form pillars of the Islamic system"[26] suggested that he wanted to blur the ideological distinctions between himself and Khatami. This effort anticipated a more ambitious project. In a speech marking the coincidence of the Persian New Year with the centennial of Khomeini's birth, Khamane'i proclaimed the "Year of Khomeini." Reminding his followers that it was because of the "Great Imam" that the "demands, ideas, interests, and dignity" of the people had finally been honored, the *faqih* then asserted that it was incumbent upon the country's leaders to "do all within their power to serve the masses and solve their problems."[27] In short, by resorting to more populist-utilitarian language, the Supreme Leader once again attempted to realign his authority with Khomeini's revolutionary legacy.

The "Year of Khomeini"

Khamane'i may have regretted that decision. By proclaiming the "Year of Khomeini," he inadvertently brought on another public struggle to reappropriate the Imam's legacy. While conservatives such as Ayatollah Mahdavi-Kani came to the *faqih*'s aid by insisting that the "Imam Khomeini . . . always believed in the absolute guardianship from the very beginning, but he advanced by steps in expressing it," reformists retorted by insisting that Khomeini's ideas had to be judged in their totality, and in light of the Imam's repeated emphasis on the role of the people and their elected *Majles*.[28] After conservatives accused reformists of supporting "de-Khomeinization," the reformists turned the tables on them by asserting that if Khomeini's ideas no longer inspired the youth, it was the conservatives' fault! After all, the conservatives—not the reformists—had failed to respect Khomeini's central dictum, namely that Islam's core values should be interpreted in the context of time and interest.[29] That the reformists had the upper hand in this contest was not merely because of their rhetorical skills, or to the elasticity of Khomeini's legacy; equally important was their adept use of the media and other civil-society-based organizations. For example, Abdollah Nuri, who established *Khordad* after his impeachment, invoked Khomeini's utilitarian populism to assail the conservatives, and to defend senior dissident clerics such as Montazeri. The presence of Islamic Leftists such as Asghar-Zadeh (and Nuri himself) on Tehran's newly elected city council added considerable weight to such efforts. It will be recalled that in 1992 Asghar-Zadeh had defended his *Majles* colleagues by suggesting that Khomeini never *forced* his followers to stop wearing Western clothing. By 1999 Asghar-Zadeh—who had been a leader of Students of the Imam's Line during the 1979–80 hostage crisis—offered a far less hesitant defense of pluralism. "We have," he told an audience of university students, "a new language for the new world. . . . And we'll try to make Islam such that it won't contradict democracy."[30]

Again outflanked, hard-line clerics responded by upping the ante. In March 1999 Mohsen Kadivar was brought before the Special Clerical Tribunal and sentenced to several years in prison. But Kadivar's trial only elicited a national outcry from lay reformists, dissident clerics, and university students. The triple alliance that constituted the reform movement thus grew more solid with each closing of an opposition newspaper or arrest of its editors. Khatami responded by insisting that the rule of law should prevail, while at the same time warning students that they should moderate their demands and political rhetoric. However, such carefully couched statements failed to either calm the hard-liners' fears or satisfy the students' aspirations. In early July some two hundred students held a protest at Tehran University to condemn the closing of the *Salam* newspaper, which in a bold act had revealed a proposal by elements within the security apparatus to enact a new, more draconian press law. Extremists linked to the conservatives seized the opportunity to create a provocation and thus discredit the reformists: on 8 July *Hezbollahi* thugs stormed a dormitory. In the bloody melee that followed, some two hundred students were wounded. Shouting "Khatami, Khatami, where are you?" and "Treason, crime . . . all under the *aba* [cloak] of the Supreme Leader," the students' cries vividly illustrated that the *faqih* and the president had yet to find a durable solution to the multiple dilemmas created by dissonant institutionalization. Faced with this sobering reality, both men once again tried to find common ground. In the weeks and months following the July protests, from their respective camps Khatami and Khamane'i denounced the extremists while praising university students in an attempt to distance themselves from the regime's radical opponents. "The young people of this country," Khamane'i declared in his characteristically patriarchal language, "whether they are students or non-students, are my sons and daughters. They are my children."[31] Khatami in turn used a modernist rhetoric that, of course, he linked to the legacy of the Imam. "What is the university?" he asked. "It is the place for young people, for the elite, for the seekers of new ideas. . . . It is obvious that [such] a center . . . should be the target of . . . narrow minded . . . individuals" who "do not comprehend national interests" and who do not "accept the late Imam Khomeini, the constitution and the Islamic Revolution."[32] At the same time, the *faqih* and the president praised each other. Their newly forged bond became manifest during a Friday sermon that Khamane'i gave in Khomeini's mausoleum before thousands of loyal followers. After celebrating what Khamane'i referred to as Khomeini's "many dimensions," the *faqih* declared that Khatami was "a pious cleric who loves the household of the Prophet and is working for the rebirth of Islam"; to reinforce this message Khamane'i then embraced the president.[33]

Khamane'i's 1 October Friday sermon, which I witnessed, was meant to herald a new phase in this cohabitation. However, the scheduling of parliamentary elections in February 2000 complicated the efforts of both men to pursue their entente. The elections presented a historic opportunity for voters to alter the domestic balance of forces: for Khatami a win might open the way to passing the political and economic reform legislation that the conservative-dominated *Majles* had thus far resisted. To forestall this potential day of reckoning, Khamane'i's allies proceeded to close down reformist newspapers such as *Neshat* and *Khordad*. They then arrested *Khordad*'s publisher, Ayatollah Nuri, in a obvious bid to prevent him from running during the upcoming Majles elections. However, Nuri's trial, during which he admonished the judge for failing to grasp and apply Khomeini's ideas, only emboldened the opposition.[34] Subsequent attempts by the Council of Guardians to undercut the reformists by disqualifying more than six hundred would-be candidates backfired: the reformists retaliated by compiling a huge list of candidates, headed by three individuals: Mohammad-Reza Khatami (the president's brother, whose wife, Zahra Eshraqi, is the granddaughter of Khomeini); Jamileh Kadivar, wife of Minister of Culture Attaollah Mohajerani and sister of the imprisoned cleric Mohsen Kadivar; and 'Ali-Reza Nuri, the brother of Abdollah Nuri. These three office seekers, who ran on the slate of the Islamic Iran Participation Front (IIPF) but as part of the Second of Khordad Front (the name of the alliance refers to the date Khatami was elected president, 23 May 1997), personified the emergence of a new generation that had inherited the mantle of the Islamic Left.[35] Inspired by their example, some thirty million people—an unprecedented 77 percent of the electorate—flooded the polls on 18 February 2000. Adopting Khatami's slogan "Iran for all Iranians" (an implicit affirmation of Khatami's idea that the system should take precedence over specific political loyalties), the Second of Khordad Front crushed its rivals, taking at least 160 out of 290 *Majles* seats. Given that 37 independents also won and that 67 seats were left to be determined in a runoff election, and given the momentum produced by the reformists' landslide, President Khatami seemed to have the majority he needed to make good on his promise of an "Islamic civil society" in which the rule of law, constitutionalism, and democracy would prevail.

Theoretical Reprise: Ideological Dissonance in a Globalizing World

Throughout the campaign, Khatami's supporters repeatedly emphasized that Khomeini had set the stage for Khatami's reform movement. "The Imam himself," Zahra Eshraqi insisted, "had a high degree of trust for Khatami."[36] However, the reformists' impressive victory hardly guaranteed a breakthrough to competitive democracy. While greater political openness is a possibility, the mere fact that the reformists now have a clear majority does not mean that they will transcend the legacy of dissonant institutionalization, of which the *Majles* itself is an integral part. Part of the challenge facing the reformists lies in the very nature of that legacy. I will return to this point in a moment, as it bears directly on several theoretical issues central to this study. However, part of the problem was also conjunctural, as an analysis of the election results suggests. The Second of Khordad Front consists of an alliance of two factions: the Islamic Left, led by the IIPF, and the center and right-of-center centrists, led by Servants of the Construction. While both factions support political liberalization, many Islamic Leftists are wary of economic reform. Reflecting such concerns, Kho'eyniha asked me whether "adopting Western-style democracy" would merely "reinforce the power of the capitalists."[37] The late entrance of former President Rafsanjani into the election campaign was designed to exploit these differences, reassure the conservatives, and blur the ideological lines between the conservatives and the Second of Khordad Front. In the end, Rafsanjani barely squeaked through—winning the thirtieth place in Tehran's thirty-member constituency. Emboldened by this symbolic

defeat, still smarting from the wounds they had suffered under Rafsanjani's presidency, and concerned that the Servants of Construction
would push for an economic reform program that imposed heavy social
costs, some Islamic Leftists were inclined to oppose rather than join
ranks with the right-of-center allies. Although a minority in the new *Majles*, the conservatives could be counted on to exploit these differences.[38]

Apart from such conjunctive factors, more profound and theoretically significant reasons exist to explain why the system of contending
authorities in the Islamic Republic will probably endure well into the
twenty-first century. The first has to do with the nature and effect of
dissonant institutionalization itself. We saw in chapters 7 and 8 that
the principle of institutionalizing competing visions of authority took
a severe beating during the late nineties. When the former editor of
Neshat argued that "we need to begin looking at Islam as just a religion,
not an ideology,"[39] he showed how popular Soroush's call for separating religion from politics had become. We also saw that the roots
of this development go back to Khomeini himself. Paradoxically, his
instrumentalist-utilitarian emphasis on interests, especially as it was
enshrined in his January 1988 edict, opened the door to this dynamic.
Exploited in 1989 by Rafsanjani and his conservative allies in the *Majles*
to reinforce the power of the *faqih*, the edict was later invoked by Islamic
Leftists to legitimate all kinds of ideas, including the very notion that
a distancing of religion from politics would protect the "interests" of
Islam. The question that remains to be answered is whether this effort
by *all players* to invoke the principle of interests has reduced religion to
little more than a shell under cover of which other kinds of interests
are rationalized.[40] And if this is indeed the case, we must also ask
whether Iran's experience of dissonant institutionalization and complex
routinization were merely passing phases along the inevitable march
of history.

Many students of the Arab world, particularly those imbued with
a Weberian understanding of religion, would make this case. Indeed,
the late Albert Hourani argued long ago that by equating Islam with
whatever form of politics served the public interest, Islamic reformists
of the "Liberal Age" such as Muhammad Abduh had unintentionally
opened "another door to secular nationalism."[41] While some observers
would argue that religion in the Islamic Republic is today submitting
to a similar fate, it seems premature to argue that disenchantment with
revolutionary Islam may have, in Ahmad Sadri's words, opened the
"gate of the secular city."[42] On the contrary, and despite the incessant
instrumentalization of Khomeini's legacy, I would argue that by the
late nineties dissonant institutionalization was so firmly embedded in

the apparatus of the state that no serious politician could risk making a case for an "Islamic Republic" in which popular sovereignty was *not* reconciled to the ultimate authority of the *faqih*. The issue is not merely that the *faqih* and his allies in the judiciary and the Council of Guardians still retain the right to veto *Majles* legislation—a veto which the *faqih* or the council may very well use against Khatami's allies in the new *Majles*. The more elemental obstacle to full democracy and secularization has been institutional and ideological—in other words, the enduring commitment of a well-organized, and thus extremely influential, minority of Iranians to a traditional conception of authority. We are reminded here of Theda Skocpol's observation that different kinds of states give "rise to various conceptions of the *meaning* . . . of 'politics' itself."[43] While in the case of Iran there was more than one such "meaning," by the late nineties the conservative clerics could still mobilize a mass constituency that favored the patriarchal vision of community represented in the office of the *faqih*, and in the person of 'Ali Khamane'i.

Moreover, far from confirming the inevitable victory of some rationalizing dynamic, it might be argued that the interminable instrumentalization of Khomeini's legacy demonstrates the *intrinsic* attraction of a charismatic *idea* that is deeply embedded in Iranian society, namely that Iran's leaders—as well as their counterparts in the international community—must respect the desire of Iranians to accommodate the exigencies of modernity to the equally vital quest for a spiritually meaningful life. Khomeini symbolizes this broad conviction. Thus while everyone makes of the Imam what they can, few of Iran's leaders on either side of the ideological divide want to let go of his memory.[44]

Still, there are different ways of sustaining, reinterpreting, and using that memory. In his effort to capture and use Khomeini's legacy, the current *faqih* and his allies have relied heavily on "manufactured charisma." Tehran is awash in posters featuring an often smiling Khamane'i next to the more austere image of the late Imam. The alliance of the two is most dramatically symbolized in Khomeini's gigantic mausoleum, at the front of which is the *faqih*'s podium flanked by a huge painting of Khomeini on the viewer's right, and an equally imposing one of Khamane'i on the left. Khatami, in contrast, has expressed a more spontaneous or "pure" form of charisma through the ballot box, while at the same time using democratic principles to make a case for placing the *faqih* above— and perhaps beyond—politics. This effort is symbolized in paintings, posters, and even buttons that situate Khatami next to Khomeini and Khamane'i, or in some cases place Khatami near a mass public that is actively engaged in exercising its democratic rights. In the coming years, we can expect that Khatami and his allies will regularly invoke Khomeini's memory to strengthen the institutional foundations of such democratic practices. Their conservative opponents will reply in kind, thus ensuring that "complex routinization" remains a central feature of Iranian politics.[45] The paradox is that this dynamic can only be ended by a change of thinking at the very pinnacle of state power: until a new *faqih* emerges to totally redefine the very foundation of his own authority, charisma as an *institutionalized* reality will remain linked to an office that Khatami and his allies cannot repudiate without impugning the very foundations of the Islamic Republic.

What can this particular story teach us about the broader realities of political change? Is the Islamic Republic of Iran an example of "Muslim" or "Middle East" exceptionalism, or can students of comparative politics look to it for more fundamental lessons about the transition from authoritarianism? To answer this question we need to return to some of the ideas outlined in chapter 1. There we noted that in recent years the quest for a grand theory of regime change has given way to more inductive analyses of how particular constellations of social, cultural, ideological, political, and economic legacies make certain kinds of transitions more or less possible. Our analysis of the Islamic Republic has not only demonstrated the validity of this new institutionalist perspective, but also accentuated the central role that organized symbolic systems play in shaping the actions, choices, or even preferences of political leaders. Beyond this important conclusion—now endorsed even by scholars of Latin America who once opposed merely uttering the phrase "political culture"[46]—our assessment of ideological change in the Islamic Republic reveals a specific lesson of particular concern to students of comparative politics.

It will be recalled that by way of implicit hypothesis, chapter 1 suggested that the dissonant institutionalization of competing visions of authority in the Islamic Republic was part and parcel of a global trend that had dramatically shaped politics in much of the Islamic if not the wider Third World. Today, despite—if not because of—growing global pressures for democratization, the political and social effects of dissonant institutionalization can be seen from Cairo to Jakarta. For example, among Arab states, particularly in the monarchies of Morocco and the Persian Gulf, the organization of charismatic, traditional, and legal-rational authority has produced systems of "contending authorities" whose eclectic foundations have been cleverly used by elites to enhance their legitimacy and at the same time hinder a transition from political liberalization to full democratization.[47] (That the rationalization of the *faqih*'s authority may have brought Iran one step closer to this pattern of rule is no small irony.) Further afield is the recent experience of Indonesia. There the June 1999 parliamentary elections, and subsequent November 1999 election of Abdurrahman Wahid to the presidency, brought to the fore a forty-million-strong *Nahdlatul Ulama* (Renaissance of the Religious Leaders) whose leader had long championed a multifaceted blend of mystical Islam, religious conservatism, and Western-inspired liberalism. What Khatami's followers said of their president—namely that "Khatami is a believer and practitioner of the Islamic laws and mystical journeys, who is interested in Alexis de Tocqueville and regards the framework of democracy as the closest available political theory to the Islamic principles"[48]—could easily have been said of Indonesia's new president. A product of "multiple imaginations," Wahid's upbringing in the mystical world of Javanese Islam, his subsequent studies at the traditional Al-Azhar University, and his experiences in socialist Iraq and liberal Western Europe, created within him a multifaceted vision of political authority that was implicitly secular and spiritually Islamic. That Wahid's vision was transmitted to a mass movement that is now represented by a political party governing in an uneasy alliance with more "fundamentalist" and secular parties, speaks volumes about the changing nature of "Islamic" politics in our postmodern world.[49]

I put "Islamic" in quotation marks because it is no longer clear that the notion of a uniquely "Islamic" politics is analytically useful. As we have seen, the quest for democracy and pluralism in the Islamic Republic of Iran has had less to do with the creation of a culturally "authentic" Islamic interpretation of democracy than it has with the struggle to make religious and modern notions of political community coexist.[50] From the very start, Iran's Islamic Revolution was not about some grand synthesis of "Islam and modernity." Rather, it was about an amalgam or "grafting" (to use Daryush Shayegan's term) of competing notions of authority.[51] (As Rafsanjani challenged the *Majles* in 1984, "Where is the precedent for parliament in Islamic history?")[52] To the extent that many in the Islamic Left looked to the West in devising one strand of this graft, Iran's revolution has come full circle under the reformists.[53] The current efforts of some Islamic thinkers in Indonesia, Malaysia, Morocco, and Kuwait to forge ideologies highlighting a largely Western view of freedom while remaining true to Islam's spiritual impulse suggest that a similar transformation from populist to pluralistic ideological amalgams might be unfolding in some quarters of the Islamic world.[54]

Facile analyses of the "end of history" notwithstanding, there is reason to believe that the social, cultural, and political dynamics constituting the most recent phase of globalization has made it easier for the leaders of Iran and other Islamic polities to sustain such eclectic ideologies and the systems of contending authorities in which they thrive. In chapters 1 and 3 we noted the decisive influence that the first wave of post–World War II globalization had on Iran's revolution. The Third Worldist discourse of the sixties and seventies, which many Islamic Leftists absorbed, was part and parcel of this process. Although in recent years the multiple biographies and shared collective imaginations initially framing the worldviews of Khatami, Soroush, and other Islamic Leftists have been largely shorn of their utopian elements, in the era of post–Cold War globalization, the increasingly rapid communication of diverse rationalities through television, radio, transnational diasporas, and the Internet has given Third World elites new tools with which to "localize" and thus "transform global processes."[55] By itself, this dynamic does not promise any particular outcome. Indeed, in many quarters of the Islamic world, globalization has sparked intolerant movements whose harmonic worldviews are manifestly absolutist.[56] But this is hardly the whole story. If today Khatami's call for a "dialogue of civilizations" has enthusiastic adherents in Iran, Malaysia, Indonesia, and some quarters of the Arab world, it is because Khatami's reformist allies know full well that this dialogue is unfolding as much *within* as between civilizations.[57] Whether their opponents are willing to accept this fact remains to be seen.

Postscript

After the first round of *Majles* elections in February 2000, President Khatami's opponents launched a campaign, the most violent manifestation of which was the attempted assassination in March of Khatami's chief advisor, Sa'id Hajjarian. Following the attack, seventeen reformist newspapers were shut down, and the Council of Guardians began reversing several reformist election victories. When the council raised the possibility that "fraud" would lead it to deny reformists many of the seats they had won in the crucial voting district of Tehran, it seemed that the conservatives were determined to deny the Islamic Iran Participation Front a leading position in the *Majles*. Paradoxically, this particular effort to thwart the reformers failed due to the intercession of Khamane'i. In the wake of the second round of elections, he declared that the results of the Tehran vote should stand, and that the new *Majles* should convene. Mehdi Karrubi, a veteran of the Islamic Left and a key member of the clerical elite, was elected Speaker of the *Majles*, and Rafsanjani quit the parliament. Although reformers had won 211 out of 290 seats by early summer 2000, these events offer a potent reminder that the Supreme Leader will continue to play a crucial role in a system of dissonant politics whose complex and contradictory dynamics are likely to endure for years to come.

Notes

Introduction

For translations of speeches given by Iranian leaders, I relied primarily on those produced by the Foreign Broadcast Information Service. The FBIS reporting areas of Near East/Asia, South Asia, and Middle East and North Africa are abbreviated in my citations as NEA, SAS, and MEA, respectively. I obtained hard-copy FBIS documents for 1979–92 from the library of Georgetown University, Washington, D.C.; the private collection of Dr. Marvin Zonis of the University of Chicago; and from the collection in the Washington Institute for Near East Policy, Washington, D.C. For the years 1992–94, I obtained hard copies from the International Forum on Democratic Studies, Washington, D.C. Documents from 1995 onward may be retrieved from <http://199.221.15.211/index.html>.

1. "Iran: Khatami Addresses Majles Hezbollah Group," *Ettela'at*, 27 February 1997, in Persian; FBIS-NES-97-053, 27 February 1997.

2. "Khamenei Speech on Politics," broadcast 3 May 1997, FBIS-NES 970086, 3 May 1997.

3. "Iran: Khatami Interviewed on Elections," *Jomhuri-ye Eslami*, 25 February 1997, pp. 14, 15, in Persian; FBIS-NES-97-047, 25 February 1997.

4. "Iran: Kani Warns Against Deviations," *Resalat,* 20 March 1997, pp. 1, 2, in Persian; FBIS-NES-97-079, 20 March 1997.
5. See, for example, the short biography of Khomeini's life written by his late son, Ahmad, in the introduction of *Kauthar,* vol. 1 of *An Anthology of the Speeches of Imam Khomeini* (Tehran: The Institute for the Compilation and Publication of the Works of Imam Khomeini, 1995), xxi–lxvii; "Biography of Imam Ayatullah Ruhullah Khomeini," in *Imam Khomeini's Last Will and Testament* (Washington, D.C.: International Section of the Islamic Republic of Iran, Solar Publishing, n.d.); and Hamid Algar, "Imam Khomeini, 1902–1962: The Pre-Revolutionary Years," in *Islam, Politics and Social Movements,* ed. Edmund Burke III and Ira M. Lapidus (Berkeley: University of California Press, 1988), 263–88. For an example of how the prophetic view of Khomeini has been paradoxically echoed by his critics, see Clive Irving's introduction to *The Little Green Book: The Sayings of Ayatollah Khomeini* (New York: Bantam Books, 1980).
6. See the speeches given by Khatami and Khamane'i before the 9 December 1997 Eighth Islamic Summit of the Organization of Islamic Conference in *Permanent Mission of the Islamic Republic Republic of Iran to the United Nations,* <www.un.int/iran/oic>.
7. "Iranian President Khatami's Televised News Conference of December 14, 1997," <http://eurasianews.com/iran>.
8. Cheryl Benard and Zalmay Khalizad, *"The Government of God": Iran's Islamic Republic* (New York: Columbia University Press, 1984), 65.
9. See Adam Przeworski, "The Games of Transition," in *Issues in Democratic Consolidation,* ed. Scott Mainwaring, Guillermo O'Donnell, and Samuel Valenzuela (Notre Dame, Ind.: University of Notre Dame Press, 1992); and Ghassan Salamé, ed., *Democracy Without Democrats?* (London: I. B. Tauris Publishers, 1994).

Chapter One

1. Robert Friedland and Robert R. Alford, "Bringing Society Back In: Symbolic Practices and Institutional Contradictions," in *The New Institutionalism in Organizational Analysis,* ed. Walter W. Powell and Paul J. DiMaggio (Chicago: University of Chicago Press, 1991), 240–41.
2. Ibid.
3. See, for example, Valerie Bunce, "Two-Tiered Stalinism: A Case of Self-Destruction," in *Constructing Capitalism,* ed. Kazimier Z. Pozanski (Boulder, Colo.: Westview Press, 1992), 25–44.
4. Frances Hagopian, "After Regime Change: Authoritarian Legacies, Political Representation, and the Democratic Future of South America," *World Politics* 45, no. 3 (April 1993): 464–500 and her "Traditional Politics against State Formation in Brazil," in *State Power and Social Forces,* ed. Joel S. Migdal, Atul Kholi, and Vivienne Shue (Cambridge: Cambridge University Press, 1994), 37–64. See also Juan J. Linz and Alfred Stepan, *Problems of Democratic Transition and Consolidation* (Baltimore and London: Johns Hopkins University Press, 1996) and Gretchen Casper and Michelle M. Taylor, *Negotiating*

Democracy Transitions from Authoritarian Rule (Pittsburgh: University of Pittsburgh Press, 1996).

5. Joel Migdal, "The State in Society: An Approach for Struggles for Domination," in *State Power*, ed. Migdal, Kholi, and Shue, 7–34. Migdal argues that a "close, historically specific treatment of power still leaves us room to . . . discern . . . the sorts of interactions among social forces leading to various patterns of domination, even if the varying combinations do lead to different results in different circumstances" (9). I would add that discovering "various patterns of domination" requires, as Migdal's essay suggests, a more inductive "anthropology" of particular states in particular sociocultural, political, and institutional circumstances.

6. See Charles King, "Review Article: Post-Sovietology: Area Studies or Social science?" *International Affairs* 70, no. 2 (1994): 291–97.

7. See Ken Jowitt, "Dizzy with Democracy," *Problems of Post-Communism* (January–February 1996): 3–8.

8. See note 18.

9. Victor Zaslavsky, "Nationalism and Democratic Transition in Postcommunist Societies," *Daedalus* (spring 1992): 97–121; Ken Jowitt, "The New World Disorder," *Journal of Democracy* 2, no. 1(winter 1991): 11–20; and Anna Seleny, "Old Rationalities and New Democracies: Compromise and Confrontation in Hungary and Poland," *World Politics* 51, no. 4 (July 1999): 484–519. Also see Bunce, "Two-Tiered Stalinism" and Richard Snyder and James Mahoney, "The Missing Variable: Institutions and the Study of Regime Change," *Comparative Politics* 32, no. 1 (October 1999): 103–23.

10. See Cheryl Benard and Zalmay Khalizad, *"The Government of God": Iran's Islamic Republic* (New York: Columbia University Press, 1984), particularly pp. 61–69. Hamid Dabashi's *Theology of Discontent The Ideological Foundation of the Islamic Revolution in Iran* (New York: New York University Press, 1993) employs a symbolic approach that is heavily influenced by Durkheim's sociology of anomie, whereas Said Arjomand's *Turban for the Crown: The Islamic Revolution in Iran* (New York and Oxford: Oxford University Press: 1988) relies on Weberian categories, as does Michael S. Kimmel and Rahmat Tavakol, "Against Satan: Charisma and Tradition in Iran," in *Charisma, History and Social Structure*, ed. Ronald M. Glassman and William H. Swatos Jr. (New York: Greenwood Press, 1986), 101–28 and Ahmad Ashraf, "Charisma, Theocracy, and Men of Power in Post Revolutionary Iran," in *The Politics of Social Transformation in Afghanistan, Iran, and Pakistan,* ed. Myron Weiner and Ali Banauzizi (Syracuse, N.Y.: Syracuse University Press, 1994), 101–51.

11. For a succinct example of structural instrumentalist analysis of Iran's revolution, see Ervand Abrahamian's *Khomeinism: Essays on the Islamic Republic* (Berkeley: University of California Press, 1993). Also see Mansoor Moaddel, *Class, Politics and Ideology in the Iranian Revolution* (New York: Columbia University Press, 1993) and Ali Rahnema and Farhad Nomani, *The Secular Miracle: Religion, Politics and Economic Policy in Iran* (London: Zed Books, 1990). Haggay Ram's *Myth and Mobilization in Revolutionary Iran*

(Washington, D.C.: The American University Press, 1994), while eschewing Marxist reduction, adopts the instrumentalist perspective by insisting on the deliberate construction and use of Shi'ite myths for political purposes.

12. For those who want to review the intellectual history of the Islamic Republic in more detail, I recommend consulting notes 10 and 11 above.
13. Abrahamian, *Khomeinism*, 13, 17.
14. Dabashi, *Theology of Discontent*, 489–90.
15. Thomas S. Kuhn, *The Structure of Scientific Revolutions* (Chicago: University of Chicago Press, 1970).
16. Friedland and Alford, "Bringing Society Back In," 241.
17. Michael Fischer, "Repetitions in the Iranian Revolution," in *Shi'ism, Resistance and Revolution,* ed. Martin Kramer (Boulder, Colo.: Westview Press, 1987), 117. Fischer was one of the few scholars during the early eighties to call for an approach that transcended the "rhetorical dead ends that characterize much of the most recent literature on the Iranian revolution." While he does not list structural instrumentalism as one of these dead ends, his multifaceted and highly empathetic view of the revolution sets a high theoretical standard.
18. Migdal, "The State in Society," 15; Hagopian, "After Regime Change" and "Traditional Politics"; Kathleen Steinmo and Frank Longstreth, eds., *Structuring Politics: Historical Institutionalism in Comparative Analysis* (Cambridge: Cambridge University Press, 1992); and Powell and DiMaggio, *The New Institutionalism.*
19. See Joseph Bensman and Michael Givant, "Charisma and Modernity: The Use and Abuse of a Concept," *Social Research* 42 (1975) 570–614. Bensman and Givant exaggerate the role that Edward Shils played in endowing charisma with a purely psychological meaning, if only because Shils emphasized Weber's broader notion in his studies of ideology or "ideological thinking" (see note 31 below). On psychological approaches to charisma see Ann Willner, *The Spellbinders: Charismatic Political Leadership* (New Haven: Yale University Press, 1984) and Irvine Schiffer, *Charisma: A Psychoanalytic Look at Society* (Toronto and Buffalo: University of Toronto Press, 1973).
20. Max Weber, "The Social Psychology of World Religions," in *From Max Weber: Essays in Sociology,* ed. H. H. Gerth and C. Wright Mills (New York: Oxford University Press, 1946), 281.
21. Ibid.
22. Ibid., 278.
23. Max Weber, *Economy and Society,* vol. 1, ed. Guenther Roth and Claus Wittich (Berkeley: University of California Press, 1978), 1111–12.
24. Weber, "Politics as a Vocation," in *Essays in Sociology,* ed. Gerth and Mills, 143.
25. *Readings from Emile Durkheim,* ed. Kenneth Thompson (Chichester, England: Ellis Harwood, 1985), 129. Quoted from Durkheim, *The Elementary Forms of Religious Life: A Study in Sociology,* trans Joseph Ward Swain (London: Allen and Unwin, 1915).
26. Ibid., 124.

27. Ibid., 128.

28. See Charles Lindholm, *Charisma* (Cambridge: Blackwell, 1990). Lindholm points out that Durkheim viewed the French Revolution as being the "prototypical example of a depersonalizing and invigorating ritual in the modern era" (30). For a collective action perspective on Durkheim, see Charles Tilly, *From Mobilization to Revolution* (New York: Random House, 1978), 17–18.

29. Karl Mannheim, *Ideology and Utopia: An Introduction to the Sociology of Knowledge*, translated from the German by Louis Wirth and Edward Shils (New York: Harvest Book, 1936), 35–36. For an overview of theories of utopia, see Barbara Goodwin and Keith Taylor, *The Politics of Utopia* (New York: St. Martin's Press, 1983).

30. Mannheim writes, "This ability to attach themselves to classes to which they originally did not belong, was made possible for intellectuals because they could adapt themselves to any viewpoint and because they and they alone we in a position to choose their affiliation. . . . [T]he fanaticism of radicalized intellectuals . . . bespeaks a psychic compensation for the lack of a more fundamental integration into a class"(*Ideology and Utopia*, 158–9).

31. Edward Shils, *The Intellectuals and the Powers and Other Essays* (Chicago: University of Chicago Press, 1972).

32. Mannheim, *Ideology and Utopia*, 192–93.

33. William Kornhauser, *The Politics of Mass Society* (New York: Free Press, 1969), 100.

34. Ibid., 209. See also his fascinating discussion of the "collective symbols" of isolated mining, maritime, and longshoring workers on p. 216.

35. Manfred Halpern, *The Politics of Social Change in the Middle East and North Africa* (Princeton, N.J.: Princeton University Press 1967), 138–39.

36. Ibid., 137–38.

37. Nadav Safran, *Egypt in Search of Political Community: An Analysis of the Intellectual and Political Evolution of Egypt 1804–1952* (Cambridge, Mass.: Harvard University Press, 1961). See Ismail Serageldin, "Individual Identity, Group Dynamics and Islamic Resurgence," in *Islamic Resurgence in the Arab World*, ed. Ali E. Hillal Dessouki (New York: Praeger, 1982), 54–66. Gilles Keppel's *Muslim Extremism in Egypt: The Prophet and the Pharaoh* (Berkeley: University of California Press, 1984) echoes Halpern's analysis by linking the emergence of Islamic radicalism in Egypt to the cultural and social alienation of declassé university graduates.

38. Consider the following citation from the opening volume of the *Fundamentalism Project*, a global study of religious fundamentalism sponsored by the American Academy of Arts and Sciences: "[A]lthough nostalgia for such an era is a hallmark of fundamentalist rhetoric . . . religious identity thus renewed becomes the exclusive and absolute basis for a re-created political and social order that is oriented to the future. . . . Fundamentalists seek to remake the world in the service of a dual commitment to the unfolding eschatological drama . . . and to self-preservation (by neutralizing the threatening 'Other'). Such an endeavor often requires charismatic and authoritarian leadership . . ." Martin E. Marty and R. Scott Appleby, eds.,

Fundamentalisms and the State: Remaking Politics, Economics, and Militance (Chicago: University of Chicago Press, 1993), 3.

39. James Burnham, *The Machiavellians* (Chicago: Henry Regnery Company, 1943).

40. Gaetano Mosca, *The Ruling Class*, trans. Hannah D. Kahn (New York: McGraw-Hill Book Company, 1939), 71; italics mine.

41. Ibid., 71.

42. Mosca's ideas were vulgarized by his contemporary Vilfredo Pareto. By transforming Mosca's pluralist view of truths into a recipe for crass elite manipulation of the masses, he helped set the stage for fascism. See Vilfredo Pareto, *Sociological Writings*, selected and introduced by S. E. Finer (Totowa, N.J.: Rowman and Littlefield, 1966), 130–37.

43. George Sorel, *Reflections on Violence*, trans. T. E. Hulme (New York: Collier Books, 1959), 165.

44. Bensman and Givant, "Charisma and Modernity," 601–3.

45. Ibid., 600–601.

46. Ibid., 607.

47. This is why, for these authors, even a personally charismatic figure like Hitler ultimately used charisma to rationalize what was, in essence, a traditional form of authority.

48. Bensman and Givant, "Charisma and Modernity," 609.

49. Ibid., 608.

50. Ibid.

51. Ronald Glassman, "Legitimacy and Manufactured Charisma," *Social Research* (winter 1975): 621.

52. The classic statement can be found in Mancur Olson's *Logic of Collective Action* (Cambridge, Mass: Harvard University Press, 1965).

53. For a fine example of instrumentalist theory in its purest form, see Abner Cohen, *Custom and Politics in Urban Africa: A Study of Hausa Migrants in Yoruba Towns* (Berkeley: University of California Press, 1969).

54. Nikki R. Keddie, *An Islamic Response to Imperialism Political and Religious Writings of Sayyid Jamal ad-Din "al-Afghani."* (Berkeley: University of California Press, 1983).

55. Paul R. Brass, *Ethnicity and Nationalism Theory and Comparison* (New Delhi: Sage Publications, 1991), 74.

56. Clifford Geertz, "Ideology As a Cultural System," in *The Interpretation of Cultures* (New York: Basic Books), 218.

57. Leonard Binder, "The Crises of Political Development," in Leonard Binder et. al., *Crises and Sequences in Political Development* (Princeton, N.J.: Princeton University Press, 1971), 38–40.

58. Antonio Gramsci, *Selections from the Prison Notebooks*, ed. and trans. Quintin Hoare and Geoffrey Nowell Smith (New York: International Publishers, 1971), 376–77. See also Walter Adamson, *Hegemony and Revolution: A Study of Antonio Gramsci's Political and Cultural Theory* (Berkeley: University of California Press, 1980) and Jorge Larrain, *The Concept of Ideology* (Athens: The University of Georgia Press, 1979), 80. Rather than speak of "false" versus "critical" consciousness, Gramsci distinguished between "organic"

and "arbitrary" ideology: the former had a constituency and served collective aims, and the latter had no constituency other than its creator.

59. Gramsci, *Selections from the Prison Notebooks,* 210.
60. Ibid.
61. Ibid., 211. Gramsci acknowledged that under some circumstances, the charismatic leader might also inadvertently create conditions that would lend themselves to social change. Most often, however, their actions served the interests of the status quo.
62. Gino Germani, *Authoritarianism, Fascism, and National Populism* (New Brunswick, N.J.: Transaction Publishers, 1978) ,91–2.
63. Ibid., 202.
64. Ibid., 203.
65. Fischer, "Repetitions in the Iranian Revolution," 131. Said Arjomand agrees, writing that "the era of chiliastic revolutions may have come to an end for the foreseeable future with the Islamic Revolution in Iran." See his "Plea for an Alternative View of Revolutions" in *Debating Revolutions,* ed. Nikki R. Keddie (New York: New York University Press, 1995), 142–54. Cited from page 152.
66. Said Amir Arjomand, "Constitutions and the Struggle for Political Power: A Study in the Modernization of Traditions," *Archives of European Sociology* 33 (1992): 75.
67. Susanne Hoeber Rudolph and Lloyd I. Rudolph, *Gandhi: The Traditional Roots of Charisma* (Chicago: University of Chicago Press, 1967).
68. This point comes across quite clearly in two collections that trace the biographies of Middle Eastern fundamentalists. See R. Scott Appleby, ed., *Spokesmen for the Despised: Fundamentalist Leaders in the Middle East* (Chicago, University of Chicago Press, 1997) and Ali Rahnema, ed., *Pioneers of Islamic Revival* (London: Zed Books, 1994). Appleby's collection includes my "Khomeini's Legacy: Islamic Rule and Social Justice," pp. 6–82.
69. Eric Hoffer, *The True Believer* (New York: Time Incorporated, 1951), 75.
70. On Islam and post-modernity see Akbar Ahmed and Hastings Donnan, eds., *Islam, Globalization and Postmodernity* (London: Routledge, 1994).
71. Harold Lasswell, *Psychopathology and Politics* (Chicago: University of Chicago Press, 1977). For an example of the application of this approach to the case of Iran, see Marvin Zonis, *Majestic Failure: The Fall of the Shah* (Chicago: University of Chicago Press, 1991).
72. Michael Fischer, "Imam Khomeini: Four Levels of Understanding," in *Voices of Resurgent Islam,* ed. John Esposito (New York and Oxford: Oxford University Press, 1983), 151.
73. Samuel Huntington, *Political Order and Changing Societies* (New Haven, Conn.: Yale University Press, 1968), 278–84.
74. This idea should be distinguished from the functional notion of tradition as a conveyer belt for modernization as outlined in Lloyd and Susanne Hoeber Rudolph, *The Modernity of Tradition: Political Development in India* (Chicago: University of Chicago Press, 1967).
75. See Akbar S. Ahmed and Hastings Donnan, "Islam in the Age of

Postmodernity," in *Islam, Globalization and Postmodernity,* ed. Akbar and Donnan, 1–20.

76. Arjun Appadurai, "Disjuncture and Difference in the Global Cultural Economy," *Public Culture* 2, no. 2 (spring 1990): 5.

77. Benedict P. Anderson, *Imagined Communities: Reflections on the Origin and Spread of Nationalism* (London: Verso, 1983), 143–44.

78. Ibid., 7.

79. I was reminded of this fact upon meeting a young cleric from Qom who was as familiar with topics such as Islamic mysticism and philosophy as he was with trends in epistemology and postmodernism.

80. After presenting this notion of "dissonant" institutionalization at a conference in Tehran, an American Islamist suggested that I might choose another musical metaphor, since, he argued, Iranian music did not use chords. He may have a point, although I rather suspect that this comment underestimates the exposure of the educated Iranians who would read this book to Western music, not to mention political thought.

81. Clifford Geertz, *Negara: The Theatre State in Nineteenth Century Bali* (Princeton, N.J.: Princeton University Press, 1980) and Theda Skocpol, "Bringing the State Back In: Strategies of Analysis in Current Research," in *Bringing the State Back In,* ed. Peter B. Evans, Dietrich Rueschemeyer, and Theda Skocpol (Cambridge: Cambridge University Press, 1985), 3–37. In *Negara* Geertz highlights the role of a "controlling political idea," but elsewhere he argues that political stability ensues when ruling elites "integrate" a wide array of symbols into one ruling doctrine. See "The Integrative Revolution: Primordial Sentiments in the New States" in *The Interpretation of Cultures,* 255–310. This idea suggests a certain level of ideological dissonance. For an analysis that accentuates the affinities between Marxist and Weberian accounts of dominant ideology, see Nicholas Abercrombie, Stephen Hill, and Bryan S. Turner, *The Dominant Ideology Thesis* (London and Boston: G. Allen & Allen Unwin, 1980).

82. See note 18 above. On new institutionalist approaches that suggest a dissonant view of authority systems, see the work of Roger Friedland, Robert Alford, Joel Migdal, and Said Arjomand cited above.

83. David Collier and Ruth Collier, *Shaping the Political Arena* (Princeton, N.J.: Princeton University Press, 1991).

84. See Lewis Coser, *The Functions of Social Conflict* (New York: Free Press of Glencoe, 1964).

85. David Laitin, *Hegemony and Culture: Politics and Religious Change among the Yoruba* (Chicago: University of Chicago Press, 1986), 175.

86. Ashraf, "Charisma, Theocracy, and Men of Power," 149.

87. Friedland and Alford, "Bringing Society Back In," 232.

Chapter Two

1. Farang Rajaee, *Islamic Values and World View* (Lanhan, Md.: University Press of America, 1983), 70.

2. See, for example, Clive Irving's introduction to *The Little Green Book: The Sayings of the Ayatollah Khomeini* (New York: Bantam Books, 1980).

3. Max Weber, *Economy and Society*, vol. 1, ed. Guenther Roth and Claus Wittich (Berkeley: University of California Press, 1978), 1112.

4. Ibid., 1113.

5. Weber, "The Social Psychology of World Religions," in *From Max Weber, Essays in Sociology*, ed. H. H. Gerth and C. Wright Mills (Oxford and New York: Oxford University Press, 1946), 285.

6. Ibid., 289.

7. Weber, *Economy and Society*, 1113.

8. Weber, "The Social Psychology of World Religions," 242.

9. Weber, *Economy and Society*, 1121.

10. For a brief account of Twelver Shi'ism, see "The Suffering of the Imams" in this chapter.

11. Works on Khomeini can be divided into at least five genres. There are popular biographies such as Amir Taheri, *The Spirit of Allah: Khomeini and the Islamic Revolution* (Bethesda, Md.: Adler and Adler, 1986). A study filled with personal and historical detail, it is inadequately documented and suffers from inaccuracies and contradictions. Forming another genre are the scholarly treatments, which run the gamut from essays to book-length biographies. Michael Fischer's intriguing "Imam Khomeini: Four Levels of Understanding," in *Voices of Resurgent Islam*, ed. John Esposito (New York and Oxford: Oxford University Press, 1983), is one of the few studies recognizing the tensions and ambiguities that stamped Khomeini's biography. "Ayatollah Khomeini: The Theologian of Discontent" in Hamid Dabashi's *Theology of Discontent: The Ideological Foundation of the Islamic Revolution in Iran* (New York: New York University Press, 1993), 404–89, offers a more one-dimensional but nuanced view of Khomeini's intellectual biography. Baqer Moin's "Khomeini's Search for Perfection," in *Pioneers of Islamic Revival*, ed. Ali Rahnema (London: Zed Books, 1994), emphasizes the mystical foundations of Khomeini's thought. Also see Hamid Algar, "Imam Khomeini, 1902–1962: The Pre-Revolutionary Years," in *Islam, Politics and Social Movements*, ed. Edmund Burke III and Ira M. Lapidus (Berkeley: University of California Press, 1988), 263–88. The above-cited essay by Moin constitutes a chapter in his *Khomeini: Life of the Ayatollah* (London: I. B. Tauris Publishers, 1999). Based on interviews and extensive analysis of Persian materials, it offer the most comprehensive and balanced analysis of Khomeini's life available in English. Mathew Gordon's *Ayatollah Khomeini* (New York and London: Chelsea House Publishers, 1990), is designed for college students and provides a balanced, straightforward overview of Khomeini's life.

   A third genre consists of official biographies such as *Biography of Ayatollah Khomeini* (Tehran: Ministry of Islamic Guidance, Council for the Celebration of the Third Anniversary of the Victory of the Islamic Revolution, 1982) and "Biography of Imam Ayatollah Ruhullah Khomeini," in *Imam Khomeini's Last Will and Testament* (Washington, D.C.: Interest Section of the Islamic Republic of Iran, Solna Press, n.d.). Also see Ahmad Khomeini's biography of his father in the introduction to *Kauthar*, vol. 1 of *An Anthology of the Speeches of Imam Khomeini* (Tehran:

The Institute for the Compilation and Publication of the Works of Imam Khomeini, 1995). The "psycho-biographical" approach is adopted in Bruce Mazlish, "The Hidden Khomeini," *New York Magazine*, 24 December 1979, 50–55.

12. "Biography of Imam Ayatollah Ruhullah Khomeini," 1. Moin's account suggests that Mostafa was murdered by two local landowners, or *khans*, Mirza Qoli Soltan and Ja'far Qoli Khan. See his *Khomeini*, 6–8.

13. The actual circumstances of Mostafa's death are far less prosaic than suggested by his official biographers. According to Ervand Abrahamian, his death arose "out of a family vendetta with the al-Riyas, the other notable household in the locality. The al-Riyas had imprisoned one of Sayyid Mostafa's men. Sayyid Mostafa had retaliated by imprisoning an al-Riya man, who had then died. The al-Riyas too revenge by killing Sayyid Mostafa." Abrahamian, *Khomeinism: Essays on the Islamic Republic* (Berkeley: University of California Press, 1993), 6. Note that this account differs considerably from that given by Moin in *Khomeini*.

14. Moin, *Khomeini*, 10–11.

15. Ibid., 13.

16. Taheri reports that Khomeini's mother in effect abandoned him to his aunt's care. If it is true that "the unloved orphan never returned to his mother's embrace," this would further explain the stoic and angry view of life that Khomeini developed as a young man. See *The Spirit of Allah*, 32.

17. Hamid Enayat, *Modern Islamic Political Thought* (Austin: University of Texas Press, 1982), 18–51 and Shahrough Akhavi, *Religion and Politics in Contemporary Iran: Clergy-State Relations in the Pahlavi Period* (Albany: State University Press of New York, 1980), 1–22.

18. M. Haroon Siddiqui, "Ayatullah Ruhullah al-Musavi Khomeini's Ultimate Reality and Meaning," in *Ultimate Reality and Meaning: Interdisciplinary Studies in the Philosophy of Understanding*, vol. 9 (Downsview, Ontario: University of Toronto Press, 1986), 118.

19. Etan Kohlberg, "Imam and Community in the Pre-Ghayba Period," in *Authority and Political Culture in Shi'ism*, ed. Said Amir Arjomand (Albany: State University of New York Press, 1988), 26. Kohlberg cites from al-Saffar al-Qummi's *Baza'ir al-darajat*, a Shi'ite text about the Imams.

20. See Mazlish, "The Hidden Khomeini," 51.

21. Moin, "Khomeini's Search for Perfection," 66.

22. Siddiqui, "Ultimate Reality," 118.

23. Moin, "Khomeini's Search for Perfection," 67.

24. Taheri, *The Spirit of Allah*, 49.

25. Alexander Knysh, "*Irfan* Revisited: Khomeini and the Legacy of Islamic Mystical Philosophy," *Middle East Journal* 46, no. 4 (August 1992): 634.

26. Moin, "Khomeini's Search for Perfection," 69.

27. Students of Islamic mysticism have translated the Arabic word *kamil* as "perfect," an apt rendering inasmuch as it emphasizes the state of spiritual perfection Arabi and other mystics had in mind. However, *kamil* also suggests completeness or wholeness, thus implying that the "perfect" man is one who had brought the spiritual and material worlds into a complete

perfect balance. As we shall see, this notion of perfect wholeness informs Khomeini's own mysticism.

28. Knysh, *"Irfan* Revisited," 634.

29. Ibid.

30. Moin, "Khomeini's Search for Perfection," 73.

31. Knysh, *"Irfan* Revisited," 644–45 n. 8.

32. Knysh uses the term *vicegerency,* although the more common term is *vice-regency.*

33. Vanessa Martin, "Khumaini, Knowledge and the Political Process," *The Muslim World* 87, no. 1 (January 1997), 9.

34. Knysh, *"Irfan* Revisited," 649, quoting Khomeini's 1930 *Misbah al-Hidaya ila al-Khalifa wa al-Waliya* (Lamp [lighting] the right way to vice-regency and sainthood), ed. al-Sayyid Ahmad al-Fihri (Beirut: Mu'assasat al-wafa', 1983). Also see Dabashi, *Theology of Discontent,* 463–66. Dabashi, as we shall discuss later, suggests that Khomeini's "revolutionary' reading of *esmat* (infallibility) crystallized in several mystical tracts he wrote in the early seventies. Clearly, the roots of this transformation go back over half a century, a fact that Dabashi implicitly acknowledges in noting the influence of Ibn Arabi and Molla Sadra on the young Khomeini.

35. Hamid Algar, "The Role of the Ulema in Twentieth Century Iran," in *Scholars, Saints and Sufis,* ed. Nikki R. Keddie (Berkeley: University of California Press, 1972) 232 n. 3.

36. Hamid Dabashi, "Mulla Ahmad Naraqi and the Question of the Guardianship of the Jurisconsult," in *Expectation of the Millennium: Shi'ism in History,* ed. Sayyid Hossein Nasr, Hamid Dabashi, and Sayyid Vali Reza Nasr (Albany: State University of New York Press, 1989), 289.

37. Roy Mottahedeh, *The Mantle of the Prophet: Religion and Politics in Iran* (New York: Pantheon Books, 1985), 300–301.

38. For a vivid and empathetic portrayal of daily life in these seminaries, see Michael Fischer, *Iran: From Religious Dispute to Revolution* (Cambridge: Cambridge University Press, 1980).

39. Dabashi, "Mulla Ahmad Naraqi," 299.

40. "Biography of Imam Ayatollah Ruhollah Khomeini," 2.

41. Knysh, *"Irfan* Revisited," 635. On Khomeini's ascetic mysticism, also see Moin, "Khomeini's Search for Perfection," in Rahnema, *Pioneers of Islamic Revival* and Mottahedeh, *The Mantle of the Prophet,* 134–85.

42. Moin, "Khomeini's Search for Perfection," 75.

43. Ibid., 67.

44. Algar, "Imam Khomeini," 268–69.

45. Moin, "Khomeini's Search for Perfection," 71.

46. Algar, "Imam Khomeini," 274; also see Taheri, *The Spirit of Allah,* 93–94. Taheri notes that in 1979, Khomeini had the commander of the troops responsible for the massacre, Captain Iraj Matbu'i, executed at the age of ninety-six.

47. Moin, "Khomeini's Search for Perfection," 77.

48. Ibid.

49. Khomeini not only resumed his lectures on ethics sometime toward the end

of the fifties or the beginning of the sixties; but also gave up the traditional *minbar* (pulpit) and lectured instead, sitting on the ground, in a corner of the room. This style emphasized both his humbleness and his quiet conviction in the righteousness of his words. See Nikki R. Keddie, *Roots of Revolution* (New Haven: Yale University Press, 1981), 207.

50. Ruhollah Khomeini, *Islam and Revolution: Writings and Declarations of Imam Khomeini*, trans. Hamid Algar (Berkeley, Calif.: Mizan Press, 1981), 349. Quoted from "Invocations of Sha'aban," a litany recited by the Imam on the month of Sha'ban. Algar notes that Khomeini always concluded his lectures on ethics in Qom with this part of the litany.

Chapter Three

1. Lezek Kolakowski, "In Praise of Inconsistency," in *Marxism and Beyond: On Historical Understanding and Individual Responsibility*, trans. Jane Zielonko Peel (London: Pall Mall Press, 1969), 233, quoted in H. E. Chehabi, *Iranian Politics and Religious Modernism: The Liberation Movement and Iran under the Shah and Khomeini* (Ithaca, N.Y.: Cornell University Press, 1990), 100.

2. Hannah Arendt, *The Origins of Totalitarianism* (New York: Harcourt, Brace & World, 1968), 353.

3. Hamid Dabashi, *Theology of Discontent: The Ideological Foundation of the Islamic Revolution in Iran* (New York: New York University Press, 1993), 145; italics mine.

4. Ervand Abrahamian, *Khomeinism: Essays on the Islamic Republic* (Berkeley: University of California Press, 1993); see pp. 23, 29, and particularly 47–48.

5. Said Arjomand, *The Turban for the Crown: The Islamic Revolution in Iran* (New York and Oxford: Oxford University Press: 1988), 50–54.

6. Imam Khomeini, *Kashf Al-Asrar* (Nashr-i Safar: 197?), 185. I have also consulted an Arabic version of *Kasfh* (n.p., 1985), 179–80.

7. Ibid, 220. Khomeini also stresses the importance of "interests" on pages 270 and 286.

8. Vanessa Martin offers a similar interpretation of *Kashf*. See her "Religion and State in Khumaini's Kasf Al-Asrar," *Bulletin of the School of Oriental and African Studies* 56, pt. 1 (1993): 34–45.

9. Hamid Algar, "Imam Khomeini, 1902–1962: The Pre-Revolutionary Years," in *Islam, Politics and Social Movements*, ed. Edmund Burke III and Ira M. Lapidus, (Berkeley: University of California Press, 1988), 276.

10. Marvin Zonis, *Majestic Failure: The Fall of the Shah* (Chicago: University of Chicago Press, 1991), 99–107.

11. Kermit Roosevelt, *Countercoup: The Struggle for the Control of Iran* (New York: McGraw-Hill Book Company, 1979).

12. Roy Mottahedeh, *The Mantle of the Prophet: Religion and Politics in Iran* (New York: Pantheon Books, 1985), 131.

13. Abrahamian, *Khomeinism*, 110.

14. Mehrzad Boroujerdi, *Iranian Intellectuals and the West: The Tormented Triumph of Nativism* (Syracuse, N.Y.: Syracuse University Press, 1996), 80–81.

15. Baqer Moin, "Khomeini's Search for Perfection," in *Pioneers of Islamic Revival*, ed. Ali Rahnema (London: Zed Books, 1994), 81–82.

16. Boroujerdi, *Iranian Intellectuals*, 80–81 and Mottahedeh, *The Mantle of the Prophet*, 236.

17. Hamid Enayat, *Modern Islamic Political Thought* (Austin: University of Texas Press, 1982), 11.

18. On Rida see Nadav Safran, *Egypt in Search of Political Community: An Analysis of the Intellectual and Political Evolution of Egypt 1804–1952* (Cambridge, Mass.: Harvard University Press, 1961), 76 and Enayat, *Modern Islamic Political Thought*, 69–83. On Afghani see Nikki R. Keddie, *An Islamic Response to Imperialism: Political and Religious Writings of Sayyid Jamal ad-Din "al-Afghani"* (Berkeley: University of California Press, 1983).

19. Sami Zubaida, *Islam: The People and the State* (London: I. B. Tauris Publishers, 1989), 13.

20. See Albert Hourani, *Arabic Thought in the Liberal Age, 1798–1939* (London: Oxford University Press, 1970), 233–34.

21. Enayat, *Modern Islamic Political Thought*, 149. I am not suggesting that the Brethren invented the concept of *maslahat*. The practice, as Asghar Schirazi has noted, "was accepted by most of the Suni schools of jurisprudence as the rule of *esteslah* (taking account of interests) and *masaleh-e morsaleh* (consideration of interests without deriving them from the *shari'a*)." Schirazi, *The Constitution of Iran: Politics and the State in the Islamic Republic* (London: I. B. Tauris Publishers, 1997), 233. However, Ghazzali appears to have pushed the concept of *maslahat* in new directions by conflating it with the *Shari'ah* (sacred law of Islam) itself.

22. Schirazi, *The Constitution of Iran*, 233.

23. This said, after Khomeini used the term *interests* during his 1963 confrontation with the Shah, Mohammad Reza Pahlavi, many of his clerical allies followed suit. See Baqer Moin, *Khomeini: Life of the Ayatollah* (London: I. B. Tauris Publishers, 1999), 96.

24. Amir Taheri, *The Spirit of Allah: Khomeini and the Islamic Revolution* (Bethesda, Md.: Adler and Adler, 1986), 97–98.

25. Ibid. Also see Chehabi, *Iranian Politics and Religious Modernism*, 116–17 and Farhad Kazemi, "The *Fada'iyan-e Islam*: Fanaticism, Politics and Terror," in *From Nationalism to Revolutionary Islam*, ed. Said Arjomand (Albany: State University of New York Press, 1984), 158–75 nn. 46, 175.

26. The *Jama'at-i Islami*, or Islamic Party, originated in India and subsequently became the chief advocate for an Islamic state in Pakistan. See Martin, "Religion and State," 42. On Mawdudi see C. J. Adams, "Mawdudi and the Islamic State," in *Voices of Resurgent Islam*, ed. John Esposito (New York and Oxford: Oxford University Press, 1983), 99–133.

27. Chehabi, *Iranian Politics and Religious Modernism*, 27.

28. Boroujerdi, *Iranian Intellectuals*, 38.

29. See Marvin Zonis, *The Political Elite of Iran* (Princeton, N.J.: Princeton University Press, 1971).

30. Ibid, 32–33.

31. Harold Lasswell and Daniel Lerner, eds., *World Revolutionary Elites: Studies in Coercive Ideological Movements* (Cambridge, Mass.: M.I.T. Press, 1965), 80.

32. Ibid., 42.

33. David Menashri, *Education and the Making of Modern Iran* (Ithaca, N.Y.: Cornell University Press, 1992), 207.
34. Ibid, 205.
35. Rather than provide comprehensive biographies, the short sketches in this section highlight the personal, cultural, social, intellectual, and political forces shaping the multiple imaginations of Al-e Ahmad, Shari'ati, Bazargan, and Taleqani. While I largely rely on several well-respected studies and biographies, in a few cases I also cited directly from original sources.
36. Boroujerdi, *Iranian Intellectuals*, 64.
37. Jalal Al-e Ahmad, *Yek Chah va Do Chaleh* (Tehran: n.p., 1343/1964), quoted in Mottahedeh, *The Mantle of the Prophet*, 288. See author's biographical essay, p. 394.
38. Dabashi, *Theology of Discontent*, 65.
39. Ibid., 66.
40. Ibid., 68. The author quotes from Jalal Al-e Ahmad's *Safar beh Velayat-e Isra'il* (Tehran: Ravaq, 1363/1984), 52. See p. 531 n. 74.
41. Mottahedeh, *The Mantle of the Prophet*, 320.
42. Boroujerdi, *Iranian Intellectuals*, 70.
43. Jalal Al-e Ahmad, *Kar-nameh-ye Seh Saleh* (Tehran: Ravaq, 1357/1978), 183, quoted in Dabashi, *Theology of Discontent*, 62.
44. Boroujerdi, *Iranian Intellectuals*, 72. Al-e Ahmad uses the word *doctors* when referring to the clerics.
45. Mottahedeh, *The Mantle of the Prophet*, 303.
46. Jalal Al-e Ahmad, *Plagued by the West*, trans. Paul Sprachman (Delmar, N.Y.: Caravan Books, 1982), 6–7, 67.
47. Ali Rahnema, "Ali Shariati: Teacher, Preacher, Rebel," in *Pioneers of Islamic Revival*, ed. Rahnema, 210.
48. Ibid., 211.
49. Ibid., 216.
50. Ali Shari'ati, *Tarikh va Shenakht-e Adyan* (History and recognition of religions), *Collected Works*, no. 14 (Tehran: Sherkat-e Sahami-ye Enteshar, 1362/1983), 52–53, quoted in Boroujerdi, *Iranian Intellectuals*, 107.
51. Dabashi, *Theology of Discontent*, 115.
52. Ibid., 114. The author cites from Shari'ati's *Shi'ah, Collected Works*, no. 7 (Tehran: Hoseyniyyeh-ye Ershad, 1357/1978), 19.
53. Rahnema, "Ali Shariati," 219.
54. Ibid.
55. Shari'ati, *Shi'ah*, 16, quoted in Dabashi, *Theology of Discontent*, 117.
56. Ali Shari'ati, *An Approach to the Understanding of Islam*, trans. Venus Kaivantash (Houston: Free Islamic Literatures, 1980), 19–20.
57. Dabashi, *Theology of Discontent*, 128. On p. 539 n. 100 the author cites from Shari'ati's *Eslamshenasi*, 3 vols., *Collected Works*, nos. 16, 17, 18 (Tehran: Entesharat-e Shari'ati, 1360/1981), 1:11.
58. Ibid., 116.
59. Ibid, 142.

60. Ibid, 115. See also Ali Shari'ati, *Man and Islam*, trans. from the Persian by Fatollah Marjani (Houston: Free Islamic Literatures, 1981), 41.
61. Shari'ati's love of mysticism was enhanced during his years in Paris where, as a student of the French Islamist and ascetic mystic Louis Massignon, he came to appreciate the universal appeal of mysticism. See Dabashi, *Theology of Discontent*, 109.
62. See Rahnema's discussion of Shari'ati's views on democracy in his "Ali Shariati," 241.
63. Indeed, *bazargan* means "merchant" in Persian.
64. Mehdi Bazargan, *Modafe'at Dar Dadgah-e Gheir-e Saleh-e Tajdid-e Nazar-e Nezami* (n.p: Entesharat-e Modarres, 1971), 52–61, quoted in Chehabi, *Iranian Politics and Religious Modernism*, 109. See also n. 18 on the same page.
65. Bahram Afrasiabi and Sa'id Dehqan, *Taleqani va Tarikh* (Tehran: Entesharat-e Nilufar, 1981), 64, quoted in Chehabi, *Iranian Politics and Religious Modernism*, 118 n. 41. The relationship between the Bazargan and Taleqani families dated to the twenties, when the fathers of Mehdi Bazargan and Mahmud Taleqani established an Islamic institute in Tehran. See Dabashi, *Theology of Discontent*, 328.
66. Chehabi, *Iranian Politics and Religious Modernism*, 156–63.
67. Mehdi Bazargan, *Jarayan-e ta'sis-e nehzat-e azadi-ye Iran* (How the IFM was founded), 17–18, in *Safehati az tarikh-e mo'aser-e Iran: Asnad-e nehzat-e azadi-ye Iran* (Some pages from contemporary Iranian history: The documents of the Liberation Movement of Iran), no. 1 (n.p., 1982), quoted in Chehabi, *Iranian Politics and Religious Modernism*, 158 n. 30; italics mine.
68. Mehdi Bazargan, *Khaneh-ye Mardom* (Houston: Book Distribution Center, 1356/1977), 56, quoted in Dabashi, *Theology of Discontent*, 335, 566 n. 52.
69. Mehdi Bazargan, *Be'that va Ideology* (Houston: Book Distribution Center, 1355/1976), 2, quoted in Dabashi, *Theology of Discontent*, 346, 569 n. 117.
70. Mehdi Bazargan, "Entezarat-e Mardom az' Maraje," in *Bahti dar Bareh-ye Marja'iyyat va Ruhaniyyat* (Tehran: Enteshar, 1341/1962), 114, quoted in Dabashi, *Theology of Discontent*, 342, 568 n. 97.
71. Ahmad Jabbari and Farhang Rajaee observe that Taleqani composed some of his best-known works in prison, relying on his memory of texts and sources. Mahmoud Taleqani, *Islam and Ownership*, trans. from the Persian by Ahmad Jabbari and Farhang Rajaee (Lexington, Ky.: Mazda Publishers, 1983), vii.
72. Seyyed Mahmud Taleqani, introduction to Sheykh Mohammad Hoseyn Na'ini, *Tanbih al-Ummah va Tanzih al-Millah: ya Hokumat az Nazar-e Islam* (Tehran: Sherkat-e Sahami Enteshar, 1334/1955), 10, quoted in Dabashi, *Theology of Discontent*, 233 n. 38.
73. Boroujerdi, *Iranian Intellectuals*, 85.
74. Menashri, *Education and the Making of Modern Iran*, 216.
75. Boroujerdi, *Iranian Intellectuals*, 91.
76. For example, in the late sixties the total number of seminary students in Mashhad was 14,000, compared with a total of 260 in the Mashhad University Faculty of Theology. See Boroujerdi, *Iranian Intellectuals*, 104.

77. Ibid., 92.
78. Shahrough Akhavi, *Religion and Politics in Contemporary Iran: Clergy-State Relations in the Pahlavi Period* (Albany: State University Press of New York, 1980), 115.
79. Ibid., 122.
80. Ibid, 120 n. 6.
81. Chehabi, *Iranian Politics and Religious Modernism*, 177.
82. Moin, *Khomeini*, 75.
83. Taheri, *The Spirit of Allah*, 126. Ayatollah Mohammad-Kazem Shari'atma-dari, a leading traditionalist cleric, also issued a statement condemning the January 26 referendum after Ayatollah Mohsen Hakim, the leading *marja'* in Najaf, sent him a telegram denouncing the Shah. The vast majority of the leading clerics remained silent. See Mohammad Borhei, "Iran's Religious Establishment: The Dialectics of Politicization," in *Political Culture in the Islamic Republic*, ed. Samih K. Farsoun and Mehrdad Mashayekhi (London and New York: Routledge, 1992), 57–81.
84. See Ruhollah Khomeini, "In Commemoration of the Martyrs of Qum," in Khomeini, *Islam and Revolution: Writings and Declarations of Imam Khomeini*, trans. Hamid Algar (Berkeley, Calif.: Mizan Press, 1981), 175.
85. Borhei, "Iran's Religious Establishment," 75–6.
86. Ibid., 76. See Khomeini's speech "The Afternoon of 'Ashura, June 3, 1963," in Khomeini, *Islam and Revolution*, 177 and in *Kauthar*, vol. 1 of *An Anthology of the Speeches of Imam Khomeini* (Tehran: The Institute for the Compilation and Publication of the Works of Imam Khomeini, 1995), 121–27.
87. Mottahedeh, *The Mantle of the Prophet*, 303.
88. Dabashi, *Theology of Discontent*, 150.
89. See Chehabi, *Iranian Politics and Religious Modernism*, 202–10.
90. Boroujerdi, *Iranian Intellectuals*, 116–20.
91. Arjomand, *The Turban for the Crown*, 97.
92. Chehabi, *Iranian Politics and Religious Modernism*, 219.
93. Dabashi, *Theology of Discontent*, 480.
94. Chehabi, *Iranian Politics and Religious Modernism*, 219.
95. Moin, *Khomeini*, 96.
96. Ruhollah Khomeini, "October 27, 1964: The Granting of Capitulatory Rights to the U.S.," in Khomeini, *Islam and Revolution*, 181–82. Also see Moin, *Khomeini*, 121–27.
97. Dabashi, *Theology of Discontent*, 427.
98. Ruhollah Khomeini, "April 16, 1967, Open Letter to Prime Minister Hov-eyda," in Khomeini, *Islam and Revolution*, 191.
99. "February 6, 1971, Message to the Pilgrims," ibid., 195.
100. "October 31, 1971, The Incompatibility of Monarchy with Islam," ibid., 202; italics mine.
101. "July 10, 1972, Message to the Muslim Students in North America," ibid., 210.
102. Chehabi, *Iranian Politics and Religious Modernism*, 205.
103. Moin, *Khomeini*, 177; italics mine. The author cites here from Hoseyn

Akhavan-e Towhidi, *Dar Pas-e Pardeh-ye Tasvir* (Paris: n.p., 1359/1981), 324 n. 36.

Chapter Four

1. Sayyad Ahmad Fehri, introduction to Ruhollah Ayatollah Khomeini, *Sharh Du'a al-Sahar* (Dawn supplication; Beirut: n.p., 1982), quoted in Baqer Moin, "Khomeini's Search for Perfection," in *Pioneers of Islamic Revival,* ed. Ali Rahnema (London: Zed Books, 1994), 76.
2. Ruhollah Khomeini, *Islam and Revolution: Writings and Declarations of Imam Khomeini,* trans. Hamid Algar (Berkeley, Calif.: Mizan Press, 1981).
3. Hamid Dabashi, "Mulla Ahmad Naraqi," in *Expectation of the Millennium: Shi'ism in History,* ed. Sayyid Hossein Nasr, Hamid Dabashi, and Sayyid Vali Reza Nasr (Albany: State University of New York Press, 1989), 288.
4. Ibid, 289.
5. The Safavid Empire (1501–1722) offers a partial exception to this historic rule. The first leader of the Safavid dynasty claimed to be the Mahdi, or Twelfth Imam, thus suggesting a close affinity between his authority and that of the Twelfth Imam. After assuming power he then moderated this assertion, claiming to be the "Shadow of God on Earth," or the forerunner of the Mahdi. Khomeini's solution to the problem of the Imamate resembles that advanced by the founder of the Safavid dynasty. See Said Arjomand, *The Turban for the Crown The Islamic Revolution of Iran* (New York and Oxford: Oxford University Press, 1988), 152.
6. See Hamid Dabashi, *Theology of Discontent: The Ideological Foundation of the Islamic Revolution in Iran* (New York: New York University Press, 1993), 116, 232, 342, 385.
7. Ayatollah Seyyed Mohammad Baqer al-Sadr was the leading Arab Shi'ite radical Islamic thinker in Najaf, and one of the few—and perhaps only— Arab Shi'ite clerics who had regular contact with Khomeini. Toward the end of the seventies al-Sadr argued that the *"marja* is the supreme representative of the Islamic ideology." Chibli Mallat, *The Renewal of Islamic Law* (Cambridge: Cambridge University Press, 1993), 66. Whether Khomeini was influenced by such ideas is hard to say, since al-Sadr had not publicly expounded his views of *velayat-e faqih* during the late sixties. One can surmise, however, that al-Sadr's radical proclivities reinforced Khomeini's radical drift during this period.
8. See Hamid Algar's translation of Khomeini's "Islamic Government" in Khomeini, *Islam and Revolution,* 27–159. Also see Hamid Enayat's "Iran: Khumayni's Concept of the 'Guardian of the Jurisconsult,'" in *Islam in the Political Process,* ed. James Piscatori (Cambridge: Cambridge University Press, 1983), 160–80.
9. Khomeini, "Islamic Government," 30–1.
10. Khomeini seem to echo here Sheykh Fazlollah Nuri, who during the 1906 Constitutional Revolution coined the term *mashru'a* ("based on religious law") to argue for a *mashruta-ye mahsru'a,* or "Islamic Constitutionalism"; in other words, a form of constitutionalism conditioned *solely* by Islamic law.

11. Khomeini, "Islamic Government," 53.

12. Shirazi led the clerical opposition to British rule in Iraq during the last years of World War I.

13. This oblique association, and others in Khomeini's "Islamic Government," may anticipate the notion of the "absolute *faqih*" that Khomeini unveiled in late 1988. See chapter 6.

14. Khomeini, "Islamic Government," 53.

15. "O you who believe, obey God and obey the Messenger and the holder of authority from among you. When you dispute with each other concerning a thing, refer it to God and his Messenger" (4:58–59).

16. Khomeini, "Islamic Government," 68.

17. Elsewhere, Khomeini insists that "the *fuquha* do not have absolute authority . . . over all other *foqaha* of their own time. . . . There is no hierarchy ranking one . . . higher than another" (64). Khomeini waited another eight years before addressing this contradiction by establishing himself as an Imam who clearly had supreme authority.

18. Ruhollah Khomeini, "Lecture on the Supreme Jihad," in Khomeini, *Islam and Revolution*, 353; italics mine.

19. Ibid., 356.

20. See Hamid Dabashi, *Authority in Islam* (New Brunswick, N.J.: Transaction Publishers, 1989), 40.

21. See Annemarie Schimmel, *Mystical Dimensions of Islam* (Chapel Hill: University of North Carolina Press, 1974), 199–213. Indeed, in Sunni Islam, the term *wali* (or *vali* in Persian) means "saint."

22. Khomeini, "Lecture on the Supreme Jihad," 353. While he discusses the *awliya* in "Islamic Government," Khomeini cites from a *hadith* in which Imam Hoseyn reportedly used the term in its broadest sense, by referring to "those who have set their faces toward God . . . not the Twelve Imams." See Khomeini, *Islam and Revolution*, 113.

23. Khomeini, "Lecture on the Supreme Jihad," 352.

24. Dabashi, *Theology of Discontent*, 463.

25. Khomeini, "Lecture on the Supreme Jihad," 357.

26. Ibid., 358.

27. See the last few pages of chapter 3 for an example of these populist themes.

28. Khomeini, "Islamic Government," 116.

29. Baqer Moin, *Khomeini: Life of the Ayatollah* (London: I. B. Tauris Publishers, 1999), 157.

30. Kambiz Afrachteh, "The Predominance and Dilemmas of Theocratic Populism in Contemporary Iran," *Iranian Studies* 14, no. 3–4 (summer–autumn 1981): 189–215, quoted from p. 195.

31. These efforts helped to drive the *bazaaris* closer to the clerical opposition. See Robert Bianchi's brief, yet incisive discussion of Iran in his *Unruly Corporatism: Association Life in Twentieth Century Egypt* (New York: Oxford University Press, 1989), 207–11.

32. According to Mansoor Moaddel, in 1972 the total number of Iranians employed in all major economic sectors was 8.875 million. It is not clear what percentage were industrial workers. See Moaddel, *Class, Politics and*

Ideology in the Iranian Revolution (New York: Columbia University Press, 1993), 123–24. Said Arjomand puts the number of these workers in 1977 at 3.5 million, one-third of the total labor force. But he notes that only government workers in the oil and tobacco industries played a major part in the revolution, while industrial labor constituted only about 7 percent of the total labor force (Arjomand, *The Turban for the Crown*, 218).

33. Arjomand, *The Turban for the Crown*, 109.
34. Ibid.
35. Ibid., 197–210. In these pages Arjomand succinctly compares the dynamics of mass society in Iran with those in Western Europe.
36. William Kornhauser, *The Politics of Mass Society* (New York: Free Press, 1969), 39.
37. Ibid., 103.
38. Marvin Zonis, *Majestic Failure: The Fall of the Shah* (Chicago: University of Chicago Press, 1991), 81.
39. Ibid., 222–23.
40. Michael Fischer, *Iran: From Religious Dispute to Revolution* (Cambridge: Cambridge University Press, 1980), 185.
41. Kornhauser, *The Politics of Mass Society*, 78.
42. The Shah's secret police.
43. Amir Taheri, *The Spirit of Allah: Khomeini and the Islamic Revolution* (Bethesda, Md.: Adler and Adler, 1986), 185.
44. Ibid., 203.
45. Karl Mannheim, *Ideology and Utopia: An Introduction to the Sociology of Knowledge*, translated from the German by Louis Wirth and Edward Shils (New York: Harvest Books, 1936), 217.
46. Arjomand, *The Turban for the Crown*, 104.
47. 19 February 1978. Ruhollah Khomeini, "In Commemoration of the First Martyrs of the Revolution," in Khomeini, *Islam and Revolution*, 213; italics mine.
48. Hannah Arendt, *The Origins of Totalitarianism* (New York: Harcourt, Brace & World, 1968), 349.
49. Dabashi, *Theology of Discontent*, 482–83.
50. Azar Tabari, "Mystifications of the Past and Illusions of the Future," in *The Iranian Revolution and the Islamic Republic: Proceedings of A Conference*, ed. Nikki R. Keddie and Eric Hooglund (Washington D.C.: Middle East Institute, 1982), 101–24, cited on p. 107.

Chapter Five

1. "Khomeyni Discusses Guardians Council Tasks," broadcast 11 December 1983, FBIS—SAS-83–060, 12 December 1983.
2. Hannah Arendt, *The Origins of Totalitarianism* (New York: Harcourt, Brace & World, 1968), 348–49.
3. Crane Brinton, *The Anatomy of Revolution* (New York: Vintage Books, 1965), 146.
4. Ezzatollah Sahabi was appointed minister for revolutionary projects; 'Ali-Asgar Haj Seyyed Javadi, minister of the interior; 'Abbas Amir-Entezam,

deputy prime minister for revolutionary affairs; Sadeq Qotbzadeh, director of National Iranian Radio and Television; Ebrahim Mohammad Yazdi, minister of foreign affairs (after the resignation of Karim Sanjabi, a leader of the Nationalist Front); and Mostafa Chamran, minister of defense. As for Ayatollah Seyyed Mahmud Taleqani, he was appointed to the "Assembly of Experts" that was responsible for drafting the Constitution, and remained—until his death from a heart attack in September 1979—an enthusiastic supporter of Mehdi Bazargan's.

5. Taleqani's heart attack occurred after he had openly signaled opposition to the principle of *velayat-e faqih*. Compelled to resign after militant students occupied the American Embassy in November 1979, Bazargan—together with Sahabi, Yazdi, Haj Seyyed Javadi, and Amir-Entezam—formed what remained of the legal opposition. In June 1981 Chamran was killed—some believe assassinated by the regime—in the Iran–Iraq War, and Abolhasan Bani-Sadr fled Iran after the *Majles* moved to remove him for the crime of treason. Finally, a year later Qotbzadeh was executed after being implicated in a failed coup d'état.

6. Cheryl Benard and Zalmay Khalilzad, *"The Government of God": Iran's Islamic Republic* (New York: Columbia University Press, 1984), 112.

7. For example, see Asghar Schirazi, *The Constitution of Iran: Politics and the State in the Islamic Republic* (London: I. B. Tauris Publishers, 1997), 22–33, which makes this case very clearly. In contrast, Robin Wright argues that during the first few months of the revolution, the "evidence indicates the imam's goals were still limited," and that his "opponents forced the debate" (*In the Name of God: The Khomeini Decade* [New York: Simon and Schuster, 1989], 72). Neither author entertains the possibility that Khomeini had multiple goals.

8. Schirazi, *The Constitution of Iran*, 24.

9. "A Military Coup Is Impossible," Paul Balta interview with Ayatollah Khomeini, Paris *Le Monde*, 10 January 1979, FBIS-MEA-79-008, 11 January 1979.

10. "Six Point Message from Khomeini, February 12, 1979," broadcast 12 February 1979, FBIS-MEA-79-031-A, 13 February 1979.

11. H. E. Chehabi, *Iranian Politics and Religious Modernism: The Liberation Movement and Iran Under the Shah and Khomeini* (Ithaca, N.Y.: Cornell University Press, 1990), 259.

12. "Khomeyni Address to Nation," broadcast 28 February 1979, FBIS-MEA-79-042, 1 March 1979; italics mine. Although Khomeini remained in Qom for nine months, beginning in late February 1979, he remained very much involved in directing the course of political events. See Baqer Moin, *Khomeini: Life of the Ayatollah* (London: I. B. Tauris Publishers, 1999), 213.

13. "Khomeyni Call," broadcast 29 March 1979. FBIS-MEA-79-062, 30 March 1979.

14. "Khomeyni Statement after Voting," broadcast 30 March 1979, FBIS-MEA-79-064, 2 April 1979.

15. This did not mean that the council was a simple tool of the clerics. Indeed, the council itself adopted the name "Democratic Islamic Republic" in one

of its first declarations, and was sharply criticized by Khomeini for this. See Schirazi, *The Constitution of Iran,* 40 nn. 37, 38.

16. "Khomeini Delivers Speech on Freedom, Plots," broadcast 25 May 1979, FBIS-MEA-79-103, 29 May 1979.
17. "Khomeini Discusses Constitution," broadcast 16 June 1979, FBIS-MEA-79-118, 18 June 1979.
18. "Khomeini Says Iran Facing 'Danger of Unbridleness,' " broadcast 24 June 1979, FBIS-MEA-79-123, 25 June 1979. Muawiyah established the Ummayad dynasty in the year 661. He opposed 'Ali's claim to the Caliphate by calling for its arbitration. Khomeini's point seems to be twofold: first, even Islamic leaders can act in an evil fashion; and second, differences within the Islamic camp can open the door to evil leaders such as Muawiyah.
19. "Khomeyni Warns Nation: Losing Key to Victory," broadcast 7 July 1979, FBIS-MEA-79-132A, 9 July 1979.
20. Shaul Bakhash, *The Reign of the Ayatollahs* (New York: Basic Books, 1984), 78.
21. "Khomeini Urges Unity in Selection Draft Constitution," broadcast 25 July 1979, FBIS-MEA-79-145, 26 July 1979
22. "Khomeyni: Army Must Act with Severity in Kordistan," broadcast 17 August 1979, FBIS-MEA-79-162A.
23. "Khomeyni Defends Concept of Theocracy in 22 October Speech," broadcast 22 October 1979, FBIS-MEA-79-206, vol 5, no. 206
24. Schirazi, *The Constitution of Iran,* 52–53.
25. Ibid., 35.
26. Mohsen Milani, "Shi'ism and the State: The Constitution of the Republic of Iran," in *Political Culture in the Islamic Republic,* ed. Samih K. Farsoun and Mehrdad Mashayekhi (London and New York: Routledge, 1992), 142.
27. Bakhash, *The Reign of the Ayatollahs,* 85.
28. Schirazi, *The Constitution of Iran,* 37–38 and Milani, "Shi'ism and the State," 142.
29. Bakhash, *The Reign of the Ayatollahs,* 84. These are Bakhash's words.
30. Schirazi, *The Constitution of Iran,* 45.
31. Ibid., 46–47.
32. Bakhash, *The Reign of the Ayatollahs,* 26. These were Rahmatollah Maraghe'i's words.
33. Schirazi, *The Constitution of Iran,* 50.
34. Ibid.
35. The quotations that follow in the text are from "Islamic Republic of Iran, 1979, " in *Constitutions of the Countries of the World,* ed. Albert P. Blaustein and Gisbert H. Flanz (Dobbs Ferry, N.Y.: Oceana Publications, 1980). I have also consulted the Persian version, *Qanoun Asasi Jumhouriyya Islami Iran 1980* (Fundamental law of the Islamic Republic of Iran, 1980).
36. Italics are mine. The use of the term *vojdan* merits special notice: it means precisely what Durkheim had in mind by the term "collective conscience"; in other words, a shared sense of morality that regulates a society.
37. The terms *rahbar* and *faqih* are interchangeable in that the leader is also the highest-ranking interpreter of the law.

38. Bahman Baktiari, *Parliamentary Politics in Revolutionary Iran: The Institutionalization of Factional Politics* (Gainesville: University Press of Florida, 1996), 63.

39. One other interpretation of Khomeini's behavior holds that he wanted no clerical competitors in the political hierarchy. While such calculations surely influenced his thinking, Khomeini's repeated statements suggest he was also genuinely concerned about the paradoxical consequences of clerical rule: he understood that any mistakes by the clergy could discredit the very idea of an Islamic Republic.

40. "Khomeyni Asks Public to Select Presidential Candidates," broadcast 4 January 1980, FBIS-MEA-80-00J, vol. 5, supplement 007, 8 January 1980.

41. See Hamid Dabashi, *Theology of Discontent: The Ideological Foundation of the Islamic Revolution in Iran* (New York: New York University Press, 1993), 384–387 and Bakhash, *The Reign of the Ayatollahs*, 93–96.

42. Baktiari, *Parliamentary Politics in Revolutionary Iran*, 67.

43. Bakhash, *The Reign of the Ayatollahs*, 98.

44. "Address by Ayatollah Khomeini on the Occasion of the Iranian New Year," broadcast 20 March 1979, FBIS-MEA-80-056, 21 March 1980.

45. "Ayatollah Khomeyni Addresses Nation," broadcast 21 March 1980, FBIS-MEA-80-038, 24 March 1980.

46. Arjomand, *The Turban for the Crown*, 143–44.

47. "Khomeyni Addresses Youth on Corruption in Society," broadcast 20 May 1980, FBIS-SAS-80-100, 21 May 21, 1980.

48. "Khomeyni Majlis Message," broadcast 28 May 1980, FBIS-SAS-80-104, 28 May 1980.

49. "Text of Khomeyni Speech to a Group of Workers," broadcast 25 June 1980, FBIS-SAS-80-125, 26 June 1980.

50. "Speech to Council," broadcast 21 July 1980, FBIS-SAS-141, 21 July 1980.

51. "20 July Speech," broadcast 20 July 1980, FBIS-SAS-80-143, 23 July 1980.

52. "25 July Speech," broadcast 25 July 1980, FBIS-SAS-80-146, 28 July 1980.

53. "Khomeyni Warns against Division," broadcast 4 February 1981, FBIS-SAS-81-24, 5 February 1981.

54. "Khomeyni Condemns National Front," broadcast 15 June 1981, FBIS-SAS-81-115, 16 June 1981.

55. "Khomeyni Message to the Nation," broadcast 11 February 1981, FBIS-SAS-029, 12 February 1981. It should be noted that Khomeini had only recently attacked those who opposed the clergy because they lacked the "technical" skills required for managing public affairs.

56. "Khomeini Addresses Pilots," broadcast 7 April 1981, FBIS-SAS-81-067, 8 April 1981.

57. Bakhash, *The Reign of the Ayatollahs*, 99.

58. Ibid., 146.

59. Baktiari, *Parliamentary Politics in Revolutionary Iran*, 69.

60. "Khomeini Speech," broadcast 25 May 1980, FBIS-SAS-80-103, 27 May 1980.

61. Ibid.

Chapter Six

1. Crane Brinton, *The Anatomy of Revolution* (New York: Vintage Books, 1965), 203.
2. "Khomeyni Issues Message on Islamization," broadcast 15 December 1982, FBIS-SAS-82-242, 16 December 16,1982.
3. "Khomeyni Speaks of Civil, Property Rights," broadcast 22 December 1982, FBIS-SAS-82-24, 23 December 1982.
4. Edward Shils, *The Intellectuals and the Powers and Other Essays* (Chicago: University of Chicago Press, 1972), 44.
5. Karl Mannheim, *Ideology and Utopia: An Introduction to the Sociology of Knowledge*, trans. Louis Wirth and Edward Shils (New York: Harvest Book,1936), 218.
6. Max Weber, *Economy and Society*, vol. 1, ed. Guenther Roth and Claus Wittich (Berkeley: University of California Press, 1978), 246. Also see pp. 1121–22.
7. Unless otherwise noted, the following citations are all from one speech: "Khomeyni to the Craftsmen," broadcast on Tehran Domestic Service 13 December 1979, FBIS-MEA-79-242, 14 December 1979.
8. See chapter 2. Khomeini frequently cited this *hadith* in his mystical writings.
9. "Khomeini Delivers Oration," broadcast on Teheran Domestic Service 4 May 1979, FBIS-MEA-79-089, 7 May 1979.
10. Marvin Zonis and Daniel Brumberg, "Shi'ism as Interpreted by Khomeini," in *Shi'ism, Resistance and Revolution*, ed. Martin Kramer (Boulder, Colo.: Westview Press, 1987), 52–53.
11. "Khomeini Tells Students of Importance of National Unity," broadcast on Tehran Domestic Service 23 December1979, FBIS-MEA-29-249, 26 December 1979.
12. Bahman Baktiari, *Parliamentary Politics in Revolutionary Iran: The Institutionalization of Factional Politics* (Gainesville: University Press of Florida, 1996), 84.
13. Ibid., 95.
14. This said, one should not underestimate the extent to which the state had succeeded in taking over "strategic" sectors of the economy by the end of 1981. By then the state had nationalized all heavy industry, including mining, oil, and shipping, as well as banking and insurance.
15. "Khomeyni Addresses Muslim Clergy on Event of Muharram," broadcast 5 November 1980, FBIS-SAS-80-217, 6 November 1980; italics mine.
16. "Khomeyni Id Ghadir Address on Islam, War," broadcast 29 October 1980, FBIS-SAS-80-211, 29 October 1980.
17. "Khomeyni Addresses Majlis Deputies March 19," Broadcast 19 March 1981, FBIS-SAS-81-282, 21 March 21.
18. See Said Arjomand, "Shi'ite Jurisprudence and Constitution Making in Iran," in *Fundamentalism and the State: Remaking Polities, Economics, and Militaries*, ed. Martin E. Marty and R. Scott Appleby (Chicago: University of Chicago Press, 1993), 96.

19. Baktiari, *Parliamentary Politics in Revolutionary Iran*, 87.
20. "Majlis Speaker Requests Khomeyni Guidance on Laws," broadcast 11 October 1981, FBIS-SAS-81-198, 14 October 1981.
21. "Khomeyni Issues Message on Islamization."
22. "Khomeyni Speaks of Civil, Property Rights."
23. "Khomeyni Addresses Majlis Deputies January 24," broadcast 24 January 1983, FBIS-SAS-82-018, 26 January 1983.
24. "Khomeyni 10 February Message to Revolution Ceremony," broadcast 10 February 1983, FBIS-SAS-83-030, 11 February 1983.
25. "Khomeyni Issues Statement on Tudeh Leaders Arrest," broadcast 4 May 1983, FBIS-SAS-83-088, 5 May 1983.
26. "Ayatollah Khomeyni Message to Council of Experts," broadcast 14 July 1983, FBIS-SAS-83-137, 15 July 1983; italics and additional explanations are mine.
27. "Khomeini Discusses Guardian Council Tasks," broadcast 11 December 1983, FBIS-SAS-83-239, 12 December 1983
28. Jahangir Amuzegar, "The Iranian Economy before and after the Revolution," *Middle East Journal* 46, no. 3 (summer 1992): 421.
29. Baktiari, *Parliamentary Politics in Revolutionary Iran*, 105.
30. Ibid.,108.
31. Ibid.,109.
32. Although IFM leaders had been effectively stripped of power, Yadollah and Ezzatollah Sahabi, Kazem Sami, and Mehdi Bazargan himself had all won seats in the First *Majles*.
33. "Khomeyni Addresses Governors, District Officials," broadcast on Tehran Domestic Service 3 January 1984, FBIS-SAS84-002, 4 January 1984.
34. Baktiari, *Parliamentary Politics in Revolutionary Iran*, 114.
35. "Khomeyni Addresses Leaders on Elections," broadcast on Tehran Domestic Service 29 April 1984, FBIS-SAS-84-015, 30 April 1984.
36. David Menashri, *Iran: Decade of War and Revolution* (New York: Holmes and Meier, 1990), 313.
37. Baktiari, *Parliamentary Politics in Revolutionary Iran*, 118.
38. Baktiari notes that "in his speech in the Majlis, Musavi had stated that some 30 percent of the 1983–1984 budget . . . was spent on the war effort. Expenditures were 14 percent higher in 1984 than in the previous year." He also notes that in March 1985, Iran lost some thirty thousand soldiers in a major offensive. *Parliamentary Politics in Revolutionary Iran*, 119–20.
39. "Khomeini Speaks," broadcast on Tehran Domestic Service 3 February 1985, FBIS-SAS-85-023, 4 February 1985.
40. "Khomeini Greets Iranian Nation on New Year," broadcast on Tehran Domestic Service 20 March 1985, FBIS-SAS-85-055, 21 March 1985.
41. "Ayatollah Khomeyni's Anniversary Message," Islamic Republic News Agency (hereafter IRNA) broadcast 11 February 1984, FBIS-SAS-84-031, 14 February 1984.
42. "Further on Khomeyni April 4 Speech on War," broadcast 4 April 1985, FBIS-SAS-85-016, 5 April 1985.

43. "Khomeini Addresses Leadership," broadcast 30 November 1985, FBIS-SAS-85-043, 2 December 1985; italics mine. Note that this was not the first time that Khomeini had made such a bold claim. In December 1983 he asserted that "[n]one of the prophets, from Adam to the Seal of the Prophets, [i.e., Mohammad] have achieved their true goals." FBIS-SAS-93-249, December 23, 1983. Cited in Marvin Zonis and Daniel Brumberg, "Khomeini, The Islamic Republic of Iran and the Arab World," *Harvard Middle East Papers, Modern Series* no. 5, 25.

44. "Khomeini Addresses Revolution Council Members," broadcast 10 December 1985, FBIS-SAS-85-238, 11 December 1984.

45. Baktiari, *Parliamentary Politics in Revolutionary Iran*, 124–26.

46. "Khomeini Speech to Majlis Deputies October 16," broadcast on Tehran Domestic Service 16 October 1985, FBIS-SAS-85-038, 17 October 1985. Also see Shahrough Akhavi, "Elite Factionalism in the Islamic Republic of Iran, *The Middle East Journal* 41, no. 2 (spring 1987): 181–204 (Akhavi cites Khomeini on p. 185) and Baktiari, *Parliamentary Politics in Revolutionary Iran*, 127.

47. Akhavi, "Elite Factionalism," 186.

48. "Khomeini Addresses Leadership"; italics mine.

49. In May 1986 the national security advisor in the Reagan White House, Robert McFarlane, secretly traveled to Iran in an effort to exchange HAWK antiaircraft missiles for a sum of cash that was destined for the "Contra" forces fighting the Sandinista government in Nicaragua. When the affair was subsequently exposed in the Iran-Contra affair, Rafsanjani was compelled to admit that he knew of the contacts between the United States and Iran. Khomeini acted quickly to cover up the affair, thus saving Rafsanjani and others from certain political demise—if not a worse fate. See Baktiari, *Parliamentary Politics in Revolutionary Iran*, 129–38.

50. "Khomeyni Addresses Members of Council of Experts," broadcast 2 July 1987, FBIS-NES-87-128, 6 July 1987.

51. "Khomeyni Addresses Friday Imams 29 September," broadcast 29 September 1987, FBIS-NES-87-188, 29 September 1987. Although Khomeini's health deteriorated during this period, it is very unlikely that his statements and edicts represented anything else but his opinion. His disciples could not risk misrepresenting his ideas, particularly since Khomeini had repeatedly demonstrated a remarkable ability to regain his strength after a long illness.

52. "Khomeyni Ruling on State Powers Report," broadcast 23 December 1987, FBIS-NES-87-247, 24 December 1987.

53. Baktiari, *Parliamentary Politics in Revolutionary Iran*, 141.

54. "Khamane'i Delivers Friday Prayer Sermons," broadcast on Tehran Domestic Service 1 January 1988, FBIS-NES-88-001, 4 January 1988.

55. "Khomeyni Answers Khamane'i Letter on Authority," broadcast 1 January 1988, FBIS-NES-88-004, 7 January 1988; italics mine.

56. See Baqer Moin, *Khomeini: Life of the Ayatollah* (London: I. B. Tauris Publishers, 1999), 96. As for the use of the term during the early years of the revolution, see Asghar Schirazi, *The Constitution of Iran: Politics and the State in the Islamic Republic* (London: I. B. Tauris Publishers, 1997), 237–41.

57. "Majlis Speaker on Khomeyni Reply," broadcast 7 January 1988, FBIS-NES-88-004, 7 January 1988.
58. "Musavi on Khomeyni's Views, Decrees," broadcast 10 January 1988, FBIS-NES-88-006, 11 January.
59. "Deputies Thank Khomeyni," broadcast 12 January 1988, FBIS-NES-88-008, 13 January 1988.
60. Ibid.
61. Indeed, Rafsanjani could have made an even bolder argument, one that was suggested by Khomeini's dictum—i.e., that "government," being a "divine injunction," was empowered to conceive all legislation, whether primary or "secondary." Rafsanjani did not go this far. In his 1 January *fatva*, Khomeini used the term *hokumat*, which can mean "state" or "government" (see Schirazi, *The Constitution of Iran*, 230). I have chosen, however, to follow the lead of other scholars such as Bahman Baktiari and Hamid Algar and use the term *government*. This is certainly the sense in which Rafsanjani and his colleagues interpreted his use of the word *hokumat*, as is indicated in Rafsanjani's emphasis on "governmental affairs" in the preceding quotation, and even more so in the quotation that follows (a "government of the people by the people"; also see note 62).
62. "First Sermon on Islamic Government," broadcast 15 January 1988, FBIS-NES-88-011, 19 January 1988.
63. Shaul Bakhash, "Islam and Social Justice in Iran," in *Shi'ism, Resistance and Revolution,* ed. Kramer, 113.
64. "Khamanei Delivers Tehran Friday Prayer Sermons," broadcast 22 January 1988, FBIS-NES-88-015, 25 January 1988.
65. See Chibli Mallat, *The Renewal of Islamic Law: Muhammad Baqer as-Sadr, Najaf and the Shi'i International* (Cambridge: Cambridge University Press, 1993), 105.
66. "Khomeyni Address on Majlis Elections," broadcast 31 March 1988, FBIS-NES-88-062, 31 March 1988.
67. David Menashri, "Iran," in *Middle East Contemporary Survey,* vol. 12, 1988 (Boulder, Colo.: Westview, 1990), 490.
68. "Khomeyni Message to Majlis," broadcast 28 May 1988, FBIS-NES-88-104, 31 May 1988. Although read by Khomeini's son, it is very unlikely that Ahmad would have contrived the speech.
69. "Khomeyni Message on Hajj, Resolution 598," broadcast 20 July 1988, FBIS-NES-88-140, 21 July 1988.
70. Baktiari, *Parliamentary Politics in Revolutionary Iran,* 173. We will return to the case of Montazeri in chapter 8. It should also be noted that in 1987 Montazeri had opposed the arrest and execution of the brother of his son-in-law Mehdi Hashemi. Hashemi was put to death on the charge of murder, although his execution probably had more to do with his having been linked to the distribution of pamphlets that associated the Musavi-Rafsanjani government with the Iran–Contra affair. Baktiari discusses this point on pp. 133–34 of his book.
71. David Menashri, "Iran," in *Middle East Contemporary Survey,* vol. 11, 1987 (Boulder, Colo.: Westview, 1989), 395.

72. "Khomeyni Letter on Guidelines for Reconstruction," broadcast 3 October 1988, FBIS-NES-88-192, 4 October 1988.
73. "Khamanei Delivers Friday Prayer Sermon," broadcast 2 December 1988, FBIS-NES-88-233, 5 December 1988; italics mine.
74. "Prosecutor General Khoi'niha Interviewed," *Keyhan,* 29 April 1989, FBIS-NES-89-088, 9 May 1989; italics mine.
75. Baktiari, *Parliamentary Politics in Revolutionary Iran,* 179–80. Ayatollah 'Abbas 'Ali Amid-Zanjani was a member of the committee to amend the Constitution.
76. It is beyond the scope of this inquiry to review the details of the debate over the Constitution. However, the dominant influence of Western democratic constitutions on this debate is clearly visible in the proceedings. See, for example, "Political Roundtable," broadcast on Tehran Television, 27 April 1989, FBIS-NES-89-084, 3 May 1989.
77. Moin, *Khomeini,* 293.
78. See "Political Roundtable," cited above.
79. "*Ettela'at* on Constitutional Amendments," broadcast 29 April 1989, FBIS-NES-89 091, 12 May 1989.
80. "Constitutional Amendments," *Tehran Times,* 18 April 1989, FBIS-NES-89-082, 1 May 1989.
81. "*Ettale'at* Cited on Leadership Issue," broadcast on IRNA 17 May 1989, FBIS-NES-095, 18 May 1989.
82. Ibid. The *Keyhan* editorial is discussed in the above-cited IRNA 17 May broadcast.
83. Mehdi Mozaffari, "Changes in the Iranian Political System after Khomeini's Death," *Political Studies* 41 (1993): 611–17. Also see Mohsen M. Milani, "The Transformation of the Velayat-i Faqih Institution: From Khomeini to Khamanei," *The Muslim World* 72, no. 3, 4 (July–October 1992): 175–90.
84. Moin, *Khomeini,* 293.
85. See "Islamic Republic of Iran," in *Constitution of the Countries of the World,* ed. Albert Blaustein and Gisbert Flanz (Dobbs Ferry, N.Y.: Oceana Publications, 1992), in English and Persian.
86. Moin, *Khomeini,* 308. Moreover, during its deliberations on the selection of a new *faqih,* the vice chairman of the Council of Experts read the letter out loud, thus giving this rationalist transformation of Khomeini's authority an official stamp.
87. Mallat, *Baqer es-Sadr,* 106–7.
88. Rafsanjani openly acknowledged his opposition to the single-leader concept following Khomeini's death and the selection of Khamane'i as *faqih.* See "Hashemi-Rafsanjani Interviewed," *Jomhuri-ye Eslami,* 16 July 1989, FBIS-NES-89-146, 1 August 1989.
89. See Ahmad Ashraf, "Charisma, Theocracy, and Men of Power in Post Revolutionary Iran," in *The Politics of Social Transformation in Afghanistan, Iran, and Pakistan,* ed. Myron Weiner and Ali Banauzizi (Syracuse, N.Y.: Syracuse University Press, 1994), 137–38.
90. Ervand Abrahamian, *Khomeinism: Essays on the Islamic Republic* (Berkeley: University of California Press, 1993), 136.

91. Ibid., 58.
92. Ruhollah Khomeini, "Islamic Government," in *Islam and Revolution: Writings and Declarations, Imam Khomeini,* trans. Hamid Algar (London: KPI, 1985), 75.
93. Arjomand, "Shi'ite Jurisprudence," 105.
94. Rafsanjani is a prosperous pistachio farmer.
95. Menashri, "Iran," 356–57.
96. "Khamanei Delivers Friday Prayer Sermon," broadcast 19 May 1989, FBIS-NES-89-097, 22 May 1989.
97. For a comprehensive overview of the social, political, and economic dynamics of post-Khomeini Iran, see Anoushiravan Ehteshami, *After Khomeini: The Iranian Second Republic* (London: Routledge Press, 1995).

Chapter Seven

1. Statement by *Majles* Deputy 'Ali Zadsar, "Resalat Reports on Majlis Debates," *Resalat,* 11 January 1993, FBIS-NES-93-028-S, 12 February 1993.
2. "Behzad Navabi's Open Letter to Rafsanjani," *Resalat,* 30 April 1992, FBIS-NES-92-098-S, 20 May 1992.
3. Max Weber, *Economy and Society,* vol. 1, ed. Guenther Roth and Claus Wittich (Berkeley: University of California Press, 1978), 266–67. This said, Weber also argued that excessive reliance on charisma could produce an authoritarian phenomenon that he called "plebiscitary democracy." Structural instrumentalist theories of charisma and populism echo this argument.
4. Juan J. Linz and Alfred Stepan, *Problems of Democratic Transition and Consolidation* (Baltimore and London: Johns Hopkins University Press, 1996), 46.
5. Adam Przeworski, "The Games of Transition," in *Issues in Democratic Consolidation,* ed. Scott Mainwaring, Guillermo O'Donnell, and Samuel Valenzuela (Notre Dame, Ind.: University of Notre Dame Press, 1992) and Ghassan Salamé, ed., *Democracy Without Democrats?* (London: I. B. Tauris Publishers, 1994).
6. See Daniel Brumberg, "Authoritarian Legacies and Reform Strategies in the Arab World," in *Political Liberalization and Democratization in the Arab World,* ed. Rex Brynen, Baghat Korany, and Paul Nobles (Boulder, Colo.: Lynne Reinner Publishers, 1995).
7. Ahmad Ashraf, "Charisma, Theocracy, and Men of Power in Post Revolutionary Iran," in *The Politics of Social Transformation in Afghanistan, Iran, and Pakistan,* ed. Myron Weiner and Ali Banuazizi (Syracuse, N.Y.: Syracuse University Press, 1994), 140.
8. See Sohrab Behdad, "The Post Revolutionary Economic Crisis," in *Iran after the Revolution: Crisis of an Islamic State,* ed. Saeed Rahnema and Sohrab Behdad, (London: I. B. Tauris Publishers, 1995), 97–128, and Anoushiravan Ehteshami, "State and Economy Under Rafsanjani," in Ehteshami, *After Khomeini: The Iranian Second Republic* (London: Routledge Press, 1995), 100–25. Both authors somewhat exaggerate the actual—as opposed to proposed—scope of Rafsanjani's reforms.

9. Bahman Baktiari, *Parliamentary Politics in Revolutionary Iran: The Institutionalization of Factional Politics* (Gainesville: University Press of Florida, 1996), 193.

10. Ehteshami, *After Khomeini*, 86.

11. "Mohtashemi Warns of Deviations from Imam's Path," broadcast on the Islamic Republic News Agency (hereafter IRNA) 23 August 1989, FBIS-NES-163, 24 August 1989.

12. Baktiari, *Parliamentary Politics in Revolutionary Iran*, 189. Note that there was also considerable continuity in the new cabinet: five ministers, the vice president, and the prosecutor general had all served in Musavi's cabinet. Nevertheless, the radicals were correct in suspecting that the new cabinet was determined to break with the policies of the previous government. See Ehteshami, *After Khomeini*, 102.

13. Baktiari, *Parliamentary Politics in Revolutionary Iran*, 190.

14. "Rafsanjani on Khomeini's Importance and Qualities," broadcast 9 June 1989 following a sermon given by Rafsanjani on June 8, *Summary of World Broadcasting, British Broadcasting Corporation (BBC)*, 12 June 1989. Unless otherwise indicated, all quotations in this section are from the June 8 sermon. Italics are mine.

15. "President's Speech on Khomeini's Character," broadcast 19 November 1989, FBIS-NES-89-226, 27 November 1989.

16. "Khamane'i Speaks in Honoring Khomeini," broadcast 22 May 1990, FBIS-NES-90 101, 24 May 1990.

17. "Inaugural Ceremony Detailed," broadcast 3 August 1989, FBIS NES 89-149, 4 August 1989.

18. "Hashemi-Rafsanjani's Prayer Sermon," broadcast 4 August 1989, FBIS-NES-89-150, 7 August 1989.

19. "Khamanei Speech on Safeguarding Nation," broadcast 23 August 1989, FBIS-NES-89-163, 24 August 1989; italics mine.

20. "Hashemi-Rafsanjani's Inaugural Speech," broadcast 17 August 1989, FBIS-NES-89 163, 24 August 1989.

21. "Hashemi-Rafsanjani Gives Friday Prayers Sermon," broadcast 29 September 1989 FBIS-NES-89-190, 3 October 1989.

22. "Khamanei Addresses Welfare Employees," broadcast 4 October 1989, FBIS-NES-89 191, 5 October 1989; italics mine.

23. "Khamanei Delivers Friday Prayer Sermon," broadcast 20 October 1989, FBIS-NES-89 203, 23 October 23, 1989.

24. "Khamanei Delivers Friday Prayers Sermon."

25. "Khamanei Speech Marking Capture of U.S. Embassy," broadcast 1 November 1989, FBIS-NES-89-211, 2 November 1989; italics mine.

26. "Khamanei Message Read at Basij Assembly," broadcast 23 November 1989, FBIS-NES-89-225, 24 November 1989.

27. "President Delivers 17 November Friday Prayer Sermon," broadcast 16 November 1989, FBIS-NES-89-226, 27 November 1989.

28. Farzin Sarabi, "The Post-Khomeini Era in Iran: The Elections of the Fourth *Majles*," *Middle East Journal* 48, no. 1 (winter 1994): 89–107.

29. Saeed Rahnema and Farhad Nomami, "Competing Shi'i Subsystems in

Contemporary Iran" in *Iran after the Revolution,* ed. Rahnema and Behdad, 65–93, 78.

30. "Mohtashemi Eulogizes Imam Husain, Khomeini," broadcast 7 August 1989, FBIS-NES-89-152, 9 August 1989.
31. "Kho'iniha Addresses Ashura Gathering," broadcast 12 August 1989, FBIS-NES-89-156, 15 August 1989.
32. "Editorial on Rationalism in Ties with France," *Tehran Times,* 19 September 1989, FBIS-NES-89-186, 27 September 1989.
33. "Majlis Deputies against Releasing Cooper," broadcast 27 September 1989, FBIS-NES-89–187, 28 September 1989.
34. "Majlis Deputies Debate Powers, Yazdi's Actions," *Tehran Times,* 5 October 1989, FBIS-NES-89-197, 13 October 1989.
35. "Khalkhali, Other Discuss Yazdi, Cooper," *Resalat,* 28 September 1989, FBIS-NES-89 201, 19 October 1989.
36. "Tehran Combatant Clergymen Issue Statement 4 November," *Ettela'at,* 29 October 1989, FBIS-NES-89 215, 8 November 1989.
37. "*Resalat* Reports on October 29 *Majles* Session," *Resalat,* 30 October 1989, FBIS-NES-89-219, 15 November 1989.
38. "Majlis Meets to Discuss Budget, Election Law," *Resalat,* 25 October 1989, FBIS-NES-89-220, 16 November 1989.
39. "Majlis Session Discusses U.S. Aggression," *Keyhan,* 1 November 1989, FBIS-NES-89-227, 15 November 1989; italics mine.
40. "Birjand Deputy Laments Passing of Khomeini Era," *Resalat,* 6 September 1985, FBIS-NES-89-230, 1 December 1989.
41. "Envoy to Romania Sacked," Paris, Agence France Press (AFP), 26 December 1989, FBIS-NES-89 246, 26 December 1989.
42. "Tehran broadcast December 24, 1989," FBIS-NES-89 246, 26 December 1989.
43. "Report on December 26, 1989 Majlis Session," *Resalat,* 27 December 1989, FBIS-NES-90-016, 24 January 1990.
44. "Khamanei Speech on East Europe," broadcast 27 December 1989, FBIS-NES-89-248, 28 December 1989.
45. "President Backs Khamanei on Foreign Policy," broadcast 27 December 1989, FBIS-NES-89-248, 28 December 1989.
46. "Yazdi on 'Irresponsible Remarks' on Leadership," broadcast 29 December 1989, FBIS-NES-89-249, 29 December 1989. These two quotations can also be found in FBIS-NES-89-249, under "Qom Clerics Support Khamanei."
47. Shaul Bakhash, "Iran: The Crisis of Legitimacy," in *Middle East Lectures,* no. 1 (Tel Aviv: The Moshe Dayan Center for Middle East and African Studies, 1995), 99–118.
48. "*Resalat* Carried Deputies' Letter to Khamanei," *Resalat,* 4 January 1990; see letter and attachment in FBIS-NES-90-010, 16 January 1990.
49. *Imam Khomeini's Last Will and Testament* (Washington, D.C.: Interest Section of the Islamic Republic of Iran, Embassy of the Democratic and Popular Republic of Algeria, Solna Print Corporation, n.d.), 16.
50. Ibid., 9.
51. Ibid., 30. This is not to say that the text is completely devoid of those other

qualities that made Khomeini such a complex thinker and leader. Thus, for example, his rationalism and utilitarianism is reflected in his warning that the leaders should take note of the "dire necessities of the country which must be undertaken by reference to secondary rules and, at times, *Velayat-i Faqih*" (p. 35). But such references to secondary rules and *velayat-e faqih* are drowned out by the document's overwhelming emphasis on the charismatic-revolutionary themes associated with fighting "enemies," defending identity, and so on. Note that the text uses the term *Shaytanic*, a direct alliteration from the Arabic.

52. See also 'Ali Akbar Velayati, "The Audience of Imam's Political and Religious Will," *Iranian Journal of International Affairs* 1 (fall/winter 1998): 297–308. The author, who at the time was Iran's foreign minister, emphasized the "simplicity of the words rules out the intermediator"; in other words, there was no need to "interpret" (as he put it) the Imam's words, since his intention was clear (p. 297). Also see Ervand Abrahamian, *Khomeinism: Essays on the Islamic Republic* (Berkeley: University of California Press, 1993), 36–37. Note that during his 9 June 1989 eulogy of Khomeini, Rafsanjani had argued that "the reading of the Imam's will solved many problems." However, throughout most of the speech, he cited from other statements and edicts rather than from the will itself.

53. "Karrubi Speaks to *Majles*," broadcast 25 February 1990, FBIS-NES-90-045, 7 March 1990.

54. "Azari-Qomi Responds to Karrubi," broadcast 26 February 1990, FBIS-NES-90-045, 7 March 1990.

55. "Ayatollah Araki Contradicts Khomeini," London *Keyhan,* 26 April 1990, FBIS-NES-90-097, 18 May 1990.

56. See Asghar Schirazi, *The Constitution of Iran: Politics and the State in the Islamic Republic* (London: I. B. Tauris Publishers, 1997).

57. See "Montazeri's Attitude to Distance Himself from Khomeini Cited," London *Keyhan,* 30 October 1986, Joint Publication Research Service (JPRS), NES-86-148, 4 December 1986. While he was something of a domestic "moderate," on foreign policy issues concerning the West and the export of Iran's revolution, Montazeri was certainly a radical. Indeed, it was precisely his link to Mehdi Hashemi, the brother of his son-in-law and head of the World Islamic Movement, that got him in trouble.

58. "Montazeri Urges Intelligence Officers against Harsh Conduct," *Keyhan,* 26 July 1986, Joint Publication Research Service (JPRS)cs-NEA-86 121, 24 September 1986.

59. "Montazeri Urges Less Harshness," *Keyhan,* 26 August 1986, JPRS-NES-86135, 27 October, 1986.

60. Baqer Moin, *Khomeini: Life of the Ayatollah* (London: I. B. Tauris Publishers, 1999), 279.

61. Ibid., 280.

62. "Khamanei Restores Montazeri's Religious Duties," broadcast on clandestine Iran's Flag of Freedom Radio 11 August 1989, FBIS-NES-89-155, 14 August 1989.

63. Baktiari, *Parliamentary Politics in Revolutionary Iran,* 202.

64. "Humiliating Treatment of Montazeri Noted," broadcast on clandestine Iran's Flag of Freedom Radio 18 January 1990, FBIS-NES-90-013, 19 January 1990.

65. "Toilers Radio Comments on Attacks on Montazeri," broadcast on clandestine Radio of the Iranian Toilers 18 January 1990, FBIS-NES-90-013, 19 January 19, 1990.

66. The Assembly of Experts was charged with selecting a successor for the *faqih*.

67. "*Resalat* on November 17 Majlis Session," *Resalat*, 18 November 1991, FBIS-NES-91-236-S, 9 December 1991, supplement, Iran, *Majles* section. There is some confusion regarding the sources from which Alviri is quoting here. He cites Khomeini's *Will*, whereas it seems that he is citing from Khomeini's letter, which he had written to Montazeri in March 1989 (published in *Abrar*, 22 November 1997). For a translation see <http://eurasianews.com/iran/montletr.htm>, "Translation of Ayatollah Khomeini Letter Dismissing Khomeini."

68. "Alviri Attacked by *Jomhuri-ye Eslami*," *Jomhuri-ye Eslami*, 18 November 1991, FBIS-NES-91-236-S, 9 December 1991.

69. Sarabi, "The Post-Khomeini Era in Iran," 94, quoted from *Ettela'at*, 9 April 1992, p. 2.

70. Ibid, 96–97.See also Baktiari, *Parliamentary Politics in Revolutionary Iran*, 214–16.

71. Forced out of the *Majles*, many Islamic Leftists became editors or writers in the semiofficial opposition press. In some ways, this change eventually gave them a wider popular audience than they had while serving in the *Majles*.

72. Sarabi, "The Post-Khomeini Era in Iran," 95, quoted from *Resalat*, 17 February 1991, p. 2, cited in FBIS, 18 July 1991.

73. Because the new *Majles* was not inaugurated until the summer of 1992, radical deputies and their supporters had ample opportunities to protest their exclusion from the elections. Although I reviewed almost two years of *Majles* debates as translated in FBIS, the following discussion represents, in necessarily brief form, the gist of the radicals' position.

74. "Iran: Majles Sessions," *Resalat*, 14 November 1991, FBIS-NES-92-015-S, 23 January 1992.

75. *Resalat*, 27 November 1991, FBIS-NES-92-005-S, 9 January 1992. Remarks by 'Ali Penahandeh, Barkhar, and Mimeh deputy.

76. "Iran Majles Sessions," *Resalat*, 18 March 1992, FBIS-NES-92-082-S, 28 April 1992. In other words, the Council of Guardians should not become the tool of any one particular political faction.

77. "Iran: Majles Sessions," *Resalat*, 20 April 1992, FBIS-NES-92-098-S, 20 May 1992.

78. "Iran: Majles Sessions," *Resalat*, 27 April 1992, FBIS-NES-92-117-S, 17 June 1992.

79. "Iran: Majles Sessions," *Resalat*, 17 February 1992, FBIS-NES-92-057-S, 24 March 1992.

80. "Iran: Majles Sessions," *Resalat,* 27 April 1992, FBIS-NES-92-117-S, 17 June 1992.

81. "Iran: Majles Sessions," *Resalat,* 23 April 1992, FBIS-NES-92-098-S, 20 May 1992.

82. "Iran: Majles Sessions," *Resalat,* 29 April 1992, FBIS-NES-92-098-S, 20 May 1992.

83. "Behzad Nabavi's Open Letter To Rafsanjani," *Resalat,* 30 April 1992, FBIS-NES-92-098-S, 20 May 1992.

84. "Iran: Majles Sessions," *Resalat,* 27 April 1992, FBIS-NES-92-117-S, 17 June 1992.

85. Ibid. Presumably, Mohammad Asghar-Zadeh was wearing a green army jacket, a garment popular among Iranian students during that period. Credited with having given the American Embassy the nickname "Den of Spies," he would emerge five years later, together with several other hostage takers, as one of the spokesmen for the reform movement. See the conclusion for details.

86. "Iran: Majles Sessions," *Resalat,* 27 November 1992, FBIS-NES-92-005-S, 9 January 1992.

87. "Iran: Majles Sessions," *Resalat,* 16 May 1992, FBIS-NES-92-117-S, 17 June 1992.

88. "Iran: Majles Sessions," *Resalat,* 16 May 1992, FBIS-NES-92-117-S, 17 June 1992. Statement by Seyyed Mohammad Neqba'i; italics mine. It seems that the speaker is referring to the speech given by Khomeini after he accepted the cease-fire with Iraq in late 1988.

89. "Iran: Majles Sessions," *Resalat,* 10 August 1992, FBIS-NES-92-178-S, 14 September 1992. These are the remarks of Seyyed Mohammad Neqba'i.

90. "Iran: Majles Sessions," *Resalat,* 13 August 1992, FBIS-NES-92-178-S, 14 September 1992. These are the remarks of Seyyed Fazel Amirjahani.

91. Peer Gatter, *Khomeinis Erban Machpolitik und Wirtschaftsreformen im Iran* [Khomeini's heritage, policymaking and economic reform in Iran] (Munster: Die Deutsch Bibliothek, 1998).

92. "Iran: Majles Sessions," *Resalat,* 22 April 1992, FBIS-NES-92-098-S, 20 May 1992. These are the words of Deputy Seyyed Akbar Parvaresh.

Chapter Eight

1. Mohammad Khatami, *Bim-e-Mowj* (Fear of the wave; Tehran: Sima-ye Javan, 1993), as translated in *Hope and Challenge: The Iranian President Speaks,* trans. Alidad Mafinezam (Binghamton, N.Y.: Binghamton University, Institute of Global Cultural Studies, 1997), 52–53, 43.

2. Abdolkarim Soroush, "Sorush on Meaning, Foundation," *Kiyan* (August–September 1995), 4–13. Translated in FBIS-NES-96-022-S, 1 February 1996.

3. "Iran: Majles Sessions," *Resalat,* 22 April 1992, FBIS-NES-92-092-S, 20 May 1992.

4. *Imam Khomeini's Last Will and Testament* (Washington, D.C.: Interest Section of the Islamic Republic of Iran, Embassy of the Democratic and Popular Republic of Algeria, Solna Print Corporation, n.d.), 62.

5. Ali Banuazizi, "Faltering Legitimacy: The Ruling Clerics and Civil Society in Iran," *International Journal of Politics, Culture and Society* 8, no. 4 (1995): 571.

6. See Kaveh Ehsani, "Municipal Matters: The Urbanization of Consciousness and Political Change in Tehran," *Middle East Report*, no. 212 (fall 1999): 22–27.

7. See "Illiteracy Rate dropped by 20 percent since 1979" Islamic Republic News Agency, 14 September 1993, in <netiran.com/htdocs/dailynews/archive/IRNA/1993/93091414RGGO7.html>. On urbanization see Ehsani, "Municipal Matters."

8. *Sobh*, no. 64 (December 1996): 58, quoted in Azadeh Kian-Thiébaut, "Political and Social Transformations in Post-Islamist Iran," *Middle East Report*, no. 212 (fall 1999): 12.

9. See David Menashri, *Education and the Making of Modern Iran* (Ithaca, N.Y.: Cornell University Press, 1992), 307–28. Also see Rasool Nafisi, "Education and the Culture of Politics in the Islamic Republic of Iran," in *Political Culture in the Islamic Republic*, ed. Samih K. Farsoun and Mehrda Mashayekhi (London and New York: Routledge, 1992), 160–77.

10. I emphasize "traditional seminary life" because during the eighties and early nineties, the teaching of Western political and social ideas within some religious seminaries encouraged seminary students to take an interest in the West. Many traditional clerics feared that this process would in effect sap the seminaries of their religious, and, most important, anti-Western, focus. See Kian-Thiébaut's "Political and Social Transformations in Post-Islamist Iran," 14.

11. See Mehdi Moayedi,'s article, "A Statistical Glance at Women's Employment in Iran," in *Zamineh* (monthly publication of the Kowsar Economic Organization) no. 39–40, pp.64–66, <netiran.com/htdocs/clippings/deconomy/940518XXDEO1.html>.

12. See Mahnaz Afkhami and Erika Friedl, eds., *In the Eye of the Storm: Women in Post-Revolutionary Iran* (Syracuse, N.Y.: Syracuse University Press, 1994) and Halah Isfandiyari, *Reconstructed Lives: Women and Iran's Islamic Revolution* (Washington D.C.: Woodrow Wilson Center; Johns Hopkins University Press, 1997).

13. By "unbridled relations," the authors mean friendships between men and women that are not controlled by the state or any form of morality police.

14. See "The Political Inclinations of the Youth and Students," *Asr-e Ma* 2, no. 13 (19 April 1995). Translated in <www.netiran.com/htdocs/clippings/social>.

15. See Messerrat Ebrahami, "The Cultural and Social Development of the Youth in the South of Tehran," *Goftogoo*, no. 19 (spring 1998). Translated in <www.netiran.com/htdocs/clippings/social>; italics mine.

16. "*Ettela'at* Publishes Sirjani Commentary," *Ettela'at*, 21 August 1989, FBIS-NES-89-178, 15 September 1989.

17. Commentaries in *Resalat* lambasted Sirjani's article and tried to disassociate President Rafsanjani from the former's liberal ideas. See "*Resalat* Rebuts Sirjani Article," *Resalat*, 24 and 26 August 1989, FBIS-NES-89-178,

15 September 1989. See also "Commentary Responds to Sirjani Article," *Ettela'at*, 23 August 1989, FBIS-NES-89-184, 24 September 1989 and "Commentary Responds to Sirjani Article," *Jomhuri-ye Eslami*, 23 August 1989, FBIS-NES-89-191, 4 October 1989.

18. See Hamid Naficy, "Islamicizing Film Culture in Iran," in Farsoun and Mashayekhi, eds., *Political Culture in the Islamic Republic*, 205.

19. Makhmalbaf was initially a keen supporter of the Islamic Revolution, but like many intellectuals of his generation, he became disillusioned by the end of the eighties. His 1989 film, *Time of Love*, was banned for five years. On Mehrju'i see Godfrey Cheshire, "Revealing an Iran Where the Chadors are Most Chic," *New York Times*, 8 November 1998. It is worth nothing that while the thirst for foreign films grew in the eighties, the number of cinemas declined, "down from 420 prior to the revolution for a population of 30 million to around 250 for nearly 65 million [in 1996]" (Farrokh Gaffari, "Special Issue on Iranian Cinema," *Iran Nameh* 4, no. 3 [summer 1996], in <www.nima3.com/IranMedia2/nameh.html>). Also see Ahmad Sadr, "Searchers: The New Iranian Cinema," *The Iranian* (September 1996), in <www.iraniam.com/Sep96/ArtsNewCinema>.

20. "Iran: Majles Sessions," *Resalat*, 28 November 1991, FBIS-NES-92-015-S, 23 January 1992. These remarks were made by Deputy Ahmad Nateq-Nuri.

21. "Iran: Majles Sessions," *Resalat*, 12 August 1992, FBIS-NES-92-178-S, 14 September 1992.

22. Ibid.

23. "Majlis Investigates Activities of Voice and Vision," *Resalat*, 3, 4, and 5 November 1993, FBIS-NES-94-016-S, 25 January 1994; italics mine.

24. It will be recalled that this deputy was one of the most vociferous critics of the *Majles* radicals.

25. Asghar Schirazi, *The Constitution of Iran: Politics and the State in the Islamic Republic* (London: I. B. Tauris Publishers, 1997), 241–42. Khomeini also argued that where music was promoted by an Islamic state, it was permissible. Thus, he implied, state interest in music could override other considerations.

26. "Iran: Majles Sessions," *Jomhuri-ye Eslami*, 8, 9, and 11 November 1993, FBIS-NES-94-016-S, 25 January 1994.

27. By emphasizing that the Imam was a "source of emulation," the response was setting up an obvious comparison with Khamane'i, who was not a *marja'* (religious guide), and whose position as *faqih* had been separated from that of *marja'* by the Constitution precisely for this reason.

28. See "The 1994 Declaration of 134 Iranian Writers, October 15, 1994," *The Iranian* (December 1998), <www.iranian.com/news/Dec98/declaration.html>.

29. See H. Stuart Hughes, *Consciousness and Society: The Reorientation of European Social Thought, 1890–1930* (New York: Vintage Books, 1958).

30. See Mehrzad Boroujerdi, "The Counter of Post-revolutionary Thought in Iran with Hegel, Heidegger and Popper," in *Cultural Transitions in the Middle East*, ed. Serif Mardin (Leiden: E.J. Brill, 1994), 236–59.

31. From Elaine Sciolino, "The Cleric Who Charmed Iranians," *New York Times*, 1 February 1998. Reprinted in <www.org/khatami/khatamistory.html>. Also see "Biography of President Muhammad Khatami," *Independent Iran Observer*, <http://home8.inet.tele.dk/huosan/khatami.html>. For a more comprehensive assessment of Khatami's early writing, see Shaul Bakhash, "Iran's Unlikely President," *The New York Review* 15, no. 17 (November 1998): 47–51.

32. I have seen numerous reports suggesting that Khatami was a close friend of Ahmad Khomeini's. Although the latter was no great thinker, in the late sixties and early seventies, he was close to the Islamic Left. Khatami's neoleftism may have been shaped at least in part by his friendship with the young Khomeini.

33. "Iran: Majles Sessions," *Resalat*, 28 November 1991, FBIS-NES-92-015-S, 23 January 1992.

34. "Iran: Majles Sessions," *Resalat*, 6 January 1992, FBIS-NES-92-021-S, 31 January 1992. Comments by Deputy Muhammad-Baqer Nowbakht.

35. "Culture, Islamic Guidance Minister on Policies," broadcast 3 May 1992, FBIS-NES-92-105, 1 June 1992.

36. "Complete Text of Khatami-Ardakani's Resignation," *Keyhan-e Hava'i*, 29 July 1992, FBIS-NES-165, 25 August 1992; italics mine.

37. Khatami, *Bim-e-Mowj*, 7, 13.

38. For a translation of Mohsen 'Alina's three-part series that appeared in the 2, 3, and 4 August 1999 editions of *Khordad*, see "Shariati Influence on Khatami Examined," FBIS-NES, 24 July 1999, Document ID: FTS 19990824000941.

39. This allusion to the "last years of his life" is clearly a reference to the "interest based" utilitarian edicts and pronouncements that Khomeini issued in 1987 and 1988.

40. Khatami, *Bim-e-Mowj*, 49.

41. Italics mine. Note the emphasis on "interests," another implicit reference to Khomeini's January 1988 edict.

42. Khatami, *Bim-e-Mowj*, 48

43. Ibid., 39.

44. See "A Biography of Dr. Abdol Karim Soroush," <www.seraj.org/biog. html>. Also see "Dr. Soroush's Interview with Seraj" (August 1977) at the same Web address. On Soroush see Valla Vakili, "Debating Religion and Politics in Iran: The Political Thought of Abdolkarim Soroush," Council on Foreign Relations, Studies Department Occasional Papers Series, no. 2, 1995; Afshin Matin-Asgari, "Abdol-Karim Sorush and the Secularization of Islamic Thought in Iran," *Iranian Studies* 30, nos. 1–2 (winter/spring 1997): 95–115; and Mahmoud and Ahmad Sadri's "Let the Occasional Chalice Break," in *Reason, Freedom and Democracy in Islam*, by Abdolkarim Soroush (Oxford: Oxford University Press, 1999). In addition to the above, a colleague interviewed Soroush on my behalf in Tehran in September 1999.

45. See Robin Wright's "Letter from Teheran: Iran's Revolutionaries Lighten

Up," *The New Yorker,* 8 November 1999, 29–47.

46. These days Soroush downplays 'Ali Shari'ati's influence on his thought, as Soroush explained during the interview mentioned in note 44 above. However, while he has clearly parted company with Shari'ati's anti-Western instrumentalism, one can still find traces of the latter's thinking in Soroush's work.

47. See Howard Schneider, "Clerics' Defense Puts Iranian System on Trial," *Washington Post,* 21 November 1999, A1.

48. "Knowledge Seen as Basis of Modernism," *Kiyan* (22 June–August 1994), translated in FBIS-NES-95-109-S, 7 June 1995.The following analysis of Soroush's thought is based on several essays that he published in *Kiyan* in 1995 and 1996, as well as several extensive roundtable discussions that he held with other scholars, and which appeared in *Kiyan* as well.

49. See "Soroush on Freedom of the Clergy," *Kiyan* (April–May 1995), as translated in FBIS-NES-95-241-S, 15 December 1995.

50. "Sorush, Farhadpur on Secularism—Sorush on Meaning, Foundation," *Kiyan* (August–September 1995), FBIS-NES-96-022-S, 1 February 1996.

51. See "Impact of Modernization on Politics," *Kiyan* 5 (June–July 1995), FBIS-NES-95-241-S, 15 December 1994.

52. Guillermo O'Donnell and Philippe Schmitter, *Transitions from Authoritarian Rule: Tentative Conclusions about Uncertain Democracies* (Baltimore and Washington, D.C.: Johns Hopkins University Press, 1986), 49.

53. "*Kiyan* on Religious, Political Pluralism: First of a Four-Part Series of Articles on Pluralism with Professors Mohammad Mojtahed-Shabestari, Mahmud Sadri, Ahmad Sadri, and Morad Farhadpur," *Kiyan* 5, no. 28 (November–December 1995, January 1996), FBIS-NES-96-123-S, 25 June 1996.

54. "Montazeri on State's Road to Destruction," London *Keyhan,* 10 October 1994, FBIS-NES-94-231, 10 October 1994.

55. "Independence of Religious Authority, a Spiritual and National Need," *Iran-e Farda,* no. 16 (February 1995): 64–66, <www.netiran.com/htdocs/clippings/social/950200XXSO01.html>.

56. See chapter 6 of this text.

57. "*Salam* Addresses Position of Vice Regency," *Salam,* 24 July 1995, p. 1, FBIS-NES-950216, 8 November 1995.

58. "Response to *Salam* View of Vice Regency," *Resalat,* 29 July 1995, FBIS-NES-95-216, 8 November 1995.

59. Dr. 'Ali-Reza Nuri-Zadeh, "Rafsanjani's Latest Battle with Khomeini's Heirs," *Al-Majallah,* 19 September 1993, Joint Publication Research Service, NEA-94–001, 6 January 1994.

60. "Ayatollah Khamenei Delivers Speech to Students," Tehran Voice of the Islamic Republic broadcast 1 November 1995, FBIS-NES-95-212, 2 November 1995.

61. David Menashri, *Revolution at a Crossroads: Iran's Domestic Policies and Regional Ambitions* (Washington, D.C.: Washington Institute for Near East Policy, 1998), 61.

62. The conservative Combatant Clergy Association won 110 to 120 of the 270 *Majles* seats; the Servants of Construction took 80; and an ideologically mixed group of Islamic reformers that included some radicals won 58 seats. While the election of Nateq-Nuri as Speaker indicated that the conservatives still could cobble together a majority, the April 1996 elections weakened the conservatives' hold over the *Majles* and opened the door to the possible creation of an alternative reformist alliance in the future. See Patrick Clawson, "Conservatives Gain Strength in Tehran," *Policy Watch*, no. 208 (20 June 1996).

63. See Bahman Baktiari and W. Scott Harrop, "Tables Turn on Iran's Islamic Extremists," *The Christian Science Monitor*, 29 May 1999, 18.

64. This is also an oblique way of reminding Khamane'i that he, as leader of the system, should not favor any particular candidate.

65. "Khatami Interviewed on Elections," *Jomhuri-ye Eslami*, 25 February 1997, FBIS-NES-97-047, 25 February 1997.

66. "Khatami Addresses Majles Hezbollah Group," *Ettela'at*, 27 February 1997, FBIS-NES-97-053, 27 February 1997.

67. "Khatami Intertviewed on Need to Address Youth Problems," *Hamshahri*, 6 March 1997, FBIS-NES-97-067, 8 March 1997. *Hamshahri*, which had a wide circulation among young intellectuals, clearly supported Khatami's candidacy.

68. "Karrubi on Ethics, Other Election Issues," *Salam*, 27 April 1987, FBIS-NES-97-088, 27 April 1987.

69. "Behzad Nabavi, Morteza Nabavi Attend Tehran University Roundtable," *Salam*, 8 February 1997, FBIS-NES-97 061, 8 February 1997.

70. "Programs and Policies 'Ali Akbar Nateq-Nouri," <netiran.com/news/election/candidates/NAT-POL.html>.

71. "Iran: Kani Warns Against Deviations," *Resalat*, 20 March 1997, FBIS-NES-97-079, 20 March 1997. Also see his first attack, published in *Abrar*, 3 February 1997, in FBIS-NES-97-024, 3 Febuary 1997. For Kho'iniha's response, see his letter in *Resalat*, 23 April 1997, translated in FBIS-NES-97-086, 23 April 1997.

72. "Iran Must Not Violate Velayat-e-Faqih's Sanctity," *Resalat*, 1 February 1997, FBIS-NES-97-066, 11 February 1997.

73. "Khamane'i Congratulates Council of Experts Session," broadcast on Iranian television 13 February 1997, FBIS-NES-97-032, 13 February 1997.

74. "Khameneí Speech on Politics," broadcast 3 May 1997, FBIS-NES-970086, 3 May 1997.

75. "Khamane'i on Elections, U.S. 'Interference,' " broadcast 7 May 1997, FBIS-NES-07-089, 7 May 1997.

76. "Khatami Interview on Elections," *Jomhuri-ye Eslami*, 25 February 1997, FBIS-NES-97-047, 25 February 1997.

Conclusion

1. "Carnival in Iran with Mickey Mouse," *Iran Weekly Press Digest*, 5 February

1999, <http://www.neda.net/iran-wpd/vol11207/il207–2.html>.

2. "Khamanei Vows to Stay on Revolutionary Path," ibid.

3. Adam Przeworski, "The Games of Transition," in *Issues in Democratic Consolidation,* ed. Scott Mainwaring, Guillermo O'Donnell, and Samuel Valenzuela (Notre Dame, Ind.: University of Notre Dame Press, 1992), 105–53.

4. "Inauguration Speech by President Khatami, 4 August 1997," <www.persia.org/khatami/speech>.

5. Statement by Seyyed Mohammad Khatami, "President's Opening Address to the OIC General Session," <www.persia.org/khatami/khatami03.html>.

6. I have used two sources for this speech: "Khatami: The Clergy Are Not Masters of the People," <http://persia.org/khatami/khatamior.html> and "Tehran Radio on Clergy's Independence, Pluralism of Society," broadcast 28 December 1997, FBIS-NES 18 December 1997, <http://199.211.15.211/cgi-bin/cqcgi>.

7. "Transcript of CNN's Interview with President Khatami," <www.persia.org/khatami/khatami06.html>.

8. "Independent Iran Observers Documentary: Cabinet Members," <http://home8.inet.tele.dk/huosan/Cabinet.htm>. Note that seven of the cabinet members had received advanced degrees in the West, five of them in the United States. With the exclusion of the most senior member of the cabinet (age 61), in 1998 the average age of the ministers was 45.

9. "U.S. Embassy Occupiers Are Iran's New 'Liberals," *CNN Interactive,* 8 February 1999, <ccn.com/world/meast/9902/08/BC-Iran-Anniversary-stud.reut/index/html>. On Ma'sumeh Ebtekar see "Who Is the Only Woman on the Cabinet and What Does She Say?" *Zanan* [Woman], no. 37 (September–October 1997): 2–5, translated in <http://netiran.com/Htdocs/Clippings/DPolitics/97100XXDPo1.html>.

10. Susan Sachs, "Many Iranian Conservatives Lose Seats," *New York Times,* 23 February 2000, A10.

11. <www.dailydavos.com/nw-srv/issue/08_99a/printed/int/wa/ov0908_2.htm>. Ganji made this statement after the government banned his publication.

12. The above citations are taken from an interview I conducted with 'Abdi on 6 October 1999, and from an Internet article cited in note 9, "U.S. Embassy Occupiers Are Iran's new 'Liberals.'" In August 1998 'Abdi held a public reconciliation meeting with former hostage Barry Rosen.

13. Iran Press Service, London, 4 December 1997, <www.iran-press-service.comarticles/azari.html>. Also see "Khatami's New Government, the Old Standing Challenges," *Peyman-e Emruz* no. 21 (January 1998), translated in <http://netrin.com/htdocs/clippings/dpolitics>.

14. "Montazeri's Speech in *Keyhan,*" 4 December 1997, reproduced in <http://eurasianews.com/iran/montadrs.html>. Also see "Khatami's New Government, Old Standing Challenges," cited in note 14, for extensive citations from Montazeri's speech.

15. Eric Rouleau, "La République Islamique d'Iran Confrontée à la So-

ciété Civile," *Le Monde Diplomatique,* June 1995, <http://www.monde-diplomatique.fr/1995/06/Rouleau/1542.html>.

16. Eric Rouleau, "En Iran, Islam Contre Islam," *Le Monde Diplomatique,* June 1999, <www.monde-diplomatique.fr/1999/06/rouleau/12105.html>.

17. "Students Call for Limiting the Power of the Leader," <http://www.iran-press-service.com/articles/students/html>. For a comprehensive history of the student movement in Iran see Ali Akbar Mahdi, "The Student Movement in the Islamic Republic of Iran," published on the Internet at *Electronic Roundtable Discussion, Student Unrest in Iran,* <http://www.sba.widener.edu/zang/default.htm>.

18. Although not a student, Kho'eyniha had been the spiritual advisor to the militant organization Students of the Imam's Line. As for 'Abdi, he was directly involved in the student movement.

19. "Anti-Montazeri Campaign Reaches the President," <http://iran-press-service.com/articles/president_reached.html>.

20. "Khatami's New Government, the Old Standing Challenges," *Peyman-e Emruz,* no. 21 (January 1998): 6–16, <http://www.netiran.com/clippings.html>. As we noted earlier, Khatami had in fact made this argument during the 1997 presidential campaign.

21. "Khatami: The Clergy Are Not Masters of the People," 27 December 1997, <http://persia.orr/khatami>.

22. See Khamane'i's speech before the 9 December 1997 Eight Islamic Summit of the Organization of Islamic Conference in <www.un.int/iran/oic>.

23. See, for example, the criticisms of remarks made by Khatami in his January 1988 interview with CNN reporter Christiane Amanpour in "*IRGC, Jomhuri-ye Eslami, Resalat* Criticize Khatami Remarks," FBIS-NES, 13 January 1998, <http://199.211.15.211/cgi-bin/cqcgi>.

24. "No More Illegalities in Iran's Culture Sphere, Promises New Culture Minister," *Iran Weekly Press Digest,* <http://www.neda.net/Iran-wpd/vol1034/1034–1.html>.

25. He was then replaced by Vice President Abdolhaveh Moussavi Lari, a Khatami loyalist.

26. "Iran: Khamanei Urges Voters Back Competent Candidates," FBIS-NES, 24 February 1999, <http://199.211.15.211/cgi-bin/cqcgi/>.

27. FBIS March 21, 1999, "Khamanei Delivers Iranian New Year Speech."

28. See "Ayatollah Mahdavi-Kani in Meeting with Members of the Islamic Coalition Association's Central Council," *Resalat,* 13 April1999, as translated in FBIS, "Ayatollah on Conformity with Khomeini Line," 18 June 1999, FTS19990618000490.

29. "The Islamic Revolution and the Serious Danger of de-Khomeinization," *Jebheh,* 5 June 1999, as translated in FBIS, "*Jebheh* on Threat to Khomeini's Legacy," 26 June 1999, FTS19990626000623.

30. Robin Wright, "Letter from Teheran: Iran's Revolutionaries Lighten Up," *The New Yorker,* 8 November 1999, 41. For a report by a scholar who witnessed the speech, see Aria Mehandoost, "From Revolution to Freedom," *The Iranian,* 24 May 1999, <www.iranian.com/featurs/199/May/rally/index.html>.

31. See Charles Kurzman, "Student Protests and the Stability of Gridlock in Khatami's Iran," as published on the Internet, *Electronic Roundtable Discussion, Student Unrest in Iran,* <http://www.sba.widener.edu/zang/default. htm>.

32. Ibid. Also see "President Warns of Identity Crisis," *Iran Weekly Press Digest,* 7 August 1999 <www.neda.net/iran-wpd/wolv1233/i1233–3.html>.

33. I attended and recorded this 1 October 1999 speech.

34. See "Abdollah Nuri: If *Khordad* Is Closed Down, I Will Defend Islam in Some Other Way," *Aftab-e Emruz,* 13 October 1999, FBIS, 5 November 1999, FTS19991105000705; and "Leading Iranian Reformist Steps Up Defiance of Conservative Court," Agence France Press, 1 November 1999, as reproduced in *Iran Mania,* <www.iranmania.com/news/nov99/011199. d.asp>.

35. The roster of victors from the IIPF includes, among others, Behzad Nabavi, Hojjat al-Eslam Hadi Khamane'i (the *faqih*'s brother), and Mehdi Karrubi.

36. See Susan Sachs, "Iran Election a Referendum on Reform," *New York Times,* 18 February 2000, A1, A10. The fact that the granddaughter of Khomeini made this case is of no small significance.

37. My interview with Ayatollah Musavi Kho'iniha, 5 October 1999. As of 24 February 2000, the Islamic Iran Participation Front had won some sixty seats, while the Servants of Construction had taken fifty-three. However, that margin was bound to increase in favor of the former.

38. See Jahangir Amuzegar, "Khatami and the Iranian Economy at Mid-Term," *Middle East Journal* 53, no. 4 (autumn 1999): 534–52. It bears repeating that despite former President Rafsanjani's talk of economic reform in 1989 and 1990, he did little to pursue it. The same initially held true for Khatami: throughout the first two years of his presidency, he not only avoided economic reforms, but also advocated populist economic policies that aggravated Iran's growing economic crisis. Clearly, he did not want to fragment his support base. However, in the fall of 1999 Khatami's cabinet proposed a bold package of stabilization and structural adjustment measures. While his allies in the reform either supported or did not oppose his policies— knowing full well that such opposition might split the reformists—it is notable *Majles conservatives* rejected Khatami's several initiatives to reduce energy subsidies. Evidently they did not want to undermine what little credibility they had left.

39. See "Iran Struggle to Find Balance between Revolution and Reform," AP News, 20 November 1999, published at <www.abcnews.go.com/wire/world/ap19991120_1154.html>.

40. "Change is good," conservative politician Mohammad Javad Larijani declared regarding the February 2000 elections. "Expediency is the first issue." See Howard Schneider, "Iran's Young Voices for Change," *The Washington Post,* 17 February 2000, A1.

41. Albert Hourani, *Arabic Thought in the Liberal Age 1798–1939* (London: Oxford University Press, 1970), 344.

42. Ahmad Sadri, "Reintroducing the Wheel," *The Iranian* (September 1996), <www.iranian.com/Sep96/Opinion/Democracy>.

43. Theda Skocpol, "Bringing the State Back In: Strategies of Analysis in Current Research," in *Bringing the State Back In*, ed. Peter B. Evans, Dietrich Rueschemeyer, and Theda Skocpol (Cambridge: Cambridge University Press, 1985), 22; italics mine.

44. This, I suppose, is what Khatami means when he insists that the reformers' February 2000 election victory will advance a reform agenda that is "in the spirit of the revolution and in no way signals a retreat from its principles." See Agence Press France, 26 February 2000, as reproduced in *Iran Mania*, 26 February 2000, <www.iranmania.com/news/feb00/260200d.asp>.

45. This may also entail another round of constitutional amendments.

46. Guillermo O'Donnell, a prominent scholar of Latin American political economy, has recently emphasized what he calls "the predominant style of doing politics" in a given country. See his "Transitions, Continuities, and Paradoxes," in Mainwaring et al., *Issues in Democratic Consolidation*, 36.

47. On the Gulf states see Michael Herb, *All in the Family: Absolutism, Revolution and Democracy in the Middle Eastern Monarchies* (Albany: State University of New York Press, 1999). On the dynamics of dissonant institutionalization in Morocco, see Guilain Denoeux and Abdeslam Maghraoui, "King Hassan's Strategy of Political Dualism," *Middle East Policy* 5, no. 4 (January 1998): 104–30. For an analysis of the efforts of Arab leaders in postpopulist states to use ideological legacies to sustain limited political liberalization, see Daniel Brumberg, "Authoritarian Legacies and Reform Strategies in the Arab World, in *Political Liberalization and Democratization in the Arab World*, ed. Rex Brynen, Baghat Korany, and Paul Nobles (Boulder, Colo.: Lynne Reinner Publishers, 1995), 229–60.

48. See article by Shahriyar Ruhani in *Neshat*, 15 May 1999, p.5, as translated in FBIS, "Identity Crisis among Iranian Youth," 7 July 1999, FTS1999070700030.

49. My interview with Wahid, 8 June 1999. On Wahid and the Nahdlatul Ulema, see Greg Fealy and Greg Barton, eds., *Nahdlatul Ulema: Traditional Islam and Modernity in Indonesia*, Monash Paper on Southeast Asia, no. 39 (Monash, Australia: Monash Asia Institute, 1998) and Douglas Ramage, *Politics in Indonesia: Democracy, Islam and the Ideology of Tolerance* (New York: Routledge Press, 1995). Nahdlatul Ulema is now represented by the National Awakening Party.

50. The "Islamic democracy" thesis is argued in John Esposito and John Voll, *Islam and Democracy* (New York and Oxford: Oxford University Press, 1996), 12–32.

51. Daryush Shayegan, *Cultural Schizophrenia: Islamic Societies Confronting the West* (Syracuse, N.Y.: Syracuse University Press, 1992).

52. Shaul Bakhash, "Islam and Social Justice in Iran," in *Shi'ism, Resistance and Revolution*, ed. Martin Kramer (Boulder, Colo.: Westview Press, 1987), 113.

53. Khatami's conservative opponents have tried to exploit this point. "There are some groups now in Iran, " Khamane'i warns, "the liberals, who repeatedly quote Western philosophers to prove that the notion of freedom is a gift from the West. This is wrong." This may be an oblique reference to

Khatami himself. See "Iran's Khamanei Says Freedom an Islamic Concept," Reuters, 3 September 1998, as published in <www.infoseek.com/content>.

54. The shift is not an easy one to make, especially for Islamists who remain emotionally wedded to a more populist Islamic vision. This has certainly been the case for Indonesia's Amin Rais, the former head of Muhamadiyya, Nahdlatul Ulema's chief rival. See Daniel Brumberg, "Islamists and Power Sharing in Comparative Perspective: A Project Report Prepared for the United States Institute of Peace" (unpublished manuscript, United States Institute of Peace, Washington, D.C., May 1999). My interviews with present and former leaders of Kuwait's Islamic Constitutional Party reveal similar splits and change.

55. Michael Fischer, "Cutting Globalization Down to Size," in *U.S.-Arab Relations and the Challenge of Globalization*, ed. Daniel Brumberg and Steven Heydemann (Washington, D.C.: The Foundation on Democratization and Political Change in the Middle East, 1997), 7.

56. See Paul M. Lubeck, "The Antinomies of the Islamic Revival: Why Do Islamic Movements Thrive Under Globalization?" (unpublished manuscript, Center for Global, International and Regional Studies, University of California, Santa Cruz).

57. The effects of dissonant institutionalization is regime- and country-specific. Moreover, while Khatami's idea of civilizational dialogue seems to have caught on outside the Middle East, there is little evidence in the Arab word that events in Iran have produced a "demonstration effect." On the contrary, the leaders of Lebanon's *Hezbollah* have openly rejected Khatami's reform message, while the leaders of Sunni Islamist groups do not seem especially interested in events in Iran. My review of three Kuwaiti newspapers, *Al-Qabas, Al-Anba,* and *Al-Watan,* over the course of December 1999 is instructive. During this period, there were numerous short articles on events in Iran, but only one analytical piece: Adullah Al-Hadliq, "Iran: Al-Mustaqbal al-Ghamid" (Iran: an ambiguous future), *Al-Anba,* 8 December 1999, p. 36. The latter piece revealed a striking lack of familiarity with Iranian events—no small point, given how close Iran is to Kuwait, and given the important role that Kuwaiti Shi'ites play in that country's parliament.

Index